This modern text is designed to prepare you for your future professional career. While theories, ideas, techniques, and data are dynamic, the information contained in this volume will provide you a quick and useful reference as well as a guide for future learning for many years to come. Your familiarity with the contents of this book will make it an important volume in your professional library.

EX LIBRIS

Effective Communication Skills

Effective Communication Skills

Daniel S. Cochran

Department of Management
Mississippi State University

Danny R. Arnold

Department of Marketing
Mississippi State University

1986

BUSINESS PUBLICATIONS, INC.
Plano, Texas   75075

© BUSINESS PUBLICATIONS, INC., 1986

ISBN 0-256-03166-5

Library of Congress Catalog Card No. 85–70976

Printed in the United States of America

1 2 3 4 5 6 7 8 9 0 K 3 2 1 0 9 8 7 6

Dedication

To our families: Melody, Steven, Heather, Aimee, Peggy, Wade, and Daryl for their support and forbearance

To our Lord and Savior, who makes all things possible.

Preface

The success of an organization largely depends on the communication skills of its individual members. More and more organizations are aware of this relationship, and as a result many are putting an increasingly high priority on more fully developing their members' communication skills.

Purpose of the Book

This textbook is designed for the basic organization communications or business communications course. Its goal is to help students improve their written and oral communication skills.

Students will find that this text is both an excellent learning tool and an excellent reference book for other courses as well as for real world situations.

Special Features

A variety of special features were designed to help achieve the authors' purpose.

1. The text has a *skills orientation* and an *application orientation*. Each chapter begins with learning objectives and a topical outline and is then designed to teach skills by using a progressive, active learning approach that involves three major components. First, relevant skills are identified and discussed. Second, applications of the skills are explained. Third, application exercises are provided at the end of each chapter to provide practice for the skills presented in the chapter.

2. A great deal of effort was devoted to making this text highly *readable*. Since a communications textbook should communicate effectively, we attempted to practice what we preach. Every attempt has been made to keep the writing clear, concise, and interesting. Numerous illustrations are included to highlight and explain material.

3. We have also attempted to keep the contents of this text highly *relevant and timely*. Inspiration for the contents of the text came from a variety of sources, including the authors' teaching and consulting experiences, industry and academic research, and communications-related articles and books.

Further, extensive class testing of the manuscript provided valuable student input.

Organization of the Text

The text is comprised of 18 chapters divided into six major parts. Part I, Understanding Effective Communication, includes three chapters that form the foundation for the development of communication skills that will be discussed in the remainder of the text. The overall communication process is discussed in Chapter 1. Chapter 2 addresses the three major ingredients needed to achieve effective communication—communication technology, communication climate or attitude, and interpersonal communication skills. Specific interpersonal communication skills are discussed in Chapter 3.

Part II, Understanding Basic Writing Skills, includes two chapters that form the foundation for letter and report writing skills. Chapter 4 examines the writing process and Chapter 5 focuses on identifying the characteristics of effective writing.

Part III is entitled Improving Letter and Memo Writing Skills, and each of the four chapters focuses specifically on a major type of letter/memo—requests (Chapter 6), favorable responses (Chapter 7), unfavorable responses (Chapter 8), and persuasive correspondence (Chapter 9).

Part IV, Report Writing Skills, examines the research and report writing process (Chapter 10), short reports (Chapter 11), and long reports (Chapter 12). The use of graphics in communication is addressed in Chapter 13.

Part V is entitled Improving Oral Communication Skills and looks at the skills needed for interviewing, small group meetings, and oral presentations in chapters 14, 15, and 16, respectively.

Part VI is entitled Improving Career Communication Skills. The career communication process is examined in Chapter 17, while Chapter 18 addresses those communication skills needed to enhance career opportunities. Each chapter integrates and applies the theories and skills discussed in the first 16 chapters.

Six appendixes are also included in the text. Appendix A is a review of basic English grammar and includes a diagnostic instrument for the students' benefit. Appendix B discusses form and style of business letters and memos. Appendix C summarizes format issues for footnotes and bibliographies. Appendix D examines key legal considerations that influence organizational communications. Appendix E summarizes relevant international business communication issues. Appendix F covers dictation skills. Several of these appendixes were the contributions of individuals who have unique expertise in the relevant area.

Supplements to the Text

For the Student. A study guide, *Exercises in Business Communication,* has been developed to help students expand their practice and application of the skills taught in the text.

For the Instructor. An Instructor's Manual is available to assist instructors in the presentation of material covered in the text. Included are basic chapter outlines (for quick reference), lecture outlines, answers to review questions, a test bank with over 1,000 questions, and transparency masters.

Acknowledgments

A project of this magnitude obviously cannot be completed by the authors alone. Many people made significant contributions. Several individuals at Mississippi State University deserve special thanks. Valuable forms of support were provided by Dean Dennis Leyden and our departmental chairmen, Dr. Dennis Ray and Dr. Henry Nash. Key insights were provided by faculty members, particularly Michael Giallourakis, Tom Hinckle, and Pepper Holland. The brunt of the production process for this project was borne by Marilyn Gentry, Tammy Smith, Ruth Green, Elaine White, Joann Elliott, and Lorri Howell. Several graduate students also made critical contributions, including Valerie Seines, Philip Halbert, Jill Austin, and Lisa Spense.

We also want to give special thanks to those who helped us prepare the appendixes. These include Janet Dolan, Associate Professor of Business and English at Pfeiffer College; Judge Denny Eshee, Professor of Applied Legal Studies at Mississippi State University; and Dr. C. Kendrick Gibson, Dean of the School of Business at Henderson State University.

Our reviewers also made numerous valuable comments throughout all phases of this project. Reviewing the text throughout various stages of development were: Nancy J. Billett, California State University, Los Angeles; Helen Diamond, Citrus College; Ronald Dulek, University of Alabama; M. W. Durso, University of South Florida; Sarah Hart, Sam Houston State University; G. Pepper Holland, Mississippi State University; Frank Nelson, Eastern Washington University; Ruthann Schlarbaum, Purdue University; and Douglas Shepard, SUNY College at Fredonia.

Daniel S. Cochran

Danny R. Arnold

Contents

Detailed Contents

PART III
Improving Letter and Memo Writing Skills 129

PART V
Improving Oral Communication Skills

Part I

Understanding Effective Communication

The three chapters included in Part I serve to prepare you to improve your communication skills. Chapter 1 captures the essence of the communication process—what actually happens when you communicate. Chapter 2 focuses on the key ingredients of effective communication. Chapter 3 addresses the key interpersonal communication skills needed to achieve effective communication in organizations.

Chapter   1

■ *Chapter Outline*

Examining the Communication Process

■ *Learning Objectives*

After studying this chapter, you should be able to:
- Differentiate between effective and ineffective communication.
- Explain why effective communication skills are vital to organizations.
- Draw and label a communication model that illustrates the major components of the communication process.
- Discuss the major barriers to effective communication in organizations.

Introduction

People have been communicating forever. From simple beginnings, communication has grown more and more complex. Individuals today not only communicate with themselves and others, but also with groups, organizations, and even machines such as the computer.

Consider the communication activities in which you might participate during a "typical day." Your day might begin, for example, waking to radio communication, such as music, a commercial, or a newscast. Additional early morning communication may occur in the forms of conversing with a roommate, reading a newspaper, and watching a television newscast. Perhaps your clothing will communicate a general mood or an impression of your lifestyle or attitudes. The walk to class may involve communicating with friends and acquaintances. The class instructor will communicate specific information and you, in turn, will provide communication feedback to the instructor through homework papers, class discussion, test taking, and term papers.

Think of other common communication situations, such as club meetings, the student senate, writing to parents, telephoning someone for a date, and preparing a computer program. In fact, you normally spend a large portion of your day sending or receiving communications. The ability to communicate effectively is an important part of a successful life and career.

Just as communication is important in your life, effective communication is a vital ingredient of successful organizations. Without it, organizations tend to flounder without direction, which often leads to chaos and even organizational death.

This text focuses on improving those skills necessary to achieve effective communication in organizations, primarily business organizations. Both oral and written communication skills are emphasized. The remainder of this chapter is devoted to the difference between communication and effective communication, expanding the discussion of the importance of communication skills in organizations, discussing a model of the communication process, and highlighting various barriers to effective communication.

Communication is important and complex.

Organizations need effective communication.

WHAT IS COMMUNICATION?

Communication can be defined in a variety of ways. Some definitions are somewhat narrow and emphasize the sender or the receiver of the message. *Webster's New World Dictionary*, for example, defines communication as:

> the act of transmitting.

Webster's definition obviously emphasizes the sender. Another popular definition is that communication:

> occurs when something has been taken into account.[1]

This definition emphasizes the receiver.

Other textbook definitions are relatively broad and can emphasize both the sender and receiver:

> the transmission and reception of ideas, feelings, and attitudes, verbally and/or nonverbally, which produce a response.[2]

Although technically accurate, none of these definitions captures the intended spirit of this book—*effective* communication.

WHAT IS EFFECTIVE COMMUNICATION?

To highlight and focus the thrust of this book, consider the phrase *effective communication*. A relevant definition is:

> Effective communication occurs when the receiver takes into account the same message the sender wanted to send.

Effective communication results in a shared understanding: the receiver understands the sender's message as the sender intended. Consequently, ineffective communication can occur when mutual understanding is not achieved.

Note that there are varying degrees of understanding, ranging from no understanding to total understanding. Truly effective communication occurs when 100 percent understanding is reached. In general, the higher the level of understanding, the more effective the communication. High levels of understanding are extremely desirable in both individual relationships and organizational and group settings. Both individual and organizational examples and situations are discussed throughout this text.

Communication can be defined in a variety of ways.

Your text focuses on effective communication.

IMPORTANCE OF EFFECTIVE COMMUNICATION SKILLS IN ORGANIZATIONS

"An unreliable messenger can cause a lot of trouble; reliable communication permits progress" (Proverbs 13:17: *The Living Bible*). The idea that effective communication leads to progress has been around for a long time. Today, more and more organizations (both business and nonbusiness) are recognizing the close relationship between effective communication and organizational success. This recognition has naturally led to increased attention to and emphasis on improving communication skills and effectiveness. Let's take a look at the general nature of an organization and how management skills, particularly communication skills, contribute to the organization's effectiveness.

What Is an Organization?

Individuals group together to form an organization when they anticipate accomplishing a common purpose more effectively by working together as a team than individually. Therefore, an *organization* can be defined as:

> a social unit that strives to accomplish a common objective and achieve relatively stable relationships among the organization's members.

An organization that has not achieved some degree of stability in its members' relationships normally experiences a great deal of difficulty in achieving a common purpose or objective.

Management's Role

Achieving a common purpose and developing and maintaining stable relationships is the function and responsibility of the organization's management. The American Management Association defines *management* as:

> getting things done through others.[3]

This definition raises two points that deserve further elaboration. First, managers are doers. They are involved in getting things done, encouraging progress, and increasing individual and organizational performance as they strive to achieve the organization's objectives.

Second, managers fulfill their responsibilities by securing the co-operation of other members of the organization. In effect, managers can be viewed as catalysts that pull together sometimes diverse organization elements. They become the force that integrates the efforts of organizational members toward accomplishing the organization's objectives.

Communication Skills Are Important

Managers "get things done through others" by using a variety of managerial tools and procedures. Many managers and organizations have found, however, that communication skills are often the most important element of managerial success. Consider these three points. First, managers spend the majority of their time (as much as 85 percent) on interpersonal communication.[4] Second, business executives contend that the most important and most desired skills for

TABLE 1.1

Newly Promoted Executives' Evaluation of Courses as Preparation for Careers in General Management

Courses	Percentage of Respondents Answering	
	Very Important	Very Important Somewhat Important (Combined)
Business communications (oral and written)	71.4%	94.1%
Finance	64.7	95.6
Accounting	57.9	90.4
Business policy/planning	47.7	86.2
Marketing	38.1	81.2
Business economics/public policy	36.5	80.0
Computer/information systems	31.7	82.6
Business law	20.9	47.1
Personnel/industrial relations	18.9	64.2
Production/operations	16.8	60.2
International business	10.5	52.0
Statistics	10.3	47.9
Advertising/sales promotion	8.6	43.2

Source: H. W. Hildebrandt, F. A. Bond, E. L. Miller, and A. W. Swinyard, "An Executive Appraisal of Courses Which Best Prepare One for General Management," *The Journal of Business Communication* 19, no. 1 (Winter 1982), p. 7.

college graduates are interpersonal communication skills.[5] Third, a large sample of newly promoted executives from leading U.S. corporations recently evaluated the importance of college courses for preparing students for a career in management. You are now taking their top choice, "Business Communications."[6] Table 1.1 summarizes the results of this study.

The above evidence highlights the key points of this chapter. First, communication skills are extremely important to organizations. Second, communication skills facilitate managers' efforts to "get things done" in order to move the organization forward to improved performance. Consider, for example, the communication flows that directly involve an assembly line supervisor. He or she must communicate horizontally with all other line supervisors as well as vertically with the plant manager (upward) and with assembly line workers (downward). In essence, communication skills can be viewed as an organization's lifeblood.

Effective communication skills help managers get things done.

A FOUNDATION FOR IMPROVING COMMUNICATION SKILLS

Efforts to improve communication skills must be based on a solid foundation. The key element of the communication foundation is the communication process. Understanding what happens when two or more individuals communicate is crucial to improving communication skills. A model of the communication process is discussed later in this chapter. To understand the communication process better, we begin with a discussion of the possible levels of communication in an organization. The last major section of this chapter discusses critical barriers to communication. Three elements—the communication process, communication levels, and communication barriers—form the foundation for improving communication skills.

COMMUNICATION LEVELS

Organizations have three interrelated levels of communication.

Studying and understanding communication is much easier if you have a clear structure or analytical framework with which to view organization communications. One popular approach involves analyzing communication at three basic levels. The three basic *communication levels* are the intrapersonal level, interpersonal level, and organizational (or group) level. Each of these is discussed briefly.

Intrapersonal Level

The ***intrapersonal communication level*** involves an individual's communication with himself or herself. Thinking and listening are the primary examples of intrapersonal communication. Intrapersonal communication is therefore a cognitive process.[7]

The intrapersonal level must be considered in analyzing organizational communications because all communication begins at this level. Effective thinking is a prerequisite to effective communication.

Interpersonal Level

The ***interpersonal communication level*** involves communications between two or more individuals. Interpersonal communication can occur in either verbal (oral or written) or nonverbal form. The communication process becomes more complex at this level of analysis because we are now dealing with the combined intrapersonal communication processes of two or more individuals. The interpersonal level of communication is emphasized throughout this text.

Organizational Level

The third level of communication can be referred to as the ***organizational (or group) communication level***. This level is even more complex than the other levels because it involves not only communications between people, but also those between departments or divisions within an organization. Although informal communications are an important part of an organization's communications, the focus here is on formal communications.

The formal communication channel is the official route of communications from top management to middle management to lower management to employees. Most of the organization's policies, procedures, and directives are disseminated through the formal channel. An overview of an organization's formal communication channel can be obtained from its organizational chart, which should relate the various authority relationships from the top of the organization to the lower levels.

The Interrelationships

Illustration 1.1 highlights the relationships among these three levels of communication in an organization. The organizational level is the broadest level in that it encompasses both intrapersonal and

ILLUSTRATION 1.1

Communication Levels

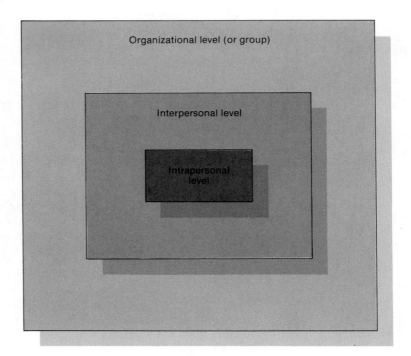

interpersonal communication. The three levels of communication influence each other, build upon each other, and essentially combine to form an internal communication system. To obtain a better grasp of organizational level communications, let's next examine a model of interpersonal communication.

AN INTERPERSONAL COMMUNICATION MODEL

Illustration 1.2 presents a model of the *interpersonal communication process.*[8] The model is designed to show in simple form the basic communication process as it occurs between a sender and a re-

ILLUSTRATION 1.2

A Model of the Interpersonal Communication Process

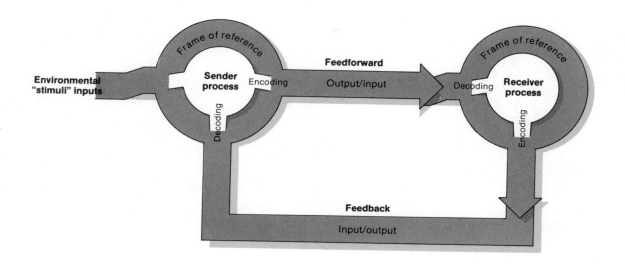

ceiver. Although all possible variables are not included, the model does integrate the four basic components: sender process, feedforward channel, receiver process, and feedback channel.

To grasp the basic flow of communication within the model, visualize yourself having a conversation with a friend. Assume that you are about to go to lunch and want to invite the friend to come along. In brief, you are the sender and must formulate (encode) the invitation and transmit it through an appropriate feedforward channel (i.e., perhaps verbal/oral). Your friend is the receiver, who will hopefully recognize (decode) your request, encode a positive response, and transmit the response through an appropriate feedback channel. Note that effective communication occurs when your friend takes into account or understands the same message you intended to send and vice versa. Now let's turn to additional details.

Communication can be viewed as a process.

The Sender Process

The *sender* is the individual who initiates the communication process. Two key elements—encoding and decoding—must be understood in the sender process.

Encoding.

Encoding.   The key element of the sender process is perhaps encoding. *Encoding* can be defined as:

> the process of building or developing a message the sender wants to send to someone else; the desired message is put into symbols, words, sentences, paragraphs, nonverbal cues, and so forth.

The overall sender process, including encoding, is heavily influenced by the sender's frame of reference.

Frame of Reference.   The sender is surrounded by his or her own frame of reference. A person's *frame of reference* can be defined as:

> an accumulated "field of experience" resulting from all past experiences, including educational, work, cultural, familial, religious, and social experiences.

The frame of reference acts as a filter through which all incoming and outgoing communications must pass. Note that both the sender's and receiver's frames of reference influence the interpersonal communication process.

The Feedforward Channel

The sender chooses a *feedforward channel* to deliver the encoded message to the intended receiver. The feedforward channel can be either verbal or nonverbal. *Verbal channels*:

> communicate to others through the use of words, either orally or in writing.

Nonverbal channels:

> communicate to others without the use of words, that is, through facial and hand gestures, posture, and eye contact.

Effective communication can be obtained only if the receiver is familiar with the specific channel. Very few of us, for example, are capable of decoding a letter written in ancient Greek.

The Receiver Process

The *receiver* is the individual who receives the message from the feedforward channel. The key element of the receiver process involves decoding. *Decoding* can be defined as:

> the process a receiver goes through to break a message into a meaningful whole, or to attach meaning to a stimulus (something that stirs action or effort).

As mentioned above, the decoding process occurs within an individual's frame of reference, which is heavily influenced by three psychological processes: perceptual, motivational, and learning. Illustration 1.3 presents a model which illustrates in more detail what happens during the receiver's decoding process.

Perception is an individual's unique interpretation of a given stimulus or situation. The interpretation is unique because every individual has different accumulated experiences (frames of reference) and needs. The process of perception can be divided into two stages that occur almost simultaneously: selective perception and perceptual organization.

Selective perception means simply that an individual chooses only certain environmental stimuli, while all others are ignored, distorted, or quickly forgotten. No one can cope with all possible environmental cues. *Perceptual organization* occurs as the individual interprets the stimuli and incorporates them into his or her frame of reference. Note that the existing frame of reference also influences

Perception is an important part of the communication process.

ILLUSTRATION 1.3

A Model of Receiver Decoding Process

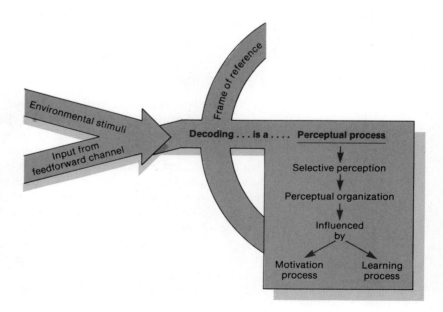

the interpretation of the stimuli. These two components of the perception process are synonymous with the decoding process.

Both the motivation and the learning processes exert a tremendous influence on the perceptual process and, therefore, on the decoding process. The *motivation process* influences decoding through an individual's needs. An individual's most important current need dictates both selection (selective perception) and interpretation (perceptual organization) of environmental stimuli. A person who is hungry, for example, is more likely to pay attention to a television advertisement for pizza or steak and may be more likely to interpret the advertisement as believable than a person who is not hungry.

An individual's *learning process* also influences his or her perceptual process. Learning has been defined as a relatively permanent change in behavior brought about by reinforced practice.[9] You may have "learned," for example, that you do not like diet soft drinks because they have an unpleasant aftertaste and/or do not taste as good as the "regular" version. If so, this learning experience will influence the way you perceive new brands of diet soft drinks. Typical advice for those interested in incorporating diet drinks in a weight loss program is "Drink diet soft drinks for which there is no regular version, such as 'wild raspberry' and 'black cherry.'"

Motivation and learning influence perception.

The Feedback Channel

The receiver selects a *feedback channel* to transmit his or her response to the original sender. Similar to the feedforward channel, the feedback channel can be either verbal or nonverbal in nature. Although the feedback channel is often identical to the feedforward channel, differences can occur. For example, a manager (sender) may send a message to an employee (receiver) by simply telling the employee something (orally); however, the message may require that the feedback be written. The employee, for example, may have to write a report.

Note also that when the sender receives the return message from the receiver, decoding occurs by the original sender. Earlier interpersonal communication models assumed that senders encoded only and receivers decoded only. More recent models, however, recognize that (1) senders must first encode a message and then decode feedback from the receiver, and (2) receivers must decode the sender's message and then encode a return message.[10]

Both senders and receivers must encode and decode.

BARRIERS TO EFFECTIVE COMMUNICATION

Obviously, organizations don't always achieve effective communication. Even when the members of an organization have a firm grasp of the communication process, effective communication is not guaranteed. A variety of *communication barriers* can cause major breakdowns in the communication process. Examples of these barriers are organized into two broad categories: organizational barriers and individual barriers.

Organizational Barriers

Organizational communication barriers arise because of some aspect of the organization itself. The four major organizational barriers involve the organization's goals, structure, size, and climate.

The organization itself can create barriers to communication.

Organizational Goals.   Perhaps the major organizational barrier to effective communication revolves around unclear organizational goals. When organization members do not agree as to what the organization's actual direction (goals) should be, it is very difficult for members to achieve effective communication.

Two questions illustrate the importance of an organization's members knowing the specific goals or direction they should be pursuing.[11] The first question an organization must address is: What business are we in? Once a satisfactory answer has been developed, a second question must be answered: Are we in the right business? Unless these broad questions can be answered specifically, effective communication is unlikely.

Even if appropriate goals have been developed and are understood by organization members, barriers can arise if effective policies and procedures are lacking. *Policies* provide guidelines for members' activities and decisions. A firm, for example, might have a policy of promoting only from within the organization (no middle- or upper-level managers will be recruited from outside the firm). *Procedures* specify how members are to accomplish certain tasks. A firm, for example, might establish purchasing procedures that specify each step needed to requisition equipment and material.

Policies and procedures that are communicated clearly to members contribute much to organizational success. Conversely, unclear policies and procedures can lead to an organization's demise.

Organizational Structure. Consider the relationship between the sales department and production department in an organization. Unfortunately, this relationship can be one marred by conflict. This conflict often arises over a disagreement regarding the most desirable inventory levels. The salespeople tend to want a large inventory of products to enable them to handle all potential customer orders, while the production manager generally prefers smaller inventories to help minimize storage costs and the amount of capital tied up in inventory. Unclear authority/responsibility relationships ultimately lead to harmful conflict, which is a major communication barrier.

Certain types of organization structures actually encourage communication problems. Consider, for example, an organization structure that requires a subordinate to answer to more than one boss. This type of structure violates a basic management principle, the *unity of command* principle. This situation puts tremendous pressure on that member to try to please two different superiors simultaneously. The structure itself can therefore become a barrier to effective communication.

Organizational Size. The sheer size of an organization can also create communication barriers. First, the geographical distance between members of organizations can be so great as to prevent effective communication, especially at a reasonable cost. Consider the plight, for example, of a corporate headquarters on the East Coast trying to discuss major strategy issues with operating divisions on the West Coast. It can be done, but it is generally expensive, involving such costs as those for long distance conference calls and executive travel.

Second, organizational communication can be victimized by barriers related to the serial communication situations inherent in large organizations. **Serial communication** occurs when a message passes through numerous parties. It occurs in an organization as messages flow from the top of the organization through various managerial levels to the lower levels. The problem is that the original message is either added to or distorted, or parts of the message are deleted. You may have played the party game in which participants sit in a circle and pass a simple message from person to person; the final message seldom has any relationship to the original message. Similar problems can occur in organizations. Effective communication is very difficult to achieve in a serial communication situation, as shown in Illustration 1.4.

Third, large organizations often have communication problems due to overly large spans of control (or management). When a manager is responsible for too many subordinates, the time available for communicating with each individual subordinate can be severely

ILLUSTRATION 1.4

Illustration of Ineffective Communication

Source: King Features Syndicated, Inc., 1983.

limited. Effective communication is practically impossible when the span of control is too large, which makes effective control, supervision, and management quite difficult.

Organizational Climate. An organization's climate can also serve as a barrier to communication. *Organizational climate* is defined as:

> the degree of trust, communication, and supportiveness that exists in an organization or group.[12]

Effective communication is extremely difficult to achieve in a closed, nonsupportive climate in which there is little trust between organization members. Managers sometimes contribute a great deal to such a defensive communication climate by deemphasizing openness in communication between members of the organization.

A good organizational climate encourages communication.

Individual Barriers

There is also a multitude of *individual communication barriers*. Five potential problem areas are discussed briefly: frames of reference, feedforward channels, physical distractions, listening habits, and feedback channels.

Individuals can erect barriers to effective communication.

Frames of Reference. The major individual barrier to effective communication occurs when the sender and receiver have different frames of reference. As discussed earlier, an individual's frame of reference is a compilation of his or her previous experiences.

Since each individual has a unique set of accumulated experiences, each also possesses a unique frame of reference. Consequently, two different individuals can perceive the same situation and attach totally different meanings to it, especially when the two individuals have different cultural backgrounds (see Appendix E).

Effective communication occurs much more easily when there is sufficient overlap between the sender's and receiver's frames of reference. Have you ever visited a town that is strange to you and had to stop and ask directions to a specific location? You may have obtained a response something like: "Go down to Harvey's store and take a left to the old oak tree; then go to the second stop sign and turn left; go past the nursery and it should be on your right." These directions would be rather simple if your frame of reference overlapped properly with that of the individual giving directions. However, if your frame of reference does not include similar location references, the directions would probably be unintelligible.

Feedforward Channel.   Another individual communication barrier relates to the sender's selection of a feedforward channel. The sender's basic alternatives include an oral channel, written channel, or multiple channels. The sender, for example, might incorrectly select an oral channel to communicate a message that actually requires a written record, such as an order for many different products. Conversely, face-to-face discussion can sometimes lead to greater understanding, such as when you need to discuss a particular problem with a teacher or boss. In essence, if the feedforward channel is not satisfactory to the receiver, the channel itself becomes a barrier to effective communication.

Physical Distractions.   Any physical distraction is referred to as "noise." Noise can be in the form of any competing sensory stimuli, such as hearing, sight, and so forth. Any significant source of noise can prevent or distort message transmission and therefore understanding.

Listening Habits.   Poor listening habits can also be a major barrier to effective communication. Although most people consider themselves good listeners, many people actually have poor listening habits. Some individuals, for example, concentrate only on major points and often miss critical details, while others do not concentrate at all. Some individuals let their minds wander if the first part of a message is not interesting enough.

Feedback Channels.   An appropriate feedback channel is an essential ingredient of effective communication. Both the sender and receiver must recognize and encourage effective feedback whether it be verbal or nonverbal. For example, a teacher or a manager is attempting to establish a feedback channel when he or she encourages questions at the end of a class period or after giving instructions. Without effective feedback, the sender has no way of knowing whether reception, understanding, and agreement have occurred.

ORGANIZATION OF TEXT

This text is intended to be *skills-oriented* rather than theoretical. We want you to learn how to apply communication skills to achieve effective communication. Good communication skills can greatly enhance your effectiveness in today's organization.

The ingredients of effective communication (both written and oral) are addressed in the next two chapters. The skills discussed form the foundation for the rest of the text.

The basic writing skills are discussed in Part II. These writing skills are then applied to letter writing (Part III) and report writing (Part IV) situations.

Part V deals with oral communication skills. Both oral and written skills are then applied to your career communication needs (Part VI).

Application Exercises

1. Bill Kelly was the administrator for a 160-bed, short-term community hospital that was undergoing a major facility expansion program. During the early stages of the expansion program, Bill began to realize that many employees were experiencing a great deal of apprehension and anxiety regarding their future role in the expanded facility.

In an attempt to reduce what Bill thought was imaginary apprehension, he contacted an organizational development center at a major university. The center arranged to provide research and consulting personnel to investigate the hospital's climate. Bill agreed to let the researchers use group decision-making procedures to obtain information from hospital employees regarding their apprehensions. The consultants were then to develop an intervention strategy and tactics that Bill would implement.

When the research was completed and the recommendations prepared, a comprehensive report was delivered to Bill. On the same day, however, Bill's attention was diverted to a major construction crisis. He immediately initiated further discussion and negotiation with the contractor, subcontractors, architects, engineers, and lawyers.

Consequently, Bill never found the time to actually implement the intervention strategy and tactics. The construction project was eventually completed and the organization's climate further deteriorated.

Answer the following questions:

a. Analyze this case relative to the communication process, communication levels, and communication barriers.
b. What are Bill Kelly's alternatives for improving the organizational climate after the completion of the construction project?

2. American RSI, Inc. is a privately owned firm that provides a variety of services and products, including insulation, storm windows and doors, fencing material, aluminum siding, and other aluminum building products. In addition, the firm provides blown, loose-fill insulation, and batt insulation for new construction and home remodeling. The firm is located in an active and growing real estate market in northwest Louisiana.

The firm is owned by Clarence Baker. Clarence is 65 years old and has been running the business since 1960. Clarence's son, Phil Baker, recently joined the business after graduating from the state university and completing a U.S. Navy enlistment. Phil normally remains in the office and tries to obtain new business, primarily via telephone inquiries. Clarence continues to supervise the delivery and installation of the various offerings. He allows few records to be kept, preferring to run the business from his "hip pocket."

Sales have been relatively stable in recent years, but monthly profits have been low or nonexistent. Phil and Clarence have begun to have frequent, heated arguments over the future direction of the firm, purchasing strategy, selling strategy, and managerial responsibilities. Tension is quite high throughout the firm and increased employee turnover of laborers and salespeople has resulted. Phil is now wondering if the business is worth the effort.

Answer the following questions:

a. Describe the communication problems encountered by Clarence and Phil Baker in terms of organizational barriers.
b. Analyze this case relative to the communication process.

3. Think of a time when you encountered difficulty in communicating because of a difference in frames of reference—yours and someone else's. Describe the incident.

4. In a group of four or five people, have one person think of an object (such as a car or a room) or a process for doing something (such as baking a cake or hitting a baseball). Have that person describe the object or process to a second person in the group, who tells a third member, and so on. Have the last group member relate his description back to the first person and analyze how it has changed.

5. Organize a group of five students for an exercise dealing with *serial communications*. Have student 1 examine a picture for a few seconds outside the room. Then have student 1 orally communicate what he or she saw in the picture to student 2. Repeat this process (2 communicating to 3, and so forth) until the message has been communicated to all five students. Have student 5 communicate what was in the picture to everyone else. Then show the actual picture to everyone. Did the message change? Was anything added, deleted, or misunderstood?

Review Questions

1. Define communication.

2. Is effective communication really different from communication? If so, how?

3. Explain why effective communication skills are so important to the success of today's organization.

4. What changes—if any—would you make in the communication model presented in this chapter? Why?

5. Describe some of your experiences with each of the different levels of communication.

6. List and define the stages in the process of perception.

7. What do you perceive to be the major barriers to effective communication in organizations today? Discuss the reasons for your selection. List some steps that may be taken to avoid each barrier.

8. Analyze the interaction of verbal and nonverbal communication. Which do you think is more important? Why?

Key Terms

communication
effective communication
organization
management
communication levels
intrapersonal communication level
interpersonal communication level
organizational communication level
interpersonal communication process
sender
encoding
frame of reference
feedforward channel

verbal channels
nonverbal channels
receiver
decoding
perception
selective perception
perceptual organization
motivation process
learning process
feedback channel
communication barriers
organizational communication barriers
serial communication
organizational climate
individual communication barriers

Notes

1. Lee Thayer, *Communication and Communication Systems* (Homewood, Ill.: Richard D. Irwin, 1968), pp. 26–28.

2. Norman B. Sigband, *Communication for Management and Business* (Glenview, Ill.: Scott, Foresman, 1982), p. 9.

3. Mary Parker Follett, quoted in Billy J. Hodge and Herbert M. Johnson, *Management and Organization Behavior: A Multidimensional Approach* (New York: John Wiley & Sons, 1970), p. 7.

4. Frank Cespedes, "Building the Communication Skills of Business Students," presented in a seminar at Harvard University sponsored by the American Assembly of Collegiate Schools of Business (AACSB), November 9–10, 1981.

5. William V. Muse, "If All the Business Schools in the Country Were Eliminated . . . Would Anyone Notice?," *Collegiate News and Views* (Cincinnati: South-Western Publishing, Spring 1983), p. 1.

6. H. W. Hildebrandt, F. A. Bond, E. L. Miller, and A. W. Swinyard, "An Executive Appraisal of Courses Which Best Prepare One for General Management," *Journal of Business Communication,* 19, no. 1 (Winter 1982), pp. 5–15.

7. Phillip V. Lewis, *Organizational Communication: The Essence of Effective Management,* (Columbus, Ohio: Grid, 1980), pp. 6–7.

8. Daniel S. Cochran and C. Kendrick Gibson, "Putting A Square Peg into a Round Hole: Communication Models and Their Application," *Journal of Business Communication,* 17, no. 1 (Fall 1979), pp. 27–36.

9. Donald V. White and William Vroman, *Action in Organizations* (Boston: Allyn & Bacon, 1982), p. 66.

10. Cochran and Gibson, "Putting a Square Peg," pp. 28–30.

11. Peter F. Drucker, *An Introductory View of Management* (New York: Harper's College Press, 1977), Chapter 5.

12. Dan Hellriegel, Judy Slocum, and Richard Woodman, *Organizational Behavior* (St. Paul, Minn.: West Publishing, 1983), p. 590.

Chapter 2

■ *Chapter Outline*

Achieving Effective Communication: Technology and Attitude

■ *Learning Objectives*

After studying this chapter, you should be able to:
■ Discuss three major ingredients needed to achieve effective communications in organizations.
■ Describe the following advances in communication technology: electronic data processing and graphics, word processing, electronic mail, and teleconferences.
■ Explain the limitations of communication technology.
■ Compare a supportive versus defensive communication climate.
■ Define what is meant by a 50/50 percent attitude toward communication responsibility.
■ Define what is meant by a 100/100 percent attitude toward communication responsibility.

Introduction

Greek mythology provides a most dramatic approach to achieving effective communication. The wing-footed Mercury would pluck a particular idea or message directly from a person's brain, secure the idea on the point of his spear, and plunge it directly into the brain of another person. Unfortunately, few of us are wing-footed today, and we must therefore seek more practical means of communicating.

The purpose of this chapter is to present and discuss the major ingredients needed to achieve effective organizational communication. An organization can seek improvements in three major areas: communication technology, employee attitudes toward communicating effectively, and interpersonal communication skills (see Illustration 2.1). Each of these three areas is discussed below.

IMPROVING COMMUNICATION TECHNOLOGY

Although computers have been around since the 1940s and technology is advancing at an incredible pace, most organizations are still at the threshold of fully realizing the potential of advanced ***communication technology***. This advanced communication technology consists of applying the latest electronic technology to facilitate the communication process, and it includes tools such as electronic data processing and graphics, word processing, electronic mail, and teleconferences.

ILLUSTRATION 2.1

Ingredients for Achieving Effective Communication in Organizations

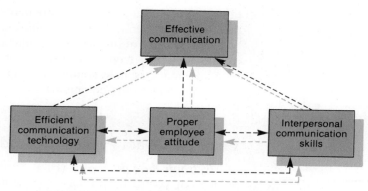

Legend: Dashed lines (––––) indicate direction of influence.

Most offices now use computer technology in communications.

Advances in technology have boosted organizations' communication abilities.

More and more organizations are now attempting to use more advanced communication technology. A 1984 survey of office managers (nonteaching members of the Office Systems Research Association), for example, found that 89 percent of the respondents either have a computerized electronic communication system or expect to have one in the near future.[1]

Advances in communication technology have also had a tremendous impact on society in general. Home computers, for example, can be and are used to enhance a variety of communication activities. On a larger scale, the United Nations demonstrated increased concern with communication technology by proclaiming 1983 "World Communications Year 1983."

Early progress in communication technology concentrated on handling and increasing information flow within an organization. More recently, however, computer and telecommunication systems technology have been combined to boost organizations' information generating and processing capabilities.[2] These improvements in information processing involve expediting access to information and enhancing message composition. Information processing technology can improve both written and oral communication throughout the firm as well as with other organizations.

Advances in communication technology offer tremendous promise to organizations. The aggregate impact of new communication technology might be even greater than the impact of the telephone when it was introduced almost 100 years ago. The use of the telephone, for example, replaced a large segment of written communications and personal contacts. Many people had to relearn and adapt their oral communication skills and change their modes of doing business because of this new communication medium. Today, many people are also having to learn new skills and techniques to take advantage of new communication technology. Several of the major advances in communication technology are discussed below.

Electronic Data Processing and Graphics

Electronic data pro-
cessing can improve
understanding.

Electronic data processing (EDP) technology has been used for a number of years. Its primary contribution has been its ability to enhance processing statistical data and generating statistical reports. More recently, graphics capabilities have been added so that the statistical reports can also be presented in graphical or figure form. The largest benefit of *graphics technology* lies in aiding understanding; complicated statistical reports often do not communicate as effectively as a well-done graphical report (see Illustration 2.2).

Word Processing Technology

Word processing technology allows written communications to be typed, edited, and formatted electronically before the document is printed. The two basic forms of word processors are computers with word processing software and "dedicated" word processors (essentially computers that have word processing capabilities only).[3] For either type of system, the basic hardware required includes:

Central processing unit (CPU). The CPU is the "brains" of the system in that it is the central element that controls data flow and executes instructions.

Keyboard. The keyboard is similar to a typewriter keyboard, but with a few extra keys. It allows you to enter text and instructions into computer memory.

Screen. The screen or monitor provides a visual display of the text you type and may show special editing symbols and codes.

Printer. The printer produces your text on paper as "output" from the computer.

ILLUSTRATION 2.2

Examples of Graphics Technology

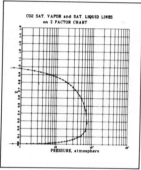

Scientific Plotting

Symbol Sets

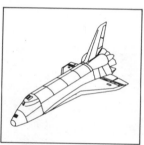

Digitizing

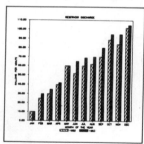

Business Graphics

Program Output

Contouring

Disk drive. A disk drive is a device that spins a magnetic disk, usually a flexible disk called a "floppy disk." Information can be "read" from the disk and "written" on the disk. It is the most common medium for storage of electronic information for small word processors.

A visual example is shown in Illustration 2.3.

The basic operating process begins with the typing of a document such as a letter, memo, or report. The document is stored temporarily in the CPU and shown on the CRT screen. The typist can therefore edit and proofread the document as it is typed and then again before printing. Mistakes can be easily corrected by inserting or

ILLUSTRATION 2.3

Illustration of Computer Word Processing System

Courtesy of Wang Laboratories, Inc.

replacing letters, words, lines, paragraphs, pages, or even entire sections. When satisfactory, the document can be printed and also stored electronically for future reference and use.

In addition to the ease of preparing new documents, word processing is especially advantageous when similar but modified letters, memos, or reports must be prepared. An old speech given by an executive, for example, can be easily and quickly updated without a complete retyping. Form letters, too, can be standardized. You have probably received such a letter in the mail. If prepared on a word processor, it probably was retrieved and simultaneously merged with a stored address file. Each resulting printed letter can also be automatically personalized by inserting the addressee's name in selected spots.

Word processing technology will probably yield even greater benefits in the future as more and more employees and managers use word processing as part of their individual workstations. As word processing becomes more pervasive in an organization, fewer communication blunders between writer and typist should occur. In addition, there should be a reduced duplication of effort.

Word processors make editing and proofreading easier.

Word processing can reduce communication errors.

Electronic Mail

Electronic mail involves the distribution of information to destinations both inside and outside the firm through electronic communication channels. Internal electronic mail becomes possible when a firm develops a fully integrated computer and word processing system. With this type of system, verbal, numerical, and/or graphical information can be transmitted from one terminal to any other terminal in the system. For example, if your office is on the second floor of your firm's building and you want to get a message to someone on the ninth floor, you could have the message typed on your terminal and transmitted directly to your receiver's terminal. Once received at that terminal, your message could be read from the screen, deleted, retained in storage, and/or printed.

Electronic mail can also be transmitted to computers outside your firm. In effect, computers "talk" to each other via telephone modem hookups. This can be done in several ways. First, one firm can have its computer transmit data directly to another firm's computer.

Second, electronic mail service can be provided by specialty firms, such as GTE Corporation's Telemail, ITT's Dialcom, and Tymshare, Inc.'s On-Tyme Service.[4]

Third, electronic transmission of mail with local printing of hard copy (on paper) can be provided by companies such as Western Union Telegraph Co.'s Mailgram and the U.S. Postal Service's Electronic Computer Originated Mail (ECOM). Both of these services emphasize mass mailouts or the sending of identical mail to many people.[5]

Fourth, such companies as MCI Communications Corp. have begun offering electronic mail to the mass market. Table 2.1 summa-

---

TABLE 2.1

Classes of MCI's Electronic Mail Service

1. Instant mail: Sent from one computer to another in electronic form. Cost: $1 for 1,000 words.
2. Four-hour mail: Sent from an organization's computer to one of 15 MCI Mail postal centers nearest the recipient. The document is then laser-printed on bond paper, even on the sender's letterhead. It is hand delivered by Purolator Courier Corp. within four hours of the time sent. Cost: $25 for five pages, major cities only.
3. Overnight: Same as four-hour mail, but with delivery by noon of the next day. Cost: $6 to 20,000 cities.
4. MCI letter: Same as four-hour mail, but mailed locally and delivered by U.S. Post Office. Cost: $2.

Source: Kevin Anderson, "MCI Delivers New Era of Mail," *USA Today*, September 29, 1983, p. 3B. Reprinted with permission of *USA Today*.

---

rizes MCI's approach. MCI can receive and send messages to and from any computer equipped with a telephone link and communications software. The company can send one letter or thousands.[6]

The major advantages of electronic mail include: (1) almost instantaneous distribution of information, (2) rapid feedback that the information has been received, (3) storage of the information until needed, and (4) retransmission of information electronically, on paper, or from a CRT screen. Disadvantages include: (1) higher initial cost, (2) inappropriate equipment in some firms, and (3) difficult to transmit letterheads and original signatures.

Teleconferences

Teleconferences have become an increasingly important aspect of corporate life as travel expenses have continued to climb and pressures on executives' time have increased. There are two basic forms of teleconferences.

First, *audio teleconferences* utilize the telephone to allow oral interpersonal communication between widely scattered groups and individuals. Audio teleconferences are beneficial when quick interactive exchange of information is necessary. The major drawback involves the inability to communicate visual information.

Second, *video teleconferences* allow both oral and visual interpersonal communication (see Illustration 2.4). A video telecon-

ILLUSTRATION 2.4

Illustration of Video Teleconference

Courtesy of AT&T Communications.

ference usually involves a large screen with advanced color projection monitors. Its major advantages are that it provides a medium that most closely resembles the face-to-face environment characteristic of normal business meetings and that it is appropriate for a large number of participants. Its primary disadvantage is its relatively high transmission cost.[7]

The Electronic Office of the Future

The technological advances discussed thus far should provide an inkling of the possibilities for the *electronic office* of the future. Most office workers, both management and clerical, will probably have individual electronic workstations. Illustration 2.5 (top) shows one possible layout. Each workstation will likely have both word processing and data processing capabilities. In addition, each workstation will likely be part of an integrated network which allows interstation sending and receiving. Each station, for example, could simultaneously receive a memo or report.

ILLUSTRATION 2.5

Electronic Office Communication Systems of the Future

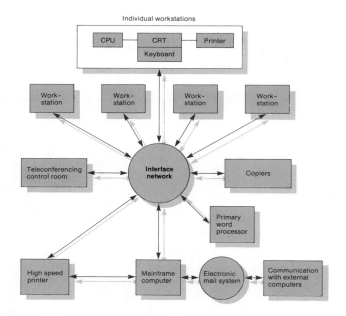

Courtesy of the NEC Corporation

A shared CPU is also likely to be part of the integrated network. Each workstation could tap the CPU for larger jobs calling for additional storage or more computing power.

The office of the future will also have interoffice communication capabilities. An engineering firm in Houston, for example, might have a variety of ways to communicate with an office in Chicago. Computer graphics transmitted directly to a CRT screen in the Chicago office could be followed by an electronic letter, a telephone call, an audio teleconference, or a video teleconference.

The office of the future will take advantage of advanced communication technology.

Limitations of Communication Technology

Despite the tremendous potential for improving communication effectiveness, communication technology is not a panacea for organizations. There are several drawbacks. First, even experienced executives and personnel must take the time to learn new systems and procedures. This *learning time* creates a short-run cost (lost time) and can be quite frustrating to some organization members. Fear of the unknown and frustration can cause organization members to resist changes in communication procedures, even if the changes are beneficial. Consequently, great care must be exercised in properly introducing and training employees to new technology.

Second, many of the advances result in communications that are basically *impersonal*. Smiles, frowns, and handshakes, for example, cannot be transmitted through electronic mail or audio teleconferencing. Nonverbal communication is therefore almost nonexistent (except for teleconferencing).

Third, the *cost* of adopting new communication technology can be relatively high. Some of the newer capabilities are now much lower in cost, but are still high relative to other alternatives. The video teleconference, for example, is much less expensive than in previous years, but it is still more expensive than an audio teleconference. The key point is that the office manager of the future will have a greater burden of analyzing the cost/benefit relationships of the new communication technology alternatives.

Communication technology can be costly, impersonal, and can provide too much information.

Fourth, organization members must guard against *information overload*. Advanced communication technology can easily produce mountains of information. Reports and other information, however, should be generated only when necessary. Too much information can create unnecessary confusion (rather than clarity) that can actually lead to worse, rather than better, decisions. In addition, the unnecessary information can be costly in terms of computer time, employee time, and so forth.

The tremendous potential combined with these limitations create a stiff challenge in implementing and utilizing communication technology in the office of the future. Organizations must focus on employee attitudes and interpersonal communication skills to meet this challenge. Otherwise, an organization may be overwhelmed with a sophisticated but ineffective communication system.

Communication Propositions

The critical conclusions relative to communication technology can be summarized in three propositions:

Proposition 1: Communication technology will continue to advance at a rapid rate, thereby providing the opportunity for increasingly effective means of improving information flow throughout organizations' communication systems.

Proposition 2: Interpersonal communication skills will have to sharpen dramatically for organizations to utilize these advances in the most effective and efficient manner.

Proposition 3: The mere presence of advanced communication technology and systems will not become a panacea to achieving effective communications within organizations. Although communication technology can be extremely helpful in achieving effective communications, the following two ingredients are absolutely necessary to achieve effective communication in organizations: (1) proper organizational climate and (2) improved individual interpersonal communication skills.

IMPROVING EMPLOYEE ATTITUDES TOWARD COMMUNICATING EFFECTIVELY

Despite the glowing accolades showered on communication technology, the most massive and technologically sophisticated communication system is useless without positive employee attitudes toward effective communication. More simply, all personnel need to have a sincere desire to communicate effectively.

Unfortunately, many people still embrace the concept of a *50/50 responsibility* toward communication. In the 50/50 concept, each party in the communication situation assumes 50 percent of the responsibility for achieving understanding. Once a ''50 percent'' effort has been expended, any shortcomings in understanding are attributable to the other party. All of us have heard comments like ''It's not my responsibility,'' ''I did my part,'' and ''Old John (or

Everyone must share the responsibility for communication.

Mary) just didn't carry his (or her) load.'' Comments like these often follow some sort of communication breakdown. Although 50/50 may sound good on the surface, it doesn't work in most communication situations.

Effective communication generally must be based on a concept of *100/100 responsibility* toward communication. Each employee must assume 100 percent, or maximum, responsibility for achieving understanding in all communication relationships. In this sense, both the sender and receiver (or listener) assume full responsibility.

Obtaining and maintaining a pervasive 100/100 attitude toward communication in an organization is obviously not easy. Organizations and individuals interested in effective communication must strive toward developing an organizational climate conducive to the 100 percent attitude.

Negative Communication Climates

An organization has a *negative communication climate* when most employees operate according to the 50/50 concept of communication responsibility. This negative climate can generally be characterized as a defensive organizational climate.

A defensive organizational climate is characterized by defensive behavior, which occurs when an individual feels threatened or anticipates a threat. The result of defensive behavior is distrust and suspicion.

The defensive behavior exhibited by one individual can have a significant impact on other individuals. In fact, it often causes other individuals to exhibit the same defensive characteristics. This phenomenon can quickly spread throughout an entire work group. Declining productivity and decreased communication effectiveness are often the result.[8]

Defensive climates are likely to occur when communication behaviors can be classified as:[9]

1. **Evaluative:** judgmental; based on personalities rather than facts.
2. **Controlling:** restricting the behavior of another due to lack of trust in one's abilities.
3. **Manipulative:** using tricks to involve another.
4. **Impersonal or detached:** expressing lack of concern for the individual.
5. **Conveying superiority:** communicating the attitude that one is superior in position.
6. **Dogmatic or close-minded:** appearing to know the answers without considering more information.

Communication characterized by these attitudes typically leads to the 50/50 attitude toward communication responsibility and, subsequently, low group performance and ineffective communication.

Positive Communication Climates

A *positive communication climate* encourages the 100/100 concept of communication responsibility. It is generally supportive in nature, which means simply that no one is defensive. It is a climate of mutual trust and confidence that stimulates creativity and encourages learning. Group members do not feel threatened, which allows them to focus more attention on the task and less attention on defending themselves in communication situations. There normally is a high level of group participation, high commitment to group and organization goals, and greater receptivity to organization changes.

A supportive climate is much more conducive to high performance and effective communication. A *supportive climate* is more likely to occur when communication behaviors can be classified as:[10]

1. **Nonevaluative:** nonjudgmental; based on descriptions of facts rather than on personalities.
2. **Problem oriented:** emphasis on solving problems and preventing their reoccurrence.
3. **Nonmanipulative:** oriented toward sincerity and freedom from deception.
4. **Empathetic:** attempting to understand others' frames of reference.
5. **Equitable:** participants have mutual trust and respect, treating each other as equals.
6. **Open-minded:** individuals are open to views that differ from their own.

Perhaps the essence of the difference between defensive and supportive organizational climates is captured by the following "Short Course in Human Relations" (author unknown):

1. The *six* most important words in the English language are:
    I was wrong—please forgive me.
2. The *five* most important words:
    You did a good job.
3. The *four* most important words:
    What is your opinion?
4. The *three* most important words:
    Can I help?
5. The *two* most important words:
    Thank you.

6. The *one* most important word:
   You.
7. The *least* important word:
   I.

The above short course could easily be called a "Short Course in Building a Supportive Organizational Climate."

Communication Propositions

The following three propositions summarize the basis for developing good employee attitudes toward effective communications:

Proposition 1: Effective communication is more likely to exist in an organization when group members take an attitude of assuming 100 percent responsibility for achieving effective communication.

Proposition 2: The more supportive the organizational climate, the greater the probability of achieving an effective communication climate in which employees possess a 100 percent responsibility attitude toward interpersonal communications.

Proposition 3: Managers who exhibit the following communication behaviors are more apt to create the proper supportive climate of trust and confidence in their organizations: non-evaluative, problem oriented, nonmanipulative, empathetic, equitable, and open-minded.

IMPROVING COMMUNICATION SKILLS

Employees should work toward improving their communication skills.

The third and final ingredient needed to achieve effective communication in organizations involves improving both verbal (oral and written) and nonverbal communication skills. *Webster's New World Dictionary* defines skill as "a great ability or proficiency; expertness that comes from training, practice, etc." Therefore, a skilled person has acquired or improved an ability through special training, practice, or experience. The key point is that communication skills can be learned. This point is the focus of this book.

This third ingredient for achieving effective communication in an organization is perhaps the most important of the three basic ingredients. The reason for its importance is that improved communication skills alone can lead to some improvements in communication effectiveness. When improved skill is combined with even small doses of advanced communication technology and/or good employee attitudes, much greater improvement in communication effectiveness can be expected. Conversely, improvements in technology and/or attitudes cannot improve communication effectiveness significantly without better communication skills.

Improved communication skills can also have a large impact on the other two ingredients. Specifically, if you can improve your communication skills, you should be able to help introduce communication technology in your organization in a way that is more likely to be accepted. Further, your attitude toward achieving effective communication and the organizational climate will probably improve when you and other organizational members acquire additional communication skills. When people can do something well, they tend to have a good attitude toward it.

Remember that all three ingredients influence each other. Improvements in any one of the ingredients often leads to improvements in the other two ingredients and, therefore, in communication effectiveness. As indicated in Illustration 2.1, all three ingredients are needed for optimum communication effectiveness.

Communication Propositions

The following two propositions state the relationship between interpersonal communication skills and the other two key ingredients—communication technology and employee attitudes toward communication:

Proposition 1: Improved oral and written interpersonal communication skills increase the likelihood that communication technology will be introduced and utilized effectively and efficiently.

Proposition 2: Improved interpersonal communication skills increase the probability of achieving a supportive climate in which employees have 100 percent responsibility attitudes toward achieving effective communication.

The remainder of this text focuses on this last ingredient of effective communication—improving your communication skills.

Application Exercises

1. John Snyder was the supervisor of the Information Services Department of a large, national insurance company. John was aware that his company was considering the development of a new automated office system in the near future. When he was asked to attend a planning session, he was eager and relieved to finally begin work on the project.

Once the entire management team was seated in the boardroom, the company CEO opened the meeting by announcing and describing the new system's design, including hardware, software, location of workstations, and other details. John was stunned. He had expected to play an integral role in developing the office system and was expecting the meeting to be an initial planning session. John's mind was completely closed for the remainder of the meeting because he felt his ability and judgment had been insulted.

When John returned to his department, his assistant supervisor, Mary Ingram, knew at a glance that something was bothering him. John responded to her concern by relating the CEO's decision. He also explained that he just could not understand why he had not been informed and involved prior to the meeting about the selection of the new office system, since his department would have major responsibilities for maintaining the system's operating effectiveness.

Mary began to apologize by telling John that when he had been out of town two weeks earlier, the CEO had called to remind John that he had not received his recommendations on the matter. Mary said that immediately after the call, an emergency had arisen in the computer room and that she had had to rush out, forgetting to make a note of the call.

a. Discuss some ways in which the above problems might have been avoided.
b. Who is responsible for the communication breakdown?
c. How can the problem be solved now?

2. Lt. Stephens, a recent college graduate, had recently arrived in South Korea for his assignment with the Second Engineer Battalion. His first major mission involved constructing a reinforced concrete bunker system for a guard post on the DMZ separating South and North Korea.

Although Lt. Stephens had eagerly anticipated beginning the mission, by dusk of the first day he was disconsolate. Day 1 had been sheer chaos. No one, including himself, had been able to get anything done despite seemingly adequate preplanning. The design was sound, dependable technical equipment and supplies were available, and sufficient manpower was also available.

Once the initial despair began to wear off, Lt. Stephens began to realize that the chaotic Day 1 was due largely to severe communication problems. He had been assigned 35 American soldiers, 15 Korean soldiers, and 40 Korean civilian construction workers. Although the language barrier was a problem, the major problem was that the mission was actually a melting pot of different cultures, subcultures, and interpersonal communication customs. The American soldiers were from all parts of the United States and all walks of life, and they did not understand each other or the Korean soldiers or civilians. Nor could the Korean nationals understand each other or the American soldiers. Lt. Stephens felt that he truly faced "Mission Impossible."

    a. How can Lt. Stephens overcome his "Mission Impossible"?
    b. How could the situation have been prevented?

3. Form a group to discuss one of the following problems:

    a. How can registration procedures at your college or university be improved?
    b. How can student advising procedures in your academic department be improved?
    c. How can the relative contribution of students on team projects be evaluated by the instructor?

Relate your discussion to the components of a positive communication atmosphere. How did your discussion exhibit or fail to exhibit these factors?

4. Examine the following quotes to determine whether they are likely to communicate a defensive or supportive climate:

    a. Don't you think 9 o'clock is a little late to start work tomorrow?
    b. Why haven't you tried this method?
    c. I'd like you to come to work at 8 tomorrow so that we can work on this budget. Do you think you can make it?
    d. There seems to be a snag here. What can we do in this case?
    e. Haven't you figured out that problem yet?
    f. I'm sure this project is behind schedule. When are you going to get caught up?
    g. Looks like we have a problem here.

h. What is the status of this project?

i. They never listen to us anyway—they think we don't know anything.

j. Could we try this idea to see if it helps?

k. Hurry up, state your problem, I've got to go.

l. We've always done it this way.

Review Questions

1. What were the three major ingredients in achieving effective communication in organizations discussed in this chapter? What would you add to these three ingredients? Why?

2. Which ingredient for effective communication do you feel is the most important? Why?

3. Discuss the four major advances in communication technology. Give the advantages of each. Which do you feel is the most important? Why?

4. Describe the limitations of communication technology. Can you provide any solutions for the problems caused by these limitations?

5. Describe the ''50/50'' concept as it relates to effective communication. Discuss the ideal communication relationship.

6. Explain the communication behaviors that are most likely to lead to a defensive organizational climate.

7. Explain the communication behaviors that are most likely to lead to a supportive organizational or group climate.

8. How can effective communication skills lead to an efficient use of communication technology?

9. Can group members communicate effectively if communication technology is unsophisticated? Discuss your answer.

Key Terms

communication technology
electronic data processing

graphics technology
word processing technology

electronic mail
teleconferences
electronic office
50/50 responsibility

100/100 responsibility
negative communication climate
positive communication climate

Notes

1. Marian C. Crawford and Robert B. Mitchell, "Computerized Electronic Communications Systems: The Impact on Organizational Communication Patterns," 1984 *Southwest Academy of Management Proceedings*.

2. John Lacy, "Preface," *IBM Systems Journal,* 22, nos. 1–2 (1983).

3. For an analysis of electronic workstation components and capabilities, see "Executive & Professional Workstations," *Data Reports on Word Processing* (Delran, N.J.: Datapro Research Corporation, 1983), pp. WP11-050-101 through WP11-050-115.

4. Kevin Anderson, "MCI Delivers New ERA of Mail," *USA Today,* September 29, 1983, p. 3B.

5. Ibid.

6. Ibid.

7. D. Anastassiou, M. K. Brown, H. C. Jones, J. L. Mitchell, W. B. Pennebaker, and K. S. Pennington, "Series/1-Based Video Conferencing System," *IBM Systems Journal,* 22, nos. 1–2 (1983), pp. 97–109.

8. William H. Baker, "Defensiveness in Communications: Its Causes, Effects, and Cures," *The Journal of Business Communication,* 17, no. 3 (Spring 1980), p. 33–43.

9. Jack R. Gibb, "Defensive Communications," *The Journal of Communications,* 2, no. 3 (September 1961), pp. 141–48.

10. Ibid.

Chapter 3

- **Chapter Outline**

Achieving Effective Communication: Interpersonal Skills

▪ *Learning Objectives*

After studying this chapter, you should be able to:

- Understand the importance of using interpersonal communication skills for achieving effective communication.
- Practice the following interpersonal communication skills:
  Seek a common frame of reference.
  Utilize feedback mechanisms.
  Recognize nonverbal cues, including
    metacommunications.
  Improve active listening and reading habits.
  Use multiple communication channels.

Introduction

You can learn specific skills to improve interpersonal communication.

Understanding and improving your ***interpersonal communication skills*** is critical to achieving effective communication in both personal and organizational settings. Recall that interpersonal communication skills form one of the three key ingredients necessary for effective communication. Good interpersonal communication skills also influence the other two key ingredients. First, they make it easier to introduce and implement advanced communication technology. Second, they foster the development of a supportive organizational climate needed for effective communication.

The purpose of this chapter is to introduce and discuss the key interpersonal communication skills necessary for achieving improved communication. The five major skills discussed are the ability to:

1. Find a common frame of reference.
2. Utilize feedback mechanisms.
3. Recognize nonverbal cues, including metacommunications.
4. Practice active listening and reading habits.
5. Use multiple communication channels.

Each of these skills should be applied to both written and oral communication. The discussion below contains examples for both types of communication.

You need to grasp three key points before studying the skills. First, although each skill is discussed separately, all five interpersonal communication skills interact with each other to form an integrated whole. When you request feedback, for example, your purpose may be to seek a common frame of reference or to ensure that active listening has occurred. Therefore, as you move through the discussion of each skill, try to relate each to those covered previously.

Second, the responsibility for using or initiating each of the major skills lies with YOU, whether you are the sender or receiver. Recall that a 100/100 responsibility attitude toward achieving effective communication is necessary for both sender and receiver.

Third, you should try to apply each of the five interpersonal skills to both oral and written communication. You should also relate each skill to both the sender and receiver.

SEEK A COMMON FRAME OF REFERENCE

The first interpersonal communication skill involves seeking a *common frame of reference*. The importance of an individual's frame of reference to effective communication was discussed in Chapter 2. Remember that your frame of reference is composed of all of your past experiences including education, work experience, family life, reference groups, and other influences.

If you do not seek a common frame of reference with other individuals, you are likely to face a major barrier to effective communication. The key to avoiding the above barrier is to first avoid assuming that your frame of reference is identical to that of your intended receiver. This assumption is normally incorrect and tends to lead to miscommunication or misunderstanding. Then, you must seek a common frame of reference and build your communications around the common points.

Consider the following example of a barrier created by the absence of a common frame of reference. Two gentlemen were watching a professional baseball game from the left field grandstands. Speaker F is a Frenchman who has never seen a baseball game. Speaker A is an American baseball fan. Both are trying to communicate despite significantly different frames of reference. A synopsis of their dialogue follows:

> *F:* "Which one is the pitcher?"
> *A:* "He's the one pitching the ball to the catcher."
> [After a brief moment of silence]
> *F:* "But they are all pitching the ball and they are all catching the ball. Which one is the pitcher?"
> [Later, after several foul balls]
> *F:* "How many strikes before a batter is out?"
> *A:* "Three."
> *F:* "Well, why did that batter just strike at the ball five times and he's still not out?"

The situation could be reversed at an exhibition of the French pastime—soccer. For example, do you know the difference between a goal kick, corner kick, penalty kick, indirect kick, direct kick, and punt?

The key issue is that neither the American nor the Frenchman recognized the disparity between their frames of reference. Consequently, neither person sought a common frame of reference. The American, for example, might have tried to find out how much the Frenchman knew about baseball. His responses could then have

Individuals have different frames of reference.

Both the sender and the receiver are responsible for seeking a common frame of reference.

been tailored to communicate more effectively. Conversely, had the Frenchman recognized the problem, he could have simply explained his frame of reference limitations relating to baseball.

The importance of seeking a common frame of reference is also illustrated in Illustration 3.1. Can a skinny doctor really understand the problems faced by patients who are overweight?

The importance of seeking a common frame of reference is illustrated in Illustration 3.2. The model highlights the idea that the overlap between a sender's and a receiver's frame of reference represents the *commonness* between the frames of reference. Further, the greater this commonness, the greater the probability of achieving effective communication. The physician in the Beetle Bailey cartoon, for example, apparently has a common frame of reference with his patient.

It is important to realize that *understanding* cannot be achieved unless a common frame of reference exists. This is a critical point. Although we generally attach meaning to words and nonverbal cues, they in themselves do not have true meaning. Even the **denotative** or dictionary meaning of a word cannot be interpreted accurately unless you know the context in which the word is used. This context is supplied by the person using the word. If you have a common frame of reference with that person, you should be able to understand the context and therefore the **connotative** meaning of specific words.

> Effective communication is based on common frames of reference.

ILLUSTRATION 3.1

Illustration of the Importance of a Common Frame of Reference

King Features Syndicated, Inc., 1983.

ILLUSTRATION 3.2

Relationship of Common Frames of Reference

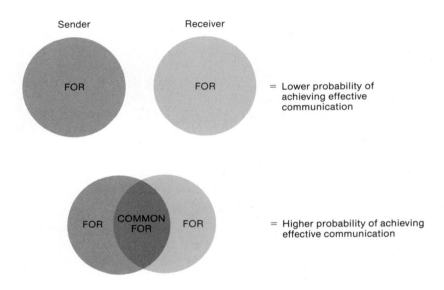

Consider, for example, the statement: I am studying.[1] Depending on the sender's frame of reference, the connotative meaning of the word *studying* could be:

1. Spending a few minutes looking at or skimming over notes or a textbook.
2. Involved in a major effort of analyzing, structuring, and learning a large mass of material over a number of hours, days, or weeks.
3. Thinking about the subject.
4. Looking at the subject.
5. Taking a specific college course.
6. Majoring in an academic discipline.

Meanings are therefore derived from people and their frames of reference. True understanding of communication can be achieved only if both senders and receivers are geared to identifying common frames of reference.

What Skills Are Needed to Obtain a Common Frame of Reference?

Developing an *empathetic attitude*, or the desire to understand other individuals' perspectives and feelings, is the overall key to achieving a common frame of reference. In the example above neither the American nor the Frenchman possessed an empathetic attitude toward communication. Without an empathetic attitude, specific types of skills needed to establish a common frame of reference probably will not be developed or used.

An empathetic attitude normally leads you to seek feedback from other individuals. Thus, the specific skills needed to establish a common frame of reference are those that help you obtain appropriate feedback. These skills are discussed in the next major section.

> You need empathy to understand another person's frame of reference.

Who Is Responsible for Seeking a Common Frame of Reference?

Both the sender and the receiver are responsible for seeking a common frame of reference. Without a 100/100 percent attitude toward responsibility, a major problem can arise. As in the above baseball example, each person might assume that the other should seek a common frame of reference. The American might assume that the Frenchman should adjust to the American's frame of reference and vice versa. When each communicator makes this assumption, little or no communication can take place.

Which Channel(s) Are Appropriate?

In which communication channels should you seek a common frame of reference? You should seek it in all *oral and written channels*. Your receiver's frame of reference is important regardless of the channel to be used. It is important, for example, when you are talking on the telephone, having a face-to-face conversation, or writing a term project, letter, or advertisement. You should always consider the potential differences between your frame of reference and your receiver's.

Communication Propositions

The following four communication propositions summarize this section. They also represent four of the most important issues regarding seeking a common frame of reference.

Proposition 1: The greater the common frame of reference between sender and receiver, the greater the probability of achieving effective communication.

Proposition 2: An empathetic attitude is the overall key to establishing a common frame of reference. The specific skills needed to establish a common frame of reference involve those needed to achieve appropriate feedback.

Proposition 3: Both the sender and the receiver are responsible for seeking a common frame of reference.

Proposition 4: A common frame of reference should be sought regardless of whether oral or written channels are being used.

The next section focuses on the second interpersonal communication skill—utilizing feedback mechanisms. Using feedback mechanisms enhances your chances of establishing a common frame of reference and improving the overall communication process.

UTILIZE FEEDBACK MECHANISMS

Feedback is one of the fundamental requirements in the communication process. Put simply, if you do not obtain appropriate feedback, you normally will not achieve effective communication. You must therefore develop your skills for using good *feedback mechanisms*.

Consider the following exclamation: "I told John exactly what to do, step-by-step, and he still didn't do it right!" This statement indicates that miscommunication has occurred. It might have been made by almost anyone, including your mother, father, or other family member, your teacher, your boss, a peer, a roommate, or even yourself. Note that the encoding and transmission of the message may have been quite efficient, but for some reason the receiver did not understand the message. This miscommunication might have been avoided if appropriate feedback had been obtained.

Communication without feedback is called *one-way communication*. Communication that includes appropriate feedback is called *two-way communication*. Several researchers have compared various aspects of one-way and two-way communication. Four of the findings are particularly important.

First, two-way communication is more accurate and effective than one-way communication. The basic reason is that you can achieve a higher level of understanding with two-way communication.

Effective communication requires feedback.

Second, two-way communication generates less frustration than one-way communication. Two-way communication reduces the chances for miscommunication and the resulting frustration.

Third, two-way communication generates confidence. When feedback mechanisms are used to create two-way communication, both communicators tend to be more confident in what they are communicating. In essence, you tend to feel better when you are sure that understanding has been achieved through effective communication.

Fourth, two-way communication takes more time than one-way communication. However, the additional time spent obtaining two-way communication can save you a great deal of time in the long run. Additional communication to correct miscommunication (and resulting erroneous activities) can be avoided.

> Two-way communication is better than one-way communication.

Skills Needed to Obtain Appropriate Feedback

Feedback can be supplied by both the sender and receiver. Similarly, either party can seek to initiate or force feedback. You should attempt to polish your skill in utilizing each of the feedback mechanisms discussed below. The mechanisms are discussed first from the standpoint of the sender and then from the standpoint of the receiver.

> Both the sender and receiver should supply feedback.

Sender-Initiated Feedback Mechanisms. The sender's general approach for eliciting feedback from the receiver involves *questioning*. Four specific categories of questions are available.

First, the sender can ask general questions that call for a *yes/no answer*. Examples of this type of question include: Do you understand? Are there any questions? Did you do it? Will you do it? Do you agree? These types of questions normally follow the transmission of a message. They can be quite effective in ensuring understanding. Seeking yes/no answers, however, does not guarantee effective understanding. Unfortunately, a yes to a question such as "Do you understand?" is not always accurate. It is sometimes given when the receiver does not want to appear slow or unintelligent to peers, superiors, or instructors. It is also sometimes given when the receiver actually thinks he or she understands, but does not. Even worse miscommunication can occur in this situation. You may have noticed this form of miscommunication in your various classes.

> Make sure your questions lead to accurate feedback.

Second, the sender can ask questions that call for a *short response*. Examples of this type of question include: Which is more effective, one-way or two-way communication? Who is responsible for seeking a common frame of reference? What time did you get here? How many courses are you taking? You can use these short response questions at any time before, during, or after transmitting the primary message. When asked before or during the transmission, they can be quite helpful in structuring your message. When used after transmitting the primary message, they can help ensure that the receiver understood the key point of the message.

Third, the sender can ask *open-ended questions* that call for a *long response*. These longer responses are sometimes asked early to help the sender structure the overall message. Examples of this form of long response questions include: What do you think about your IBM PC? What are you looking for in a new car? What are you looking for in a company? Note that the first two questions might be asked by a salesperson and the third asked by a college recruiter. Their overall purpose is to understand your frame of reference so they can tailor their presentation more effectively. If accurate information can be obtained, these questions can be quite effective. Sometimes, however, the receiver cannot or will not provide full information.

Fourth, questions can also be used to get the receiver to paraphrase the message. *Paraphrasing* is sometimes referred to as *maximum feedback* and does indeed provide you with the maximum possible feedback. It involves restating the sender's message in the receiver's own words. The sender's role is to actively listen to the paraphrasing to ensure that it in fact represents the intended message accurately. Examples of questions that call for paraphrasing include: John, would you please explain the difference between one-way and two-way communication? Helen, how would you seek to obtain a common frame of reference?

Paraphrasing is extremely useful and important when the message is detailed or complex, or when the need for accuracy is critical. In these situations, the time spent on paraphrasing can actually save a great deal of time, energy, and frustration in the long run. Recall situations in which you have been given specific instructions for activities such as preparing a term project, operating a computer or word processor, finding the location of an unfamiliar building or house, or playing a new card, board, or video game. If you listened halfheartedly and began the activity immediately, you may have encountered some problems. Conversely, if you listened well and took the time to talk about the instructions, including paraphrasing them, you probably experienced fewer problems.

Receiver-Initiated Feedback Mechanisms.
One way the receiver can participate in the feedback process is to simply respond to the sender's use of feedback mechanisms. In addition, the receiver can initiate the feedback with several different mechanisms.

First, the receiver can voluntarily offer such simple *declarations*

Good questions can help you (as a sender) formulate your message.

Paraphrasing allows the sender to judge the receiver's level of understanding.

as "I understand" and "I don't understand." This type of feedback can help the sender with the encoding process and to gauge the best rate of transmission.

Second, the receiver can interrupt the sender with *questions*. Examples include: Would you clarify that last point? What do you mean? When did you learn about this? Can you verify that? Note that these questions normally ask the sender for a clearer explanation of something or for additional information.

Third, the receiver can interject *unsolicited information*. The following dialogue illustrates this point:

> **Salesperson:** "The Apple IIe comes with 64k."
> **Prospect:** "I read an article about the hardware specifications. I want to know more about the software alternatives."

Unsolicited information can save time by helping the sender encode a more appropriate message.

Fourth, the receiver can voluntarily *paraphrase* the message. Any gaps or inaccuracies can then be corrected by the sender.

Nonverbal feedback can also help the sender in encoding and transmitting. Nonverbal cues are discussed later in this chapter.

Who Is Responsible for Obtaining Feedback?

Again, both the *sender and receiver* are responsible for obtaining feedback. Unfortunately, some people believe the responsibility lies solely with the sender. Their attitude is: "If she wants to know how I feel about it, she will ask." Others feel the responsibility lies with the receiver. Their attitude is: "If he doesn't understand, he will say so." Neither of these 50/50 attitudes is appropriate.

The likelihood of achieving effective communication is enhanced greatly when both the sender and receiver assume total responsibility for initiating the feedback process. You should assume the responsibility for utilizing the feedback whether you are the sender or the receiver.

Which Channels Can Be Utilized?

Which message channels can be utilized for initiating the feedback mechanism? Any specific form of both verbal (oral and written) and nonverbal channels can be used. A variety of message/feedback channel combinations are possible.

Oral Message/Oral Feedback. Oral feedback for a message transmitted via an oral channel is a common pattern. Practically every conversation you participate in involves this pattern.

Receivers can help the sender by volunteering feedback.

Both the sender and receiver are responsible for obtaining feedback.

Feedback can be provided via any communication channel.

Oral Message/Written Feedback. Written feedback for a message transmitted is sometimes appropriate. Business people, for example, often discuss items such as dates, contract terms, and other agenda items via oral channels either face-to-face or by telephone. Feedback is then often supplied via written channels for confirmation.

Written Message/Oral Feedback. Oral feedback is sometimes appropriate for a written message. If you have ever written home asking for additional funds, for example, your parents may have telephoned with an oral response.

Written Message/Written Feedback. Written feedback is the only appropriate form for certain written messages. If you write a company requesting information for a term project, for example, you might expect to receive a packet of written information.

Nonverbal Feedback. Feedback can also be obtained via nonverbal channels. When you are talking to someone, for example, you might judge their level of interest in your message by the amount of eye contact maintained. Nonverbal channels will be discussed more fully later in the chapter.

Communication Propositions

Four key communication propositions summarize the importance of using appropriate feedback mechanisms.

1. Maximum feedback or paraphrasing is the most accurate feedback mechanism and should be used in communication encounters.
2. Senders who encourage feedback will increase the probability of achieving effective communication.
3. In an organizational context, managers influence the amount of feedback in the communication process. They can either encourage or discourage the degree of feedback within their group.
4. Managers who encourage feedback mechanisms in their organizations will increase the probability of having the proper organizational climate—one that is free from frustration, one that is conducive to trust and open communications.

RECOGNIZE NONVERBAL CUES AND METACOMMUNICATIONS

Words or verbal messages are the primary communication tool. However, messages can also be transmitted *without* the use of words. These messages involve **nonverbal communication**. Nonverbal messages can be conveyed via both oral and written channels.

Conflicts between Verbal and Nonverbal Cues

Verbal messages and their related nonverbal messages (or cues) are not always consistent. Research indicates that when there is a conflict between the verbal and the nonverbal cues, the receiver tends to put more reliance on the nonverbal cues.[1]

Verbal and nonverbal messages may conflict.

Consider the following example. Mr. Kelly, the office manager, arrives at the office at 7:58 and greets two employees, Mary and Jane, with a "Good Morning!" as he passes their respective desks. Although it might appear that both should react similarly, what might make them react differently? Mary might react positively because the greeting was delivered with positive nonverbal cues, such as a smile, positive eye contact, and positive voice inflection. Jane's negative reaction might be traced to various negative nonverbal cues, such as a frown, averted eyes, and negative voice inflection. Other possibilities are shown in Table 3.1.

TABLE 3.1

Examples of Positive and Negative Nonverbal Cues Delivered with Positive "Good Morning" Greeting

Positive	Negative
Boss smiles, nods, and looks directly at Mary when greeting her.	Boss frowns and looks at Jane's desk as he greets her.
Boss approaches within three feet of Mary.	Boss approaches within about 15 feet of Jane.
Boss knows that Mary often arrives early.	Boss knows that Jane usually arrives late and his surprise is apparent.
Boss emphasizes the word *good* and uses rising inflection on *morning*.	Boss emphasizes the word *morning* with decreasing inflection.

What Skills Are Needed?

Improving your ability to recognize nonverbal communication cues is based on improving your understanding and awareness of the different types of nonverbal cues. Although nonverbal communication probably pre-dates verbal communication, scholarly investigation has only recently focused on this area. The major nonverbal cues identified to date can be organized into six broad categories: (1) kinesics, (2) proxemics, (3) chronemics, (4) paralanguage, (5) artifacts, and (6) metacommunication. Each of these categories is discussed below.

Kinesics. *Kinesics* is the study of *body language,* or of body movements and the visual aspects of behavior. It typically applies to face-to-face, oral communication. The effects of posture, facial expressions, movement, and gestures are normally included.

Your body language can either support or contradict your verbal communication. If you say that you "like" something, for example, you may also support your statement by smiling and nodding approval. Conversely, what if you say, "I am interested in what you are saying," but look out the window, tap your fingers on the desk, or continually glance at your watch or other material? Your nonverbal message would contradict your verbal statement.

Although body language can be quite revealing, judgments about the meaning of particular body movements must be made carefully. Differences in frames of reference, for example, can cause misinterpretations. The key point is that no single body movement should be considered as an absolute indication of an individual's attitudes, feelings, or emotions.

Proxemics. *Proxemics* is the study of *spatial relations,* or of how people structure and use physical space in relation to other individuals. Key spatial relations include the distance maintained between individuals during the communication process and the use of space in houses, offices, buildings, and cities.

You probably have learned through experience what is considered to be the appropriate distances for various communication situations. Visualize the relative distance you maintain in conversations with close friends, passing acquaintances, and virtual strangers. The distance tends to increase as the level of familiarity decreases.

You also probably maintain more distance from those that you dislike and from those you consider to have higher status. You may speak to your boss, for example, while standing near his or her door. Your boss, however, will typically walk up to the edge of your desk or work area to talk.

You can learn to recognize nonverbal cues.

Body language cues can be revealing, but be careful in interpreting them.

What happens when you get too close to someone according to his or her distance standards? They back up! Although you may desire a smaller distance, the other person will probably be more comfortable (and can communicate better) if you let him or her determine the distance.

What happens when two people have different ideas about the desired spatial distance and both want to determine the distance? Usually, one tends to get uncomfortable and begins to move away. The other tends to move forward to reestablish the closer spatial relationship. The repetition of this pattern creates a "spatial dance."

People get uncomfortable if you "violate their personal space."

TABLE 3.2

Zones of Spatial Distance

Zone	Description
1. Intimate zone	a. Close-intimate: actual contact; for very close friendships, children clinging to a parent or each other, and making love.
	b. Far-intimate: from 6 to 18 inches; for intimate friends; female/male and female/female normally acceptable, but male/male not normally acceptable.
2. Personal zone	a. Close-personal: 18 to 30 inches; touching is relatively easy.
	b. Far-personal: 30 to 48 inches; the limit of physical domination; the difficulty of touching creates privacy, but does not preclude conversation.
3. Social zone	a. Close-social: 4 to 7 feet; normal for transacting impersonal business, meeting business colleagues, at casual social gatherings, and boss to employee.
	b. Far-social: 7 to 12 feet; for formal social and business relationships; typical zone created by "big bosses" and receptionist desks (if closer, receptionist would have to stop work and talk to visitor).
4. Public zone	a. Close-public: 12 to 25 feet; suited for informal gatherings, such as in classroom or for boss addressing employees at a conference.
	b. Far-public: more than 25 feet; for formal public situations, such as political speeches and stage acting.

Source: From *Body Language* by Julius Fast. Copyright © 1970 by Julius Fast. Reprinted by permission of the publisher, M. Evans and Co., Inc., New York, N.Y. 10017.

Although there are no precise spatial rules, several general guidelines have been developed. Four categories of spatial zones are described in Table 3.2. Note that these spatial zones do not have universal application. In other countries, for example, business people may conduct business in what most Americans would consider the far-intimate zone.

Chronemics.

Chronemics involves the use of time. The importance of *time* is illustrated by factors such as specific beginning and ending times for classes, completion dates for term projects, and establishing specific times and dates for tests, dates, games, meetings, and other appointments. Similar factors in an organizational setting also include time clocks and establishing specific times for pay periods, working hours, coffee breaks, and lunch periods.

People are judged on how they use time.

You are judged on your ability to meet both formal and informal time standards. Completing projects on time or early can influence your performance evaluation, both at school and on the job. Arriving early for a meeting can communicate interest and respect for the person holding the meeting. Conversely, arriving late for work, a meeting, or class often communicates unreliability, disinterest, and disrespect. Failure to observe the formal and informal time standards communicates nonverbal messages that can reduce your chances for success.

Paralanguage.

Paralanguage involves use of the *voice*. It is concerned with *how* something is said rather than what is said. The way the voice is used is an important element in understanding the total message.

The meaning of a spoken sentence can differ significantly according to the particular word stressed. Consider the following variations in emphasis (in boldface):

> **How** did she do the job?
>
> How **did** she do the job?
>
> How did **she** do the job?
>
> How did she **do** the job?
>
> How did she do **the** job?
>
> How did she do the **job**?

By shifting the emphasis, the same combination of words can convey at least six different meanings.

The multitude of paralanguage elements can be divided into four major categories:

1. *Voice qualities:* tone, rhythm, resonance, and tempo.
2. *Vocal characteristics:* crying, laughing, whispering, sighing, yelling, yawning, and others.
3. *Vocal irregularities:* um-m-m, uh, uh-um, er-r-r, ah-h-h, and others.
4. *Vocal qualifiers:* intensity (how loud or soft), rate (how fast or slow), and pitch (how high or low).

Individuals have unique speech patterns because of the way in which they combine these four elements.

Many people tend to make relatively quick judgments about another individual based on general paralanguage characteristics. As you might expect, these judgments based on paralanguage stereotypes are often inaccurate. Greater accuracy can be achieved when observing paralanguage cues from an individual with whom you are familiar. Familiarity allows you to detect unusual or abnormal paralanguage cues in a person that can be interpreted fairly accurately.

Artifacts. The term *artifacts* refers to *object language,* which is the communication that results from the display of material things. Examples of objects that often influence communication (or even communicate themselves) include clothes, chairs, desks, podiums, methods of transportation, and architectural arrangements. The arrangement of furniture in a classroom or conference room, for example, can affect the communication patterns during the class or meeting. Similarly, furnishings and their arrangement in apartments, offices, and homes convey messages about an individual.

Consider the communication influence of an office desk. If you walk into an office and the executive's (or professor's) desk is positioned between him and you, the desk serves both as a physical and a communication barrier. It can also serve as a psychological barrier because its size can be construed to represent authority and power.

Metacommunication. *Metacommunication* involves messages that can be picked up "between the lines" of *verbal communication.* Although the metacommunication message is not expressed in words, it must always accompany a message that is executed in words, either oral or written. Table 3.3 provides several illustrations of metacommunication.

Note that the column on the right is labeled Possible Metacommunication Message because not everyone would get the same between-the-lines message from the worded message on the left. Table 3.4 presents some tongue-in-cheek business metacommunications.

TABLE 3.3

Examples of Metacommunications

Written message	Possible metacommunication meanings
"I hope you can make it on time."	"Past experience has led me to believe that you probably will be late."
"I was under the impression that our meeting was scheduled for 1:00 P.M."	"I know that our meeting was scheduled for 1:00 P.M. It is a shame that you are so unreliable that you cannot keep scheduled appointments."
"The report was fine overall, but a couple of points need clarification."	"The report was full of errors and is therefore useless."
"I have no problems with the overall concept, but I still don't understand all of the details."	"It sounds like a scatter-brained idea."

Characteristics of Nonverbal Cues

The six categories of nonverbal communication cues have several common characteristics that you should keep in mind.

1. Nonverbal cues are present in all messages, whether written or spoken.
2. Nonverbal cues vary in meaning according to the individual.
3. Nonverbal cues vary in meaning according to the situation.
4. Nonverbal cues transmit clues about the sender.
5. Nonverbal cues may make a greater impression than the worded message.
6. The obvious interpretation of nonverbal cues may be unintended by the sender.
7. Verbal and nonverbal cues may not be consistent.

There are no dependable rules on how to interpret nonverbal cues, but you should be aware of their presence and their influence. You can then more easily avoid conflict between verbal and nonverbal cues.

TABLE 3.4

A Glossary of Modern Office Terminology and Their Metacommunications

Terminology	Metacommunication
It is in process.	So wrapped up in red tape that the situation is hopeless.
We will look into it.	By the time the wheel makes a full turn, we assume you will have forgotten about it, too.
Program.	Any assignment that can't be completed by one phone call.
Expedite.	To confound confusion with commotion.
Channels.	The trail left by interoffice memos.
To activate.	To make carbons and add more names to the memo.
To implement a program.	Hire more people and expand the office.
Under consideration.	Never heard of it.
Under active consideration.	We're looking in the files for it.
A meeting.	A mass mulling by the masterminds.
A conference.	A place where conversation is substituted for the dreariness of labor and the loneliness of thought.
To negotiate.	To seek a meeting of minds without the knocking together of heads.
Reorientation.	Getting used to working again.
Reliable source.	The guy you just met.
Informed source.	The guy who told the guy you just met.
A clarification.	To fill in the background with so many details that the foreground goes underground.
We are making a survey.	We need more time to think of an answer.
Note and initial.	Let's spread the responsibility for this a little.
Let's get together on this.	I'm assuming you're as confused on this as I am.
See me, or let's discuss.	Come down to my office—I'm lonesome.

Who Is Responsible?

In this context, responsibility involves avoiding conflicts between verbal and nonverbal cues. Both the sender and receiver should assume the responsibility for addressing and surmounting any such conflicts. If the sender, for example, detects that the receiver has misinterpreted the intended message because of interference from nonverbal cues, the sender should clarify the intended message. This clarification often involves restating the message in different terms or elaborating on the basic message and removing the conflicting nonverbal cues.

Similarly, when the receiver detects conflicts between the verbal and the nonverbal cues, he or she should try to determine which set of cues represents the real message. This can involve any of the mechanisms discussed earlier for initiating feedback. It can also involve direct confrontation, such as: "Steve, although you said that you will be at the meeting, I get the impression that you are not that interested. Perhaps we should discuss it more fully."

Why is it important to confront apparent conflicts between verbal and nonverbal cues? The answer involves the importance of developing the right climate for communication relationships, as discussed in Chapter 2. When verbal/nonverbal conflicts are frequent, the parties involved begin to distrust each other. Individuals often begin to either consciously or subconsciously believe that the other communicators are insincere and cannot be trusted. When trust is lost, communication flow and the probability of achieving effective communication is reduced substantially.

Which Channels Are Appropriate?

Although specific types of nonverbal cues may be rather unique to a specific channel, nonverbal communication of some type occurs in all communication channels. Body language, spatial relations, and paralanguage, for example, are normally more relevant to the face-to-face, oral channel. Chronemics and artifacts might influence meaning in both oral and written channels. Metacommunication, by definition, relates to written channels. You should therefore be alert for nonverbal cues in all communication situations and from any channel.

Communication Propositions

The relevance of nonverbal communication skills can be summarized with the following six propositions.

Both the sender and receiver are responsible for detecting conflicts between verbal and nonverbal cues.

Conflicts between verbal and nonverbal cues reduce communication effectiveness.

Proposition 1: If you are aware of and understand nonverbal cues, your chance of interpreting verbal messages accurately is greater.

Proposition 2: You should verify the meaning of nonverbal cues by initiating appropriate feedback mechanisms.

Proposition 3: You are more likely to remember the nonverbal message when there is a conflict between verbal and nonverbal cues.

Proposition 4: You should address and solve any conflicts between verbal and nonverbal cues before they adversely affect the trusting relationship (i.e., climate) between you and other communicators.

Proposition 5: Both the sender and receiver are responsible for alleviating conflicts between verbal and nonverbal cues.

Proposition 6: Nonverbal cues are relevant to both oral and written channels.

PRACTICE ACTIVE LISTENING AND READING HABITS

Most of what we learn is derived from listening.

Most people consider themselves to be good listeners. Controlled research experiments, however, indicate that most people are *not* particularly good listeners. In fact, average listening effectiveness is only about 25 percent—people typically understand about 25 percent of the average message. This is a rather alarming situation when you pause to consider that *most of what we learn comes from listening* rather than from reading and using the other senses combined.[2]

Business leaders recognize the importance of good listening skills.

Business leaders have recently begun to recognize the importance of **listening skills**. Many feel that poor listening habits are costing businesses millions of dollars each year. Many corporations are also trying to do something about it. In 1982, Sperry Rand Corp. invested millions of dollars in a worldwide program to train 16,000 managers in effective listening skills. Other firms that have been pioneers in the development of listening skill training include New York Life Insurance Company, Honeywell Inc., and Xerox Corporation.[3]

There are two major reasons why most people do not listen as well as they think they do. First, many people assume that speaking is an *active* process and that listening is a *passive* process. Listening is therefore inaccurately perceived as something that does not require energy—all you have to do is sit back, relax, and open your ears. Much of the burden for this inability to listen actively falls on our educational system, which has apparently failed to teach both

Listening is an active
process.

the importance of active listening and the needed skills. The problem is compounded because students are in too many classroom situations where passive listening is acceptable.

Second, there is a significant mismatch between the average rate of speech and your ability to comprehend words. Most people speak at a rate of 125 to 250 words per minute. But you can probably comprehend a rate of around 500 words per minute and can think even faster.[4] Consequently, you are left with a great deal of "idle" time during most conversations. Unfortunately, many people do not use this time constructively; rather, they allow their attention to wander to unrelated subjects and therefore experience significant lapses of attention.

What Are the Skills for Active Listening and Reading?

Although there are no magic formulas or rules for good listening and reading, there are several practical guidelines. The listening guidelines described in Table 3.5 and the reading guidelines described in Table 3.6 do not provide an easy way to active listening—they are simply guides to the hard work that listening requires.

Remember that good listening and good reading are not passive activities. Your level of understanding can be improved with active listening and active reading based on the guidelines shown.

Who Is Responsible?

Both the sender and
receiver must use listening skills.

Listening Responsibility.   The receiver has a major responsibility for active listening, but it is also important to understand that the sender has a major responsibility for active listening. A good speaker, for example, "listens" for nonverbal cues from his or her audience. If you fail to listen actively as a sender, you will probably have greater difficulty finding a common frame of reference, miss critical feedback, and miss many nonverbal cues. Without active listening from both the sender and the receiver, the level of understanding will be less.

Reading Responsibility.   The receiver (or reader) obviously has a major responsibility for reading and should follow the guidelines presented in Table 3.6. Of course, the sender (or writer) must also assume a primary responsibility. The sender's responsibility involves careful editing and proofreading. The writer should make the message easy to understand and eliminate factors such as misspelled words and jargon that can distract the receiver. Much of the remainder of this textbook focuses on this latter issue.

TABLE 3.5

Listening Guidelines

1. *Stop talking.* You cannot listen while you are talking.
2. *Empathize with the speaker.* Put yourself in the speaker's place by seeking a common frame of reference.
3. *Ask questions.* Providing feedback shows that you are interested and encourages the speaker.
4. *Concentrate.* Actively focus your attention on the concepts, ideas, attitudes, and feelings related to the spoken message.
5. *Look interested.* Put the speaker at ease and show that you want to listen. The key is positive nonverbal feedback.
6. *Control your emotions.* Strong emotions, especially anger, lead to message distortion and misinterpretation.
7. *Get rid of distractions.* Put down papers, pencils, and other objects that can distract you and eliminate as many outside distractions as possible.
8. *Seek areas of agreement.* Do not mentally argue with the speaker. It creates a barrier to understanding, especially if detected by the speaker.
9. *Avoid snap judgments.* Listen to the complete message before evaluating and drawing conclusions. Premature evaluations tend to push the listener ahead of the speaker, which creates a barrier to further communication.
10. *Listen for the main points.* Avoid focusing on only the illustrative material, stories, statistics, and so forth. Minor details can sometimes obscure the main issue.

Source: Adapted from Ralph G. Nichols, "Listening Is a 10-Part Skill," pp. 554–60; Carl Rogers and Richard Farson, "Active Listening," pp. 561–76; and Sherman R. Okum, "How to be a Better Listener," pp. 582–86, all in *Readings in Interpersonal and Organizational Communications*, 3d ed., ed. Richard C. Huseman, Cal M. Logue, and Dwight L. Freshley (Boston: Allyn & Bacon, 1977).

Which Channels?

Listening skills are relevant primarily to oral communication channels. Reading skills are relevant primarily to written communication channels. Also note that your ability to observe and understand nonverbal cues in the various channels enhances both listening and reading skills.

Communication Propositions

The following communication propositions serve to summarize active listening and active reading skills.

TABLE 3.6

Reading Guidelines

1. *Determine your best reading speed.* You can *scan* by reading headings, lists, boldface words, and other indicators of key points. *Careful reading* involves slower, more analytical reading to optimize comprehension.
2. *Determine the amount of time available.*
3. *Control your environment.*
4. *Control your physical and psychological condition.*
5. *Improve your vocabulary.* Read more.
6. *Practice reading.*
7. *Read in logical blocks or phases of words.*
8. *Focus on words and phrases long enough to get the key points.* Skip short transitional words and phrases—let your mind fill in the blanks.
9. *Keep your eyes moving smoothly.* Breaking eye movement with periodic stops generally reduces speed and comprehension.
10. *Read silently.* Don't talk or move while reading—your speed will be reduced.
11. *Underline and take notes sparingly.* It reduces your speed and breaks your concentration.

Source: Adapted from Bobbye D. Sorrels, *Business Communication Fundamentals* (Columbus, Ohio: Charles E. Merrill Publishing, 1984), pp. 54–61.

Proposition 1: Active listening requires a 100 percent responsibility attitude. Both sender and receiver are responsible for effective listening.

Proposition 2: Active listening and reading requires energy and involves hard work.

Proposition 3: Listening and reading skills can be applied to both the oral and written channels of communication.

USE MULTIPLE CHANNELS

The use of more than one channel is often a good way of ensuring effective communication.

One of the key decisions in the communication process involves selecting the appropriate communication channel(s). You might, for example, choose a verbal channel. Then you must decide whether to use an oral or written medium. If you choose an oral medium, the specific medium could be face-to-face, telephone, or teleconference. If you choose a written medium, your choice could be a memorandum, letter, or report sent through regular mail, courier service, telegraph, computer linkups, or others. The key issue in this section, however, involves deciding whether or not to use multiple channels to communicate.

What Skills Are Relevant?

Perhaps the key relevant skill involves simply recognizing when multiple channels would be beneficial. Multiple channels would probably be useful in the following situations:

1. If miscommunication is likely.
2. If the potential negative consequences of miscommunication are significant.
3. If the potential lost opportunities (positive consequences) of miscommunication are significant.
4. If time pressures permit the use of a second channel.

To illustrate the potential benefit of using multiple channels, consider the following hypothetical situation. Assume that your boss calls you on the telephone and tells you to prepare a bid for constructing a small office building. You then carry out the instructions as you understood them by preparing and submitting the bid and then reporting back to your boss. His reaction is: "You idiot! That's not what I told you to do! What's wrong with you?" Since you are not an idiot and you carried out the instructions as you understood them, how could this situation have been avoided? You assumed that the boss wanted you to prepare and submit the bid, but the boss only wanted you to prepare the bid for his review.

First, the boss could have avoided misunderstanding by using an additional communication channel. He could, for example, have sent you a brief memo that summarized the instructions. Note also that he could have initiated a feedback mechanism by having you paraphrase the instructions over the phone or by having you send him a brief memo outlining your intended actions.

Second, you could have avoided embarrassment and stress by asking the boss to send you a memo, voluntarily paraphrasing the instructions, or by sending the boss a memo outlining your intended actions. Any of these actions by either party would have increased the probability of effective communication.

Who Is Responsible?

Who is responsible for deciding whether to use multiple channels? The above example clearly illustrates the necessity of a 100 percent attitude. Both the sender and receiver are responsible—either party can initiate the use of additional channels.

Which Channels Are Appropriate?

Regardless of which channel is chosen as the primary channel, any channel can be chosen as an additional channel. The key involves choosing the additional channel that is most likely to reinforce and increase understanding and that meets time and budgetary constraints.

Communication Propositions

The following communication propositions serve to summarize the use of multiple channels:

Proposition 1: When multiple channels of communication are used, the probability of achieving effective communication is increased.

Proposition 2: Both the sender and receiver have the responsibility for initiating the use of multiple channels.

Application Exercises

1. Analyze your ability as a listener as demonstrated in your business communications class. Be sure to use the guidelines for effective listening.

2. Describe a situation in which multiple communication channels would be appropriate and tell which channels would be best to use.

3. With a partner, discuss an issue of your choice while standing face-to-face. The issue might be a football game, a person, or an automobile. After two or three minutes, turn back-to-back and continue the conversation for two or three minutes more. Discuss any changes in the way you felt before and after the change in physical position. Could you assess your partner's comments better before or after the switch? Do some senses change in importance after the switch?

4. Spend a day with some proxemics experiments of your own. As you meet and speak with friends and acquaintances, vary the distance you maintain from them. Note their reactions and adjustments to your position.

5. Form into small groups. Have one individual use a real or fabricated map as the basis for giving other group members directions for locating a particular place. After the instructions have been completed, each group member should draw a map to correspond with the original. Compare the maps to find out who can listen well.

6. Divide into small groups. Choose one person to draw a relatively simple arrangement of geometric shapes such as those shown.

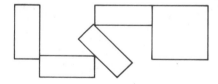

Part A: Without showing the drawing to the group, the artist should describe the drawing. The group should then draw the geometric shapes from the artist's description, but NO QUESTIONS ARE ALLOWED.

Part B: Repeat Part A with a new but similar drawing, but ALLOW THE GROUP TO ASK QUESTIONS. Compare the accuracy of the drawings made in each part. What other differences do you notice between the two parts of the exercise. What part did feedback play in this exercise?

Review Questions

1. How do interpersonal skills affect the other two ingredients of effective communication?
2. What is the difference between the denotative and the connotative meaning of a word?
3. On what basis do people derive meanings for words?
4. Who has the responsibility for establishing a common frame of reference, the receiver or the sender? What kinds of problems can arise if the responsibility is shirked?
5. Describe the advantages of two-way versus one-way communication.
6. Discuss the practice of paraphrasing. When is it most useful?
7. Describe the various receiver-initiated feedback mechanisms.
8. Define the six types of nonverbal communication.
9. Discuss the failure of people to listen effectively. Why do people not engage in effective listening?
10. How does the sender play a part in active listening?

Key Terms

interpersonal communication skills
common frame of reference
denotative meaning
connotative meaning
empathetic attitude
feedback
feedback mechanisms
one-way communication
two-way communication

questioning
nonverbal communication
kinesics
proxemics
chronemics
paralanguage
artifacts
metacommunication
listening skills

Notes

1. Robert W. Rasberry, "A Collection of Nonverbal Communication Research: An Annotated Bibliography," *Journal of Business Communication,* 16, no. 4 (Fall 1979), pp. 21–29.

2. Jackie Schmidt-Posner and Nancy Schmidt, *Instructor's Film Guide for the Power of Listening* (Del Mar, Calif.: CRM McGraw-Hill Films, 1978); G. M. Morgan, "Therapeutic Listening—A Communication Tool," *Training and Development Journal,* August 1983, pp. 44–46; and Gail Gregg, "They Have Ears, But Hear Not," *Across the Board,* September 1983, pp. 56–61.

3. George Headric, "Let's Learn to Listen!" *Kiwanis,* February 1983, pp. 18–20.

4. Schmidt-Posner, "Instructor's Film Guide," p. 2.

Part II

Understanding Basic Writing Skills

The two chapters in Part II deal with preparing you to write more effectively. Chapter 4 focuses on improving your understanding of the writing process. Chapter 5 stresses the output of the writing process, focusing on the major characteristics of effective written correspondence.

Chapter 4

Understanding the Communication Process

- *Learning Objectives*

After studying this chapter, you should be able to:
- Envision the steps involved in the writing process.
- Describe the steps involved in the planning stages of writing.
- Develop an effective organization plan for writing.
- Describe the stages of the writing phase.
- Use effective editing techniques.

Introduction

Good writing skills can yield benefits to you during and after your college career. These benefits come from three basic areas. First, good writing skills can help you directly in your remaining courses. Have you noticed that the number of essay tests and term projects tends to increase as you progress through your academic career? Superior knowledge is often useless if you cannot effectively communicate that knowledge.

Second, good writing skills can help you when you begin job hunting. Your skills will be apparent in items such as your resume, cover letter, letter of application, and thank you notes. These items are critical in portraying your potential contribution to the prospective employer.

Third, good writing skills can provide an important boost to your career progress. A college diploma may help you obtain a job, but further progress depends on your performance. Your overall communication skills, including writing skills, will play an important role in your performance evaluations.

Most evidence indicates that, despite its importance, basic writing skills have declined over the past 10 years in the United States. In essence, today's students do not write as well as students in similar grades 10 years ago, which means that when these students graduate they will bring their declining skills with them into the business world. This problem began to receive widespread notice in the 1970s because of articles such as *Newsweek's* "Why Johnny Can't Write."[1]

Business organizations, as a result, are finding that far too many employees, including higher level managers and executives, have poor writing skills. These companies must spend millions of dollars each year to send their employees back to school to improve their writing skills.[2]

Why are businesses so concerned with writing skills? The major reason is that executives spend a large proportion of their time communicating. Much executive communication involves writing memos, letters, and reports. Inadequate writing skills generate a negative image of the writer and the company. Business firms, your potential employers, are putting a premium on good writing skills.

Good writing skills can benefit you now and in the future.

Businesses want their employees to have good writing skills.

Regardless of your present writing ability, you should be concerned with improving and polishing your skills. This chapter focuses specifically on improving your understanding of the overall writing process. Research has shown that understanding the overall process is the first requirement for improving writing skills.[3] The six major parts of the writing process are: (1) dealing with writing apprehension, (2) applying creativity, (3) planning to write, (4) organizing to write, (5) writing, and (6) editing.

DEALING WITH WRITING APPREHENSION

Many people experience a great deal of apprehension when they have to write. Writing even a short letter or memo can cause a great deal of stress for some individuals. If this apprehension becomes severe enough, it can restrain the writer's thought processes, make it difficult to begin writing, and reduce the effectiveness of the writing.

Although there are many specific causes of apprehension, two myths appear to be major contributors. You must recognize and conquer both.

Myth Number 1: A good writer is born, not made. Those who believe this myth feel that those who are born without the knack for writing cannot develop good writing skills. Consequently, they write with little confidence and a great deal of stress. Fortunately, research has shown that this perception is false.[4] A more accurate statement is: Good writers are made, not born. Good writing skills are actually learned.

Myth Number 2: Writing is harder for me than it is for you. This myth is related to Myth Number 1, but focuses more directly on an "I can't" attitude. Some individuals feel that they simply cannot write well. They are likely to have a negative attitude toward writing and to experience high levels of frustration and stress.

This perception may be true in specific situations, but it does not have to be "written in stone." Any activity, such as swimming and skating, is difficult if you do not know how to do it the right way. But most of you probably learned to swim and skate at a relatively young age.

Develop a positive attitude toward writing and improving your writing skills.

It is important to keep in mind that good writing is usually the result of hard work. Professional writers normally have to work hard to develop and polish their writing skills. Most of them also have to work hard on a piece of writing to make it effective.

Your Challenge. Your challenge is to overcome any negative preconceptions and develop a positive attitude toward developing your writing skills. The key point is that you can learn the basic skills and, with hard work, learn to apply them effectively.

APPLYING CREATIVITY

Creativity is vital to successful communications, particularly writing. **Creativity** involves *bringing something new into existence.* Although most people recognize the importance of creativity, few fully comprehend what it really means and how it comes about. The creative process focuses on solving a problem.

Creativity is an important element of good writing.

The creative process consists of four basic steps:[5] (1) preparation, (2) incubation, (3) illumination, and (4) verification. In the *preparation* stage, you must recognize that something new (a good piece of writing) or the solution to a problem does not come into existence instantaneously. You must define and analyze the problem and gather relevant data. Assume, for example, that you need to write a letter of recommendation for an individual who has worked for you in the past. Although the person was a good worker and you want to give a good recommendation, you know that his qualifications and experience are not particularly impressive. Your problem is to write a truthful letter that highlights the person's positive characteristics. Your initial preparation to write the letter may not provide you with the ideas you need.

Your creativity can be improved.

When the preparation step does not yield a quick solution, you enter an *incubation* stage. You simply "shelve" the problem temporarily and divert your attention to some form of relaxation or recreation. Many new ideas and approaches are often generated during this stage. Unfortunately, many people who consciously use an incubation stage often use it only during the planning phase of writing. Problems and issues arising in the other stages can sometimes be addressed effectively with incubation.

An *illumination* stage often follows the incubation stage and is characterized by a sudden flash of insight or spontaneous solution. It normally cannot be forced—you must simply be aware that it can happen and be ready to take advantage of it. In the problem of writing a letter of recommendation mentioned above, for example, you might realize that your emphasis in the letter should be on the individual's dependability, initiative, and ambition rather than on skills and experience.

The final stage of the creative process normally involves **verification**. Your ideas generated in the illumination stage must generally be verified and revised to make them meaningful.

As you move through the remainder of the writing process, you will see that the entire creative process applies to each individual step of the writing process.

PLANNING TO WRITE

Good writing is generally the result of good planning.

Once you have dealt with your apprehension, you are ready to begin thinking about the specific task at hand. All writing begins with some degree of planning. It can occur in a few seconds, or it may take hours or even days. It may also be conscious or subconscious. The three major phases of planning are: (1) determine the purpose of your message, (2) anticipate reader reaction, and (3) choose the major points to be covered.

Determine the Purpose of Your Message

Although all written correspondence has a general purpose of achieving a high level of understanding, you must also develop a specific purpose. The specific purpose of a letter, for example, might be any of the following:

- Provide information about an upcoming event.
- Request something from someone.
- Persuade someone to do something.
- A combination of all three above purposes.

The key issue is that every piece of written correspondence must have a specific purpose to serve as a guide for all aspects of the writing process. If you cannot verbalize a specific purpose, your reader will surely have similar problems. For example, the letter shown in Illustration 4.1 lacks a clear purpose.

The major purpose is usually stated early. It can, however, be stated in the middle or at the end of certain types of correspondence. These exceptions are discussed in later chapters.

A clear purpose guides the remainder of your writing process.

Anticipate Reader Reaction

The interpersonal communication skills (i.e., common frames of reference, feedback) discussed in Chapter 3 provide the means to

ILLUSTRATION 4.1

A Letter without a Clear Purpose

Dear Mr. Davis:

How are you? I saw where you were entering the Summer Fling Golf Tournament. How did you do? Maybe we can play sometime.

As you know, a major aspect of life insurance involves sales. Although only a part of our group makes a career of it, everyone has to be sales-minded.

Therefore, I know in building a file for you for an interview, they would like to have the benefit of an aptitude index test to determine your sales potential. Accordingly, I am attaching a little folder which tells the story of the aptitude index, which I would like for you to read. Then if you will read the test book which is also being enclosed, and then fill out the answer sheet and fill in the attached score report card in line with the instructions, and return to me in the attached self-addressed envelope, we will then send it on to the Life Insurance Agency Management Association, who will advise the company of your rating.

This will require about three weeks after we receive it to have it processed and to get further advice from our home office.

By the way, I went ahead and bought that new van we talked about. The family really likes it, especially our teenager.

Thank you for your cooperation and the prompt way in which you answered.

                                        Sincerely,

anticipate the reader's reaction. Specifically, you must try to visualize the reader's frame of reference and strive for sufficient empathy to understand how he or she will react to your message. You should then be able to plan your writing to build goodwill, minimize possible antagonism, and achieve your specific purpose. For example, ask yourself:

- What is the reader's educational level?
- How much interest does the reader have in the correspondence?
- Why is the reader interested?
- Under what conditions will the correspondence be read?
- What does the reader really want to read?

The answers will help you decide how to present your message in a manner that maximizes your chances of achieving your desired reader reaction. You might also ask yourself: How much detail should be included? Should a conclusion be presented? Should it be at the beginning or end? If both are relevant, should good or bad news be presented first?

Choose the Major Points to Be Covered

The previous step should have helped you think of the major points to be covered. Now you must choose all of the key ideas needed for your writing.

A few seconds or minutes of simple brainstorming may generate a sufficient number of key ideas. A simple aid involves asking the following classic questions:

- To *Whom* am I writing?
- *Why* am I writing him or her?
- *What* is happening?
- *Where* is it happening?
- *When* is it happening?
- *How* is it going to happen?
- *How much* will the reader be affected?

The right information, however, might sometimes be obtained only through extensive research. It is imperative in either situation (brainstorming or research) that the key points be written down so they can be organized later.

Anticipating reader reaction is based on visualizing the reader's frame of reference.

DEVELOPING AN EFFECTIVE ORGANIZATION

Understanding can be improved with a good organization plan.

The order in which your major points are presented can have a significant impact on your reader's ability to understand the message. Consequently, the second major phase of the writing process involves developing an effective organization for your writing. This phase obviously draws heavily on the first phase discussed earlier: an organizational plan cannot be devised until you have determined your purpose, collected all necessary information, and analyzed your reader.

Choose Your Overall Approach

Your overall approach or structure should be based on the reader's frame of reference. The two major approaches are the direct plan and the indirect plan. In the *direct plan*, the main idea or purpose is located at the beginning. In the *indirect plan*, the main idea or purpose is located later in the writing.

Remember that these plans are not rigid patterns, but are simply intended to serve as guides. Guidelines for selecting the most appropriate approach are covered in subsequent chapters.

Develop an Outline

Once you have chosen an overall approach, you are ready to develop a logical presentation format. For most writers, the most efficient technique for organizing ideas involves outlining.

Outlining helps improve organization, ensures completeness, and saves time.

Several benefits can be derived from outlining. You have greater assurance that the information is presented in a logical manner. You can determine whether your message is complete. If key points have been omitted inadvertently, the omission is easier to detect in an outline. Lastly, an outline can sometimes save you a great deal of time. It is easier to rearrange, add to, or delete information from an outline.

Perhaps you have heard of individuals who write quite well but do not use an outline. Rather than following our suggested order of outline-write-edit, they follow a write-edit sequence. Their philosophy might be to first get the ideas on paper and then worry about rearranging them to create a logical order of presentation. This approach can work. It is important to note, however, that many of these writers have gained enough proficiency to create and maintain extensive outlines in their minds. Most of us do much better when relying on a written outline.

Thus far, the discussion of outlining has focused on longer reports and letters. Shorter letters and memos can often be prepared without using the outline-write-edit sequence. Because of their brevity and simplicity, the write-edit sequence is often sufficient.

Choose an Outline Format. You need to find or develop an outlining format that you are comfortable using. Although the mechanics may vary a great deal, an acceptable format is one that allows you to distinguish between the major and minor points to be covered.

There are, however, a number of well known outline formats. The *roman numeral outline* is used most frequently. It uses roman numerals for each major point with capital letters for the important minor points. As shown in Illustration 4.2, additional subtopics can be included by using Arabic numbers and lowercase letters.

The *decimal outline* is another popular format especially with engineers and other individuals with technical backgrounds. It uses whole numbers for major topics and decimals for subtopics (see Illustration 4.3).

Although the mechanics of these outline formats differ, the end results are the same. You should choose a format that makes outlining, writing, and editing easy for you.

There are several useful and acceptable outline formats.

ILLUSTRATION 4.2

A Roman Numeral Outline

```
I. First Main Heading
   A.  First subtopic under main heading
   B.  Second subtopic under main heading
       1.  First subtopic under B
       2.  Second subtopic under B
           a.  First subtopic under 2
           b.  Second subtopic under 2
               (1)  First subtopic under b
                   (a)  First subtopic under (1)
                   (b)  Second subtopic under (1)
II. Second Main Heading
```

ILLUSTRATION 4.3

A Decimal Outline

1. First Main Heading
    1.1 First subtopic under first main heading
    1.2 Second subtopic under first main heading
        1.21 First subtopic under 1.2
        1.22 Second subtopic under 1.2
            1.221 First subtopic under 1.22
            1.222 Second subtopic under 1.22
2. Second Main Heading
    2.1 First subtopic under second main heading
    2.2 Second subtopic under second main heading
        2.21 First subtopic under 2.2
        2.22 Second subtopic under 2.2

Choose an Outline Type.   You must also choose the type of outline to construct. The two major types of outlines are the topical and the sentence outlines.

In a *topical outline*, a few words or phrases are used to describe each point. The primary benefit of the topical outline is that it can be constructed fairly quickly. The primary disadvantage is that you may forget what a phrase means by the time you begin writing, especially if the outline is long and detailed or if there is a long delay between outlining and writing. For example, assume that one topic on an outline is "Do's and Don't's" and that your subject is "Starting Your Own Business." Several weeks later you might wonder if the topic involves legal issues, financial issues, or management issues. An example of a topical (roman numeral) outline is shown in Illustration 4.4.

Choose an outline type that fits your needs.

The *sentence outline* consists of complete sentences for each point. Although it takes longer to develop, it can enhance understanding during the writing phase. This is especially beneficial if the writer is somewhat unfamiliar with the general topic. Perhaps the major disadvantage of the sentence outline is that it is more difficult to examine the overall logical flow. An example of a sentence outline is shown in Illustration 4.5.

Determine the Appropriate Length.   How long is a good out-line? It depends on several factors. Good outlines tend to be long when (1) there are many major points to be covered; (2) a large amount of detail is needed for each major point, thereby creating many levels of subtopics for each major point; and (3) there will be a significant time lapse between outlining and writing, thereby requir-ing a sentence outline. If these conditions are not present, you prob-ably need only a short outline. The key point is that the outline should be sufficient to make the writing phase easier and quicker without unnecessary time spent on outlining.

WRITING

With outline in hand, you are now ready to begin the writing phase. The overall writing phase consists of four basic steps.

Prepare Yourself to Write

Make sure that *you* are ready to write. For example, review your planning and organizing phases to ensure that they generated what you need. In addition, make sure that you have with you all physical

ILLUSTRATION 4.4

A Topical Roman Numeral Outline

I. Introduction
    A. Status
    B. Guidelines
II. Brainstorming
    A. Definition
    B. Development
    C. Rules
    D. Procedures
    E. Application
    F. Criticisms
III. Synectics
    A. Definition
    B. Development
    C. Steps
    D. Analogies

ILLUSTRATION 4.5

A Sentence Outline

   I.   Introduce the need for creative thinking techniques and for formal guidelines.
        A.   Advances in the application of creative techniques are lagging far behind advances in the quantitative techniques.
        B.   There have been very few attempts to establish formal guidelines. One of these attempts involves the following rules.
             1.   Recognize psychological barriers, primarily cultural and perceptual blocks.
             2.   Concentrate on one attribute of the problem at a time, preferably the key attribute.
             3.   Be alert for serendipity.
  II.   Brainstorming is one of the two major creative techniques for individuals.
        A.   Brainstorming was defined originally as "the use of the brain to storm a creative problem and to do so in a commando fashion, with each stormer audaciously attacking the same objective."
        B.   Brainstorming was developed by Alex F. Osborn to help trigger creative ideas in the field of advertising.
        C.   Maximum individual creativity is possible only by following four critical rules.
             1.   Judicial judgment is ruled out. Criticism of ideas must be withheld until later.
             2.   "Freewheeling" is welcomed. It is easier to tone ideas down than to think them up.
             3.   Quantity is wanted. The greater the quantity of ideas, the more the likelihood of winners.
             4.   Combination and improvement is sought.
        D.   Other procedures can be quite helpful.
             1.   Sessions as short as 15 minutes can be productive and a one hour limit is usually needed.
             2.   The problem to be discussed should generally not be revealed before the brainstorming session.
             3.   The problem should be stated clearly and specifically.
             4.   Use a small conference table.
             5.   Have samples available, if appropriate.

items necessary, including your outline, extra notes, reference material, and writing supplies.

Prepare Your Writing Environment

Next, make sure that your writing environment is appropriate. One of the major considerations is that it should be quiet and free from interruptions and other distractions. Good writing requires periods of uninterrupted concentration. Since you probably do not want to alienate your friends, you should not try to write in the same place you socialize. If your dormitory room or apartment is frequented by friends, for example, you may have to consider a location such as the library. In an office you might have to close your door and have a secretary or receptionist screen out all but major interruptions.

Find a good atmosphere in which to write.

Plan the Mechanical Stages

Third, consider the mechanical steps between your encoding and the final draft and transmission to the receiver. Years ago there was one basic method of getting your thoughts into written form—you wrote by hand. Over the years, alternatives for creating a first draft have been developed.

- You can type it on a typewriter.
- You can type it into a word processor and have a draft printed.
- You can dictate to a secretary and have him or her type a draft.
- You can dictate into a dictation machine (tape recorder) and have a secretary type a draft.

Learn more than one way to create a first draft.

If one of these alternatives does not appeal to you, the technology is being developed to allow you to speak into a computer, which can then print a draft.

If you have all of the above alternatives available, your choice will depend on several factors. Unless you develop typing or dictating skills, you will be limited to writing by hand (dictating skills are discussed in Appendix F).

The *time* available is an important consideration. You may need to type a short memo or letter yourself if it must be transmitted as soon as possible.

Also consider the entire *mechanical sequence*. Many combinations are possible. For example, the text you are now reading was dictated into a cassette recorder. The dictation was then typed by a

The mechanical se-
quence should fit your
needs and skills.

secretary. After each author read the first draft and made comments
(handwritten on the draft), the coauthor created a second draft by
simultaneously rewriting and typing directly into a word processor.
Subsequent editing involved a combination of handwritten comments on the printed copy and changes typed directly into the word
processor.

Write

Now you are ready to begin the first draft. Your planning and
organizing is complete, the outline is in front of you, and your environment is right—there is no reason to delay any longer.

One of the most critical issues of writing involves deciding how
much care you should take in writing the first draft. Some writers
believe the first draft should be ''good enough'' to qualify as a final
draft (except for proofreading for typos). If your writing is good
enough, you might be able to do this.

Unfortunately, most of us cannot create a perfect first draft. How
many times have you sat down to write something and found yourself rewriting the opening lines three or four times because they just
did not sound right? Striving for perfection at this point typically
leads to a variety of unpleasant results, including inhibited creativity, delays, frustration and stress, writing apprehension, and a full
wastebasket.

Don't try to edit while
you are writing the
first draft.

Since you probably cannot avoid the editing stage(s), you do not
have to be as careful while writing the draft. Consequently, you can
concentrate more on *getting the ideas on paper* (or on tape or in the
word processor). This is the best approach for most people. Its
primary advantage is that your creativity is given free rein to help
you generate a continuous flow of ideas. Do not worry about spelling
or grammar or anything except your ideas.

EDITING

The final phase of the writing process involves *editing*. Good
planning, organizing, and writing will make editing somewhat easier,
but they do not eliminate the need to edit. Conversely, good editing
skills make the other three phases easier to handle, especially the
writing phase. As you are writing you will be confident that rough
spots in your writing can be easily handled later.

Good editing skills are
just as important as
good writing skills.

Editing is somewhat analogous to the control function in the management process. Essentially, it is a monitoring activity that involves determining whether the original objectives have been met.
As such, it might be construed as the most important part of the
overall writing process.

Sometimes too much editing can occur. Overediting occurs when the editing phase becomes so lengthy that your overall objectives are not met. Second, it can occur when the additional editing is not yielding improvements or moving you closer to achieving your objective.

The greatest problem related to editing, however, involves too little rather than too much editing. Most people devote far too little time to editing. Like any other activity, however, editing skills can be learned and improved. Commonly used editing and proofreading marks are shown in Illustration 4.6.

Editing skills can be learned.

For many writers, too little editing occurs because of inadequate time. Good editing takes time and concentration. You should analyze the various tools at your disposal to find ways to minimize time consumption while maintaining high quality. Word processing technology, for example, is a significant time saver. Once a draft is entered into the word processor, even major revisions can be assimilated much more quickly than through a complete retyping. If you can type, you can compose and enter revisions directly without any intervening handwritten changes.

Revise

When *revising* you should focus your attention on whether the content is sufficient to accomplish your objectives. Specifically, you should address several questions, including:

- Is the material presented in the most logical fashion?
- Does the material fit the reader's frame of reference?
- Is all of the necessary information included?
- Are there issues or information that detracts from your overall objectives?
- Is the purpose clear to the reader?

Any deficiencies indicated by your answers should be corrected by revising.

Probably the worst approach to editing is to try to make all needed revisions in one pass through the manuscript. Most people cannot look for all of the various types of revision possibilities during one reading of a manuscript. Your train of thought tends to become too scattered, thereby reducing your efficiency.

Develop a revising pattern that works for you.

The most effective approach to revising an early draft involves reading it several times. During each reading, you should focus on one major issue. Does your information, for example, flow in a consistent and logical sequence, such as by chronological order or by importance? Then you might check the accuracy of each date,

ILLUSTRATION 4.6

Commonly Used Editing and Proofreading Marks

Mark	Meaning	Mark	Meaning
∧	Insert marginal addition	wf	Wrong font
℘	Delete	x	Broken letter; bad type
℘	Delete and close up	tr	Transpose (Mark letters ⌣ in text) or
⌒	Close up	⌐⌐	Transpose (Mark in margin and also mark words in text)
#	Insert space	=	Straighten line
⌒/#	Close up and insert space	‖	Align type
∨∧	Space evenly	↓	Push down space
℧	Reverse; turn upside down	⌐⌐	Lower
¶	Paragraph	⌐	Raise
no ¶	Run in same paragraph or	]	Move to right
run in	No paragraph	[	Move to left
sp	Spell out	□	Indent 1 em
?	Query to author	□□	Indent 2 ems
⊙	Insert period	bf	Set in bold-faced type or
⌃	Insert comma	‿‿‿	Set in bold-faced type (Indicated by wavy line under word or letter)
:	Insert colon	rom	Set in roman type
;	Insert semicolon	ital	Set in italic type or
=	Insert hyphen	——	Set in italic type (Indicated by one line under word or letter)
'	Insert apostrophe	lc	Set in lower case (Used in margin; draw slant through letter in text)
" "	Insert quotation marks	caps	Set in capitals or
?/	Insert interrogation mark	≡	Set in capitals (Indicated by three lines under word or letter)
!/	Insert exclamation mark	sc	Set in small capitals or
[/]	Insert brackets	=	Set in small capitals (Indicated by two lines under word or letter)
(/)	Insert parentheses	c+sc	Set in caps and small caps
em	Insert em dash	stet	Let it stand; restore words crossed out or
en	Insert en dash	......	Retain words under which dots appear (Write "stet" in margin)
2	Insert superior figure or letter		
3	Insert inferior figure or letter		
⌒	Use ligature (Mark ff, æ, etc.)		

Source: *Author's Manual* (Homewood, Ill.: Richard D. Irwin, 1980), 3d ed, p. 74.

calculation, or quote. These multiple reviews tend to greatly increase the efficiency of your revising.

Revising does not necessarily imply rewriting. A complete rewriting of a poor draft is often much more difficult and less efficient than revising. An original draft, revised draft, and final draft of a memo are shown in Illustration 4.7.

ILLUSTRATION 4.7

An Original, Revised, and Final Draft of a Memo

Original Version of Memo

TO: All Employees
FROM: K. Clark, Safety Inspector
DATE: May 1, 1987
SUBJ: Buying of Safety Glasses and Safety Shoes and Discount Therefrom

This memo is to inform all construction employees of a new policy beginning June 1, 1987, involving the buying of safety glasses from the firm of Professional Opticians and safety shoes from the Traditional Shoe Store.

Beginning June 1, we will pay 50 percent of the purchase cost of safety glasses purchased from Professional Opticians and limit you to two pair per year.

Beginning June 1, we will pay 50 percent of the purchase cost of safety shoes bought from the Traditional Shoe Store, but limit you to two pair per year.

Purchase request forms for both safety glasses and safety shoes must be approved by your section chief. Forms for said purchases are available from the appropriate person in the personnel department.

Edited Memo

TO: All Employees
FROM: K. Clark, Safety Inspector
DATE: May 1, 1987
SUBJ: ~~Buying~~ of Safety Glasses and Safety Shoes ~~and Discount Therefrom~~

Discount Purchase ^

~~This memo is to inform all construction employees of a new policy beginning June 1, 1987, involving the buying of safety~~

ILLUSTRATION 4.7 (concluded)

~~glasses from the firm of Professional Opticians and safety~~
~~shoes from the Traditional Shoe Store.~~ *your*

Beginning June 1, we will pay 50 percent of ~~the~~ purchase *price for*
~~cost of~~ safety glasses purchases from Professional Opticians
~~and~~ (limit ~~you to~~ two pair per year).

purchased   ~~Beginning June 2, we will pay 50 percent of the purchase~~
~~cost of~~ safety shoes ~~bought~~ from ~~the~~ Traditional Shoe Store,
~~but~~ (limit ~~you to~~ two pair per year).

Purchase request forms for both ~~safety glasses and safety~~
~~shoes~~ must be approved by your section chief. Forms ~~for said~~
~~purchases~~ are available ~~from the appropriate person~~ in the
personnel ~~department.~~ *office.*

Final Memo

TO: All Employees
FROM: K. Clark, Safety Inspector
DATE: May 1, 1987
SUBJ: Discount Purchase of Safety Glasses and Shoes

Beginning June 1, 1987, we will pay 50 percent of your
purchase price for:

    Safety glasses purchased from:
      Professional Opticians
      (limit: two pair per year)
    Safety shoes purchased from:
      Traditional Shoe Store
      (limit: two pair per year)

Purchase request forms must be approved by your section
chief. Forms are available in the personnel office.

Proofread

Once you are satisfied with the overall content of your draft, you
are ready for the final phase of the editing process—proofreading.
Proofreading involves examining the more mechanical aspects of
your writing. Essentially, proofreading applies those tools your

teachers have referred to as grammar, composition, and language arts. Examine things such as paragraph structure and flow, sentence structure and flow, subject/verb agreement, spelling, and correct word usage. A checklist of common proofreading errors is shown in Table 4.1.

You should also address the question, Is this the best way that I can say what I want to say? You should create and evaluate alternative ways to make a statement. You might be surprised how often you will then modify a sentence or word.

Ask yourself the right questions.

TABLE 4.1

A Checklist of Common Proofreading Errors

Typing Errors

Typographical errors. Some typographical errors, such as *thet* instead of *that,* are relatively easy to detect. Others, such as the following, are far more elusive: *that* instead of *than, than* instead of *then, is* instead of *if, think* instead of *thing, now* instead of *not.*
Because the context does not come to the reader's aid, typographical errors in numbers (*12,459,* for example, instead of *12,348*) can be particularly troublesome.

Transpositions. A transposition such as *hte* instead of *the* offers considerably less difficulty than one such as *form* instead of *from.* The proofreader must be particularly alert to spot transposed numbers (*12,438,* for example, instead of *12,348*).

Additions. Sometimes letters or words are added: *your recent orders* instead of *your recent order,* for example, or *your your recent order.*

Omissions. Frequently letters or words are omitted: *you request* instead of *your request* or *we were able* instead of *we were not able.*

Strikeovers. Except on practice work, striking over an error simply compounds the error and is therefore not acceptable.

Raised capitals. Capital letters that float above the line (a problem usually restricted to manual typewriters) are unsightly and are therefore generally regarded as errors.

Spacing errors. Although less noticeable than other kinds of typing errors, too much or too little space left between words or sentences is also an error.

English Errors

Spelling errors. Misspelled words, such as *accomodate* instead of *accommodate* and *alloted* instead of *allotted,* are among the most common English errors found in typewritten work.

Words frequently confused. Unusually careful attention should be given to words that are commonly misused, such as *affect* and *effect, principle* and *principal,* and *advice* and *advise.*

TABLE 4.1 (continued)

Capitalization errors. Examples of capitalization errors are *Summer* instead of *summer* and *chapter 15* instead of *Chapter 15.*

Punctuation errors. There are numerous opportunities for errors in punctuation. For example, a needed comma may be omitted, an unnecessary or incorrect comma may be inserted, or a comma may be used when another mark of punctuation (a semicolon, perhaps) should have been used.

Errors in forming plurals. Particular caution should be exercised to spot such errors as *attornies* instead of *attorneys* and *sister-in-laws* instead of *sisters-in-law.*

Errors in forming possessives. At times an apostrophe denoting possession may be omitted entirely, such as *students books* instead of *students' books.* Another frequent error is the incorrect use of the singular possessive form for the plural (*boy's clothing* instead of *boys' clothing*).

Word division errors. Many word division errors occur as the result of the failure to divide words according to their pronunciation. Common examples of this type of error are *know-ledge* instead of *knowl-edge* and *child-ren* instead of *chil-dren.*

Errors in agreement. A prevalent type of error is the lack of agreement between pronouns (*Everyone should do their best* instead of *Everyone should do his or her best*). Another is the lack of agreement between subject and verb (*Neither of us have solved the problem* instead of *Neither of us has solved the problem*).

Content Errors

Names. Errors in typing persons' names are particularly serious because they can cause embarrassment and result in poor public relations. A person whose name is *William D. Greene,* for example, might well be offended to see his name typed as *William D. Green* or as *William C. Greene.*

Facts. Unusual care must be taken to insure that all factual information is accurate. For instance, dates should be carefully checked against a calendar so that no parts of a date are expressed incorrectly. A letter that includes the date *Friday, November 14, 1981,* for example, contains a factual error because November 14 fell on Saturday, not Friday, in 1981.

Inconsistencies. Although inconsistencies are easy to overlook, they must be avoided because they give the reader an impression of carelessness. It would be inconsistent and incorrect, for example, to refer to *Journal of Business Education* in one paragraph of a communication and *The Journal of Business Education* in another.

Addresses. All the elements of an address should be checked to prevent incorrect delivery or delayed delivery. The typist must be certain, for example, that a street designation such as *East Lafayette Street* is not inaccurately typed as *West Lafayette Street.*

TABLE 4.1 (continued)

State abbreviations. Every typist should have close at hand a list of the approved two-letter state abbreviations and should consult it when in doubt. *MI,* for example, stands for *Michigan,* not Minnesotat (MN), Mississippi (MS), or Missouri (MO).

Zip codes. An incorrectly typed ZIP Code (*24606,* for example, instead of *24060*) could cause delivery problems.

Dollar amounts. It is imperative that all dollar amounts be typed with absolute accuracy. An example of one of the most serious errors that can occur in a document is a misquoted price, such as *$1,000* instead of *$1,100.*

Dates. Dates must be checked with great care. To type *January 30* when *January 31* was intended could have unfavorable consequences for both the writer and the recipient of a communication.

Telephone numbers. A common error is to transpose two digits in a telephone number: *961-5741,* for example, instead of *961-5471.* Another is to type a digit incorrectly: *951-5471,* for example, instead of *961-5471.*

Other numbers. Some of the most frequent errors in the typing of numbers have been mentioned above. In addition, the final typed copy should be checked carefully against the source document to insure the accuracy of all other numbers, such as weights, measures, dimensions, distances, fractions, decimals, ages, times, and computations.

Form Errors

Letter style. After a letter has been typed, it should be checked to insure that the chosen style (block or modified block, for example) has been faithfully followed. The implication here, of course, is that the typist should thoroughly understand the distinguishing characteristics of the major letter styles that are employed in business and personal use.

Punctuation style. Only two styles of punctuation are commonly used in business correspondence today—open and mixed. A check should be made to determine whether or not the appropriate marks of punctuation, if any, have been included after the salutation and the complimentary close.

Paragraph indentions. A frequent error in typing a letter is forgetting to indent a paragraph that should be indented or indenting a paragraph that should not be indented.

Positioning of letter parts. All parts of a letter should be properly placed. Often a typist will position incorrectly one or more of the special parts of a letter; for example, an attention line, a subject line, an enclosure line, or a copy notation.

Headings. The main heading in a table or report, for example, should be correctly centered and typed in all caps. Column headings in a table should be correctly centered over the items in the columns.

TABLE 4.1 *(concluded)*

The subheadings in a report (centered, side, and paragraph) should be properly typed and positioned.

Spacing. Among the points to be noted are the following: single spacing or double spacing of the text, double spacing between paragraphs (regardless of whether the copy is single or double spaced!), correct spacing before and after headings and subheadings in reports and tables, and equal spacing between columns in tables.

Margins. Particular attention should be given, for example, to the margins in a report, in which it is especially important that the proper side, top, and bottom margins be maintained.

Appearance Errors

Corrections. All corrections should be neatly made. Messy corrections are unsightly, denote carelessness, and leave the reader with a negative impression.

Smudges. A well typed piece of work contains no smudges to detract from its overall appearance. Particular caution must be taken when erasable paper is being used because of its susceptibility to smearing and smudging.

Typescript. The typescript should be of equal intensity. Uneven typescript is associated primarily with manual typewriters; the problem does not ordinarily arise with electric typewriters.

Vertical placement. The vertical placement on the page should be attractive—neither too high nor too low. Correct placement can usually be judged satisfactorily through visual inspection.

Margins. The side and top margins should be neither too wide nor too narrow; they should be appropriate for the kind of work being typed. The left and right margins should be approximately equal. The right margin should be relatively even rather than ragged.

Source: Walter Shell, "Improving Students' Proofreading Skill," *Journal of Business Education*, May 1982, pp. 305–7.

If time permits, you might want someone else to proofread your draft. Another person is likely to catch mistakes that you miss, just as you probably could proofread someone else's writing more easily than your own. Also, another person might find certain areas that are confusing, even though they are clear to you.

Conclusions on Editing

The editing phase is a critical ingredient of the overall writing process. It helps ensure that your desired final product—effective communication—is actually achieved.

Although you may be an excellent writer, you still should not omit the editing phase. Even professional writers often revise their manuscripts numerous times before they are satisfied with the final product. It is believed that *War and Peace,* for example, was revised five times. James Thurber is said to have rewritten stories as many as 15 times.

Although 15 revisions are probably excessive for most of your writing, you still have an obligation to yourself, your reader, and your employer. Your image and your employer's image are on the line every time you send a memo, letter, or report. Since readers tend to identify writing qualities with individual qualities, unorganized and sloppy writing will reflect negatively on you and your company. The editing phase is your last opportunity to ensure that your communication efforts have been effective.

Application Exercises

1. Assume that you intend to write a letter to a friend at another university. Your purpose is to invite him or her to attend a party next weekend back in your hometown. Using the questions suggested in the text to help anticipate a reader's reaction, develop a list of major points to be covered.

2. Use the major points developed in Exercise 1 to develop an outline with the following characteristics: inductive, roman numerals, topical.

3. Use the major points developed in Exercise 1 to develop an outline with the following characteristics: deductive, decimal, sentence.

4. Use the major points developed in Exercise 1 to develop an outline with the following characteristics: inductive, decimal, sentence.

5. Use the major points developed in Exercise 1 to develop an outline with the following characteristics: deductive, roman numerals, topical.

6. What types of revisions need to be made in the following paragraph?

> And per our company directive of Dec. 18, I find that adverse evaluations of these articulative abilities evade the average perceptory powers of those executives into whose purview it falls to determine what those aforementioned abilities, carried to their consummative performance, should ultimately and finally achieve.

7. Proofread the following paragraph:

Doc. Meridith Lucian
State university
Business administration and Business Education Dept.
Monroe, Mi. 12345

Dear Meridith,

Thank you for returning my call last week. As I told you, I am trying to publish more textbooks on Business Education. I can do several different book.In some cases I have experts in a particular area, but the writing frightens the. With your writing experience your could be a big help as an author or coauthor.

I want to contract with several authors for books yet this year or in the first quarter of next year. Among those would be books in Office Procedures, Business Communications, Records Management, and Office Management jst to name a few.

If your interests and time committments fit any of these projects I would be happy to discuss them further.

Sincerely,

8. Form into groups of three to four. Have each person make a list of the times he or she has had to write something (other than class notes) in the previous semester. Compile a master list of written items. Swap items and edit each other's writing.

9. Form into groups of three to four. Assume that your group must cooperate to write a term paper of 20 to 30 pages. Have the group analyze the writing process and then the group's collective writing skills. Develop an overall writing plan that integrates the group's skills.

10. Make a list of your strengths and weaknesses relative to each part of the writing process. How do you rate overall? Which skills need to be upgraded?

11. Recall the last time you wrote a report or letter. Once you sat down to write, how many times did you have to get up to find additional items. What were they?

12. Recall the last time you wrote a report or letter. Describe your writing environment. How could it have been improved?

13. Form into groups of five or six. Have each person relate how he or she normally prepares a first draft of a report or letter. Prepare a list of alternative means of preparing a first draft. Have each person discuss his or her ability to use each method.

Review Questions

1. List and describe the three key benefits of good writing skills.
2. What is the status of basic writing skills in the United States today?
3. List and briefly describe the four major parts of the writing process.
4. List and briefly describe the four major phases of the planning process.
5. Describe the two major myths associated with writing apprehension.

6. Develop a list of questions that can help you choose the major points to be covered in your writing.
7. Define and contrast the deductive and inductive approaches to writing.
8. Describe the benefits of using an outline for writing.
9. Describe and contrast a roman numeral outline and a decimal outline.
10. Describe and contrast a topical outline and a sentence outline.
11. How do you determine how long an outline should be?
12. Describe an ideal writing environment.
13. What is the difference between editing, revising, and proofreading?

Key Terms

creativity   *roman numeral outline*
preparation   *decimal outline*
incubation   *topical outline*
illumination   *sentence outline*
verification   *editing*
direct plan   *revising*
indirect plan   *proofreading*

Notes

1. "Why Johnny Can't Write," *Newsweek,* December 8, 1975, pp. 58–65.

2. John Barbour, "School Teaches Bosses to Communicate," *Northwest Arkansas Times,* October 3, 1976, p. 7B.

3. Richard VanDeWeghe, "Writing Models, Versatile Writers," *Journal of Business Communication,* 20, no. 1 (Winter 1983), p. 13.

4. Kathleen Booker and Wilma Davidson, "11 Myths About Writing and How Trainers Can Debunk Them," *Training,* April 1982, pp. 40–43.

5. Graham Wallas, *The Art of Thought* (New York: Harcourt Brace Jovanovich, 1926), p. 80.

Chapter 5

■ *Chapter Outline*

Identifying the Major Characteristics of Effective Writing

- **Learning Objectives**

After studying this chapter, you should be able to identify and describe the following major characteristics of effective writing:
- Completeness
- Conciseness
- Clarity
- You Attitude
- Tone
- Grammar and Mechanics
- Attractiveness

Introduction

Effective writing can
yield you benefits now
. . .

. . . and later in your
career.

Written communication serves as an important vehicle for securing and maintaining positive relationships with other individuals. Effective written communication will help you minimize misunderstanding and achieve high levels of understanding. On an essay test, for example, your writing must show your instructor what you know. Have you ever taken an essay test on which your grade did not fully reflect your knowledge? If you have, the grade was probably attributable to ineffective writing.

When you begin your professional career, the importance of effective writing remains just as great as it was in school. It may, in fact, be even more important. Internal correspondence to superiors, subordinates, and peers must be clear and understandable—they will probably not react like the gentleman in Illustration 5.1. Similarly, correspondence with individuals and groups outside of the organization must exhibit effective writing characteristics. Poor writing can and will negatively influence your relationships with others.

This chapter presents and discusses the major characteristics of effective writing: (1) completeness, (2) conciseness, (3) clarity, (4) you attitude, (5) tone, (6) grammar and mechanics, and (7) attractiveness. If you carefully develop each step of the writing process discussed in Chapter 4, your final product should exhibit these seven characteristics. This list can actually serve as an excellent checklist for the last step of the writing process—editing.

COMPLETENESS

The first critical characteristic relates to the *completeness* of your correspondence or report. If you have included all information necessary to achieve full understanding, you will save both time and money in the long run. An incomplete message, for example, often requires additional communication, such as follow-up correspondence, a telephone call, or even a personal visit. The memo in Illustration 5.2, for example, is missing a critical element. Note that the

ILLUSTRATION 5.1

Avoid This Reaction to Your Memos

Courtesy USA Today, Sept. 25, 1984. Reprinted with permission of USA Today.

ending date for the Christmas holidays is not included. Even if this ineffective communication were caught early enough, additional memos or phone calls would be necessary to correct the miscommunication. It could also lead to several problems, such as some teachers returning to school late.

In addition to the time and cost of additional communication, errors or mistakes caused by incomplete communication can result in lost sales, shipping errors, and wrong products. One of the most detrimental aspects of an incomplete message is that it can irritate the receiver, which damages you and your organization's image.

Incomplete communication can be costly.

ILLUSTRATION 5.2

An Incomplete Memo

To: University Colleagues:

Revised Christmas holidays begin on December 19 (for certain purposes this is defined as 1 A.M., December 18). This arrangement is designed to conserve energy.

In cases where work must be performed during these holidays, responsible officials are authorized to keep offices open and to require members to work.

Wage payrolls will be available Friday, December 16, as scheduled. Salary checks will be in the post office Tuesday morning, December 20.

Use your outline to check for completeness.

There are several approaches to ensuring that your message is complete. One of the best approaches involves comparing your written document to the outline developed as part of the writing process. Your outline makes an excellent checklist for completeness. The outline in Illustration 5.3, for example, probably should have been followed for the letter shown in Illustration 5.2.

ILLUSTRATION 5.3

An Outline for a Memo

Revised Christmas Holidays
I. Announce revised Christmas holidays
    A. Dates: December 19–January 2
    B. Times
    C. Purpose
II. Exceptions
III. Pay dates
    A. Wage payrolls
    B. Salary checks

If you began writing without an outline, you might want to develop a series of questions like the following:

1. What questions should be addressed by this communication?
2. Have all questions been answered?
3. Is the information presented sufficient to enable the receiver to take any necessary action?
4. Have the five "Ws" been answered (who, what, why, when, and where)?
5. Has the "how" question been answered (i.e., if you or the receiver are to do something, how should it be done)?

Accuracy is a fundamental aspect of completeness. In one sense, inaccurate information can be more devastating than incomplete or missing information, because inaccurate information is often more difficult to detect. An inaccurate time, date, or place, for example, can cause the reader to make embarrassing and costly mistakes. This embarrassment is likely to be focused back on you, the sender, in the form of antagonism. If you arrange a meeting, for example, and tell the guest speaker the wrong time, date, or place, irreparable damage to your relationship with the speaker could occur.

Inaccurate correspondence can be embarrassing and damaging.

CONCISENESS

A written message that uses as few words as possible and is easily understood is *concise*. Imagine going into a retail store to purchase a new stereo system with $500 in pennies. You could do it, but it would waste your time as well as the clerk's time. In this context, five $100 bills would be more concise. Writers often waste their time and their readers' time by overloading sentences and messages with unnecessary words and phrases.

Some writers appear to believe in the classic myth: More words (especially big ones) equal better writing. Those who practice this myth also tend to think that the major objective of written communication is to impress the reader. To help dispel this myth, remember:

Avoid wordy sentences and unnecessarily complex phrases.

- The overall objective of written communication involves communicating effectively, not impressing the reader.
- Effective communication leads to understanding, not to reader confusion.
- Too many words can cause readers to lose their train of thought, which leads to confusion.

- Complicated words may not be understood by the reader, thereby increasing confusion and reducing understanding.
- People are more impressed with writing they understand than with big words and complex sentences.

Do not assume that your readers have sufficient education and interest to cope with complex, wordy writing. If they do not, you probably will alienate them. Further, even if you know that your readers are highly educated, do not assume that they have highly developed reading comprehension skills. To achieve your objective of effective communication, you must write with conciseness and simplicity. Consider the following illustrations:

> *Even if your readers can read complex writing, they may not* want *to.*

Wordy: After many long hours of tedious investigation and research, we found that several different organizations and companies were satisfactory, and offered programs that were designed to improve the ability of our technicians in the vital and important area of technical report writing.

Concise: We learned that 10 Boston area firms were qualified to offer programs in report writing for technical personnel.

Wordy: It should be observed that not very many, in fact only 21, cases of shoplifting took place in the second month of this year, February; the very month, in fact, when the new system was evaluated.

Concise: Only 21 cases of shoplifting were recorded during February, the month the new system was started.

Conciseness is also enhanced if you avoid cluttering phrases, needless repetition, and roundabout wording. For example:

Cluttering Phrase	Shorter Substitution
Along the lines of	Similar to, like
In view of the fact that	Since, due to
In very few instances	Rarely
On the basis of	By, because

Repetitious: By making a move now we can finish sooner, perhaps today, than if we wait until a later date.

Better: By acting now we might finish today.

Repetitious: As a matter of interest, I am interested in learning more about your new system.

Better: I am interested in learning about your new system.

Roundabout: Reference is made to your first report in which you concluded that the new software is worthless.

Better: Your first report concluded that the new software is worthless.

Roundabout: The managers should take necessary action to determine whether the job is being completed properly.

Better: The managers should determine whether the job is being completed properly.

Fog Index

The Fog Index can help you evaluate the readability of your writing.

Robert Gunning developed the simple and now well-known *Fog Index* to measure the level of reading difficulty.[1] Essentially, the Fog Index system generates a number that represents the number of years of formal education necessary to understand and respond to written material. Sentence length and word complexity form the basis for the index figure. Table 5.1 illustrates how the Fog Index works.

Let's calculate the Fog Index for the above paragraph:

1. Number of words: 62.
2. Number of sentences: 4.
3. Average number of words per sentence: 15.5.
4. Number of hard words: 11.
5. Number of hard words per 100 words: 17.7.
6. Sum or word average and hard word percent: 33.2 percent.
7. *Fog Index:* 13.3.

The above paragraph therefore requires approximately 13.3 years of education to be understood.

Can You Be Too Concise?

Don't seek conciseness at the expense of completeness and clarity.

Writing can be too concise. You must not forget completeness and clarity. Too much conciseness can be a barrier to completeness and clarity and, therefore, understanding. Big words and longer sentences should not necessarily be avoided at all costs—they can sometimes enhance understanding. Don't forget that conciseness should not be pursued at the expense of the other key ingredients of effective writing (see Illustration 5.4).

TABLE 5.1

Fog Index Readability Appraisal*

A. Find the average number of words per sentence in a sample of your writing 100 to 200 words long. Treat clearly independent clauses as separate sentences. Example: "In school we read; we learned; we improved." This counts as three sentences.
   1. Number of words _____
   2. Number of sentences _____
   3. Average number of words per sentence (item 1 divided by item 2) _____
B. Calculate the percentage of words having three or more syllables. Don't count capitalized words, easy combinations like *pawnbroker,* or verbs that reach three syllables by addition of *-es* or *-ed.*
   4. Number of hard words _____
C. Add the average sentence length to the percentage of big words and multiply the total by 0.4. The resulting number is the years of schooling needed to understand what you've written. If the piece of writing you are analyzing is lengthy, take other samples at random, repeat the process, and average the results.
   5. Number of hard words per 100 words (item 4 divided by item 1 times 100) _____
   6. Sum of word average and hard word percent (item 3 plus item 5) _____
   7. Fog Index (item 6 multiplied by 0.4) _____

* The Fog Index measures readability of a given text in terms of approximate years of schooling needed to read it with ease.

Adapted from "How to Take the Fog out of Writing" by Robert Gunning and Douglas Mueller. Chicago: Dartnell Corporation, rev. ed. 1981. Used by permission of the copyright owners.

CLARITY

Clarity improves understanding.

A message has *clarity* if the intended receiver can be reasonably expected to interpret it correctly. If a message can be easily interpreted in more than one way, however, it lacks clarity. Although a message may be complete and concise, it may not necessarily be clear to the reader. Consider, for example, the following paragraph:

The professor was notorious for using 20 words when 10 would do and for using words of five syllables when three syllables would be perfectly adequate. One bright spring day, the professor sent a note to a student during class: "Mr. Garrett, you hold the key to ventilating

ILLUSTRATION 5.4

Don't Seek Too Much Conciseness

Courtesy USA Today, *September 18, 1984. Reprinted with permission of USA Today.*

this room in a more grandly efficient manner. Would you please exercise your exclusive and innate ability.'' The student was quite perplexed. It took Mr. Garrett several moments to realize that the professor simply wanted him to open the window.

Frames of reference influence clarity.

Careful consideration of the intended reader's frame of reference can greatly enhance your chances of achieving clarity. For example, the following statements might be interpreted differently by two individuals:

Statement A: This is a bad movie!
Interpretation 1: The speaker thinks the movie is no good.
Interpretation 2: The speaker thinks the movie is great.

Statement B: I like baseball.

Interpretation 1: The speaker likes to occasionally watch a baseball game on television.

Interpretation 2: The speaker likes to play baseball occasionally, coach Little League, watch baseball on television, and attend all the local professional games.

You can check all your written correspondence for clarity by asking yourself three questions. First, do you understand what you are trying to say? Surprisingly, a lack of understanding is a major problem in the area of writing clarity—writers too often do not fully grasp what they want to say. If *you* do not understand, how can you expect the reader to understand? You can alleviate this problem with additional thought or study and with the development of an adequate outline before you begin writing.

Second, ask yourself if you have considered the reader's frame of reference. As discussed earlier, frames of reference can have a major influence on message interpretation.

Finally, ask yourself if you have any doubt regarding the clarity of your message. If you have any doubt, you might consider asking someone to read your message before you send it. If that reader can't understand the message, you should consider changing words or revising sentences, paragraphs, or the overall flow.

YOU ATTITUDE

In general, the **you attitude** involves examining a situation from another individual's point of view. This should help you generate a consideration and respect for other points of view.

A you attitude shows concern for the reader.

The you attitude can only be accomplished by anticipating the reader's frame of reference. Effective consideration of your reader's frame of reference should provide you with a writing style that demonstrates empathy and concern for the reader.

A you attitude is important because most people naturally have an "I" or "we" attitude. Consequently, it is generally safe to assume that your reader will have an I attitude. If you construct a message with an I attitude (the writer's), then the reader cannot interpret that you feel he or she is important. Remember who is "Number 1" to the reader. As shown in the examples below, the you attitude, as embodied by the word *you*, makes your writing easier to understand.

Avoid the "I" or "we" attitude.

We: We are happy to have this order for Cagle products, which we are sending today by FastLine Freight.

You: Your selection of Cagle products was shipped by Fast-Line Freight today and should reach you by Saturday.

We: We sell the Moore cutlery set for the low price of $6 each, and we suggest a retail price of $10.

You: You can reap a nice $4 profit on each Moore set you sell at $10, for your cost is only $6.

Do you remember ever having received a letter that was written with an I or we attitude? If so, it probably turned you off. Consider the we letter shown in Illustration 5.5. Compare the we attitude to the you attitude shown in the letter in Illustration 5.6.

To effectively incorporate a you attitude in your writing, you should keep two key points in mind. First, concern and respect for

ILLUSTRATION 5.5

A We Attitude Letter

Dear Mr. Lee:

For several years we have shipped you and our other customers quantities of your Quentil line from our Birmingham manufacturing plant and our Shantron line from Atlanta.

Although we have been happy to do this, you can appreciate that the cost to us for double shipping has often been excessive. This is especially true when orders are small, and our profit margin is consequently completely absorbed. We certainly are not happy with such a situation.

Beginning August 15, however, we will consolidate shipping procedures and we will forward both the Quentil and the Shantron line from Atlanta. This will certainly save us money and will afford faster delivery of our merchandise. In addition there will be fewer billing as well as other bookkeeping procedures for our firm to carry through.

We believe that you will agree that this new arrangement will prove wiser and more satisfactory for us.

Sincerely,

ILLUSTRATION 5.6

A You Attitude Letter

Dear Mr. Martin:

A change in our shipping procedure should prove beneficial to you in many different ways.

For the past several years, our Quentil and Shantron lines have been shipped from warehouses in Birmingham and Atlanta. Processing your order from two different cities sometimes resulted in service that was not always the most expedient.

Beginning August 15, however, all products will be shipped directly to you from Atlanta. This will result in several definite benefits to you:

Your orders will be filled and sent within 24 hours of receipt. Shipping costs will be reduced, and the savings achieved will be passed on to our customers in the form of lower prices. A new price list will be sent to you next month. Complete selections will be available at all times due to our carrying larger inventories.

It is our pleasure to add this new procedure to our list of services. This, plus our high-quality products sold at very competitive prices, assures you of fast merchandise turnover and top profit margins.

Sincerely,

the reader's welfare must be projected with sincerity. Insincerity is difficult to hide, and it can cause the reader to distrust the writer and the writer's organization.

Second, adopting a you attitude does not necessarily mean that you agree with the reader. In fact, a you attitude can be especially critical when the message expresses disagreement or is unfavorable for the reader.

TONE

Even though your message may be complete, concise, and possess a you attitude, it still may not communicate effectively. Effective communication requires a fifth key characteristic—tone. The *tone* of a message involves its emotional flavor or mood. Three of the most critical aspects of tone are naturalness, optimism, and tactfulness.

Natural Tone

A natural tone makes your writing easier to read and understand.

A written message possesses a ***natural tone*** if it resembles the way a person speaks. Perhaps the primary benefit of a natural tone involves eliminating stiffness and artificiality.

An unnatural tone tends to project an artificial and formal image that most organizations prefer to avoid. Examples of unnatural phrases and expressions used frequently in business and governmental writing are shown below.

> According to our records.
>
> As per.
>
> Attached hereto.
>
> Attached please find.
>
> At you earliest convenience.
>
> Avail yourself of this opportunity.
>
> Enclosed please find.
>
> Esteemed order.
>
> Hand you herewith.
>
> Hereby acknowledge.
>
> Permit me to say.
>
> Pursuant to.

These and similar expressions can quickly destroy an otherwise natural tone as shown in the following examples:

> **Unnatural:** The undersigned wishes to advise that the afore-mentioned report is at hand.
>
> **Natural:** I have the report.
>
> **Unnatural:** Submitted herewith is your notification of our compliance with subject standards.
>
> **Natural:** Here is your notification of our compliance with the standards.
>
> **Unnatural:** We deem it advisable. . . .
>
> **Natural:** We suggest. . . .

Positive and Optimistic Tone

Effective writing also tends to possess a *positive and optimistic tone*. Most messages are expressed in either a positive and optimistic tone or a negative and pessimistic tone. Department stores, for example, often have a department to handle various customer questions, problems, and complaints. Would you rather visit the Customer Service Department or the Customer Complaint Department? The positive and optimistic image projected by the Customer Service Department promises a much more helpful and favorable experience than the latter.

In a similar vein, consider the following excerpt: "We hope you won't be dissatisfied with your new Brand X stereo system." These beginning words project an extremely negative tone. One possible metacommunication would be: "We hope you won't be dissatisfied, but you might be and maybe you should be." A much more positive statement is possible, such as: "With the purchase of your new Brand AAA stereo system, you join 50,000 other happy and satisfied customers." Other examples of a positive versus a negative are shown below.

> **Negative:** We regret to inform you that we must deny your request for credit.
>
> **Positive:** For the time being we can serve you only on a cash basis.
>
> **Negative:** We don't believe you will encounter trouble and difficulty in the installation of the new equipment.
>
> **Positive:** For quick and efficient installation of the new equipment, please follow the directions shown in the owner's manual.
>
> **Negative:** You should have known that the Lawton Cooker cannot be submerged in water for it is clearly explained in the instructions.
>
> **Positive:** The instructions explain why the Lawton Cooker should be cleaned only with a cloth.

Notice in these examples that positive words create a positive tone. Consequently, you should strive for a positive and optimistic tone by trying to use positive and optimistic words and expressions.

Tactful Tone

Writing that possesses a *tactful tone* says the right thing at the right time and in the right way. For example, how do you think your

---

A positive tone can help improve your reader's image of you.

 This text is being sent to you with the compliments of Business Publications, Inc.

Future requests for desk copies, teaching aids, and other inquiries concerning the subject matter of these books should be directed to:

Business Publications, Inc.
1700 Alma Road
Suite 390
Plano, Texas 75075

If your plans should include adoption or purchase of this text, please advise your bookstore to direct their order to:

Business Publications, Inc.
1820 Ridge Road
Homewood, Illinois 60430

BUSINESS PUBLICATIONS, INC.
1700 Alma Road • Suite 390 • Plano, Texas 75075

We are glad to make available for your consideration this copy of

EFFECTIVE COMMUNICATION SKILLS
By Daniel S. Cochran and Danny R. Arnold

Using a mainstream, skills/applications-oriented approach, this new basic business communications text devotes two-thirds of the material to written skills and one-third to oral communication skills. Communication theory and interpersonal skills are integrated and applied to both written and oral skills.

The material is applications oriented — both good and bad examples are included. There is a detailed chapter on integrating graphic aids into business communications. Letters and memos are discussed together. Six special appendixes cover grammar (including diagnostic test), form and style (letters and memos), international communication, legal aspects. dictation skills, and footnote and bibliography format.

Supplemental aids include:

1) *Instructor's Manual* — with lecture outlines, answers to text questions, additional exam questions, and transparency masters;

2) *Study Guide* — with chapter outlines, review questions, and application exercises.

12-1800-01

We will greatly appreciate it, if after examining this book, you will use the attached reply card to give us a brief comment and an indication of adoption possibilities.

- -

I have received the copy of:

EFFECTIVE COMMUNICATION SKILLS — Cochran & Arnold

After examining this book, I wish to comment as follows:

I plan to require my students to purchase this book as a ☐ basic text ☐ supplementary text

in my course _____

starting _____ enrollment_____

NAME _____

SCHOOL_____

You do ☐ do not ☐ have my permission to quote the above in future promotional material professor feels when you ask, "Dr. Carson, will you be doing anything important in class today?"

Although the concept of tact is relatively abstract, it is extremely important for achieving a positive, trusting relationship with others. Consider the following excerpt from a business letter: "We were surprised that you did not understand the well-written instructions we sent you last week." The metacommunication meaning derived from this obviously tactless statement might be: "We were surprised you did not understand the well-written specifications we sent you, you dummy!" A more tactful statement might begin with: "Please accept our apologies for providing you with unclear (or incomplete) instructions." A positive tone like the one expressed in this last statement helps maintain desirable positive relationships. Additional examples of tactless versus tactful statements are shown below.

> **Tactless:** We received your letter in which you claim we did not send. . . .
>
> **Tactful:** Thank you for your letter concerning our shipment of March 31.
>
> **Tactless:** You failed to indicate the size you preferred.
>
> **Tactful:** Please indicate the size you prefer and we will ship immediately.

GRAMMAR AND MECHANICS

The sixth major characteristic of your writing involves using correct *grammar and mechanics*. The most common grammatical errors are incorrect spelling, run-on sentences, sentence fragments, and subject/verb disagreement. Table 5.2 uses a humorous approach to illustrate some of these errors. Although intended to be humorous, the "un-rules" are unfortunately typical of much of today's writing.

What effect does incorrect grammar have on your reader? It's usually negative. Just as poor grammar in a term paper or on an essay test often results in a lower grade, poor grammar can hurt you professionally. If you are communicating as the representative of an organization, the reader's response to poor grammar might be:

- Do I really want to do business with someone who cannot even write a simple letter without numerous grammatical mistakes?

- Do I really want to promote someone to a responsible position in this organization who cannot even write a simple report without numerous distracting grammatical mistakes?

A positive tone helps maintain positive relationships.

Using poor grammar has a negative effect on your reader.

TABLE 5.2

Un-rules for Writers

1. Don't use no double negatives.
2. Make each pronoun agree with their antecedent.
3. Join clauses good, like a conjunction should.
4. About them sentence fragments.
5. When dangling, watch your participles.
6. Verbs has to agree with their subjects.
7. Just between you and I, case is important too.
8. Don't write run-on sentences they are hard to read.
9. Don't use commas, which aren't necessary.
10. Try to not ever split infinitives.
11. Its important to use your apostrophe's correctly.
12. Proofread your writing to see if you any words out.
13. Correct spelling is esential.

Source: Professor E. Reber Casstevens, "Un-Rules for Writers," *The ABCA Bulletin,* December 1980, p. 1.

- Am I so unimportant to this writer that he or she did not even bother to edit this letter for grammatical errors?

These and similar questions typically evoke negative answers.

You might be asking yourself, "Why should I be so concerned about correct grammar? I am not an English major and, besides, my secretary will take care of it." Although you may be fortunate enough to have a secretary with excellent grammatical skills, many secretaries do not have these skills, since they are not necessarily English majors. Even if your secretary is quite skillful, you must remember that you are the one who signs your correspondence—the responsibility for your outgoing correspondence lies with *you.*

Appendix A presents a concise review of basic English grammar. The appendix reviews the principles of business English and provides opportunities for practicing various grammatical skills. The self-administered Business English Exam can provide you with an indication of your strengths and weaknesses relative to grammar.

Everyone can improve his grammar.

ATTRACTIVENESS

Although discussed last, *attractiveness* is by no means the least important characteristic of effective writing. Your reader's first im-

The physical appearance of your written communication affects your reader's evaluation of the contents.

You are responsible for all aspects of your written communication.

pression is often quite important in determining his or her overall reaction in a variety of situations. People do, in fact, judge a book by its cover. In this context, the "cover" refers to the overall appearance of your writing. If it is attractive, the contents may benefit from a positive first impression.

An unattractive appearance tends to automatically put the reader in a negative frame of mind. Even if your writing possesses all of the characteristics discussed in this chapter, poor appearance can create a negative image that can damage the way the message will be received. In fact, the negative frame of mind can be so negative that the receiver may decide not to read your message.

What makes a written message unattractive? Careless erasures or typos, insufficient white space, unbalanced or unfamiliar format, or incorrect spacing all contribute to unattractiveness.

Although most secretaries are well versed in correct style and format, the basic style and format decisions are the responsibility of the writer. Consequently, you must become familiar with acceptable style and format alternatives. Appendix B provides a brief overview of these alternatives.

Application Exercises

1. Calculate the Fog Index for the following paragraph:

As Jeremy meandered through the antiquated establishments, he felt like a typical overawed tourist. Although the native population attempted to demonstrate condescension, their demeanor could not totally mask their enthusiasm for separating the unsuspecting from their accumulated wealth.

2. Evaluate the following letter relative to the major characteristics of effective writing. List each characteristic with your evaluation and summarize the letter's overall effectiveness:

Dear Mrs. Hester:

I was happy to receive your letter and to learn that you are doing so many worthwhile things with your seventh grade science class.

I agree with you that your students would benefit from a visit to our utility to see the coal and nuclear generators and other equipment. However, we do have government regulations to contend with: they strictly prohibit children 14 years of age or less from visiting potentially dangerous areas.

Although these regulations do not apply to all parts of our plant, I wonder how much each child would really observe if he or she had to compete with 25 others. And of course there is the factor of the slight disruption of routine created by such a large group.

May I suggest an alternate plan, Mrs. Hester? We have an excellent film entitled, "A Powerful and Safe Giant." This tells the story of what goes on in electricity generating facilities. Although it was made to recruit employees of all types, your students would find it very valuable and interesting. The camera gives the viewer close-ups of all types of equipment and processes, and the commentary is excellent.

One of our staff could bring the film to your class, or if you wish, you may use our conference room. In both cases, a competent person would be present to answer questions.

Just call me at 111-4444, extension 500, and we can make arrangements for showing the film at a time that will suit your schedule.

Sincerely,

3. Evaluate the following letter:

Dear Mr. Conners:

We received the knee brace which you returned to us.

We are sorry that it has given you no comfort during the last two months. However, we are at a loss to know what to do with the item. Surely this soiled unit cannot be returned to stock and sold again. In addition, local government regulations make it impossible for us to resell an article of this type.

We are returning the brace and we hope you will understand why we cannot take favorable action in this case.

Sincerely,

4. Find three words of fewer syllables to use in place of each of the following words:

a. antiquated
b. procrastination
c. unbelievingness
d. incredulously
e. ventilator

5. Rewrite the following paragraph to get a lower Fog Index:

In terms of economic and historical importance, the Mississippi–Missouri river system has few rivals. Its drainage basin extends all the way from the Appalachian Mountains in the east to the Rocky Mountains in the west. Covering an area of 1,244,000 square miles (3,222,000 kilometers), it takes in the agricultural and industrial heartland of the United States and a bit of Canada as well. The rivers played a crucial role in the country's westward expansion, were responsible for the growth of many of its major cities, and still are important shipping arteries.

6. Form groups of three to four. As a group, prepare a checklist for evaluating each of the characteristics of effective writing discussed in the chapter. Your checklist, for example, could require a yes-no response, or it could force you to give a rating (e.g., 1–5, 1–10) for each component. Then, use your checklist to evaluate something each of you has written.

7. Rewrite the following sentences in a natural and more conversational style:

a. Attached please find receipt of your March 10 invoice.
b. Anticipating your visit in early May, I remain. . . .

c. Referring to your correspondence of June 15, I wish to state that this office has no responsibility.

d. Please be advised of the up and coming balloon race.

e. You are hereby advised to endorse subject report and return same to the undersigned.

8. Write *you-attitude* sentences for each of the following sentences and situations:

a. So that we can sell at discount prices we cannot permit merchandise to be returned.

b. Services desired should be checked on the enclosed order form.

c. Our long experience in the stereo business has enabled us to provide the best customer service possible.

d. We give a 3 percent discount when payment is made within 14 days.

e. I am pleased to inform you that I can grant your request for a sabbatical.

9. Underline all *negative words* in the following sentences. Then rewrite the sentence situations for positive effect. (Make up information if necessary.)

a. Your misunderstanding of our April 25 report caused you to make this mistake.

b. We hope this delay has not inconvenienced you.

c. You cannot visit the plant except on Sundays.

d. We are disappointed to learn from your recent letter that you are having trouble with our Model 707 lawnmower.

e. Do not smoke in the studio.

Review Questions

1. List and briefly describe the seven major characteristics of effective writing.
2. Why is effective writing important to you?
3. Discuss the issue of completeness. Why is it important?
4. Discuss the issue of conciseness. Why is it important?
5. What is the Fog Index? What does it tell you?

6. Can you achieve too much conciseness? Why or why not?
7. Discuss the issue of clarity. Why is it important?
8. Discuss the issue of a you attitude. Why is it important?
9. Discuss the issue of natural tone.
10. Discuss the issue of a positive and optimistic tone.
11. Discuss the issue of a tactful tone.
12. Discuss the issue of grammar and mechanics. Why is it important?
13. Discuss the issue of attractiveness. Why is it important?

Key Terms

completeness	*tone*
accuracy	*natural tone*
conciseness	*positive and optimistic tone*
fog index	*tactful tone*
clarity	*grammar and mechanics*
you attitude	*attractiveness*

Notes

1. Robert Gunning, *How to Take the Fog Out of Writing* (Chicago: The Dartnell Corporation, 1964).

Part III

Improving Letter and Memo Writing Skills

The four chapters included in Part III focus on helping you write more effective letters and memos. A *letter* is defined as written correspondence to an individual or group outside the writer's organization. A *memo* (or memorandum) is defined as written correspondence to an individual or group inside the writer's organization. The organizational plans for effective letters and memos are essentially the same, but the formats are different.

Each chapter in Part III concentrates on one of the basic types of letters and memos:

Chapter 6—Letters and memos of request.
Chapter 7—Favorable response letters and memos.
Chapter 8—Unfavorable response letters and memos.
Chapter 9—Persuasive letters and memos.

The body of each chapter has three basic components: (1) the psychology of the specific type of letter or memo, (2) basic organizational plans, and (3) common situations requiring the type of letter or memo being discussed (with examples). Recommended formats for both letters and memos are included in Appendix B.

Chapter   6

■ *Chapter Outline*

Writing Letters and Memos of Request

■ *Learning Objectives*

After studying this chapter, you should be able to:
- Understand the psychology of a letter or memo of request.
- Describe the different situations that require request letters or memos and the different types of organizational plans.
- Write effective letters and memos for common situations involving requests for information, adjustments, orders, attendance, or credit.

Introduction

Many letters and memos are *requests*.

Letters and memos of request represent one of the most common forms of business writing. A ***letter of request*** is designed to obtain information and/or action from an individual or group outside the writer's organization. A ***memo of request*** is designed to obtain information and/or action from an individual or group within the writer's organization. For the sake of your reading convenience, the acronym "LMR" will be used throughout this chapter to represent "letters or memos of request."

A well-written LMR will generate the information or initiate the action needed by its author. A poorly written LMR typically generates several unfavorable results. First, additional communication is usually necessary. This follow-up communication—such as another LMR, a telephone call, or a personal visit—costs you both time and money.

Second, the poorly written LMR can have a devastating impact on the relationship between you and the receiver, generating distrust and frustration.

This chapter contains three major parts: (1) the psychology of LMRs, (2) basic organization plans for LMRs, and (3) common situations requiring LMRs. Five common situations are discussed. The primary emphasis in the discussion of each situation involves designing an appropriate organization plan and includes examples of both good and bad LMRs.

Throughout these discussions, remember that the characteristics common to effective written communication (discussed in Chapter 5) apply to each type of LMR. These characteristics are reinforced throughout the chapter.

PSYCHOLOGY OF LETTERS AND MEMOS OF REQUEST (LMRs)

Consider the psychological state of your reader.

To write an effective LMR, you must understand the underlying psychological aspects. If you can incorporate these issues into your planning process, you will likely improve your chances of achieving your objectives and reduce the probability of an irate response. A good approach is to address several questions while planning the LMR. Remember to keep your reader in mind while addressing these questions.

Is the LMR Complete?

The first question you must address is, Is the LMR complete? In other words, have you included enough information in the LMR for the receiver to act on your request? To answer this question, you must determine the type and amount of information the receiver needs to respond to your request. You must try to understand the receiver's frame of reference, especially the knowledge or information already in the reader's possession.

One day several years from now, for example, you might have to write to one of your college professors requesting that a letter of reference be sent to a firm. You probably should consider providing information such as:

1. Your name.
2. Social security number.
3. When you were in the professor's class.
4. Your grade.
5. Your grade point average or a transcript.
6. A picture.
7. A current resume.
8. The firm's name and address.
9. The type of job you are applying for.
10. A name to address the letter to.
11. A deadline for the letter.

This list might appear rather long, but your professor may not actually remember you, your face, and your activities after several years. Even if a little is remembered, you want enough information available to ensure a good reference letter.

Is the Situation Simple or Complex?

The next question to ask is, Is the relevant situation simple or complex? The purpose of asking this question is to help you determine how much detail to provide in the LMR.

In a simple situation, for example, the amount of detail should usually be kept to a minimum. Unnecessary detail can confuse your reader, thereby reducing your chances of having your request granted. Consider, for example, the memo in Illustration 6.1. In this memo to parents, three different times are given. Are they neces-

Your reader needs adequate information to fulfill your request.

Simple situations require minimal information.

ILLUSTRATION 6.1

A Memo with Too Much Detail

TO: Parents of Youth Choir
FROM: Youth Choir Director
DATE: May 17, 1987
SUBJ: Sunset Manor Visit

Too much information can result in confusion.

Our children's choirs will be singing at the Sunset Manor Nursing Home on Sunday, May 27, 1987, at 4:30 P.M. The older patients there like the children's visits so much. Following our performance we will return to the church to play games and have a picnic supper. At 7:15 P.M., we will sing in the worship service the same program presented at Sunset Manor. Please have your child at the Sears parking lot at 4 P.M. in order for us to go to Sunset Manor to sing.

sary? Actually, only the 4 P.M. time is needed because that is when the children are to be picked up by the choir director.

Complex situations re-quire more information.

Complex situations typically require more details. Even though concise, a detailed LMR for a complex situation can run several pages. If the situation calls for even more details, you might want to consider putting the details into a report and structuring the LMR as a cover letter.

A special variation of the complex situation arises when the situation is also highly sensitive, such as when the request or the details could have high emotional impact. For example, asking someone to step down from a leadership position due to incompetency is likely to be quite a sensitive problem. In this situation, you should consider using a more personal channel such as the telephone or a personal visit.

To ensure complete understanding, you should provide all necessary information. If you make responding difficult for any receiver, your chances of obtaining a timely, accurate response (or any response at all) is greatly reduced.

Is the LMR Concise?

The third question you must address is, Is the LMR concise? You must try to balance the requirement for completeness with the need for conciseness. The psychological rationale behind the need for conciseness is simple: Time is valuable to people who are busy, and business people tend to be busy. Most people are not interested in reading a long, complex document. Others cannot read writing that is difficult.

Conciseness alone does not guarantee your desired response, but the lack of conciseness does significantly reduce the chance of achieving your objective.

Concise requests tend to be more effective.

Is the LMR Clear?

An LMR must be clear to the reader to minimize the probability of an incorrect response from the reader. A lack of clarity can result in a variety of unpleasant situations. First, the reader may not know what kind of response to provide. Consider a situation, for example, in which you must ask an individual to present a speech or program for your campus organization. One point that must be clear is the manner in which the potential speaker should confirm or deny your request. Should the speaker contact you or will you contact him or her?

Lack of clarity may cause the reader to respond incorrectly. In the previous example, if you had asked the speaker to be ready to begin at 7:30, the speaker might assume that the time was 7:30 P.M. Yet you could have been inviting him or her to speak at a 7:30 A.M. breakfast meeting. Lack of clarity in this situation could leave everyone dissatisfied—you are embarrassed, the speaker is embarrassed, and your organization may be somewhat irritated.

Unclear requests cause unnecessary problems.

Summary of Psychological Aspects

All letters and memos of request have a specific objective. To improve the chances of attaining your objective, your LMR should be complete, concise, and clear so the reader can act on the request. Without these characteristics, your LMR might generate a variety of undesirable results.

Perhaps the key point is that you must make it easy for the reader to respond to your request. The easier it is for the receiver to respond, the more likely the receiver will be able to respond in the desired manner.

BASIC ORGANIZATIONAL PLANS

The most appropriate organizational plan for an LMR depends on the situation. As shown in Illustration 6.2, two general categories of situations exist—routine situations and nonroutine situations.

The situation dictates the proper organizational plan.

ILLUSTRATION 6.2

Organization Plans for Request Letters and Memos

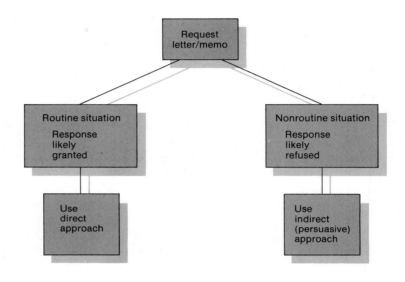

Routine Situations

A ***routine situation*** is one in which your request is likely to be granted. If you were the purchasing agent for a successful company, for example, a potential supplier would probably grant your request for more product information, service information, or a salesperson's visit.

The organizational plan for routine situations is based on a ***direct (or deductive) approach***. Illustration 6.3 presents an example of the direct approach. Since the receiver is expected to accept or grant your request, the request is positioned at the beginning of the LMR. Other information and details fill out the remainder of the space. This approach gets right to the point and makes your reader immediately aware of your request. The direct approach is particularly appropriate in simple situations and when the receiver is relatively busy.

Use a direct approach for routine situations.

ILLUSTRATION 6.3

Routine (Direct) Approach for Letter Memo of Request

**Routine (Direct) Approach
for
Letter/Memo of Request**

1. Request itself

2. Reason for request

3. Details and action statement
    (date by which reply is needed)

4. Assurance information will be considered confidential
    (if necessary)

5. Friendly close

Nonroutine Situations

A *nonroutine situation* arises when your request is likely to be refused. Assume again that you are the purchasing agent for a successful company and that you are preparing to write a letter to one of your suppliers requesting that the 12-month warranty be honored even though it has been 14 months since your firm purchased the product from the supplier. This is a nonroutine situation because your request would normally be refused by the supplier. Since the supplier does have the discretion to honor the warranty, however, an appropriate persuasive letter has a chance of succeeding.

The recommended organizational plan for nonroutine situations is based on an *indirect (or inductive) approach*. Since your reader is predisposed to refuse your request, you must soften his or her attitude before presenting the request. You might first state your reasons for the request and why the reader should grant the request (see Illustration 6.4). After these reasons have set the proper psychological tone, your request can then be presented. If appropriate, you might want to assure the reader that the information will be held in the strictest confidence. Your close should be warm and friendly and assure the receiver that granting your request is the appropriate decision.

Use an indirect approach for nonroutine situations.

ILLUSTRATION 6.4

Nonroutine (Indirect) Approach for Letter/Memo of Request

> **Non-Routine (Indirect) Approach**
> **for**
> **Letter/Memo of Request**
>
> 1. Reason for request
>
> 2. Request itself
>
> 3. Other details and action statement
>   (date by which a reply is needed)
>
> 4. Assurance information will be considered confidential
>   (if necessary)
>
> 5. Friendly close

COMMON SITUATIONS REQUIRING AN LMR

You are probably familiar with most of the common situations that require an LMR. They are requests for information, adjustments, an order, attendance, or credit. As these situations are discussed, the emphasis will be on the appropriate type of organizational plan.

Requests for Information

The first common situation calling for an LMR involves *requests for information*. Most requests for information involve products (or services) and people.

Requests for Product or Service Information. Requests for descriptive information on products and services are quite common. Examples of these requests include information about vacation spots, personal computers, on-line computer data bases, stereo systems, or hotel/motel reservations.

The direct approach is best for most requests for information.

The most appropriate organizational plan for these routine requests tends to be the direct approach. Since companies are generally eager to sell their products and services, a short, concise letter with the request positioned early is best (see Illustration 6.5).

Requests for Information about People.   Letters requesting information about people can be quite sensitive because they involve moral, ethical, and legal human rights issues. You must exercise extreme care in planning and writing these letters.

Three suggestions can help you avoid potentially unpleasant situations. Since many requests for information about people relate to job applicants, the following suggestions are structured around such situations.

First, ask questions that pertain only to the job for which the person is applying. In fact, this is more than a suggestion, it is a legal requirement. You must carefully analyze the specific job requirements and structure your questions around those requirements. Fur-

ILLUSTRATION 6.5

A Letter of Request for a Product

Request and reason
for request.

> Dear Mr. Green:
>
>   Would you please send us a complete list of models and specifications for Kemp Tractors. We are planning to add yard and garden tractors to our line of leased equipment and will feature Kemp Tractors.
>
>   It would be helpful to have the following data as soon as possible:

Details.

> 1. Horsepower/range of job function.
> 2. Commercial/homeowner equipment.
> 3. Contract samples/sale terms.

Close and action
statement.

>   Since the publication date for our catalog is scheduled for November, your reply by September 1 will be appreciated.
>
>   Sincerely yours,

ther, you must make sure that the requirements are real—employers sometimes have to defend the relevance of certain stated job requirements to the job itself.

Second, ask questions that deal only with facts about job-related performance. Again, this is a legal requirement. Any other questions may run afoul of each individual's right to be free from malicious gossip and unjustified attempts to undermine his or her reputation. Any breach of this right is referred to as defamation. When defamation is spoken it is slander; when it is written it is libel. Appendix D presents a brief overview of the major legal considerations pertaining to written correspondence.

Third, explain the job requirements. Your readers can provide you with better responses if they understand the nature of the job. For example, consider the following question: Do you think John Smith will make us a good employee (or manager)? Without knowing something about the job John Smith is applying for, the reader cannot give you a reasonable, specific, and truthful response.

Most inquiries about people are considered to be routine situations. The organizational plan for most LMRs about people would therefore involve the direct approach. An example of a poor letter requesting information about a person is shown in Illustration 6.6. It does not contain enough information about the position. Compare the weak letter to the letter shown in Illustration 6.7, which shows careful study of the job and the person.

> Be careful of individuals' rights when requesting information about them.

ILLUSTRATION 6.6

A Poor Letter of Request for Information about a Person

Dear Mr. Bush:

Miss Amanda Blake has applied to us for employment and has given us your name as a reference. She indicates that she worked under your supervision during the period 1984–86.

> A weak letter with too little information.

We would be most appreciative if you would give us your evaluation of Miss Blake. We are especially interested in her ability to handle responsibility, knowledge of sales procedures, work habits, and morals.

Thanking you in advance for your courtesy, I remain,

Sincerely yours,

ILLUSTRATION 6.7

A Good Letter of Request for Information about a Person

Dear Mr. Bush:

Will you help me evaluate Miss Amanda Blake for the position of sales manager? In authorizing this request, Miss Blake indicated that she worked for you from 1984 to 1986. Your candid answers to the following questions will help me determine whether Miss Blake is the right person for this job.

Does Miss Blake have the leadership ability and human relations skills to run a sales force of 17 people?

A good LMR with ample details.

Can Miss Blake manage a rapidly expanding sales force? The person who manages our sales force will need good sales and sales management skills and also must be able to adapt to changing conditions.

Does Miss Blake have the stamina and drive to cope with a high volume, pressure-filled operation?

Is Miss Blake reliable? Our sales manager is responsible for our sales force equipment as well as some company funds.

We shall, of course, hold your answers in strict confidence.

Sincerely,

Questions Are Important.   Most letters of request involve the use of questions. Asking the right question(s) in the right manner is critical to the success of your request. The following suggestions should prove quite helpful.

First, questions should be as specific as possible. General questions tend to elicit general responses. Remember the question, Do you think John Smith will make us a good employee (or manager)? This is a general question that is likely to get a response like, Yes, he's pretty good. Although such a response may be somewhat helpful, you will generally want much more specific information. If you do, you must ask for it.

The way you ask questions is important.

Second, consider organizing multiple specific questions into a numerical list. Scattering a large number of questions throughout your letter reduces the probability of getting all of them answered and perhaps of even obtaining a response at all. If your list is too long, you should consider putting it on a separate page rather than in the body of the letter.

Third, do not ask yes/no questions when you want a detailed answer. Although a yes or no answer is sometimes desirable, more detailed information generally must be obtained through a different type of question. Compare these similar questions. Two ask for a yes/no response and two ask for a detailed response, yet the wording is only slightly different.

Yes/No Question	Detailed Question
1. Are you going out tonight?	1. Where are you going tonight?
2. Are there specific instructions?	2. What are the specific instructions?

Fourth, each question should focus on only one topic. Consider the potential confusion created by the following question: What are the specific operating instructions for your equipment, can I have a set of instructions, and are they simpler than the instructions for Brand X? This question should obviously be restructured into three separate questions. Remember that you must make it easy for your reader to understand your request to make sure he or she can respond correctly.

Fifth, when you have multiple questions, begin with the easiest question unless logic dictates otherwise. Putting the more difficult questions first can discourage the reader from responding at all. The obvious exception to this suggestion involves a series of questions that build upon each other (when each answer depends upon previous answers).

Sixth, make your questions as neutral as possible. If you bias your questions, you can normally expect biased answers. Consider the following question: Although we question John Smith's ability, do you think he would make a good employee? Such a question makes it extremely difficult for the reader to respond in any way but a negative manner.

Requests for Adjustments

The second type of common situation calling for an LMR involves a *request for adjustment* or a *claim adjustment*. It is a fact of life that businesses make mistakes and that products do not always perform up to expected standards. When you or your firm experiences such a problem with a supplier or his product, you must do something to get the supplier to take corrective action. One possible course of action involves a written request for an adjustment in the form of a claim letter. The letter could ask for a refund, a replace-

Poor performance causes requests for adjustment.

ment product, an exchange, additional service, payment for damages, and so forth.

Depending on the specific situation, a claim letter can involve either the routine or nonroutine situation.

Routine Requests for Adjustments.   A routine situation occurs when a product is still under warranty or when you feel that an adjustment should be and will be granted. An organizational plan incorporating the direct approach, as discussed earlier, would be most appropriate. The claim should be made first, followed by the justification and other relevant details. The specific action requested should end the body of the letter. The example shown in Illustration 6.8 uses the direct approach.

Remember that business firms are interested in pleasing their customers. Mentioning any legal obligations or remedies, therefore, would likely be counterproductive.

ILLUSTRATION 6.8

A Routine Request for Adjustment

Dear Mr. Foster:

Subject: Request for replacement of faded Sunproof drapes, your invoice 3333 dated May 1, 1987.

Note the direct approach.

The Sunproof drapes you installed for us last May have faded badly. The original sandstone beige color now is streaked with varying shades of white and brown. The streaking is especially heavy in areas adjacent to the glass walls. The sun has probably caused the damage, but your written warranty says that the color will "withstand the effects of sun and water."

As the product clearly has not lived up to the warranty, please replace the Sunproof drapes with more suitable drapes. If you are unable to find satisfactory drapes, please refund the full purchase price, including installation.

I shall appreciate your usual promptness in correcting this problem.

Sincerely,

Nonroutine Requests for Adjustments. A nonroutine situation arises when you feel that your claim has a reasonable chance of being refused. Assume, for example, that your company car is just out of warranty when the air conditioner breaks. Although neither the automobile dealer nor the manufacturer has to honor an expired warranty, you still might want to send a claim letter.

Your claim letter in such nonroutine situations should have an organizational plan that uses the indirect approach. You should begin the letter by explaining the situation and your specific problem. This explanation should contain all of your reasons for making the request. It should be followed by your request for an adjustment.

Why would a firm want to grant your request if they are not legally bound? They may not. They may, however, weigh your (or your firm's) future worth or value as a customer against the cost of honoring your request. If the firm feels that they can recoup their cost and still make a profit from your business, they might honor your request. Other business people might honor your request rather than hide behind a legal technicality because of feelings of moral or ethical responsibility. More and more business people appear to be taking the longer term view that they should do what is right from the customer's perspective rather than just from a legal or short-term profit perspective.

> Use an indirect organizational plan for nonroutine requests for adjustment.

Requests for an Order

A *request for an order* involves a written order for products or services. Although much ordering is done by telephone, face-to-face, or on standard order blanks, written orders are still common in today's business world.

Written orders typically occur in routine situations. Since most firms are anxious to sell their products, you normally do not have to give a variety of persuasive reasons for the order. Your letter should therefore utilize the direct organization plan. Make your request at the beginning of the letter. In planning the remaining details of the letter, you should remember the following key considerations.

Make It Clear that You Are Ordering Something. The first key consideration involves ensuring that the reader understands that you are requesting products rather than product information. For example, avoid phrases like "I am interested in. . . ." Phrases such as "Please ship. . . ." and "Please send. . . ." are much better.

Make Your Order Easy to Fill.   Include all necessary product-related details. If you are ordering stationery, for example, you might include the following information:

1. Size.
2. Amount.
3. Name of style (if appropriate).
4. Style description.
5. Rag content.
6. Weight.
7. Whether you want letterheads.
8. Whether you want backing sheets for letterheads.
9. Whether you want envelopes.
10. Color of ink.

Failure to include any of this information will make your order more difficult to fill correctly.

Include Shipping Instructions.   The third key consideration involves shipping instructions. The most important information to include is a clearly stated and easy-to-find address. Other important information includes special instructions about the preferred transportation mode and the timing of the shipment.

Specify the Manner of Payment.   If you know the supplier's standard terms and are willing to accept them, your acceptance should be clearly stated in the letter. If you offer the supplier better terms than normal for the industry or trade, no problem should arise. However, if you do not know the supplier's standard terms, you probably should mention how and when you intend to negotiate the terms. The letter in Illustration 6.9 shows an *urgent* request for an order.

Requests for Attendance (Invitations)

The fourth common situation calling for a letter of request involves *requests for attendance (invitations)*. These invitations arise in a variety of situations.

Simple Invitation.   A simple invitation is appropriate when attendance is requested at such situations as a meeting or event as part of the audience, a social function, a standard membership meeting, or a committee meeting.

ILLUSTRATION 6.9

A Letter of Request for an Order

An urgent request using the direct approach.

Dear Ms. Davis:

Please accept this order for immediate shipment via Osage Trucking to Stubbs Cabinets, 1234 West Vinson Road, High Point, California 39762.

Quantity	Description	Unit Price	Total
1,500	No. 888 hinges, brass plated	$1/pair	$1,500
500	No. 34 braces, brass plated	1.50 each	750
Total			$2,250

An unexpected flurry of orders has depleted our stock. Therefore, any assistance that you can give in expediting our order and delivery will be greatly appreciated. We are assuming your normal credit terms are applicable.

Sincerely,

Simple invitations generally involve routine situations and, therefore, a direct approach. In fact, they are often no more than simple announcements. The example of a request for meeting attendance in Illustration 6.10 uses the direct approach.

Sometimes, however, nonroutine situations can arise. Consider, for example, a simple invitation to a club or organization member who has not attended a meeting in several months. If you do not anticipate that this individual will respond to an announcement, you should consider the more persuasive indirect approach. Persuasive letters are discussed in Chapter 9.

Request for Speaker. Individuals are sometimes asked to attend a function and actively participate as a speaker, panel member, session chairperson, or in some other active role. This is often a routine situation, especially if the activity benefits the individual directly, such as furthering his or her career aspirations.

Other situations, however, can be nonroutine. The benefits of having the speaker, for example, may accrue only to the group and not to the speaker. An indirect approach would probably be more

ILLUSTRATION 6.10

Memo of Request for Attendance

TO: Barbara Blount
      Nancy Means
      Angela Osborn
      Bill Persons
      Ed Rushing
      Henry Stevens
FROM: Richard Lewis
DATE: January 6, 1987
SUBJ: Executives' Strategic Planning Meeting

Note the direct approach.

The Executives' Strategic Planning Committee will meet Friday, January 15, at 11 A.M. in the Lighthouse Room of the Barons Building in Dallas. Luncheon will be served.

If you cannot be with us, please call 333-8888 no later than January 10.

An agenda is enclosed. Also, you will find a map with complete travel directions and a description of the parking facilities at the Barons Building.

---

effective than a direct approach in such situations. The letter shown in Illustration 6.11 uses the indirect approach.

Key Issues in Planning Requests for Attendance. In both routine and nonroutine requests for attendance, you must consider several issues. The reader's frame of reference influences the amount of detail that should be included. If the receiver knows nothing about the nature of the event you are inviting him or her to, for example, you will have to describe the event in detail.

The five Ws—who, what, when, where, and why—can help ensure that sufficient information is included.

Requests for Credit

The fifth common situation calling for an LMR involves *requests for credit*. Buying merchandise on credit is an integral part of our business world. Although most requests for credit take the form of standardized forms, letters requesting credit are still common. (Let-

ILLUSTRATION 6.11

A Letter of Request for a Speaker

Note the indirect approach.

Dear Mrs. Robinson:

On November 3, Starlight Corporation's middle management employees will begin a week long workshop. The workshop will consist of talks and discussions on various phases of business. The seminars are to be led by persons prominent in each subject area.

A discussion of "Women in Management" has been scheduled for Tuesday afternoon, November 4. Would you present this 20-to-30-minute talk and then answer questions for a brief period?

The meeting will begin at 1:30 P.M. in the Falcon Room of the Seashore Inn. The group consists of 20 men and women managers. Please plan for you and your husband to attend the dinner afterward.

Can you let me know by October 1? Thank you.

Sincerely,

ILLUSTRATION 6.12

A Letter of Request for Credit

Note the direct approach.

Dear Mr. Ross:

After inspecting your recent exhibit of fine cabinets at the International Hardware Convention in San Diego last month, I would like to add your line of merchandise.

Please consider this letter an application for a charge account within the $2,000–$3,000 range. Of course, credit references will be supplied upon request.

Ross merchandise should be quite successful in this state.

Sincerely,

ters requesting or ordering products often contain requests for credit, making them dual-purpose letters; the credit request portion of such a letter should still follow the principles discussed below.)

If you and the supplying firm consider the request for credit a mere formality, a routine situation exists. You could therefore employ the direct approach for your organizational plan. State your request up front, followed by appropriate supporting information. The letter in Illustration 6.12 uses the direct approach.

If approval of your request is not a sure thing, a nonroutine situation exists. A nonroutine situation would exist, for example, when you are writing a firm that does not normally offer credit or has previously turned down your request for credit.

The supplier's frame of reference is critically important in nonroutine situations. The supplier wants satisfied customers and the resulting sales volume. At the same time, the supplier understands that granting credit is a risk—the supplier must be sure that your firm can repay the money owed.

Your letter requesting credit in nonroutine situations must therefore use an indirect approach. Your logic should focus on reducing the supplier's perceived risk. Once this is accomplished, your request can be stated.

Application Exercises

1. You own a small appliance store and have recently purchased a personal computer which you plan to use to maintain household as well as business records. SofTech, Inc. provides a service through which it gathers information from software producers about new software packages. A listing of new offerings is sent each month to those who subscribe to the service. Write a letter to SofTech's marketing manager, George Jones, asking for more information about this service. Be specific in your request.

2. The leisure time you spend in bird watching would be much more enjoyable if you owned a high-powered birding scope. In the September 1986 issue of *Wings* magazine, you found an advertisement for a scope that is exactly what you need. The price of the Birding Scope, Model 23, is $230. UPS shipping charges will amount to $30.45. Write a letter to Bill Clark of TeleProducts ordering the scope.

3. You are the financial manager for a small firm that has recently decided to begin an employee payroll savings program. Each participating employee will receive a quarterly statement (along with that month's paycheck) that lists total and quarterly contributions, withdrawals, interest earned, and the current balance. You must order the blank forms for preparing these statements. Write to Alice King of Cockrell Bros. Printing (your regular printer) asking for a cost estimate for each 1,000 forms. Be sure to give the printer an idea of what is to be printed on the forms.

4. You are a member of the National Book Club, a mail-order house. Last month you ordered a new edition of the *American Road Atlas* from the firm's monthly catalog. Three weeks ago you received a copy of the *New World Atlas*. You immediately returned this book with a letter explaining the mistake and requesting that the other volume be sent.

You have just received a statement from the book club requesting that you pay for the *New World Atlas*. Write a letter in which you explain the situation, requesting again that the *American Road Atlas* be sent and that your account be corrected.

5. You are a buyer for Brinkman and Co., a retail sporting goods store. You are responsible for buying a wide range of merchandise from both wholesalers and manufacturers. You recently transmitted an order (#2355) to Lenoir Sport Products for 50 Arkel X-5 tennis rackets. When the shipment arrived, however, the receiving department found that 14 of the rackets had been cracked or severely damaged during shipping. Write a letter to Lenoir requesting credit for the damaged rackets and instructions for their disposal.

6. Shortly after moving to Minnesota, you placed an order with Craigman Bros., an outdoor clothing mail-order house. Your order was for a medium, navy blue, down-filled parka (catalog no. B2074). You received, however, a forest green parka. Write a letter explaining that your are returning the jacket and requesting that Craigman ship one in the correct color.

7. As the program chairperson of your university's chapter of the Business Management Society (BMS), you are responsible for arranging a dinner and for a guest speaker. Write to Dr. Laura Franks, president of the southeast region of BMS. Ask her to attend the dinner and to present a short talk on ''The Next Five Years for the Business Management Society.'' The dinner will be on January 23, 1987, at 7 P.M. You have been authorized to reimburse Dr. Franks for her travel and hotel expenses.

8. You are the assistant director of recruiting for Allied Company, a manufacturer of chemicals and textiles. You feel that it would help your recruiting efforts if university placement officials had a better understanding of your firm's structure and activities.

Write a letter to Dr. Eric Osborn, placement director for Central State University. Invite him to attend a special program that will consist of several tours and short programs by divisional representatives. The program will be March 28 from 9 A.M. to 3 P.M. A complimentary luncheon will be served.

9. Using the information in Exercise 8, change the focus to college of business faculty. Write a letter inviting Dr. Mary Hayden, Professor of Management, to the special program.

10. Dr. Gary Cobb is a widely recognized authority on lightweight aircraft. You are the secretary of the Mayville Pilots Association. The association would like to host a panel discussion on various safety issues, including regulation of this type plane. Since Dr. Cobb is a proponent of the safety of lightweight aircraft, write a letter asking him to be a member of the panel. You have already asked Dr. James C. Miller, another noted authority, to present opposing arguments. Mr. Thomas Warren of the Federal Aviation Administration has agreed to discuss safety regulations.

11. Since you are in your last semester of college, you have decided that you should begin to establish credit. You have accepted a job with CaliCo, a large California-based oil firm. AmeriBank, Inc. offers a widely accepted charge card (the TourCard) that you feel would be perfect for your needs. Write AmeriBank to request the TourCard.

12. You have recently opened ComputerTech, a retail store offering personal computer hardware and software in a small city.

CompSoft Company produces a large number of software packages compatible with the hardware sold in your store. They have recently launched an interesting new program called NuComp. You feel that you will need to deal extensively with CompuSoft in the future and want to establish credit. Write a letter requesting credit privileges.

13. You are a buyer for Crump's, a large department store. Crump's is planning to open a candy counter in the immediate future. Write Zevenbergen, Inc. (a distributor of imported Swiss chocolates) to place an order and a request for credit.

14. Write a memo to your firm's marketing vice president asking him to speak for approximately 20 to 30 minutes at the Kiwanis club next month (June 4 at 12 A.M.) on your newest product line. You are also the program chairman of the local Kiwanis club in Crabs Prairie, Texas.

Review Questions

1. Describe the major problems associated with a poor letter or memo of request.
2. Relate the concept of completeness to letters and memos of request.
3. Relate the concept of conciseness to letters and memos of request.
4. Relate the concept of clarity to letters and memos of request.
5. Describe the major problems associated with lack of clarity in a letter or memo of request.
6. Describe the direct or deductive approach to organizing a letter or memo of request.
7. Describe the indirect or inductive approach to organizing a letter or memo of request.
8. List and explain three ways to help avoid potentially unpleasant situations when making requests for information about people.
9. Discuss the importance of using questions in letters of request. List and explain the six relevant suggestions.
10. Discuss nonroutine requests for adjustments.
11. List and explain the four key considerations in writing a request letter for an order.
12. List and explain the key considerations in planning a request for attendance.

Key Terms

letter of request
memo of request
routine situation (LMR)
direct approach (LMR)
nonroutine situation (LMR)
indirect approach (LMR)

requests for information
requests for adjustments
requests for an order
requests for attendance
requests for credit

Chapter   7

Writing Favorable Response Letters and Memos

■ *Learning Objectives*

After studying this chapter, you should be able to:
■ Explain why building goodwill is important when writing yes letters and memos.
■ Outline several organizational plans for yes letters and memos.
■ Write yes letters and memos for the following common situations:

General requests

Claim requests

Order requests

Invitation requests

Credit requests

Introduction

Now that you have a firm grasp of the techniques used to write various types of letters/memos of request, you are ready to examine how to respond to letters/memos of request. The two primary types of response letters/memos are favorable and unfavorable. This chapter focuses on favorable responses, and Chapter 8 addresses unfavorable response letters and memos.

This discussion of favorable responses consists of three major sections: (1) the psychology of favorable response letters and memos, (2) the basic organizational plans, and (3) the different responses to each type of request letter and memos.

PSYCHOLOGY OF FAVORABLE RESPONSE LETTERS AND MEMOS

Writing an FRLM can be easy, but beware of subtle problems.

On the surface, *a favorable response letter or memo* (FRLM) may appear to be the easiest type of correspondence to write. In one sense, such a correspondence is easy and pleasant to write because saying yes is easier than saying no. On the other hand, writing a *good* FRLM presents some subtle problems. Let's first address these problems and the need to examine your reader's frame of reference.

Examine Frames of Reference

You must consider the frame of reference of the person who made the request. For example, was it positive or negative? An individual writing a claim letter, for example, could have a negative frame of mind. You probably would not write the same FRLM to an irate person as you would write to a person who is quite positive toward your firm.

A related consideration involves people's expectations regarding your response. If they expect a yes, for example, and your standard response is yes, your FRLM could be relatively short and to the point.

Your reader's frame of reference dictates your organizational plan.

Conversely, if they expect a no but your response is yes, you face a different situation. You have a tremendous opportunity to build goodwill beyond simply saying yes. People receiving the yes tend to be more receptive to additional information about your firm, products, or services. You should take advantage of this to cultivate future relationships.

Build Goodwill

Goodwill refers to a firm's relationships with other firms and individuals. Even though an FRLM offers tremendous opportunity to build goodwill, companies sometimes find ways of turning this opportunity into a disaster. Consider, for example, the letter shown in Illustration 7.1.

Don't miss opportunities to build goodwill.

The author of this letter has a we attitude and is quite tactless—goodwill is therefore not projected. It is sure to unnecessarily upset the reader, even though the author is granting the claim. Examples of letters that build goodwill are shown later in this chapter, particularly for adjustment or claim letters.

ILLUSTRATION 7.1

A Letter that Does Not Project Goodwill

Dear Mr. Heller:

We received your letter of June 5 in which you requested that we credit your account for $33.67 for discounts on orders which were delivered to you in March and April.

Condescending   and
. . .

As you may or may not know, the standard policy throughout the computer industry is that a 3 percent discount is granted only when bills are paid within 15 days of date of invoice. If we did not follow this policy, and gave such discounts to everyone who walked in off the street, we would surely lose money. The discounts which you claim you are entitled to are all for orders which you paid late. Surely you are aware of this.

. . . insulting.

However, we are granting your claim and we hope this satisfies you. We also hope you will be less careless in the future.

Sincerely,

When writing an FRLM you must concentrate on building good-will and preventing a negative response. The four following suggestions can help.

Answer Requests Promptly.

Although simple promptness can help build goodwill, too many business people appear to feel that since they intend to say yes, they can delay responding. This delay can, in fact, generate negative reactions, despite the fact that a yes answer is being delivered. For example, program chairpeople need quick responses to requests for speakers so they can find another speaker if necessary. Similarly, requests for information about people—especially when involving employment—tend to be urgent.

Sometimes, you might have to delay a response because you simply do not have the final answer. When this occurs, you should write a letter of acknowledgment. This letter provides you with an additional opportunity to build goodwill. (It also is an excellent example of utilizing the feedback mechanisms discussed in Chapter 3.) You should explain the reason for delaying your decision, that you are taking steps toward making the decision, and approximately how long your decision will take.

Don't keep your reader waiting.

Put Good News Up Front.

Since you know the reader wants to receive a favorable response, you should provide that information at the very beginning of your letter. In other words, you should use the direct approach in most FRLMs. The letter in Illustration 7.2 uses a poor approach. Why keep the reader in suspense? This letter not only delays the good news, it seems to be leading to a rejection. The acceptance should be placed at the beginning of the letter.

If you have good news, use a direct approach.

Use a Tactful and Positive Tone.

Although tact is important in all types of letters and memos, it is far too easy to downgrade the importance of tact in FRLMs. For example, you should strive to avoid giving a yes response that sounds like you begrudge having to say yes. Here are three examples of tactless and negative sentences. Each is followed by an improved version.

> **Poor:** Although you were in error, we are giving you the money.

> **Better:** We are pleased to make the adjustment under these circumstances.

> **Poor:** If you had read the specifications, this would never have happened. We are going to go along with you anyway. I trust you have learned your lesson.

ILLUSTRATION 7.2

A Poor Yes Letter: Good News Is Not Up Front

Good news is at the
end of this letter.

Dear Dr. Rodriguez:

Thank you for submitting your manuscript entitled
"Communication Conflicts in Organizations" to the
Management Division of the 1987 Southwest Management
Association meeting. There were numerous manuscripts
submitted and, as a result, the process of choosing those to be
part of the program was highly selective. Each manuscript was
reviewed by at least two different individuals. Enclosed you will
find evaluation sheets as completed by the reviewers. It was
decided to accept your paper as part of this year's program.

Congratulations! See you in New Orleans.

Sincerely,

Better: The adjustment has been made as you requested. May
we suggest that the specifications be followed carefully for
complete satisfaction in the future.

Poor: To err is human, but this is ridiculous. We can't imagine
why you would feel your claim is justified. Regardless, we
have credited your account.

Better: Mistakes are certainly made from time to time and on
this basis we have credited your account.

Completeness.   Although the above characteristics may be
present, your opportunity to build goodwill with a favorable response letter can still be lost if your letter is not complete and
accurate. Imagine, for example, receiving a response to a claim that
says "Yes, we are going to give you an adjustment," but which
neglects to give enough information for you to take further action. In
situations like this, the reader's response can quickly become unpleasant.

Although these four suggestions for writing a favorable response
letter are extremely important, remember that all of the characteristics of effective writing apply to favorable response letters. However, these four suggestions are frequently neglected in commonly
written favorable response letters or memos.

ORGANIZATIONAL PLAN

The most effective organizational plan for FRLMs normally involves a variation of the direct approach. The good news or the yes should occur very early. Illustration 7.3 presents the sequential components for an FRLM.

Put good news up front.

The first part of the letter consists of an *introductory statement* acknowledging the request. This statement is needed to alert the reader to the purpose of the letter. It is important because many organizations receive hundreds of letters every day, and your reader may need reminding of his or her request. It is also important for filing purposes in that it can help the reader find the correct file folder more easily.

Remind the reader of his or her request early.

An alternative to putting an introductory acknowledgment statement in the first sentence or paragraph of the letter involves using a *subject line* to acknowledge the request. The subject line serves the same purpose as the acknowledgment statement. Its primary advantage lies in allowing the first sentence of the letter to contain the grant itself. A subject line is shown in the abbreviated letter in Illustration 7.4.

Good FRLMs can include more than a simple yes. You most often respond to multiple questions. One approach to responding to multiple questions is to answer the most important question first. This approach allows you to put the major emphasis at the beginning

ILLUSTRATION 7.3

Organizational Plan for a "Yes" Letter/Memo (Direct Approach)

**Organizational Plan for a Yes Letter/Memo
(Direct Approach)**

1. Introductory statement acknowledging the request

2. Grant itself

3. Listing necessary information

4. Sales appeal
   (if appropriate)

5. Friendly close

ILLUSTRATION 7.4

An Abbreviated Letter with a Subject Line

Subject line alerts
reader to contents.

Dear Mr. Thatcher:

SUBJECT: Your inquiry about a tire adjustment.

   Please come in anytime this week for your free tire
adjustment.

                                    Sincerely,

Respond to all ques-
tions.

of the letter. If, however, the request letter includes a list of questions, you may need to address the questions in the order they were
originally requested. In other situations, you may have to use a
logical approach. For example, you would need to answer the following two questions in the order listed, regardless of the order in
which they are asked:

1. Which entrance exam must I take to apply to your university?
2. What is the minimum acceptable score for admittance to your
   university?

Whether the first item is an introductory acknowledgment statement or the subject line, the *grant* itself should immediately follow.
The paragraph that includes the grant should be short and to the
point. For example, you might begin the FRLM with a subject line
and have a one-sentence opening paragraph such as "Congratulations! Your credit application has been accepted by the Sunshine
Corporation."

The third major component of an FRLM is any information the
reader needs in order to take action. Assume, for example, that you
must write a letter granting someone credit. If a credit card is not
included in the mailing, the reader would need answers to questions
such as:

1. Will a credit card be mailed?
2. Should the card be picked up? Where?
3. Where does he or she go to activate credit?
4. Whom should one see?
5. How much credit is granted?

Don't miss the selling opportunity.

The fourth part of the organizational plan is a *sales appeal* or at least an appeal for goodwill. Remember, you have the reader's attention and probably a very positive attitude. A tremendous opportunity exists to present a sales appeal to the reader.

The last part of the FRLM should be a *friendly close*. It should show your appreciation for the letter of request and the interest in your situation or company. Each of these parts of the organizational plan is illustrated in letter examples shown in the remainder of this chapter.

COMMON SITUATIONS

The remainder of the chapter discusses the five major situations that call for FRLMs:

1. Responding to general requests for a product, service, or person.
2. Responding to claim letters.
3. Responding to orders for products.
4. Responding to requests for credit.
5. Responding to invitation requests.

Answering General Requests

The format of this section follows that of the companion section on general requests in Chapter 6. Thus, the two major subsections involve answering: (1) requests referring to products or services and (2) requests for information about people.

Answering Product/Service Requests. A common letter of request involves asking for information about a product or service. Most organizations are very interested in answering this type of request with a favorable response. As a result, FRLMs regarding product or service information are common in today's business organizations. Because they may be the reader's first direct exposure to your company, they can be the deciding factor in whether the reader buys from your firm or from a competitor.

Since you have good news, the best organizational plan for this type of letter involves the direct approach—put the good news up front. In addition, you have the opportunity to present a strong sales appeal. Remember that the reader is probably a potential customer. If so, he or she may base a purchase decision solely on the information received from you and perhaps one other firm. You generally

Make your sales appeal strong.

should provide more information than is asked for, including brochures, catalogs, order forms, and other detailed information.

Although including a strong sales appeal may appear rather devious, many firms fail to take full advantage of what is really an opportunity. For example, the short request shown in Illustration 7.5 was sent to 10 companies. The purpose of the request was to obtain enough information to choose an on-line data base to access with a personal computer and a modem. Most firms sent only an advertising brochure and perhaps an order blank. Only one firm really viewed the request as a sales opportunity. This firm sent a packet containing: (1) an overview of the service, (2) an order form, (3) ordering instructions, (4) a detailed price list, (5) a comprehensive and detailed list of specific data bases available, (6) a description of how to use the service, (7) a cover letter, (8) a description of hardware and software requirements, (9) a pamphlet describing national training seminars, and (10) a seminar reservation form. No other firm included more than a cover letter and two other items (which varied in nature). Some firms did not even include a cover letter.

Answering Letters/Memos about People. This type of response is included as an FRLM because you essentially provide the information requested. In other words, the reader is satisfied because you respond, even though your response may be positive or negative. Use the following guidelines when you write a letter evaluating an individual.

Include only job-related information. Focus your comments only on the person's job-related performance. In addition, you

ILLUSTRATION 7.5

A Short Request Letter

Dear Staff:

I am trying to choose one of the on-line data bases, but cannot find adequate information about them. Would you please send me information that tells me why yours might be appropriate.

Thank you.

Sincerely,

should restrict your observations to facts. As mentioned in Chapter 6, hearsay and unfounded opinions could result in a libel suit.

Emphasize a key issue early. After your introductory acknowledgment statement, you should mention a key issue. You might mention, for example, your qualifications to evaluate this person. Or, you could include your overall evaluation at this point.

Use a logical order. Your personal evaluation of the individual's job-related performance should be presented in a logical order. Reply to specific questions in the order that they were posed or group your evaluations into categories, such as performance-related qualifications and personal qualifications. Remember that the personal qualifications must relate to the individual's potential performance on a specific job. An example of a good memo about a person is shown in Illustration 7.6.

Answering a Claim

A *claim* is a customer request for a monetary refund, product replacement, or other adjustment because of a product defect. Writing an FRLM to a claim request can involve two different approaches—the routine and the nonroutine.

Answering a Routine Claim Request. A *routine claim request* arises when your company (as the seller) is clearly at fault. You should therefore respond immediately with a FRLM. Routine

ILLUSTRATION 7.6

A Good Memo Answering a Request for Information about a Person

Yes, I'd be happy to recommend Jerry Wade as a member of your accounting staff there in Baltimore. He has worked with me since July 1986 and has worked on just about every type of oil and gas accounting problem we've encountered. He's self-motivated, thorough in his research, and knowledgeable in all aspects. Although not particularly articulate, Jerry does communicate effectively in writing. I only wish there was a way to give him the promotion here that he deserves; I hate to lose him.

I wish both of you the best when his transfer is approved.

claim requests should generally generate an FRLM that uses a direct organizational plan.

Since your company is at fault in these situations, you must do everything possible to regain any lost confidence. Do not *overemphasize* the fact that your company made a mistake. Instead, employ a highly positive tone throughout the letter.

Your FRLM should immediately inform the reader that your firm has agreed that the claim is warranted. In other words, say yes to the claim immediately. You might mention that corrective action has been taken so that the particular problem will not occur in the future. You could then mention something more positive, such as a new product or an upcoming sale.

The key point is to remove any remaining negative thoughts because of the mistake or deficient product. Illustration 7.7 shows an example of a poor letter answering a routine claim request.

The letter shown in Illustration 7.8 is a much better revised version of a routine claim request letter.

Answering a Nonroutine Claim Request. A *nonroutine claim request* occurs *when the buyer is at fault*, but the firm still intends to grant the claim. As you probably have recognized by now, the standard organizational plan for an FRLM involves the direct approach. An FRLM for a nonroutine claim, however, is the one major exception. The indirect approach is generally better for these FRLMs. If you use the direct approach and mention immediately that your firm will accept the claim, your reader may not read the remainder of the letter and it is important that he does.

Admit the mistake and remain positive.

The indirect approach is often better for a favorable response to a nonroutine claim request.

ILLUSTRATION 7.7

A Poor Routine Claim Request Letter

Dear Mr. Ruthven:

In your letter of March 6 you claimed that the merchandise you purchased for $73.76 on February 1 was paid for on that date. Our records indicated that this was not so.

However, a detailed check revealed that you were correct in your claim. A member of our clerical staff neglected to enter your payment on our books.

We hope that this error caused you no undue concern.

Sincerely,

Positive tone is missing.

ILLUSTRATION 7.8

A Good Routine Claim Request Letter

Dear Mr. Ruthven:

A positive tone improves the letter.

You are right, Mr. Ruthven. After checking your file, we discovered that you did pay for the merchandise on the day it was purchased, just as you said.

Please forgive us—you can be sure that steps are being taken to see that this does not happen again.

Sincerely,

The indirect approach for FRLMs begins with a review of the situation that brought about the claim request. From your company's point of view, it is important that you let readers know that you realize they are at fault, but that you want to correct the situation to their satisfaction. You can do this only by explaining the situation, including the cause or reason for the problem.

After the situation has been clarified, you can tell the reader that you are accepting the claim and are proceeding with the adjustment. The positive psychological effect of goodwill should be greater if the reader first understands that he or she is at fault, and then finds out that you are still going to accept the claim.

Maintaining a positive tone is critical.

When presenting the case to show the reader that he is at fault, remember to be positive and tactful. You must not state your case in a way that makes the reader lose credibility. Assuming a grudging approach will cause you to lose all positive benefits of the FRLM. Illustration 7.9 shows an ineffective response to a nonroutine claim letter.

Compare the letter to Mrs. Pickett with the much better example shown in Illustration 7.10. Note that the customer is tactfully told he is at fault *before* the grant is made. If the grant had been made first, the customer might have stopped reading and thus never become aware of his error.

Answering an Order

The third major request letter discussed in Chapter 6 involved requests or orders for products. **Routine orders** are filled as promptly as possible. **Nonroutine orders** are expected to be filled,

ILLUSTRATION 7.9

An Ineffective Response to a Nonroutine Claim Letter

Dear Mrs. Pickett:

We are happy to tell you, in reference to your letter of April 2, that we have credited your account for $105.78.

We can understand how you felt when the merchandise you purchased was not operational.

Little tact.

However, your maintenance personnel should not have tried to correct whatever was wrong with the #555 switching unit. This is a highly complex piece of electronic equipment, and it is for this reason that we carefully place the statement on every cover which says: "To be opened by a qualified manufacturer's representative only; call manufacturer for service."

For your best interests, we suggest that you follow our recommendations in the future.

Sincerely,

ILLUSTRATION 7.10

A Good Response to a Nonroutine Claim Letter

Dear Mr. Ellis:

We were sorry to learn that the ⅓ h.p. motor did not prove satisfactory. In your letter, however, you indicated that it was used to power a Stark-Cannon Industrial Press, model #567.

This letter is tactful and . . .

The manufacturer of the press recommends that a ¾-to-1 h.p. unit be used with this particular model. Apparently this was overlooked by the people in your shop and our ⅓ h.p. unit was used. Of course, we realize that incidents such as this occur and we are sending out the larger motor as you requested. However, for your satisfaction and the most efficient operation of equipment in the future, we strongly suggest that the manufacturer's recommendations be followed.

. . . the grant is made after the explanation.

The new motor should be delivered to your warehouse no later than November 10; at that time our driver can pick up the original unit. If we can assist you in any way in the future, Mr. Ellis, please call on us.

Sincerely,

but only after additional actions by the ordering firm or individual. Your response to orders should involve more than simply filling and shipping the order. Assuming you are interested in filling the order, you should consider sending one or more FRLMs.

When filling an order, always consider including an FRLM.

Routine Orders. Upon receiving an order and verifying your firm's ability and willingness to fill it as quickly as possible, the order can be treated as routine. You should determine the approximate shipping date and send an FRLM immediately.

Following the direct approach for your organizational plan, your letter should begin by acknowledging receipt of the order. Your opening line, for example, might be something like, "Thank you for your order of October 1."

The next two items—the grant and any necessary information—can often be covered together. The additional information could include details such as shipping mode, when delivery can be expected, and confirmation of the sales terms. Your second sentence, for example, might be, "One dozen widgets were shipped to you today via Jones Trucking Company."

The sales appeal might consist simply of a general offer to be of future service. A more involved sales appeal might include a variety of material such as catalogs or brochures announcing new products and a specific mention of related products your firm carries.

Nonroutine Order. A nonroutine order occurs when your firm wants to fill the order, but cannot until another event takes place. Your firm, for example, might be experiencing a shortage of the ordered product, causing shipping delays. Or the customer may have supplied inadequate information (e.g., on shipping, credit, product specifications) with his or her order.

A favorable response to a nonroutine order calls for an indirect organizational plan. As with indirect approaches for other types of FRLMs, you should begin with an introductory acknowledgment statement.

The second major element of your letter should involve development of the situation that will cause you to eventually state that you cannot ship now but still want to fill the order. This section of your letter, for example, might begin, "Demand for widgets is at an all-time high. This unprecedented situation has created a temporary production backlog."

The remaining components of your FRLM are similar to other indirect approaches. An example of an entire indirect FRLM is shown in Illustration 7.11.

ILLUSTRATION 7.11

A Nonroutine Letter Responding to Order

Dear Mr. Duhon:

Thank you very much for your order of five dozen Carlisle baseballs. However, you did not indicate whether you wanted the day-light model #7 or the night-light model #22. If you will check your merchandise and shipping preference on the enclosed airmail card, your order will be processed and shipped immediately.

I am also enclosing a flyer describing our new line of soccer balls. If you wish to order a quantity of these fast-moving items, simply mark the appropriate boxes on the same card.

Sincerely,

Answering an Invitation Request

Business people must frequently respond to requests to attend meetings and perhaps to make a speech or presentation at a meeting or convention. Many organizations encourage their employees to accept these invitations because of the public relations benefits.

Favorable responses to invitation requests normally call for a direct organizational plan. First, you should acknowledge the invitation. For example, you might begin with, "The invitation to speak to your group is quite flattering."

Next, you should make your response clear. For example, your second sentence might be simply, "I would be delighted to deliver the speech."

You should confirm all necessary details related to the invitation. The basic W questions, for example, can help your confirmation efforts. Although the letter of request may have contained all the necessary information, it is important that you give the reader feedback to reconfirm these details.

Rather than a sales appeal, you should present any action statements that are needed. These statements might involve your needs relative to attending the meeting or speaking to the group. For example, if you need any special equipment, you say so in the letter.

Finally, you should always include a friendly close. The close should enhance your firm's relations or goodwill with the organization to which you have been invited to attend or speak. The memo in Illustration 7.12 shows a good answer to an invitation request.

Answering Credit Request

Replying favorably to a credit request normally requires a direct approach. The introductory acknowledgment statement and the grant (or yes answer) should be the first two components. In this type of letter, there is really no reason to delay the good news you have for the reader. This point is demonstrated in Illustration 7.13.

The third component, listing necessary information, should involve details regarding the credit terms. It is important that these details be explained in a very clear and effective manner. By communicating the terms clearly, you can prevent (or at least reduce) misunderstandings and collection problems later. For example, is it sufficient to simply state that your credit terms are the usual 2/10, net 30 (a 2 percent discount is given if the bill is paid within 10 days and the net or total bill is due in 30 days)? Actually these terms can

ILLUSTRATION 7.12

A Good Example Answering an Invitation Request

TO: Mary Whittle, Public Relations Director
FROM: John Clyde, Director of Research
Subject: Presentation to the Golden Roundtable

Acknowledgment, response, and details confirmed.

It isn't every day that one is honored by an invitation to address the Golden Roundtable! I am extremely pleased to accept your invitation to address your group on Friday, August 16, 1987, at 5 P.M. in Roundtable Hall in Omaha.

After reflecting on a topic, perhaps "Ethics and Technology" would be of interest to your members. As you know, our division has done considerable research in this area.

An action statement.

As soon as my travel arrangements are confirmed, I shall send you further information regarding any special needs.

Friendly close.

Thank you, once again, for the opportunity to participate in your 50th Annual Conference. May I offer my congratulations to you for the splendid contributions that the Golden Roundtable has made to the field of business.

ILLUSTRATION 7.13

A Good Letter Answering a Credit Request

Dear Miss Kim:

Acknowledgment and grant.

It's a pleasure to open a credit account for your firm with Brown Products.

The next time you give your Brown salesperson an order, simply say, "Charge it." He will be happy to do so.

Details confirmed.

All bills are payable by the 15th of the month for merchandise purchased during the previous month. Bills handled in this manner enjoy a profit-making 2 percent discount. Net payments are required by the 25th.

Sales appeal.

We are also pleased to offer you many other Brown services. Our Consumer Sales Advisory Department representative will visit you periodically or when you have a special problem. And the Brown Display Department will supply you with sales-building materials for your place of business and items for direct mail distribution.

Friendly close.

We are here to serve you in the years to come.

Sincerely,

Be sure to include a sales appeal.

be easily misunderstood if the date the invoice terms begin is not specified. Is it based on the invoice date? The shipping date? Delivery date? Or from the end of the month? It is important that you be specific.

Answering a credit request is a tremendous opportunity to enhance your chances for additional sales. You are not only granting credit, you are also encouraging the purchase of your products and services. Sales promotion material such as sales announcements and special offers for seasonal merchandise can be included as part of the letter or in the same envelope.

The last item—friendly close—should be future oriented. Explain that you want to provide continuing service and would appreciate the opportunity to do so.

Application Exercises

1. You are the assistant traffic safety director for your state. Recently, you received a letter from Ralph Richardson, an auto shop instructor at Samson High School in Thomasville. He requested that you send him 50 copies of the pamphlet *Maintenance for Safety*. Write a letter to Mr. Richardson to accompany the pamphlets you are sending.

2. Respond to the following memo:

Subject: Reference Request for Sales Rep Transfer

As I mentioned to you during our phone conversation last month, I have had my eye open for a sales job for some time. At last, I have had the opportunity to interview with Jerry Ferguson for such an opening in the Mideastern Division. I gave your name as a reference.

Should he contact you about previous work under your supervision (February 1984–June 1986), I'd appreciate any comments you can make about my interpersonal skills in dealing with customers there in the office. My product knowledge gained in relaying such information from headquarters to field personnel is also important. The sales rep job, of course, heavily depends on skills in these areas, as well as on initiative and organizational ability in handling a larger territory.

Thanks so much for any help you can give in arranging this transfer.

3. As owner of a small town radio station, you have a policy of regular involvement in community service projects. Frances Kilmichael, a local Girl Scout leader, has written to request that your disc jockeys conduct a 24-hour dance marathon sponsored by her troop. Proceeds of the event will go to a children's cancer foundation. The marathon will begin at 7 P.M. on August 29. Write to Ms. Kilmichael, granting her request.

4. You are the sales manager for Best Products. William Smiley, owner of Smiley Appliances, has written you concerning your recent shipment of toaster ovens. Of the 100 ovens shipped, 23 were irreparably damaged during shipment. Mr. Smiley has requested credit for the ovens and information regarding their disposal. Reply to Mr. Smiley. Assure him that his account will be credited and answer his question regarding disposal.

5. One of your customers, Linda Gelko, has requested that you replace her newly purchased lawnmower with a new one. Her mower has a "blown" engine because she incorrectly added oil to the gasoline, rather than putting the oil directly into the oil pan. Even though she did not follow the instructions, which clearly state *not* to combine the oil with gasoline, you have decided to grant her request. Write a letter to her granting the request, while making sure that she knows to read and follow the instructions carefully.

6. You are the sales manager for Radiotronics, a mail-order retailer. Joanna Simms ordered an AM–FM stereo radio, Model F100, for $67.80. She actually received a car radio, Model A100, along with a bill for $108.72. She returned the radio and asked that her account be credited and the correct merchandise shipped. She also requested that her account be credited for the shipping charges incurred in returning the incorrect merchandise. Reply to Ms. Simms granting each of her requests.

7. You are the credit manager for a small department store. Bernard Soames, having recently moved to your city, has applied for credit. He has supplied you with various credit references, and your checking found him to be an acceptable credit risk. Write to Mr. Soames to grant him credit.

8. You are the credit manager for Outlines, Inc. Sandra Jenkins has recently opened a store selling needlework and sewing supplies. She has written your firm stating her intentions that you will be one of her major suppliers, and she has requested credit. Write to her to grant her credit.

9. As director of recruiting of Barnwell Industries, you have been invited to a meeting at Cromwell College by your vice president of personnel. The purpose of the meeting is to introduce you and other recruiters to Cromwell's new placement director. The meeting will be held in the faculty room in Cromwell's student union on April 5 from 9 to 11 A.M. Write a memo to Jan Avery, your vice president of personnel, to accept the invitation.

10. You are the associate editor of a newspaper in a large city. You have been invited to attend the annual journalism conference at McClung University. You have been asked to present a 15- to 20-minute lecture entitled "Interviewing for a Job in Journalism." Your presentation will be made to a student group on October 15 at 2 P.M. on the McClung campus. Write to Dr. Jeremy Wallace, conference coordinator, to accept the invitation.

11. Critique the following letter regarding the characteristics of effective writing and its organizational plan:

Dear Sir:

   Your application for Rural Home Administration services has been favorably considered. This favorable consideration does not necessarily mean that a loan will be made to you.

The following items will be needed to further process your loan:

1. _____ All items have been completed and submitted
2. _____ Option or Purchase Agreement
3. _____ Information on property
4. _____ Bid from licensed contractor
5. _____ Deed
6. _____ Appraisal has been scheduled for

   _____

7. _____ County Health Department Certificate
8. _____ Mortgage Survey
9. _____ Termite Report
10. _____ Direction Map
11. _____ Pending the availability of loan funds
12. _____ An interview has been scheduled for

    _____

13. _____
14. _____

Please note only the items checked will affect your loan processing. If you have any questions, please feel free to contact this office. The telephone number is

_____.

Sincerely,

12. Critique the following letter regarding the characteristics of effective writing and its organizational plan:

Dear Sir:

The Rural Home Administration has approved a loan to assist you in the purchase of a home at the address shown below. Before approving the loan, a member of our staff made an appraisal/ inspection of the property—the appraisal to determine the maximum loan value and the inspection to determine the physical condition of the dwelling.

Major defects observed during the inspection were noted, and you were directed to obtain cost estimates to make the required corrections to bring the property into substantial compliance with our standards. Such requirements are necessarily limited to conditions detected by the appraiser during the inspection. There may be additional defects which you will want repaired to meet your satisfaction.

Rural Home Administration cannot guard against *possible* defects of the property. Therefore, will you please sign below indicating your understanding that *Rural Home Administration does not warranty or guarantee the condition of the property.* Return one copy of this letter to our office prior to the date of loan closing.

Sincerely,

13. Critique the following letter regarding the characteristics of effective writing and its organizational plan:

Dear Professor Hildebrand:

It is good to know of your interest in the *Annual Report* of the Orleans Corporation for use by the students in your research seminar.

As you requested, a dozen copies of Orleans' *Annual Report* were mailed to you today. Since these reports were labeled Priority Mail, you will have them well in advance of the target date for their use.

Each year, if you will let us know the number of these reports that you will need, it will be our pleasure to send them. We feel that the material will be our contribution to the business and economic understanding of your students.

Sincerely,

Review Questions

1. Discuss frames of reference as they pertain to favorable letters of response.
2. Discuss the idea of building goodwill with favorable letters of response.
3. What is the best organizational plan for a favorable response letter? Why?
4. List the major components of a favorable response letter.
5. Discuss the major characteristics of favorable response letters to requests for information about products.
6. List and explain three important guidelines for writing a favorable response letter to requests for information about people.
7. Describe the ideal favorable letter of response to a routine claim request.
8. Describe the ideal favorable letter of response to a nonroutine claim request.
9. Describe the key features of a favorable response letter to a routine order.
10. Describe the key features of a favorable response letter to a nonroutine order.
11. Describe the key components of a favorable response letter to an invitation.
12. Describe the key components of a favorable response letter to a request for credit.

Key Terms

favorable response letter

friendly close

goodwill

claim

introductory statement

routine claim request (FRLM)

subject line

nonroutine claim request (FRLM)

grant

routine order (FRLM)

sales appeal

nonroutine order (FRLM)

Chapter 8

Writing Unfavorable Response Letters and Memos

- ## *Learning Objectives*

After studying this chapter, you should be able to:
- Understand the psychology of saying no in writing.
- Discuss the logic behind the indirect approach of writing "no" letters and memos.
- Describe an exception to the indirect organizational plan.
- Write "no" letters and memos for the following common situations:

  Refusing a general request.
  Refusing an order.
  Refusing a request for credit.
  Refusing a request for a claim adjustment.
  Refusing an invitation request.

Introduction

An *unfavorable response letter or memo* (URLM) involves saying no to someone who has made a request of you. Although some believe the myth that writing business correspondence is rather uncreative, writing an unfavorable response letter or memo takes a great deal of creativity. How do you tell customers no, for example, and still maintain their goodwill? It is not easy and creativity is a must.

Refusals require creativity.

This chapter will help you write effective no letters and memos. Your major objective for this type of letter or memo is to deliver the unfavorable news in a manner that will maintain positive relations and minimize antagonism.

PSYCHOLOGY OF SAYING NO

Although your primary objectives are to minimize antagonism and maintain any existing goodwill, you are not necessarily trying to make your reader happy. Few people like to be told no, but many people can accept a no without disliking it *if they understand why you are saying no*. You should therefore strive to construct a letter that focuses on providing this understanding. In a few situations, however, you might be able to use your creative skills to generate a little reader happiness (such as when you can offer an attractive counter-proposal).

Your reader must understand why you are saying no.

The following guidelines can help you write effective URLMs:

1. Refuse the request (or situation), not the individual.
2. Reply quickly.
3. Avoid too much abruptness.
4. Include alternatives.
5. Cushion the reader.
6. Make it personal.
7. Emphasize the positive.
8. Show confidence in the reader.

The guidelines are designed to take into consideration the reader's psychological framework as he reads your response and the reader's potential reactions. The key link between each of the guidelines involves the reader's frame of reference. As mentioned in earlier chapters, you must seek a common frame of reference with your readers. Maintaining a you attitude is also critically important in letters of refusal.

Refuse the Request (or Situation), Not the Individual

Aim your refusal at the request, not at the individual making the request. This focus should be obvious to the reader, whose ego and pride must be protected. Consider the focus of the following brief refusals:

> **Bad:** No, we do not have any rooms. If you had written two months earlier, we might have been able to help. You will probably have to wait three or four weeks before we will have more rooms available.

Don't emphasize the individual's problem.

> **Better:** Unfortunately, there are no accommodations available for the weekend you requested. Accommodations are available, however, for the weekends immediately before and after. If you like, we can assist you by checking with other area establishments.

The bad example focuses too directly on the individual's shortcomings.

Reply Quickly

If you must send a refusal, send it as promptly as possible. The reader will appreciate knowing quickly so other arrangements can be made. Consequently, you should not yield to the common tendency to put off the delivery of bad news.

Avoid Too Much Abruptness

The URLM should normally be a little longer than a yes letter or memo. This additional length is often necessary to clearly explain the reasons for the refusal. A brief, abrupt refusal can generate negative metacommunication, such as, "The writer has very little concern for my feelings."

Include Alternatives

Most requests are made because of an existing or potential problem. If you must refuse the request, you should attempt to address the problem in another manner. General suggestions and alternative solutions to the problem can sometimes be quite helpful to the reader. Even if your suggestions and alternatives do not solve the problem, they might provide a partial solution. They can also help generate positive metacommunication by showing readers that you are concerned with their situation and welfare.

Cushion the Reader

By providing a *reader cushion* you help insulate the reader from the potential shock of receiving bad news. One of the most effective ways to do this is to "read the individual into the situation" and provide some good (or, at least, neutral) news. This *buffer* allows you to gradually lead the reader to the no. Letters/memos without proper cushioning normally carry harsh personal metacommunication to the reader.

If cushioned properly, readers will realize that their request is being refused before no is stated. Note, however, that cushioning does not imply that your letter should be vague. The refusal and the reasons behind it should be clear to the reader.

Make It Personal

Although your refusal should be directed at the request, you should also demonstrate concern, empathy, and sympathy for the reader's situation. One of the best ways to do this is to use personal pronouns. Phrases such as "your project," "your organization," and "your situation" can be quite helpful. "American United Manufacturing, Inc. might consider. . . .," for example, is much less personal than "Has your organization considered. . . ."

Emphasize the Positive

Unfortunately, this guideline is frequently violated in business writing, especially in letters of refusal. As discussed earlier, an abrupt early statement of refusal is not desirable; nor should your letter/memo conclude with your refusal. The refusal should come closer to the middle of your letter/memo so you can conclude on a more positive note.

Your letter/memo should not end with negative or apologetic statements. Consider, for example, the following statement: "I hope this situation will not cause you any undue hardships." This ending has at least two major shortcomings. First, it demonstrates that the writer knows the person will suffer—wishing the problem away sounds rather ridiculous. Second, the reader is reminded again of the bad news—in this case, the word "hope" has negative connotations.

Show Confidence in the Reader

You should not psychologically attack the integrity or intelligence of the reader. Further, you should not imply that a mistake has been made, either intentionally or unintentionally. For example, avoid sentences such as, "You could have avoided this problem if you had followed the manufacturer's instructions."

THE ORGANIZATIONAL PLAN

Once you understand the psychology of writing a letter or memo of refusal, you are ready to consider the organizational plan. To gain the proper perspective, consider the following scenario: You have applied for your first loan after graduation from a respected university. You intend to use the loan to buy your first new car. Upon finding a letter from your bank in your mailbox, you excitedly open it and begin to read: "Your application for a loan has been refused."

An indirect approach is generally best.

The author of this refusal letter, who obviously employed the direct approach, violated most of the guidelines of a good letter of refusal in the first sentence. The only worse beginning lines would have been something like, "You have been refused a loan by the ABC Bank." This beginning adds a personal attack to the other violations. The indirect approach is generally much more appropriate for letters of refusal.

The Indirect Approach

The *indirect approach* for a URLM is shown in Illustration 8.1.

Acknowledge the Request. You should begin a letter of refusal with an acknowledgment of the request. The purpose of the acknowledgment is to simply remind the reader of his or her request. The acknowledgment can also include a review of the situation surrounding or leading up to the request.

Include a Buffer. Next comes the buffer or cushion. This buffer should be something positive or at least neutral. It should help put

ILLUSTRATION 8.1

Organizational Plan for a "No" Letter/Memo (Indirect Approach)

**Organizational Plan for a No Letter/Memo
(Indirect Approach)**

1. Acknowledging request

2. Reader oriented "buffer" or "cushion"

3. Explanation of situation which makes refusal necessary

4. Refusal (implied or expressly stated)

5. Constructive suggestions

6. Sales appeal (if appropriate)

7. Friendly (positive) close

The indirect approach allows you to cushion your reader.

the reader in the right frame of mind to accept the refusal. Four common types of buffers include:

1. **Agreement.** Include a statement with which the reader is likely to agree, such as "Decreasing interest rates are helping your industry."

2. **Appreciation.** Show the reader that you appreciate the initial request, such as "Thanks for the substantial order you placed with our firm."

3. **Assurance.** Assure the reader that you have carefully considered the situation before a decision was made, such as "A thorough examination of your creditworthiness has been made."

4. **Compliment.** Compliment the reader on something, such as "Your recent advertising campaign has surely gotten your customers' attention. Congratulations on an excellent effort."

Although these buffers can be quite helpful, a word of caution is needed. Do not mislead the reader into thinking that you are about to say yes with too strong a buffer. In addition, do not include irrelevant information.

Explain Your Situation.

An explanation of the situation that makes the refusal necessary should be factual and reader-oriented. Your explanation should be as specific as possible. Simply stating that your refusal is based on "company policy" is an unacceptable, but common, mistake. Readers cannot understand this reason and obviously cannot relate it to their situation. If company policy is, in fact, the reason for your refusal, then you should explain the logic or reasoning behind the policy.

The Refusal.

When making the actual *refusal*, you can use an *implied refusal* or an *expressly stated refusal.* An implied refusal is simply a refusal that is not stated expressly or directly. In can and should, however, be strong enough to leave no doubt in the reader's mind that it is a refusal. If you want to use an implied refusal, a thorough and well-organized explanation is necessary. *An implied refusal is preferable* because you can omit the negative implications associated with a direct refusal. Consider the following alternatives to refusing an invitation to speak at a banquet:

> **Implied:** I have another speaking engagement arranged for that night.

> **Expressly stated:** No, I cannot speak at your banquet because I have another speaking engagement arranged for that night.

The implied refusal is clear and understandable. If you cannot make the implied refusal clear and understandable, however, you will have to use the expressly stated approach. To make the expressed refusal more digestible, you should be tactful, give a logical reason for the refusal, and provide a constructive suggestion.

An implied refusal makes it easier to keep a positive tone.

Constructive Suggestions.

If there is any way you can help the reader other than granting the request, make the offer. If, for example, you have to refuse an invitation to speak, as in the above illustration, you might offer the services of one of your partners or colleagues. This part of your letter might read as follows:

> I have another speaking engagement arranged for the same night. However, you might ask one of my colleagues. Either Tom Barnes or Jerry Cales would be capable substitutes.

Even if you must refuse a request, try to help the reader.

Sales Appeal.

If you are dealing with a customer or potential customer, you should attempt to incorporate an appeal for future sales into the letter. This appeal can help redirect the letter toward a more positive conclusion, and you can show your interest in granting the request in the future or as conditions change. In the example of the invitation to speak, for example, you might offer to speak at next month's or next year's banquet.

Friendly Close. A friendly close implies a positive close. You should avoid rehashing or reintroducing the negative aspects of the situation. You might summarize the sales appeal or add an action statement. If further action by the reader could change the refusal into a yes, tell the reader what to do. Similarly, if you have provided constructive suggestions or alternatives, tell the reader how to act on your suggestions. If you have offered to help arrange a substitute or replacement speaker, for example, give the reader a name, phone number, time, and date to call. Examples of no letters are shown in the illustrations below.

An Exception: The Direct Approach

Although most no letters should use the indirect approach, the *direct approach* can sometimes be used effectively. Two situations illustrate this point. First, the direct approach is more appropriate when you know that the reader prefers a direct and frank answer or when the issue is such that it will have negligible impact on goodwill. As shown in Illustration 8.2, this approach is most common in writing memos to people the writer knows well.

Second, the direct approach is more appropriate when the unfavorable message is urgent and understanding the main idea is of primary importance. A bank, for example, might need to send a letter to all its customers informing them that the regulatory agencies will no longer let them pay interest on checking accounts.

ILLUSTRATION 8.2

A Memo Containing an Unfavorable Response

The direct approach can sometimes be used effectively, especially for memos.

```
      TO:  George Dollar
    FROM:  Tom Penny
    DATE:  July 28, 1986
    SUBJ:  August Meeting of Strategy Planning Committee
```

I will not be able to attend this meeting since I will be in Chicago working on the Abby account. I will check back with you when I return. Jerry has my schedule for the remainder of the month if you wish to reschedule the meeting.

COMMON SITUATIONS

An indirect organizational plan is generally used to refuse requests. The most common situations include refusing a general request for information about a product, service, or person; refusing an order; refusing a credit request; refusing a claim request; and refusing an invitation request.

Refusing a General Request

Refusing general requests can occur in several situations, including requests for a product or service and for information about an individual.

Product or Service.   This type of refusal can occur in two types of situations. First, the request might be incomplete or unclear. In this situation, you should point out the areas for which you need additional information.

Second, the information requested might be unknown or unavailable at this time (i.e., because of patents or copyrights). The specific reasons for your refusal should be made clear. If possible, suggest who might have the information or where and when it might be available.

Information about an Individual.   Requests for information about an individual often involve letters of reference or recommendation. There can be several reasons for refusing to provide this information: (1) you may have a concern about possible libel suits, (2) you may have nothing but bad news to provide, or (3) you may not know the individual well enough to give a positive recommendation or reference. Regardless of the specific reason, you should provide a clear explanation for your refusal.

Remember that you have a responsibility to the requesting organization as well as to the individual being evaluated. What you say must be fair and *job-related*.

Refusing an Order

Occasionally you may have to refuse an order for a product or service. Usually this is because the product is out of stock or you cannot provide the service now. Again, a clear explanation and creative suggestions are important. You can offer, for example, to fill a *substitute order*. This would be a viable suggestion if your firm sells other products of similar quality at equivalent or lower prices.

Or, you might offer to *back order* the product. Essentially, you tell the customer that you will be able to fill the order at a date later than requested. Be sure to avoid negative statements such as: "We are temporarily out of stock." Instead, rely on remarks such as "We will be happy to send you the books you ordered by August 15. The factory has guaranteed to fill and ship our reorder by the end of July."

If you do not plan to stock the requested product, you can suggest a firm that can provide it. This can help build goodwill with a potential customer. A good letter illustrating the acknowledgment of an order for merchandise not handled is shown in Illustration 8.3.

Refusing a Credit Request

Since all individuals and firms who apply for credit are not good credit risks, you may have occasion to write a letter refusing a credit request. This is one of the most difficult refusal letters to write

ILLUSTRATION 8.3

A Good Letter Acknowledging an Order for Merchandise Not Handled

Dear Mr. Hutto:

Good acknowledgment.

Thank you for your April 24 order #789; all the merchandise, with one exception, will be on its way to you by this afternoon.

Implicit refusal and explanation.

Although we handle all types of tools, we have never stocked the Chilton Super Wrench. This is recognized as an excellent tool; however, our customers' needs at this level have always been fulfilled by the Kenny Line, which we do stock.

Alternative suggested.

We can fill your order for Kenny products immediately. However, if you prefer the Chilton brand, these may be purchased from Francis Machine Tools in St. Louis.

Friendly close.

It has been a pleasure doing business with you, and we know that you will be satisfied for many years to come with the consistently high quality of tools we handle and the competitive prices we offer. Please call collect if you would like to purchase the Kenny items.

Sincerely,

because it is often perceived as an evaluation of personal character. You must exercise extreme care to emphasize the reasons for the refusal. Although your primary reason will be that the applicant is a poor credit risk, the focus of this letter must be on the risk situation, not on the individual.

You should be aware of two potential pitfalls when refusing a credit request. First, you face the possibility of lawsuits for libel or discrimination. Second, refusing a request for credit can easily create sufficient antagonism to negate goodwill.

You should strive to maintain customer goodwill, even though an individual or company is not a good credit risk. Remember that even poor credit risks often have cash or can obtain loans from other sources to purchase your products or services. Further, many poor credit risks are small and perhaps new firms or young men and women just starting careers. Situations do change—small firms can become big firms (such as IBM), and young, struggling individuals can become wealthy.

Constructive suggestions and alternatives are particularly critical in letters refusing credit. You could suggest, for example, that the individual or firm provide additional information or apply for a different type of credit.

More and more firms are beginning to use the telephone to refuse credit applications. The telephone tends to be more personal than a letter, and you are better able to answer other questions promptly.

Always try to make a letter refusing credit reader-oriented and as positive as possible. Before sending such a letter, make sure it follows the "golden rule" for unfavorable response letters: "Write unto others as you would have them write unto you."

Retail Credit Refusal.

Perhaps the dominant characteristic of responding to applications for retail credit is that you are dealing with an individual who has a personal stake in the refusal. Minimizing personal antagonism is therefore a must.

Remember that many poor credit risks have legitimate, and often temporary, reasons for their situation. In your situation, for example, if you do not have credit experience, you might initially encounter difficulty in obtaining retail credit after graduation. In the long run, however, you will probably be a good credit risk.

There are two basic approaches to writing a letter refusing credit. First, you can emphasize the standard criteria used for considering credit (such as financial condition and history). This approach can help keep potential embarrassment to a minimum. It can also help reduce the probability of libel suits because you do not use personal traits in stating your reasons for refusing the application. The major disadvantage of this approach is that the individual might not understand the exact reason his or her credit was not approved. Individ-

---

Try to maintain good-will.

uals now have the legal right to demand the specific reasons for refusal. Also, individuals usually would like to know what they can do to improve their credit situation.

Second, you can provide the specific reasons for which you are refusing the application for credit. This approach is generally more appropriate because it avoids the disadvantages associated with the general approach. When using this approach, be careful to use objective, factual, credit-related information. Avoid alluding to personal traits such as dishonesty, unreliability, and so on.

Illustration 8.4 shows an example of a good letter refusing an application for retail credit.

Company Credit Refusal.   Refusals of credit applications from other companies can generally be more forthright than refusals to individuals. Most executives understand that evaluations of company credit applications are based on their financial statements or published credit ratings (such as Dun & Bradstreet) and not on personality. Illustration 8.5 presents a poor letter refusing company credit. The letter shown in Illustration 8.6 refusing a company credit application is much better.

ILLUSTRATION 8.4

A Good Letter Refusing an Application for Retail Credit

Dear Mr. Parker:

Palmeiro's appreciates your recent request for a charge account.

A careful check of the information you submitted, however, revealed that you now carry several open accounts with rather heavy balances.

Implied refusal.

Rather than burden you with an additional account, which would require your end-of-month attention, we suggest that you continue on a cash basis with Palmeiro's. In this way your transactions will be completed immediately.

I am enclosing our January brochure describing our Annual Celebration Sale. You might be interested in the remarkable savings available on Palmeiro's fine quality clothing.

Sincerely,

ILLUSTRATION 8.5

A Poor Letter Refusing Company Credit

Direct approach not good.

Suggestions poorly stated.

No goodwill created.

Dear Mr. Roark:

We received your letter and completed credit information forms. We examined these and have concluded that you should buy on a cash basis.

As you know, you are heavily overextended at the present time. If you could borrow the necessary funds to pay off some of your debts, your financial situation would look much better. Of course, you would want to watch high interest rates, for they will only increase your financial problems.

We also feel that the receivables which you have are probably higher than they should be. Have you considered putting more pressure on your debtors and secure cash in this manner?

We have the merchandise in stock about which you inquired.

If you want it, you can come get it or we can send it out COD.

Sincerely,

Refusing a Claim Request

Claim requests should be granted if at all possible. Occasionally, however, you will encounter claim requests that are not legitimate. Common situations calling for refusal include the following:

- The product is out of warranty.
- The customer abused the product or did not follow operating instructions.
- The product cannot be returned because of legal or company reasons (e.g., special sales merchandise and undergarments).

Since most claim requests are considered legitimate by the person making the request, your letter must explicitly and clearly state the reasons for the refusal. These reasons must be logical and objective.

ILLUSTRATION 8.6

A Good Letter Refusing Company Credit

Implied refusal.

Dear Mr. Roark:

Thank you for the completed order and credit application blank.

After checking the references which you listed, we find that your references speak highly of you. However, your ratio of assets to liabilities, plus the debts you have incurred in your new location, would seem to indicate that it would be in your best interests to purchase on a cash basis.

The advantages of doing so are important. A 3 percent cash discount, low inventory, and no end-of-month bills all add up to money-making features.

Please call me collect and I will see to it that the merchandise you ordered is on its way to you, on a COD basis, almost immediately.

Sincerely,

ILLUSTRATION 8.7

Letter of Refusal Showing Little Concern for Reader's Feelings

Direct approach seems harsh.

Reasons are weak and probably irritate the customer.

The close is negative and accusing.

Dear Ms. Van Cleve:

I regret to report that we must reject your claim for refunding your money on the Heritage fabrics.

We are refusing your claim because Heritage fabrics are not made for using outside. It is difficult for me to understand how you overlooked this limitation. It was clearly stated in the catalog from which you ordered. It was even stamped on the back of every yard of fabric. As we have been more than reasonable in trying to inform you, we cannot possibly be responsible for your negligence.

We hope that you will understand our position. We regret very much the damage and inconvenience your carelessness has caused you.

Sincerely,

ILLUSTRATION 8.8

A Tactful Letter of Refusal

Indirect approach.

Dear Ms. Van Cleve:

You certainly have the right to expect the best possible service from Heritage fabrics. Every Heritage product is the result of years of research. And each yard is manufactured under the most careful quality control system in the industry. We are determined that our products will do for you what we say they will do.

Since we do want our fabrics to satisfy our customers, we carefully ran the samples of Heritage fabric 007 you sent us through our laboratory. Research shows that each has been subjected to long periods of extreme heat and sunlight. This limiting feature of Heritage is clearly noted in all our advertising. You will find it in the catalog from which you ordered and in a stamped reminder on the back of every yard of the fabric. Under the circumstances, all we can do concerning your request is suggest that you change to one of our outdoor fabrics. As you can see from our catalog (pages 105–35), all fabrics in the 100 series are recommended for outdoor use.

You may also be interested in the new DuckBack cotton fabrics listed in our 300 series. These plastic-coated cotton fabrics are most economical, and they resist sun and rain remarkably well. If we can help you further in your selection, please call on us.

Sincerely,

Refusals of claim requests must also be highly reader-oriented, especially when the reason for refusal involves the customer not following the instructions. Unfortunately, far too many firms send letters that carry negative metacommunications because they imply that the customer is stupid. The letter in Illustration 8.7 shows little concern for the reader's feelings. The letter in Illustration 8.8 is much better. It is indirect and more tactful.

Refusing an Invitation

Business people receive a variety of invitations, including those to speak at a meeting, attend a meeting, be an officer in an organiza-

ILLUSTRATION 8.9

A Memo Refusing Invitation (Direct Approach)

TO: James Hill
FROM: Brice Horace
DATE: September 5, 1987
SUBJECT: Absence at Promotion Strategy Meeting

Direct approach works
well for this memo.

I will be unable to attend the upcoming promotion strategy committee meeting to be held on Monday, June 17, at the Montclair in Detroit. Due to my recent kidney ailment, my physician has restricted my work schedule to four hours a day and has advised me not to travel.

I'll be in touch with Sarah Crosser, however, after June 17 to catch up on discussion and decisions made in my absence.

Enclosed you will find my nominations for the upcoming scholarships our branch would like to offer. Also, I'm returning my marked ballot for the ATS election.

Best wishes for a productive meeting.

---

tion, serve on committees, and judge an event. Occasionally, you will have to refuse such invitations. The indirect approach is generally recommended for this letter of refusal. If possible, the no should be implied. Suggestions and potential alternatives are also important.

In special circumstances, the direct approach can be appropriate. If you receive a request to attend a committee meeting from another employee of your company, for example, you would probably respond by memo or telephone. The direct approach would probably be best for either communication vehicle (see Illustration 8.9).

Application Exercises

1. You are the owner of a small-town radio station. John Mitchell is planning the grand opening of his new grocery store and has requested that you provide the station's mobile broadcast unit. Unfortunately, you have committed the mobile unit to broadcasting a dance marathon sponsored by a local Girl Scout troop on the same date. Write to Mr. Mitchell to decline his request. Suggest an alternative date for the broadcast.

2. You are an assistant in the order processing department of a large wholesale sporting goods distributor. Samuel Gooden has written to order a certain type of cricket bat for which you are the only wholesale distributor. Because of agreements with retail clients, however, you are unable to sell your sporting goods to individuals. Write to Mr. Gooden informing him that your company cannot sell him the cricket bat.

3. As senior vice president of a large oil firm, you are in charge of administering the program through which the firm makes charitable contributions. Sandra Anspach, director of the Children's Charity, has written to ask that you present an address on "Corporate Social Responsibility." The meeting will be attended by administrators from many different charity organizations. You have already committed yourself to speak at a management seminar on the same date. Write to Ms. Anspach to decline her request.

4. You are a public accountant and have recently moved from Oklahoma to Texas. One month before your move, you attended a statewide oil and gas accounting seminar in Oklahoma City. You have received a letter from Charles Davis, director of professional programs for the Texas Board of Public Accounting (TBPA). The letter is an invitation to attend a TBPA-hosted oil and gas seminar in Houston. You really do not want to attend because of your recent attendance at a similar conference and the recent move. Write to Mr. Davis declining the invitation.

5. You are a claim representative for a large mail-order clothing concern. You have just received a letter from Mr. Roger Bannister concerning his purchase of a three-piece wool suit. The suit was shipped three months ago and Mr. Bannister claims that it does not fit. Your firm, however, has a policy that states that all claims must be postmarked within 15 days of the shipping date. Since Mr. Bannister failed to meet this requirement, you must write him a letter denying his request for an adjustment.

6. You are the owner of a small retail store. Mary Jane White has just moved to your community and is requesting credit. Although her credit references are quite good, you have a credit policy of "no credit." Write to Ms. White denying her request.

7. EmCo Products has just sent your company, Riley Appliances, an order for 100 BRQ501 blenders and 50 TRQ toasters. Accompanying the order was a letter stating that EmCo expected to do a large amount of business with Riley and requesting a credit agreement for this and future orders. Riley has made it a policy to confirm the financial position of all applicants before granting credit. Write to Emma Thomas, purchasing director for EmCo, declining the request.

8. Write a memo to your firm's president refusing his request for you to attend a legal contracts seminar in Kansas City next month. The meeting conflicts with a court hearing regarding your firm's pollution control system in the Atlanta plant. Remember that he is your boss and the meeting is important. You might offer to send your assistant to the meeting.

Review Questions

1. Explain the basic concept of an unfavorable response letter/ memo.
2. Describe and explain the primary objectives of a URLM.
3. Explain the following statement relative to URLMs: Refuse the request or situation, not the individual.
4. Defend the inclusion of alternatives in URLMs.
5. Explain the idea of cushioning the reader.
6. How can you make a URLM personal and not refuse the individual?
7. Why is the indirect approach better for URLMs?
8. Contrast an implied refusal with an expressly stated refusal.
9. When might the direct approach be appropriate for a URLM?
10. What kind of creative suggestions might be used in a URLM to a request for a product or service?
11. Why might you refuse to provide information about an individual?
12. What are the major problems associated with writing a URLM to a request for credit?
13. Describe the two basic approaches for writing a URLM to a request for retail credit.

Key Terms

unfavorable response letter or memo (URLM)
reader cushion
buffer
indirect approach
refusal
implied refusal
expressly stated refusal

Chapter 9

■ *Chapter Outline*

Writing Persuasive Letters and Memos

■ *Learning Objectives*

After studying this chapter, you should be able to:
■ Explain the concept of the psychology of persuasion as it applies to writing persuasive letters and memos.
■ Describe the AIDA organizational plan for persuasive messages.
■ Write letters and memos for the following common situations involving persuasive correspondence:

Persuasive Request Letters and Memos
Sales Letters
Collection Letters
Goodwill Letters

Introduction

Persuasion plays an integral role in our everyday lives. It can take both the verbal (oral and written) and the nonverbal forms of communication. For example, you might use oral communication to persuade someone to help you with an assignment or to meet you for a game of tennis. Written communication could be used to persuade your parents to send you more money, to persuade a business person to speak at a club meeting, or to persuade someone who owes you money to pay his or her bills. Furthermore, nonverbal cues can also be persuasive—a smile might convince someone that you would like to have a pleasant interchange or a large desk might convince someone that you hold an important position in your firm. A *persuasive message* is therefore

> a message that attempts to convince a person or an organization to take action beyond the routine.

This chapter focuses on improving your skills in writing persuasive letters and memos (PLM). Although most communications involve persuasion to some degree, the primary emphasis in this chapter is on nonroutine situations—those in which you feel that there is a chance the individual will not respond positively to your request.

Writing an effective persuasive letter in a nonroutine situation is not particularly easy. Your success depends heavily on understanding the psychology of persuasion and the development of a reasonable organizational plan.

Persuasion is an important part of communication.

You can learn to write more effective persuasive letters/memos.

PSYCHOLOGY OF PERSUASION

Persuasion involves getting an individual to act in a specific manner by creating or stimulating the individual's desire. That desire can result in a physical or direct action, such as visiting your store or buying your product, or it can result in a mental or indirect action, such as accepting an idea.

Effective persuasion often takes a great deal of creativity. Persuasion is a matching or integrating process—you must match your reader's needs and desires with your objective. This matching is best accomplished through a general three-step process that involves analyzing the reader's frame of reference, your objective, and the persuasive appeal.

Analyze the Reader's Frame of Reference

Successful persuasion depends upon knowing your reader's frame of reference.

The first major step in the matching process involves gaining an understanding of the reader's frame of reference. As with other types of effective communication, you must seek a common frame of reference with the reader. Perhaps the most important aspect of this step involves understanding the reader's desires and motives relative to your objective.

The key to this step involves obtaining information regarding the other person or organization. For example, as you get involved in the job market, you will need to do some research to determine what a particular company does and is looking for before you write them asking for an interview. This research might involve asking people (such as professors) who might know the company and reading published information (such as annual reports). Through this process you will be analyzing the firm's frame of reference.

Analyze Your Objective

Convert your objective into reader *benefits*.

Both tangible and intangible products, services, and ideas can be analyzed with the *feature-advantage-benefit (FAB) approach*. Essentially, the FAB approach involves analyzing the features and advantages of a specific action or object and translating them into benefits that match the reader's motives. Note the following descriptions:

1. *Feature:* A physical characteristic that answers the question, What is it?
2. *Advantage:* A performance characteristic that answers the question, What does it do? and/or, What makes it better than key alternatives?
3. *Benefit:* An asset characteristic that answers the question, What does it mean to the reader?

Consider, for example, a self-propelled lawnmower. The self-propelled mechanism is the feature. Its advantage can be described as "causing the mower to propel itself at a speed equal to the average person's walk" or as "the only variable speed self-propelled mower." The customer's benefits from the mechanism might involve time saved and reduced fatigue. Anytime you are trying to persuade someone to do something it is vitally important that you emphasize how he will benefit.

Develop a Strategy

The two basic methods of persuasion are logical reasoning and suggestion.

Logical Reasoning.   The *logical reasoning* approach tends to be more appropriate when you expect your reader to analyze, compare, and evaluate your request and other alternatives. A few general guidelines can help you decide when to use logical reasoning:

If your reader uses a logical approach, you must use a logical reasoning approach.

1.   When attempting to persuade readers who are likely to think in a logical pattern.
2.   When your action objective is complicated.
3.   When your request involves the expenditure of large amounts of money.
4.   When presenting something new to the reader.

Logical reasoning can take three basic forms. First, you can attempt to formulate a logical syllogism for your reader. A *logical syllogism* is an argument consisting of three parts: a major premise, a minor premise, and a conclusion. The following is perhaps the classic example:

> *Major premise:* All men are mortal.
> *Minor premise:* I am a man.
> *Conclusion:* Therefore, I am mortal.

This approach can be used to develop a straightforward appeal, such as the following:

> Every driver likes a car that is economical on gas.
> You are a driver.
> Therefore, you want a car that is economical on gas—this car delivers 54 miles to the gallon.

For some letters, you might want to develop each of the three components fully. For others, such an appeal may be illogical. For example, developing the minor premise "You are a driver" is not needed and you should consider another form of logical reasoning. The second form of logical reasoning involves the *if-then approach*. This approach is based on an assumed premise. Consider the following: If you delay your purchasing decision for six months, the price could go up and you would pay more. Arguments like this are logical if you accept the assumed premise. Be careful, however, not to exaggerate this premise. It could cost you the confidence of your reader.

The third basic approach involves *comparing alternatives*. First, limit the number of alternatives to two or three. Then help the reader compare them and choose one of the possibilities. Compare the following with the if-then example above: Let's examine what you have to gain and lose by waiting six months and compare it with what you will gain and lose by buying now.

Suggestions.   A *suggestion* tends to be more appropriate if minimum resistance is expected or if an emotional appeal is needed. Before discussing the types of suggestions, let's review the key principles of suggestion:

1. People tend to accept ideas or conclusions as true unless a contradictory idea blocks their acceptance. If they are merely indifferent, they often go along with the suggestion.
2. The acceptance of a suggestion depends upon the source of the suggestion. You should establish your credibility, expertise, and trustworthiness to enhance the chances of your suggestion being accepted.
3. The acceptance of a suggestion is influenced by the intensity with which it is made.
4. If several suggestions have been made over a period of time, people are more likely to accept the most recent suggestion.
5. A suggestion is more likely to be accepted if it is repeated.
6. A suggestion that appears to be natural and spontaneous is more likely to be accepted than one that appears to have been planned or contrived.

A number of types of suggestions are possible. A *positive suggestion* asks the reader to do or believe something. It implies that the reader is moving toward a favorable decision or position. Conversely, a *negative suggestion* asks the reader *not* to do or believe something. Consider the following examples:

Positive: This roof is guaranteed to stay tight for at least five years.

Negative: Don't worry about this roof leaking during the next 5 years; we guarantee it won't.

A *pleasant suggestion* should motivate people to gain the things that are held out before them. Conversely, an **unpleasant suggestion** should call attention to happenings that people naturally avoid or try to get away from. Consider the following examples:

> **Unpleasant:** If your tires are getting thin, you might have a bad blowout any day now. You know what that means, don't you? Don't gamble with the lives of your loved ones. Buy now.
>
> **Pleasant:** If your tires are getting thin, think of the peace of mind that driving on a steel-belted radial tire gives! No worry, no fear, no further expense. That is what you would prefer.

Although a pleasant suggestion has a wider application, the unpleasant suggestion can be quite effective in the earlier part of your letter in persuading the reader to be dissatisfied with things as they are. Later, you can associate your request with more pleasant suggestions.

Other types of suggestions include:

1. **Countersuggestion:** Used in the hope of eliciting an opposite response or reaction (can be either positive or negative), such as "I'm not sure that trying to make all As is worth the effort" (but I want you to make all As).
2. **Direct suggestion:** Immediate aim is stated in an explicit, straightforward manner, such as "I think you should come home this weekend."
3. **Indirect suggestion:** Objective is not stated explicitly, such as "Janie and I talked about going to the concert" (therefore I need some money and the car).

Key Considerations

A variety of other issues must be considered when making suggestions. Two major considerations are research and ethics.

Research.   It takes a great deal of planning and research to develop an effective persuasive strategy. To effectively appeal to customers, for example, you must know something about such factors as their buying habits, their preconceptions about your product and competing products, and their potential reactions to various types of appeals. Firms often call on specialists in research and appeal strategies, such as advertising agencies and marketing research companies and departments, for assistance.

Research may be needed to develop a persuasive strategy.

Ethical Considerations.   You must be constantly aware of the ethical ramifications of your approach while planning your appeal strategy. The concept of *ethics* used here relates to the motives underlying an individual's actions. If an individual's motives in developing the appeal strategy are sincere and honest, then the persuasion process is basically ethical. Conversely, if the motives are devious or dishonest, then an unethical approach has been used.

There is nothing unethical in trying to show people how a product, service, or idea can benefit them. If you can actually deliver the claimed benefits and these benefits can actually generate satisfaction, you might even look upon your persuasion activities as a good deed. However, if you cannot deliver what you promise, your offer is probably unethical and, perhaps, illegal. You must therefore do enough research to make sure that your appeal is entirely truthful.

THE ORGANIZATIONAL PLAN

All of the organizational plans discussed in previous chapters utilize basic persuasion techniques to some degree. A PLM simply has persuasion as the major objective.

In practice, the specific organizational plan used in writing PLMs varies a great deal from situation to situation. Although both the direct and indirect approaches can be used, the indirect approach tends to be used more frequently.

Both the direct and indirect organizational plans must accomplish the same persuasive objective. Each must obtain the following:

Both the direct and indirect approaches can work.

1. **A**ttention of the reader.
2. **I**nterest in the product, service, or idea.
3. **D**esire or conviction.
4. **A**ction by the reader.

The acronym *AIDA* (for attention-interest-desire-action) is commonly used to summarize these steps. The letter shown in Illustration 9.2 was written according to the AIDA organizational plan. Each AIDA step is discussed below.

Attention

All PLMs, especially persuasive letters, must gain the reader's *attention*—they must have some means of ensuring that the entire letter is read. Otherwise, your persuasive objectives cannot be

ILLUSTRATION 9.1

A Letter Using the AIDA Approach

Dear Mr. Parker:

Attention.

Who says you can't take it with you?

Further, who says you can't take a grill with you when you hike, hunt, or climb a mountain?"

Interest.

You can now! You can take the same grill that is standard equipment for all Idaho Mountain Rescue Patrol units—the Blue Ridge Compact Grill.

The Blue Ridge Compact Grill was designed specifically for sportsmen and other outdoor enthusiasts. It is small (16-inch-by-16-inch carton), handy (with carrying handle and folding legs), sturdy (stainless steel body and steel legs), and has a full 200-square-inch grill surface.

Desire.

Want to cook while doing something else? The Blue Ridge Compact Grill also comes with a spit, a motor, and its own battery! You can roast game on the slowly rotating spit and baste and season to taste.

Over 200,000 of these grills have been sold in less than two years. Many of these were purchased by satisfied owners as gifts for others.

Action.

The Blue Ridge Compact Grill is available either with or without motor and spit. Just check your preference on the enclosed card and return it today.

Sincerely,

achieved. Examples of proven attention getting techniques are shown in Table 9.1.

Although getting attention is critically important, do not go overboard in your pursuit of attention. Artificial techniques, for example, can actually be a barrier to further reading. Attention getters should be dynamic and colorful, but not unrealistic. Ways to avoid common weaknesses in attention getting paragraphs are listed below.

TABLE 9.1

Attention Getting Techniques

1. Use attractive nonverbal symbols, such as color, letterhead, layout, graphs, and size and kind of type.
2. Open with a natural, conversational lead-in: "Don't you agree that . . .," "You are right, we should . . .," and others.
3. Tie the message to a current topic, such as how inflation affects all of us.
4. Use a striking subject line: Money Market Certificates: Exciting Alternatives to Traditional Savings Accounts.
5. Raise a question: How often have you wished you could write letters on your own personalized stationery?
6. Insert the receiver's name: Take a look at the enclosed catalog, Mrs. Kelly, and you will. . . ."
7. Set a scene: Have you ever been stuck at home on Saturday night with nothing to do? Then you should. . . .
8. Use action words, such as control, save, strike, or reach.
9. Make a dramatic or unexpected statement: You may be one of the millions who have high blood pressure and do not know it!
10. Spotlight a single, dramatic key word, such as energy, growth, security, or hunger.
11. Use common courtesies, such as please and thanks.
12. Enclose something in quotation marks: "To err is human"—and are we ever human!

Source: Adapted from Bobbye D. Sorrels, *Business Communication Fundamentals* (Columbus, Ohio: Charles E. Merrill Publishing, 1984), p. 213.

1. Avoid first paragraphs that are too long.
2. Avoid questions that have obvious answers, such as "Would you like to increase sales?"
3. Avoid obvious statements, such as "To make a profit, you have to move merchandise."
4. Avoid writer centered or we-attitude openings, such as "We are proud to announce the opening of our new store."
5. Avoid slow and wordy openings, such as "We have received your inquiry about our products and we are writing to give you the information you requested."
6. Avoid constructing openings that just surprise or startle without regard for relevance or those that do not tie in with following paragraphs.

7. Avoid insincere and obvious flattery, such as "A person with your social position, Mr. Smith. . . ."
8. Avoid negative openings, such as those that mention disadvantages of your product or service.
9. Avoid referring to the price of the purchase, unless it is to be used as the central selling point.

Interest

Once you have the reader's attention, you must generate *interest* in the product, service, or idea. One of the best ways to do this is to emphasize its benefits to the reader.

People are usually interested in their personal *benefits*.

The attention- and interest-getting steps are closely related to the reader's perceptual process discussed in Chapter 1. *Selective perception*, for example, has a large effect on the attention-getting step. Similarly, *perceptual organization* has a strong influence on the potential for generating interest. It both influences reader awareness and attaches meaning to the information.

Desire

The third step involves developing or stimulating the reader's *desire* or conviction to take the action you recommend. For example, you must make the reader want your product or service, or believe that your idea is right and beneficial and should be accepted and believed. Accomplishing this step involves using the appeal strategy you developed earlier.

Your product, service, or idea must be described to the reader in a manner that allows the reader to visualize it positively. You might, for example, develop the FABs and present them to the reader with either an emotional or rational appeal.

Offer proof for all claims.

Many people are skeptical of unjustified claims, especially regarding products and services. Perhaps the best way to avoid this skepticism involves using the *benefit-proof technique*. Essentially, any time you make a claim about product features, advantages, or benefits, you should also offer proof or support of the claim. The claim and proof can often be combined in a single sentence, such as, "Independent laboratory tests have shown that our pharmaceutical products contain fewer impurities than any other nationally advertised brands."

Remember the importance of psychological benefits. Anything new has a better chance of being accepted if you can show that it fits the reader's present psychological patterns. You should *describe your product, service, or idea in terms of psychological values*. To do so, you must consider *why* someone would respond to your request positively. Why do people buy a product? What are they really buying? Consider the following:

Benefits do not have to be tangible.

1. People buy *knowledge,* not *books.*
2. People buy *comfort,* not *air conditioners.*
3. People buy *cleanliness,* not *soap.*
4. People buy *hope,* not *cosmetics.*
5. People buy *round holes,* not *drill bits.*

The key point is that people can relate better psychologically to comfort than to a bulky, expensive air conditioner. Therefore, emphasize the benefits of what you have to offer.

Action

Finally, you need to provide the reader with reasons and an avenue to take **action**. To accomplish this you should emphasize the reader's interests, make sure the action objective is easy for the reader to pursue, and emphasize the need for prompt action. The following statements stimulate action by emphasizing the reader's interests:

This offer is good until. . . .

Send no money. . . .

Your money will be refunded if you are not fully satisfied. . . .

You can make sure your objective is easy to pursue by providing the reader with an option that initially requires little time or investment on his or her part. The following statements emphasize simple action:

Make it easy for your reader to take action.

Our toll-free number is. . . .

Order with the enclosed easy-order blank. . . .

Take advantage of our deferred-payment plan. . . .

Emphasize prompt action. While you have got the reader's attention is the time to get him or her to act. The following statements suggest immediate response:

Get your free copy by returning the enclosed card today. . . .

Rush the enclosed card today. . . .

Send your order today. . . .

AN ILLUSTRATION OF THE PSYCHOLOGY AND ORGANIZATIONAL PLAN FOR A PERSUASIVE LETTER OR MEMO

Consider a situation in which you have designed a computerized monitoring system to be used in drilling oil wells. Your problem is that you do not have sufficient capital to market your invention. You must write a letter to potential investors.

Your *objective* is to attract funds from potential investors. Your *readers* will be individuals who are interested in providing venture capital to small firms pursuing the development and marketing of technological innovations.

The *features* of your system involve the physical attributes, such as a computer, keyboard, monitoring wires, communication hardware and software, software for calculations, and a carrying case. Features of your firm would also have to be mentioned, including the size, history, organization, personnel, sales and cost projections, and tax situation.

The *benefits* that can be mentioned are threefold. First, the benefits to drillers (the potential customers) will be cost savings, improved safety, greater accuracy and speed for reports, and greater convenience. The second benefit is that there is little competition for your firm. Third, the investor can benefit from an immediate tax write-off (because your firm qualifies as a Limited R&D Partnership and will lose money for the first several years) and high potential profits.

The above analysis should be transformed into an outline such as the AIDA format below:

I. Get *attention*—mention tax savings and potential profitability
II. Generate *interest*
    A. Discuss Limited R&D Partnership
    B. Discuss product
        1. Description of features
        2. Description of customer benefits
        3. Proof
    C. Discuss advantages enjoyed by firm
III. Arouse *desire*
    A. Tax situation
    B. Potential profitability
IV. Get *action*
    A. Small number of partnerships available

ILLUSTRATION 9.2

A Letter that Follows the AIDA Approach

Dear Mr. Walker:

Attention.

Interested in an immediate tax write-off that has tremendous profit potential in a few years?

Interest.

The IRS is now allowing tax write-offs for investments in qualified limited R&D partnerships. Madrill Company qualifies because of our planned development of a new product—Drillmaster.

The Drillmaster will be a computer-based monitoring system for oil drilling rigs. It will have the capability to automatically monitor a variety of factors currently being checked manually. Calculations will be instantly sent to engineering headquarters for further analysis.

The Drillmaster system has the potential to save drilling firms hundreds of thousands of dollars each year. It will also result in improved safety for well blowouts, greater accuracy and speed of reports, and increased convenience. One of the petroleum engineers who analyzed the technical plans commented, "Why hasn't someone done this already?" A major driller told us, "Hurry up and get one working. I will lease the first one off the line."

If we can move soon, we will be first on the market.

Desire.

Your tax write-off for one $5,000 share (of 100 partnership shares) will be equal to 1 percent of Madrill's losses during the development phase. As you can see in the enclosed projections, the first year's write-off should be around $3,000, the remaining $2,000 being written off the second year.

By year three, the Drillmaster should begin to reap profits. Your return on investment by year five should reach an average of 45 percent.

Action.

If you are interested in finding out more about Madrill and Drillmaster, please call me at (111) 333-4444. Reservations for partnership shares will be accepted until May 1.

Sincerely,

      B. Call owner for additional information

      C. Reserve partnership by May 1

This outline forms the basis for the letter shown in Illustration 9.2.

COMMON SITUATIONS

The four common business situations that require persuasive letters and/or memos are requests, sales, collections, and goodwill.

Persuasive Requests

A *persuasive request letter* is essentially a nonroutine letter of request. It is appropriate when you feel that there is a reasonable likelihood that your request will *not* be received favorably by the reader, therefore an indirect organizational plan is generally best. Persuasive request letters would be appropriate in situations when you are asking (1) a reluctant individual to speak to your club, (2) someone to invest in your business, or (3) someone to vote for or against a certain issue.

Focus on creating desire.

You should begin writing this letter after analyzing your action objective and your reader, developing an overall appeal strategy (FAB), and outlining your organization plan (AIDA). A major portion of this letter should focus on building the reader's desire. You should therefore describe your request's FABs in a specific, clear, and reader-oriented manner.

Sales Requests

A sales letter simply asks someone to buy something and generally falls into one of two categories—solicited or unsolicited.

Unsolicited Sales Letters. *Unsolicited sales letters* are often part of mass direct-mail campaigns, and in all cases the receivers have not previously contacted your company about the subject of the letter. An effective unsolicited sales letter is difficult to write for several reasons.

Generally sent to many people.

Since unsolicited sales letters are often mailed to a large group of people, it is extremely difficult to identify the typical frame of reference (including needs and values). Without a specific, consistent frame of reference, developing an effective appeal strategy is difficult because the major selling point is more obscure. If the mail campaign is large enough to justify the expense, research and/or

Key problems are vague frames of reference and . . .

consulting specialists are often hired to help develop the appeal strategy.

Another problem is obtaining and maintaining the reader's attention. This is difficult when the reader has not previously expressed interest in the issue. Because of this, you generally must devote careful attention to developing a dynamic and colorful attention getter. Because of lower production costs, many unsolicited sales letters are form letters (everyone gets the same standard letter). Readers often consider these letters impersonal, and letters that are not personalized have greater difficulty obtaining and maintaining attention.

. . . obtaining attention.

Unsolicited sales letters are often longer than other letters and often include enclosures, such as brochures and leaflets. The length and breadth of the overall package serves as a barrier to complete reading.

An effective unsolicited sales letter is based on a well-conceived appeal strategy and organization plan, such as shown in the unsolicited sales letter sent to an office supply and equipment distributor presented in Illustration 9.3. This letter has a unique opening (including a subject line) that attracts the reader's attention. It also offers benefits and provides the reader with a chance to see the product. The close encourages the reader to take positive action right away.

Solicited Sales Letters.   A *solicited sales letter*, although similar in some ways to an unsolicited sales letter, is generally aimed at a single individual. It is also usually more personal and individualized. Since this type of letter is usually a response to the reader's request, it is much easier to identify the reader's frame of reference and to develop an effective appeal strategy.

Generally sent to one individual.

Designing an effective attention getter is also much easier because the reader is already interested in your response. This ease, however, does not imply that an attention getter is not needed. A good attention getter is just as important in a solicited sales letter as in the unsolicited sales letter, but it is easier to write since you can refer to the reader's original request.

Collections

Collection letters are designed to get customers to pay delinquent or past-due accounts. Firms expend a great deal of effort in collecting delinquent accounts. Collection letters are generally an integral part of this effort.

Collection letters are not particularly easy to write. The greatest problem involves *conflicting objectives*. On one hand, you are inter-

ILLUSTRATION 9.3

A Good Unsolicited Sales Letter

Dear Mr. Aker:

WHAT'S NEW FOR THE OFFICE?

Attention.

Today's office supply and equipment distributors are constantly challenged by this question. Brenlys Office Management Services is a recognized authority on the subject.

Interest.

Each month a newsletter entitled Office Products News summarizes new office equipment and supplies to help busy office managers like you make good decisions fast. This month's edition is enclosed. Please accept it with our compliments.

Desire.

Get ahead with summarized information on the latest office products. It won't take long for everyone to recognize you and your firm as leaders in what's new for the office.

Action.

Office Products News can be yours each month for the special introductory fee of $10 per year. If you use the enclosed special subscriber's card within the next 10 days, you will get two extra issues at no extra cost. May we hear from you soon?

Sincerely,

ested in receiving your money as soon as possible. On the other hand, you must maintain customer goodwill because of potential sales revenue. Because of this problem, you must exercise extreme care and tact.

Collection letters vary from simple, routine reminders to sometimes complex, threatening letters. In fact, an individual firm will often have a standard series of letters beginning with reminders and gradually evolving to heavy threats.

Beware of conflicting objectives.

Before discussing the series of collection letters, let us identify some key guidelines for all types of collection letters:

1. List the *specific dates* when the payment was originally due and when further company action can be expected. Further action implies more drastic action.
2. List the *precise amount* due the company.
3. Include the *account number* or transaction number for easy reference.
4. Make the tone of the letter *courteous and restrained*.
5. Include a *you attitude* that clearly shows the reader benefits to be reaped from making a prompt payment.

Collection letters should not unnecessarily harass, accuse, or defame the reader. Unnecessary and empty threats can generate unpleasant lawsuits.

As mentioned earlier, a collection letter often forms part of a series of collection letters. Firms actually vary regarding the number of stages of collection letters and the number of letters involved in each stage.

The firm's assessment of the risk involved influences its choice of a collection letter pattern. If the firm perceives, for example, that the debtor otherwise has a good credit rating and is a good credit risk, it will probably allow more time between collection reminders or letters. It will also probably send fewer letters. If, however, the firm perceives the debtor as being a poor risk, the collection series might be considerably speeded up. To facilitate discussion, three stages or categories are used to describe series of collection letters: (1) early-stage collection letters, (2) middle-stage collection letters, and (3) late-stage collection letters.

You may have to send more than one collection letter.

Early-Stage Collection Letters.   *Early stage collection letters* are generally routine, informing the reader that the firm has not received the last payment. These letters often come in the form of a short note, short letter, or a note attached to a monthly statement. They are usually brief, mild, and friendly. Many even use resale techniques to help show the customer that he or she is still valuable to the firm and thus to enhance future sales. The letter shown in Illustration 9.4 is an example of a good early-stage collection letter.

These are often simple reminders.

Middle-Stage Collection Letters.   *Middle stage collection letters* use persuasive techniques to a much greater extent than early stage collection letters. They tend to be longer and more individualized or personalized. Their primary focus is on convincing the reader to either pay the account or at least explain why the account has not been paid.

ILLUSTRATION 9.4

A Good Early-Stage Collection Letter

Dear Mr. Balch:

This brief note is just to call your attention to your past-due balance of $234. Perhaps you have just overlooked the balance due in the normal rush of things; however, we would appreciate receiving your remittance by return mail.

Burney's prices and products have never been more attractive. Why not check your needs and call your Burney's representative today.

Sincerely,

Short, mild, and friendly.

Often focuses on getting the customer to explain their nonpayment.

Most customers try to pay their bills, yet even solid, desirable customers can sometimes have delinquent accounts. A variety of mitigating factors could prevent timely payment from an otherwise solid and responsible customer. The following is a list of reasons that some customers become delinquent:

1. They forget.
2. They are experiencing a temporary cash flow problem.
3. They have been out of town or otherwise incapacitated.
4. They moved and have not received a bill.
5. They know that they do not owe anything (a billing error).
6. They have a complaint regarding the product and want an adjustment, but have not formally filed the complaint.
7. They are bankrupt or out of a job.

You must find out why an account is delinquent before using heavier threats. Premature threats can lose you a customer forever. The letter shown in Illustration 9.5 is a good example of a middle-stage collection letter.

Late-Stage Collection Letters. *Late-stage collection letters* should not be used until opportunities for early- and middle-stage collection letters have been exhausted. When this occurs, the objective of maintaining customer goodwill becomes much less impor-

ILLUSTRATION 9.5

A Good Middle-Stage Collection Letter

Dear Mr. Balch:

The head of our bookkeeping department has just called me about your delinquent account of $234.

I was quite surprised; there must be a very good reason for your nonpayment. Why don't you jot a note on the back of this letter telling me what the problem is. We want to help in any way we can.

Positive and asks how your firm can help.

You have been one of our valued customers for many years. We want our relationship to continue in the future. Won't you help me to help you by sending me a check today or an explanation for the nonpayment of your bill for $234.

Sincerely,

tant. Late stage collection letters are therefore generally shorter and more direct and demanding. The appeal is stated in a firm and urgent manner and can sometimes even be threatening. The company might state, for example, that the account will be turned over to a collection agency if it is not paid by a specific date.

These are more action oriented.

The close of a late stage collection letter should be very action oriented. The tone of the entire letter, if possible, should remain positive and incorporate the you attitude. A late-stage collection letter is shown in Illustration 9.6.

Although maintaining customer goodwill is less important at this stage, it should not be completely ignored. In an attempt to maintain some goodwill, some firms will use the telephone to substitute for or supplement late stage collection letters. The telephone can be more personal and can create a greater sense of urgency.

Goodwill

A *goodwill letter* is similar to a collection letter. Rather than selling a product or service, however, its purpose is to create a favorable perception of the sending firm. It focuses on selling friend-

ILLUSTRATION 9.6

A Good Late-Stage Collection Letter

Dear Mr. Balch:

After several reminders and letters concerning your past-due bill of $234, we now must consider taking more drastic steps. This means turning your account over to our attorneys for legal action.

This step is not desirable for either of us. For you it means the payment of not only the sum overdue, but also court costs of an unknown amount.

Why not save yourself these problems by sending us your check for $234? If we do not hear from you within the next two weeks, your account will be turned over to Cooper, Jones and Cooper for legal action.

Sincerely,

ILLUSTRATION 9.7

A Goodwill Letter

Dear Mr. Pearce:

Yesterday's Daily Sentinel announced the exciting news of your appointment as president of First State Bank. Congratulations!

It is well known that great strides were made at First State Bank while you were the vice president of marketing. The recognition you are now receiving is certainly well deserved.

Again, you have my sincere congratulations and best wishes for continued success.

Sincerely,

ILLUSTRATION 9.8

A Goodwill Memo

Subject: Memorial Donation in the Name of Brian Stevens

Julie, our department was so sorry to hear of the airplane accident and Brian's death. I remember meeting him at our Thanksgiving banquet last year, and at that time thinking what a warm, intelligent person he was. In fact, we talked of your plans to move into the position you now hold. From what you've said of him, too, I know he must have provided inspiration, meaning, and emotional support in so many of your career accomplishments. I can only imagine what a great loss this will be to you and your two girls.

All of us here in the office want to express our sympathy by making a contribution to the American Heart Fund in your name. If you can think of anything that we can do as far as notifying other colleagues or clients, please let us know.

---

liness, trust, and sincerity. The goodwill letter in Illustration 9.7 shows the idea of focusing on commending the recipient of an honor or promotion.

A goodwill letter or memo can also be appropriate for extending sympathy for illnesses or death, natural disasters, and other problems. Some firms, for example, have offered help immediately following damaging floods in the Mississippi River Valley by extending or delaying victims' scheduled monthly payments. Goodwill letters that extend sympathy should offer assistance if possible and should try to end on a comforting note. Illustration 9.8 shows a good example of a memo expressing sympathy to a fellow employee.

Goodwill letters can also be appropriate for expressing appreciation for orders. These should reinforce the reader's self-esteem, offer further services, and close in a friendly but not effusive manner.

Application Exercises

1. You are the owner/manager of a successful landscape architecture firm. You feel that the doubling in size of your firm over the last five years has been due primarily to the quality of your services as well as an aggressive sales approach. Although you can no longer personally select the variety of plants used in each landscaping project, you still find time to oversee the design and actual planting of the projects. Last year, your expertise was rewarded with the Golden Achievement Award for Landscape Architecture by the State Developers Association.

You have found through contacts at city hall that a large, new office complex will be built in the city within the next year. The developers are Allen & Sons of Sharonsburg, West Virginia. Write to Allen & Sons to persuade them that your firm is the contractor that will do the best job of landscaping the complex.

2. You own an auto body repair shop in a small town. The contract for the repair of the city's police cars is up for renewal this year. Although your shop is small, your are on good terms with the local insurance adjusters and are recommended by them to customers who need body work after accidents. The city commissioner is in charge of awarding contracts to private firms for city services. Write the commissioner, Jerry Williams, in an attempt to convince him that your shop deserves the contract.

3. You are the president of your business fraternity's pledge class. The pledge class is responsible for planning the annual banquet. You must secure a speaker for the banquet. Your university has recently been forced to eliminate or curtail certain programs because of state budget cuts opposed by the governor. You feel that if you can persuade the governor to speak on the budget cuts, you, your fraternity, and your university would benefit from the publicity. The governor, however, is quite busy and might not want to speak at this time on such a controversial subject. On the other hand, the business school at your university is the largest in the state and is ranked among the top 20 in the nation. Write to the governor to persuade him to attend the dinner and give the speech.

4. Since you started your chain of fried chicken restaurants with one store in your hometown of Nellville six years ago, you have added three stores in adjoining towns. You are currently building four outlets in Baris, a major city in the state. The expansion means that your current supplier of chicken just cannot fill the bill. You are therefore forced to find another producer.

RicChic Farms is a huge operation supplying grocery stores throughout the state with fryer and broiler chickens. In the past, RicChic has dealt only with large chain operations. In addition, because of the money you have tied up in constructing your new stores, a credit agreement will be necessary if you are to deal with RicChic on the large-scale basis you foresee. Write to Rick Current, owner and financial director of RicChic, keeping in mind the request for credit, and persuade him that his firm should become your primary fryer supplier.

5. You are the credit manager for Coign Bros., a building materials wholesaler. Coign deals with several local contractors and has good relations with each. One of the contractors, Henry Johnson, has failed to pay last month's bill for $979.60, which is now three weeks past due. Write to Mr. Johnson to remind him that his bill is overdue.

6. Henry Johnson (see Exercise 5) has still not paid last month's bill for purchases from Coign Bros. Two weeks have passed since you sent him a reminder letter. Write to Mr. Johnson a second time requesting payment.

7. Rita Simpson recently moved to your town and immediately opened a charge account at your clothing store. Billing on charge accounts is on a ''payable upon receipt'' basis. Bills for the previous month were sent out three weeks ago, and no payment has been received from Ms. Simpson. Her bill amounts to $107.10. Write an appropriate reminder to Ms. Simpson.

8. Four appeals to Ms. Simpson (see Exercise 7) have not elicited a response. The last two were middle-stage letters. Write Ms. Simpson a late-stage message requesting payment of $107.10.

9. Your firm has carried on a satisfactory credit relationship with Rutgers Hardware for years. You supply the retailer with kitchen cabinets and cabinet hardware. Rutgers' last order, for door handles and hinges, totaled $276.11 and has not been paid. Three letters, the last one quite strong, have failed to elicit payment. Write an appropriate message to Hal Snyder, the manager of Rutgers.

10. You have just been appointed advertising manager for your college newspaper. You are responsible for helping the paper make enough money to cover all expenses during the school year. To cover costs, at least 55 percent of each eight-page edition must be sold as advertising space. It is important to keep local merchants interested in your advertising space. Write to Rebecca Dodd, owner of a local women's clothing shop. Encourage her to renew her contract for a quarter-page ad in each weekly edition of the paper. Consider suggesting that she might benefit from increasing the size of her ad.

11. You are director of the state system of boys' ranches and have decided that the state will give each of the boys a fishing rod and reel for Christmas this year. You will need 200 units. In an attempt to keep costs down, you have decided to write Robert Pelle, president of Sportco, a large wholesale sporting goods distributor.

Sportco usually distributes only to retail stores, but you feel that the nature of the request and the large number of rods and reels desired might make a difference. The models you are interest in are the BY150 Little Angler (75 units) and the XJ Caster (125 units). Write to Mr. Pelle with your request.

12. An employee in your department, Johnny Tuder, has lost her father in an automobile accident. Write a memo showing your sympathy and concern.

Review Questions

1. Define and describe the concept of a persuasion letter.
2. Discuss the feature-advantage-benefit approach.
3. Discuss logical reasoning as it relates to persuasion.
4. Discuss suggestions as they relate to persuasion.
5. How does research relate to persuasion?
6. Relate ethics to persuasion.
7. Discuss the AIDA approach.
8. Discuss the benefit-proof technique.
9. Distinguish between unsolicited and solicited sales letters.
10. Why is an unsolicited sales letter difficult to write?
11. Give an overview of the idea of writing a series of collection letters.

Key Terms

persuasive message *logical syllogism*
FAB approach *if-then approach*
feature *comparing alternatives*
advantage *suggestion*
benefit *positive suggestion*
logical reasoning *negative suggestion*

pleasant suggestion
unpleasant suggestion
AIDA
ethics
attention
interest
selective perception
perceptual organization
desire
benefit-proof technique

action
persuasive request letter/memo
  (PLM)
unsolicited sales letter
solicited sales letter
collection letter
early-stage collection letter
middle-stage collection letter
late-stage collection letter
goodwill letter

Part IV

Report Writing Skills

Executives and employees in many organizations spend countless hours writing reports. Although a few firms may have professional report writers, the majority of reports are written by people like you—college graduates of business disciplines such as accounting, marketing, management, or finance. This part of your text focuses on improving your report writing skills.

Part IV is divided into four chapters: Chapter 10 examines the research process needed to generate professional reports; Chapter 11 focuses on the scope and format of short reports; Chapter 12 covers long reports; and Chapter 13 discusses using graphics to present information.

Chapter 10

■ *Chapter Outline*

Examining The Research and Report Process

- ### *Learning Objectives*

After studying this chapter, you should be able to:
- Understand the relationship between research and report writing.
- Identify and discuss the four major steps in the research process.
- Describe the difference between secondary and primary research.

Introduction

Research has become an integral part of our society. Business reports based on in-house research are quite common, and probably early in your career you will be asked to prepare a report. You might be asked, for example, to report on the feasibility of establishing a store or plant in a new location, the frequency of employee turnover, or the strengths and weaknesses of your major competitors. Unless you already have all of the necessary information, you will have to initiate a research process to gather the information needed to write the report.

To help clarify the term *research*, consider its definition in *Webster's New World Dictionary:*

> a careful, systematic, patient study and investigation in some field of knowledge undertaken to discover or establish facts or principles.

The key word in this definition is *investigation*, which implies that research has a guiding motive or purpose. Your professors, for example, may perform *academic (or pure) research* to test a particular theory or concept. Conversely, an organization is more likely to perform *applied research* aimed at solving a present or potential problem.

The result of most research involves writing a report. *Webster's New World Dictionary* defines a *report* as:

> a formal or official presentation of an investigation or as a formal statement or official account of the results of an investigation.

Without a report, research benefits no one other than the researcher. A well-written research report, however, can greatly benefit the researcher, the researcher's organization, and others.

Essentially, the overall research and report writing process begins with either a problem or a potential problem. The research process is then initiated, and usually this generates a report that either recommends a solution to the problem or spurs further action. This relationship is shown in Illustration 10.1.

A thorough understanding of the research process forms the base for gaining a better understanding of developing and writing reports. Consequently, the major purpose of this chapter is to examine the research process in detail. The major steps of the research process are: (1) identify and define the problem; (2) design and implement the research methodology; and (3) prepare the research report.

The research process discussed in this chapter focuses primarily on gathering information for nonrecurring or special problem areas.

ILLUSTRATION 10.1

The Research Report Process

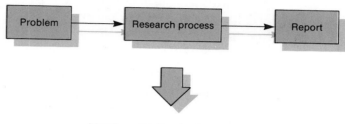

Identify and define the problem area

    Recognize that a problem exists
    Define the specific problem
    Develop a problem statement
    State hypotheses

Design and implement the research methodology

    Determine information needs
    Identify sources of information
    Gather information

Analyze information

Prepare the research report

Other types of regular or routine problems or potential problem areas can also require a constant flow of information. Many firms, for example, want regular reports on topics such as their financial condition, competitive products, and their sales situation. This information is generally supplied by the firm's management information system (MIS).

IDENTIFY AND DEFINE THE PROBLEM

Problem identification comes first.

The first step of the research process involves identifying the problem. A ***problem*** can be defined as the difference between a desired objective or situation and the anticipated or existing condition. To identify a problem area you must recognize that a problem exists, define the specific problem, develop a problem statement, and state a hypothesis.

Recognize that a Problem Exists

Let's use a fairly typical situation to illustrate problem recognition. If a firm has an employee turnover objective of 5 percent, this firm does not want to lose more than 5 percent of its work force in any one year due to resignation, dismissal, retirement, leaves, or other causes. If an employee turnover problem exists at this company, executives might recognize this fact in several ways—from simple observation of events, through discussion with the personnel department, or from regular reports from the personnel department. Since low employee turnover is an objective, the firm might monitor employee turnover as part of their overall control system. A monthly report reflecting the current turnover, for example, might be sent to a key executive. As long as employee turnover stayed below 5 percent, no action would be taken. However, if employee turnover suddenly jumped to 20 percent or began to show a sharp increase, the need for action would be reflected in the monthly report.

An executive seeing a jump in employee turnover from 5 percent to 20 percent would recognize that a problem existed and would react in one of two ways. If the executive already has adequate information, an immediate decision could be made on how to handle the situation. Or, the executive might recognize that additional information is needed before he can decide on a solution, which would launch the remainder of the research process.

Define the Specific Problem

Preliminary investigation helps to narrow problem.

At times the specific problem is determined relatively easily. For example, a report showing that employee turnover has risen to 20 percent may clearly define the basic problem area. If an executive wants to know the causes of employee turnover, he might need more information than is available in the regular report. He might request a brief report listing terminations from all departments. This report might point out that the specific turnover problem might be confined to one department that has had 100 percent turnover. Thus, the preliminary investigation leads to a narrowing of the problem's focus.

Develop a Problem Statement

The third component of identifying the problem involves developing a problem statement. Continuing with the above example, an appropriate *problem statement* would be:

> The organization's employee turnover rate is 20 percent, which is 15 points or 4 times greater than the objective of 5 percent. The problem is confined to the dietary department, which has experienced a turnover rate of 100 percent during the past six months.

The problem statement forms the basis for the next step, stating your hypothesis.

State Hypothesis

A *hypothesis* is an educated guess or tentative solution to the problem, which the researcher attempts to prove or disprove. A hypothesis may be written in either a positive or a null manner. A positive hypothesis is written more as an educated guess. For example: High turnover in the dietary department is caused by poor working conditions. The problem with such a positive statement is that it can cause the researcher to introduce bias into his or her research effort.

To help alleviate the potential bias, most researchers write hypotheses in the null manner. For example: No significant differences exist in the working conditions of the dietary department and the other departments in the hospital. Most sophisticated statistical tests are more applicable to hypothesis testing than they are to general research objectives.

In summary, you must begin your research process by defining what to research and why. Determining your specific problem involves (1) identifying the problem area through the use of information feedback which tells the organization that a significant difference exists between actual results and expected results, (2) narrowing the identified problem area to a specific area in the organization, (3) developing a specific written problem statement, and (4) finally writing a specific hypothesis that your research design must prove or disprove. The next section discusses how to design and implement a research methodology appropriate for testing your hypothesis.

DESIGN AND IMPLEMENT THE RESEARCH METHODOLOGY

The research methodology affects the usefulness of the investigation.

A *research methodology* consists of the planned procedures that lead to the gathering of the desired information. The steps involve determining information needs, identifying sources of information, gathering information, and analyzing information.

Determine Information Needs

Determining information needs is one of the most critical aspects of methodology design. Achieving the research objective requires focusing on the right information. Too little information or inappropriate information leaves the problem unanswered, while too much information can obscure the desired answers.

Determine General Information Needs. Essentially, you will need information on all major factors that influence the problem. For the ongoing example, therefore, your list of general information needs would contain all of the key influencing factors for employee turnover.

Determine Specific Information Needs. Your specific information needs are obviously derived from the list of general information needs. Consider the two factors: compensation system and prevailing wage rates. For these two general information needs, you might need specific information regarding the following:

1. Characteristics of compensation system for each division and department in the firm (e.g., salary, commission, bonus).
2. Comparison of compensation levels with similar positions in the firm, in the industry, and in the local area.
3. Comparison of fringe benefits with similar positions in the firm, in the industry, and in the local area.
4. Analysis of trends regarding raises.
5. Employee attitudes and expectations regarding direct compensation, fringes, and raises.

Determine Relative Importance of Specific Information. Not all information is of equal importance. Although some information might be interesting, it may have little relevance to the research objective. You should therefore analyze each type of specific information to determine its importance. If it is not needed, do not collect it.

Identify Information Sources

The third step in research methodology involves identifying the sources of information needed to achieve the research objective. We can classify information by location or by purpose. Information can be from *internal sources,* those that exist within an organization, or from *external sources,* those that exist outside the organization.

Information can be obtained from many different sources.

Information can also be classified as *primary data,* gathered originally to solve current problems, and as *secondary data,* data gathered originally for another purpose. Both primary and secondary data are available from both internal and external sources. Thus, the four major sources of information are:

1. **Internal secondary sources:** inside sources of previously gathered data.
2. **Internal primary sources:** inside sources for new or ungathered data.
3. **External secondary sources:** outside sources of previously gathered data.
4. **External primary sources:** outside sources of new or ungathered data.

Before addressing each of these sources, note that many researchers go directly to expensive, time-consuming sources for information. The search for information should actually begin with internal secondary sources because they are inexpensive and readily available. External secondary sources should be consulted next, followed by internal primary sources. External primary sources are the last sources to pursue because more time and expense are involved in obtaining them. The search for information is complete when sufficient data are available to solve the problem, regardless of whether all sources have been pursued.

Consider the time and expense of each potential source.

Internal Sources.   Organizations gather large quantities of internal data to make routine decisions. Information about sales, inventory, production costs, profits, and employee turnover are just a few. Much of this information may not be in the form necessary for decision making, but it should not be overlooked.

Internal secondary data are plentiful in most organizations, and with some manipulation they can provide a good information base for decision making. This data can be found in sales slips, written customer order forms, cash register tapes, credit records, accounting records, personnel records, production reports, sales reports, and previous research reports completed for other purposes.

Employees are another excellent, but often underutilized, source of information. Salespeople, cashiers, checkers, delivery people, and credit and office personnel all come into contact with customers, and they hear many comments about the organization and its products. Purchasing agents, financial and accounting personnel, computer operators, and production personnel are other good sources of information.

Employees can be excellent sources of information.

External Sources.   Although internal information is more accessible and often less costly, sources outside the organization may have to be consulted. There is an enormous amount of external secondary data available, from library sources to computer simulations. External secondary sources should be searched first because they are more available and less expensive than primary sources. If this information is insufficient when combined with the internally generated information, external primary sources must be used.

The use of secondary data is normally a part of any research process. There is a wealth of information available in external secondary sources, much of it at no expense. The advantages of using external secondary data include quick access and low costs, which extends the time and money resources and provides an increased range of information otherwise unavailable to most organizations.

The problems with secondary data include unavailability of data to meet specific needs, differences in definitions, dissimilar units of measure, questionable accuracy, and lags in time between data gathering and use of the data. In many cases, decisions can be made using only secondary data, but the researcher must keep in mind the disadvantages of secondary data sources.

Table 10.1 lists examples of useful references and guides. Excerpts from the *Business Periodicals Index* and *The Wall Street Journal Index* are shown in Table 10.2. Many libraries now provide the means for computerized searches of multiple data bases. Software for personal computers that allows the search of commercial data bases is also available. Although these computerized searches can save hours of library time, they can also be quite expensive.

Examples of both general and specific sources of business and economic information are shown in Table 10.3. Much information is available from various levels of the government and from trade associations.

An organization may often need private organizations to gather data for decision making. In some cases the charges for these services may be considerable, which is one reason that it is important to know exactly what information you need to make a decision. Table 10.4 gives examples of various private organizations that provide commercial data and the types of information they supply.

Primary data can come from a variety of sources and, depending on which source is used, may present advantages or disadvantages. Basically, the usability of this data depends on such factors as the timeliness of the data and ability to control measuring techniques, the method of data gathering, the information sample, and the over-

---

External secondary sources can be extremely productive.

External primary data sources are generally the most expensive and time-consuming.

TABLE 10.1

Examples of Useful References and Guides

Accountants' Index and supplements
Accounting articles
AMA 10-Year Index of AMA Publications
Applied Science and Technology Index
Bibliographical Index
Business Education Index
Business Periodicals Index
Cumulative Index of the National Industrial Conference Board Publications
Data Sources for Business and Market Analysis
Education Index
Engineering Index
Engineering Index Annual
Index of Corporations and Industries
Index of Economic Journals
Management Index
Marketing Information Guide
New York Times Index
Poole's Index to Periodical Literature
Public Affairs Information Service Bulletin
Readers' Guide to Periodical Literature
Social Science and Humanities Index
Sources of Business Information
The Wall Street Journal Index

all accuracy of the research. Disadvantages of external primary sources include the cost and time involved in gathering the data and the limitations in research scope that the organization can undertake.

External primary data sources should be the final information source utilized. However, if the secondary sources and internal primary sources provide insufficient or inadequate information, gathering external primary data will be required.

Gather Information

Gathering information from primary and secondary sources requires entirely different approaches.

TABLE 10.2

Examples from Two Common Business-Related Indexes (Both Using the Key Word *Communication*)

Excerpt from
Business Periodicals Index

Netherlands
Dutch approach to switching. R. J. Raggett. il Telephony 196:97–9+ Mr 12 '79
COMMUNICATION in management
Are staff meetings ho-hum sessions? Purchasing 86:111 Ja 24 '79
Behavior training: refining communication skills in an industrial setting. R. H. Keppler. il Train & Devel J 32:58–60 S '78
Benefit messages offer broader corporate aids. E. Simon. Bus Insur 12:42+ My 29 '78
Better communications: better productivity. W. H. Weiss. Supervision 40:1–2 Ja '78
Body talk—the unspoken language. C. Hurston and G. Wilson. Mgt World 7:14–17 Jl '78
Can you manage in a fishbowl? H. Sargent. Mgt R 67:55–62 My '78
Chrysler Marine revamps communications program. Ind Mkt 64:70 Mr '79
Communicating in the employee benefits world. H. H. Simanek. Pension World 14:52+ Je '78
Communicating telecommunications ideas to your top management. J. E. Jewett. tabs Comms N 15:24–5 Jl '78
Communication and the small business manager. T. H. Inman. J Small Bus Mgt 16:50–2 Jl '78
Communication in the corporate budgetary system. L. D. Parker. tab Acct & Bus Res 8:191–207 Summ '78
Communication: panacea or pain in the neck? A. Tsaklanganos. Accountancy 89:146–8 N '78
Communications and costs can alter the bottom line. K. W. Bennett. Iron Age 221:28–9 Je 26 '78
Communications conference [BI Employee Benefits; special report] Bus Insur 12:13–28 N 27 '78
Controlling the sycophant: policies and techniques of corporation president. R. P. Newman and L. Sussman. SAM Advanced Mgt J 43:14–21 Aut. '78
Costs upstage benefit story. M. E. McKee. Bus Insur 12:1+ N 27 '78
Deep sensing: a pipeline to employee morale. Bus W p 124 Ja 29 '79
Despite need, most benefit execs keep low profile. R. A. Fannin. Bus Insur 12:49+ Ap 3 '78
Dialogue with workers can pay dividends. L. Kleber. Bus Insur 12:61+ My 29 '78
Effects of pay disclosure on satisfaction for sales managers: a longitudinal study. C. M. Futrell. tab Acad Mgt J 21:140–4 Mr '78
Employee reports: no panacea. D. Harvey. Director 31:22 F '79
Employee reports still to find the right formula. M. Burne. il Int Mgt 33:42–4 S '78
Employee sounding boards: answering the participative need. D. G. Curley. Pers adm 23:69–73+ My '78
Exec views of worker communications vary. Ind W 199:36 D 11 '78
Finance for the non-accountant: the need to communicate. Accountant 179:142 Ag 3 '78
Firms communications project well taped [Philips Industries] Pers Mgt 10:13+ Ag '78
Ford employees quiz brass. R. W. Irvin. Automot N p3+ F 12 '79
Getting the word to the top. J. B. McMaster. Mgt R 68:62–5 F '79
Getting your benefit programs understood and appreciated. R. C. Huseman and others. tabs Pers J 57:560–6+ O '78
Good idea + poor presentation = 0 good idea + good presentation = !!. J. Ruth. Banking 70:82–4+ Ag '78

Excerpt from *The Wall Street Journal Index*

COMMON MARKET
(*see* European Common Market)

COMMUNICATIONS
(*see also* **Facsimile Transmission, Media, Radio, Telegraph, Telephone, Television**)

Western Union Corp. said it plans to launch its third satellite for domestic communications service in August; cost was put at about $30 million, including hardware and launch expenses. 1/3-5;2
ITT Space Communications Inc. was awarded a $5 million contract to install a satellite communications ground station in Cyprus. 1/3-33;2
FCC's moves to reduce regulation of the broadcast industry won't lead to weaker equal-employment enforcement, FCC chairman Charles Ferris said; Ferris outlined recent FCC actions intended to provide greater opportunity for minorities to acquire broadcast properties. 1/17-18;4
McGraw-Hill and a Free Press: Editorial page feature article by Fred Friendly on McGraw-Hill, American Express merger battle and the repercussions for journalism. 1/26-14;4
FCC voted to study whether shareholders or rate payers should pay legal costs incurred by communications carriers. 2/15-6;1
An International Telephone & Telegraph Corp. unit said it is offering a new service, Infotex, through which telex users in nearly 200 foreign countries can have access to U.S. data banks. 2/28-21;2
Daily newspapers hired 3,600 journalism and communications graduates from the class of 1978's 15,924 grads, says the Newspaper Fund. (Labor Letter) 3/6-1;5
The FCC told the U.S. Postal Service to keep its hands off certain electronic communications. 3/14-22;4
The U.S. Postal Service shouldn't restrict competition in the delivery of electronic communications, the Justice Dept. said. 3/15-7;1
Ranking members of the House Communications subcommittee introduced a scaled-back proposal to overhaul federal communications law; AT&T wouldn't be forced to divest itself of unit under House proposal. 3/30-3;1
Hottest new tool in employee relations is the in-house, corporate TV newscast. 4/13-7;5
Litton Industries Inc. said it signed a contract to provide a command control and communications system for Saudi Arabia with a value of more than $1.64 billion. 4/18-14;3
The head of Japan's state-run Nippon Telephone & Telegraph Corp. indicated he is willing to let U.S. companies bid to supply NTT with communications equipment, apparently opening the way for a settlement of one of the knottiest trade issues between the U.S. and Japan. 4/23-6;1
The FCC is weighing rule changes that would further widen the competition among common carriers of communications, including AT&T. 5/7-10;2
Book review of 'The Powers That Be,' by David Halberstam. (Knopf) 5/7-20;4
FCC moved on two fronts to increase competition in the communications common carrier industry; agency tentatively approved proposal that would allow AT&T and other carriers to provide wide variety of sophisticated computerized communications services and equipment; rejected staff proposal to ease rate filing requirements for AT&T competitors. 5/18-12;1

TABLE 10.3

Examples of Sources of Business and Economic Information

American Register of Exporters and Importers
American Retail Federation publications
Business Conditions Digest
Business Statistics
Census of Business
Census of Retail Trade
Census of Selected Services
Census of Wholesale Trade
Chase Econometric Associates' publications
County and City Data Book
Economic Indicators
Economic Outlook
Federal Reserve Bulletin
Foreign Economic Trends
Food Marketing Institute publications
Guide to Foreign Trade Statistics
Handbook of Basic Economic Statistics
Handbook of Labor Statistics
Index of Economic Articles
Kiplinger Washington Letter
Long Term Economic Growth
Marketing Economic Guide
Monthly Labor Review
National Home Furnishings Association publications
National Retail Merchants Association publications
National Sporting Goods Association publications
Small Business Administration (SBA) publications
Statistical Abstract of the U.S.
Survey of Business
Survey of Buying Power
Survey of Current Business
Survey of Manufacturers
U.S. Industrial Outlook
Worldcasts
Yearbook of International Trade Statistics

TABLE 10.4

Example of Commercial Sources of External Secondary Data

Sources	Use of Data
A. C. Nielsen: Conducts a retail index service; generates continuous data on food, drug, cosmetic, tobacco, toiletry, other products sold in food stores and drugstores.	Market share based on consumer purchases, changing market share, evaluation of price, and promotion changes.
Audits and surveys: Provide physical audits of merchandise in stores.	Merchandise line of competition, merchandise movement.
Market Research Corporation of America: Examines purchasing behavior via a large consumer panel; computes consumer and store data.	Consumer habits, changes, demographic relationships to purchases, geographical purchases.
R. L. Polk: Provides mailing lists and automobile registrations.	New automobile purchasers, related products.*
Selling Area—Marketing, Inc. (SAMI): Gathers information on flow of products to retail outlets.	Market share based on channel movement, effectiveness of promotion on movement of merchandise.*
Standard Rate and Data Service: Collects information on advertising rates for various media; consumer data include income, retail sales, etc.	Information on advertising rates and costs, media usage for advertising and segmentation.
Dun & Bradstreet, Inc.: Information about specific customers and credit ratings.	Extension of credit.
Daniel Starch and Staff: Magazine and newspaper readership data.	Awareness and impact of advertising.*
American Market Research Bureau: Target Group Index covers purchase, usage, and demographics and psychographics for 400 product categories.	Demographic and psychographic consumer segmentation, identification of purchasing and usage behavior.*

* More applicable to large retailers.

Source: Reprinted with permission of Macmillan Publishing Company, from *Retail Management* by Barry Berman and Joel R. Evans, p. 170. Copyright © 1979 by Macmillan Publishing Company.

Data from Secondary Sources.   Efficient collection of data from secondary sources is important. The following practical steps can help ease your venture to the library:

1.   Identify key words for your research topic.
2.   Look for your key words in available indexes, abstracts, and so forth.
3.   Identify likely sources (write them down).
4.   Locate books or journal articles in bound volumes.
5.   Skim material to determine if it is useful.
6.   Take as many notes or make as many photocopies as you feel are needed.

Although you want to be thorough, you do not want to be overwhelmed with data. Following are some hints to help you keep the volume of data to a minimum.

Use cue notes.   A cue note is simply an abbreviation or symbol designed to help you recall information. It should be the smallest record you can make that will later serve as a recall cue. Examples of common cues include *$* for dollars, *%* for percent, and *USA* for United States of America. You can develop many additional abbreviations unique to your objective.

Use a card system.   Card systems are particularly useful for library research. Standard 3 by 5 or 5 by 8 cards are most effective. You might begin by compiling a bibliography from the card catalog or appropriate reader's index. Place only one source or entry on each card and make the bibliographic entry as complete as possible to save return trips to the library. A complete entry should contain the author's name, the title of book, publisher's name and location (or title of article and journal name), the date of publication, and the page of reference. In addition to the bibliographic entry, it is helpful to jot down the key subject area covered by the entry. This makes it easier to organize the cards later.

Learn, rather than accumulate.   When filling out your cards, be careful that you do not develop a pattern of accumulating *all* information provided by a source. Your primary purpose is to learn or gather information pertinent to your research objective, not to accumulate all possible knowledge on the subject.

When you take notes, follow these four steps:

1.   Read the material rapidly.
2.   Put the material aside.
3.   List the main and supporting points from memory.
4.   Review the material to determine whether all significant points have been included.

Cue notes can save time.

Develop an effective card system.

The rapid reading forces concentration. Taking notes from memory reinforces learning and reduces the temptation to rely heavily on the words of others.

Be sure to check the references at the end of articles and book chapters. They can be valuable in providing additional sources. It is also helpful to peruse current issues of journals. If you can find an article on your topic, it will often list many additional references.

Survey Method.   The *survey method* is a technique whereby information is gathered from respondents. Because of the versatility of the survey method, it is the most common technique for gathering primary data. Survey information is gathered by personal interview, by telephone, or by mail. Some type of questionnaire is usually developed as a mechanism for gathering survey data.

Surveys are often used to collect primary data.

There are a variety of survey data collection methods. The *personal interview* is a face-to-face method that makes it possible to gather a wide range of data. A higher response rate is obtained from personal interviews than from telephone or mail techniques. On the negative side, the personal interview is expensive and time-consuming compared to other data collection methods, and interviewer bias is possible.

The *telephone survey* is relatively inexpensive and requires only a short time to gather simple types of information. It allows person-to-person contact for explanation and probing in the questioning process. However, the time allotted to the interview must be kept short, thereby limiting the amount of information you can gather.

Mail questionnaires offer the possibility of reaching nearly all respondents over a wide geographical area. Economy and versatility make mail questionnaires a widely used technique. Interviewer bias is also eliminated.

Problems do exist with mail questionnaires, however. Obtaining addresses or mailing lists for sampling can be expensive and time-consuming. Because most questionnaires must be relatively short to maintain interest on the part of the respondent, there is little opportunity to probe and explain questions. And, nonresponse rates run as high as 80 percent or more for many surveys. Furthermore, it is entirely possible that those answering a questionnaire are more interested in the subject, more educated, or more articulate so that their responses may not be similar to the answers the nonrespondents might have given. Therefore, there is a chance of obtaining erroneous data for decision making.

A number of methods can be used to increase response to mail questionnaires including introductory letters, personally addressed questionnaires, stamped return envelopes, incentives (money, coupons, gifts, contest entries), assurance of anonymity, and, if possible, short easy questions.

Each survey method has strengths and limitations. The choice of a data-collection technique is often a compromise between cost, time, and accuracy. Certain data requirements must be met for effective decision making and they should form the basis for selecting a data-gathering technique. The need for highly accurate information may dictate the use of an expensive technique such as personal interviewing. Time requirements must be lengthened accordingly. If budget constraints are quite restrictive, the telephone may be the most appropriate method. You must keep in mind the objective of the primary research process—accurate data for decision making—in choosing a survey method.

Questionnaire design is a critical issue. The organization and overall design of the questionnaire follows from the information required and the data-gathering method chosen. The questionnaire design must focus on obtaining the appropriate information in as clearly interpretable a form as possible.

The major design issue involves *questionnaire structure*, which refers to the degree of standardization of the questions. A highly *structured questionnaire* consists of questions and allowed responses predetermined by the researcher (see Table 10.5). A highly *unstructured questionnaire* involves little predetermination of answers; the questions asked are less definite and may even be developed during the data-gathering process.

A structured questionnaire is appropriate when the specific information is known and the options are straightforward. If time is restricted, a structured questionnaire can use the time most efficiently. A structured questionnaire would be appropriate, for example, in determining how far shoppers drive to shop at a retail store. Unstructured questionnaires are suitable in situations where the expected answers are not well defined.

Each type of questionnaire can be effective depending on the specific situation. Identifying the research situation and consumer's possible answers dictates the selection of the questionnaire design.

The effectiveness of a questionnaire will greatly affect the quality of data gathering. Poorly worded questions, leading questions, and broad open-ended questions may not generate the information needed for effective decision making. Use of proven questioning and measurement techniques can decrease the incidence of wasted effort. Seven types of structured or closed questions are shown in Table 10.5.

Regardless of the type of questionnaire chosen, remember that *all questions must relate directly to the hypotheses* stated earlier. Asking a question just because you are curious should be avoided.

The specific wording and arrangement of your questions can have a significant impact on the quality of your information and on the percentage of returned questionnaires. Here are a few suggestions:

Evaluate each survey method carefully before choosing one.

Make sure the questionnaire design fits your needs.

Carefully evaluate the type of questions needed and their wording.

1. *Make the questionnaire easy to complete.* The easier it is to complete, the more likely it will be completed. Accuracy will also be enhanced. Ways to make a questionnaire easy to complete include: (*a*) making numbering easy to follow, (*b*) making it easy to find where to place the response, (*c*) asking for objective rather than subjective responses, (*d*) providing checklists where possible, (*e*) using easy to understand words, (*f*) including instructions where appropriate, and (*g*) keeping the number of questions to a minimum.

2. *Use a logical order.* An illogical series of questions can reduce the probability of the respondent completing the questionnaire. For example, it is illogical to ask a person what university he or she attended in question 4 and how many years of education were completed in question 9.

3. *Put easy questions first.* Easy questions can be answered quickly and people are less likely to discard the questionnaire when they reach a difficult question if they have already answered 8 or 10 questions.

4. *Avoid the skip-and-jump pattern.* People can only take so much of the following pattern: If you answered no to question 6, skip questions 7 through 9 and go directly to question 10, unless you also answered no to question 5, in which case you should not answer question 10.

5. *Make each question deal with only one issue.* Avoid questions such as, Would you like movies shown in the student union for a $2 charge? What if the respondent answers no? What does he or she dislike—Movies? Movies in the student union? The $2 charge? The question may be frustrating to the respondent, and the researcher probably will not be able to interpret the results.

6. *Avoid questions that introduce bias.* The following questions introduce bias by leading the respondent to specific answers: Do you prefer foreign sports cars? Do you usually buy box seats when attending ball games? Do you always drink moderately? Providing a list of choices can help eliminate this bias.

7. *Ask questions that the respondent is willing and able to answer.* Many people might be unwilling or unable to answer the following questions: When did you take your first drink? How much do you spend in an average week at the grocery store? How many times have you played golf during the past 12 months?

8. *Avoid personal questions.* Unless absolutely necessary, you should avoid questions regarding items such as individuals' income, age, political or religious affiliation, and sex habits.

TABLE 10.5

Types of Structured or Closed Questions

1. **Two-way question:**
   Do you think New Orleans will win the Super Bowl?

   　　　　　　Yes　　　No

2. **Multiple Choice:**
   If the following men were running for president, for whom would you vote?

   a. Washington　　d. Truman
   b. Adams　　　　 e. Jefferson
   c. Lincoln　　　 f. Other ___

3. **Forced Choice:**
   When you go out to eat, do you prefer steak or seafood?

   _____ Steak　　_____ Seafood

4. **Likert Scale:**
   What is your reaction to the present administration's economic program?

   _____ Strongly agree
   _____ Agree
   _____ No opinion
   _____ Disagree
   _____ Strongly disagree

5. **Semantic Differential Scale:**
   Please circle the number closest to the adjective that describes your attitude toward a woman president.

   Positive　1　2　3　4　5　6　7　Negative
   Active　　1　2　3　4　5　6　7　Passive
   Hope　　 1　2　3　4　5　6　7　Fear

6. **Checklist:**
   Please check all of the following adjectives which apply to your home.

   _____ Warm _____ Cold _____ Noisy _____ Large _____ Small
   _____ Quiet

7. **Situation Questions:**
   A male student with shoulder-length hair sits down in front of you. Your immediate reaction is:

   _____ He's weird.
   _____ He makes me sick.
   _____ I admire him.
   _____ I pity him.
   _____ I don't think anything about him.
   _____ Other _____

A promise of anonymity and placing these questions at the end of the questionnaire may help, but the respondents still might not answer.

9. *Avoid generalized questions.* A generalized question, wording, or word is open to a variety of interpretations. The question, Do you drive carefully? can obviously be interpreted in different ways.

10. *Avoid emotionally laden words.* Certain words can sometimes have a powerful impact because of positive or negative connotations. These words are often abstract (e.g., *happy, morality, patriot, communism*) or relate to sex, race, religion, or politics.

Collect data from a sample rather than from the entire population.

To gather primary data, you must select respondents to answer the survey questionnaire. Collecting data from all possible respondents (a census) is too costly and time-consuming, but a sampling of the population is appropriate. The manner in which the sample is selected will influence the representativeness of the data collected.

A sample selection procedure known as **probability sampling** gives each member of the population a chance of being selected. While this procedure is complex and time-consuming, it gives answers that are representative of the actual population. **Nonprobability sampling** may be more convenient and less costly, but it does not have the accuracy of a probability sample. Table 10.6 provides a short description of the two types of sampling.

Another issue with questionnaire design involves the validity and reliability of the questionnaire. **Validity** is concerned with the question, Are we measuring what we think we are measuring? **Reliability** is concerned with the consistency, accuracy, and predictability of the research findings.

Observation Method. Rather than questioning respondents, the **observation method** employs simple recording of behavior. Observing people can be done personally or with mechanical devices such as cameras and mechanical counters (e.g., turnstiles).

Respondent cooperation is not required, and interviewer and questioning biases are not present in the observation method. Observation does, however, limit sample selection because the respondents must be part of the setting being observed, and only limited information can be gathered when no questioning is involved.

There are three types of observation. *Personal observation* involves watching and recording individuals' behavior while not interacting with them. The observer may pretend to be doing something else while observing others' behavior. This direct observation can be used, for example, to determine shopping patterns or movement

TABLE 10.6

Selected Sampling Techniques

Probability sampling techniques

1. *Simple random sample:* Select from list of population on a random basis, such as by assigning every member of the population a number and selecting the sample from a random number table.
2. *Stratified random sample:* Group population into subsets; select from subsets (or strata) of population on a random basis. For example, stratify population by sex and randomly select a certain number of males and females to survey.
3. *Cluster sampling:* Group population into subsets and select the subset to sample.

Nonprobability sampling techniques

1. *Convenience sample:* Select sample at convenience of interviewer ("person on the street" or whoever is available to interview).
2. *Judgment sample:* Select a sample based on judgment of expert. For example, have a sales manager select respondents who are typical customers or preferred customers.
3. *Quota sample:* Select sample in proportion to some population characteristic(s), such as sex, income, age. For example, if 15 percent of the population is between the ages of 17 and 21, 15 percent of the sample would be from that age group.

---

in a store. Some researchers have used this technique to observe child-parent interaction in selecting cereals. *Mechanical observation* can be used to gather data by using mechanical techniques, such as movie cameras that film individual behavior and interactions. Electronic sensors are also used for making various kinds of traffic counts.

Unobtrusive observation involves observing things rather than people. Periodically observing the number of free samples or coupons taken in a time period or observing the carpet or tile wear to determine traffic patterns are some uses of unobtrusive measures.

Experiments. An *experiment* is used as a data-gathering technique to establish a cause-and-effect relationship. Factors can be manipulated under controlled conditions to allow the desired relationship to be tested.

While experiments have an advantage over the survey and observation methods for testing cause and effect, experiments are not easily conducted. High costs, artificiality, and problems in controlling all extraneous variables in the experimental setting make experiments difficult to conduct.

Simulation.   *Simulation* techniques offer exciting potential for analyzing systems or processes. Simulation is the process of conducting experiments on a model of a system, a model being anything used to represent reality. The essentials of simulation are (1) a mathematical model of the process or system being studied and (2) a sample of inputs. The inputs may be actual data or hypothetical data. Changes are entered into the simulation system to determine the effect on the system or process. In most cases the simulation is computer based.

Analyzing Information

Once the data is gathered, it must be analyzed and interpreted. Computerized statistical analysis is becoming more common, but this topic is beyond the scope of this text.

PREPARE THE RESEARCH REPORT

The final step in the research process is the preparation of the research report. Communicating effectively to your audience(s) is a critical step many researchers appear to neglect. An excellent research effort is all too frequently overshadowed by a poorly written report. You must put the same effort into writing your report as you did into designing and conducting your research. The following chapter focuses on creating and writing a clear and concise report.

Research has limited value unless an effective report is prepared.

There are several points you should keep in mind as you move into the next chapter. Reports are submitted through oral, written, or a combination of oral and written channels. Frequently, for example, a written report will be supplemented with an oral presentation of the report. This portion of the text, however, focuses on the written report.

Remember that the organization of written material is very important. The two most common organizational plans are the *direct plan* and the *indirect plan*.

The direct (or deductive) plan places conclusions and recommendations at the beginning of the report; the details and analysis of the research effort follow. This approach is normally used for longer, more complex reports.

The indirect (or inductive) plan has details, information, and analysis placed first, followed by the conclusions or the recommendations. This approach is frequently used in short reports. Short re-

TABLE 10.7

Guidelines for Using Headings

FIRST–DEGREE HEADING

The title of your whole report, book, or article is the first-degree heading. Since there is only one title, no subhead should be written in the same form. As illustrated here, the title is written in the most superior form and position. The heading above this paragraph is a good choice for a first-degree heading.

Second-Degree Heading

If you use solid capitals centered on the page for the first-degree heading, a good choice for the second-degree headings is caps and lowercase, as illustrated here. Preferably, it and any other uncapitalized head should be underscored to make it stand out, though some people say it should be only if its immediate superior is. Of course, if you do not need the five-level breakdown here, you could start with this form for the first-degree heading.

Third-degree heading

To distinguish the third-degree headings from their superiors, you may wisely choose to change position and put them at the left margin above the text, underscore them to make them stand out, and write them in initial-cap form (as here) or in cap and lowercase (which would require capitalizing the H in Heading).

Fourth-degree heading. For further breakdowns into a fourth level, you may place headings at the paragraph indention on the same line with the text and write them as caps and lowercase or as straight lowercase. They definitely need to be underscored and separated from the first sentence, preferably by a period and dash, as here. Some people drop the dash.

The fifth-degree headings can be well handled as integral parts of the sentence of the first paragraph above a topic. If they are underscored (which means italic type when printed), they will stand out sufficiently without further distinctions in form.

Good headings make a report easier to read.

---

ports are discussed in Chapter 11, and long reports are discussed in Chapter 12.

The effective use of *headings and subheadings* can yield several benefits. Headings make a report more readable—a 10-page report that contains no headings is usually difficult to understand. Headings can be used to emphasize key topical areas and to signal the reader that a new topic is being addressed. Further, headings can help you locate a specific topic more easily. Guidelines for using headings are shown in Table 10.7.

Remember that it is possible for an organization to generate too many reports. *Report overload* has become a more acute problem in recent years with the increased utilization of communication and information systems technology. Before generating another report, you should address the following questions: Is the report necessary? Who will use the information from the report? How will the information be used? and Do the benefits of the report outweigh the cost involved in generating the report?

In addition, organizations should frequently examine existing routine reports and the reporting system. *Report pruning* should be conducted frequently in any organization. The result is that often some reports are deleted entirely, while others are streamlined and/or combined with others.

Application Exercises

1. Prepare five annotated bibliography cards for one of the topics listed below, using the *Business Periodicals Index* and *The Wall Street Journal:*

   a. Accounting
   b. Computer technology
   c. Finance
   d. Marketing
   e. Word processing

2. Prepare a one-page description of your attack on the problems listed below (a–e). Use the following headings: Statement of the Problem, Hypotheses, Sources of Information, and Research Method.

   a. As marketing director of International Leisure, owner of a large group of luxurious vacation condominiums, you want to determine what previous customers liked and disliked about their stays at your units.
   b. Burger King plans to open a new outlet in your town in one of three possible locations: (1) in a downtown shopping district, (2) on an interstate highway, or (3) next to the university campus. You must prepare and submit a recommendation.
   c. As the marketing director of the First National Bank, you must decide whether to give gift certificates or the actual gifts as incentives to encourage customers to open new savings accounts. Incentives cannot exceed $5.
   d. As the advertising director for a regional chain of small department stores, you have discovered that in some small towns advertising in newspapers is best, but that in others radio yields the best results. Your firm is opening a new store next month in a new town.
   e. You own a lumber yard that obtains 80 percent of its business from contractors and 20 percent from ultimate consumers. You want to convert the business into a home improvement center and obtain 80 percent of your business from ultimate consumers. You must find out what kind of handyman projects your potential customers like to do.

3. Write a clear statement of the problem and list the problems involved for each of the following situations. You may supply any additional information necessary.

    a. Ace Furniture Manufacturers, Inc. must prepare a report on its credit relations with the Boardtown Showroom.

    b. As a supervisor in your firm's computer division, you must prepare a report evaluating the performance of each computer programmer.

    c. You must prepare a study that focuses on determining why your firm's employee turnover is increasing.

    d. As an investment consultant, you must advise a client on whether or not to invest in the early development stages of a ski resort.

    e. As a restaurant owner, you want to learn how your business can increase sales.

    f. As a restaurant owner, you want to learn how your business can decrease costs.

    g. Your firm, a producer of men's skin care products, wants to determine the characteristics of its customers.

    h. As the director of marketing for a large bank, you want to determine which types of media your customers use.

Review Questions

1. Discuss the relationship between research and reports.
2. Briefly outline the five basic steps of the research process.
3. Describe briefly the three components needed to identify a problem.
4. Describe the three key substeps necessary for analyzing a problem.
5. Discuss the 5 Ws approach.
6. Briefly describe the four activities needed to determine information needs.
7. List the order in which sources of data should be consulted. Defend your answer.
8. Discuss data collection procedures from secondary sources.
9. What is the survey method?
10. Discuss the advantages and disadvantages of personal interviews.

11. Discuss the advantages and disadvantages of telephone interviews.
12. What are the advantages and disadvantages of mail questionnaires?
13. Discuss the major issues of questionnaire design.
14. Compare structured and unstructured questionnaires.
15. What are the various types of structured or closed questions?
16. What factors make a questionnaire easy to complete?
17. Why is sampling used?
18. Distinguish between probability and nonprobability sampling.
19. Discuss three types of observation.
20. Discuss the major advantages and disadvantages of experiments.

Key Terms

research
investigation
academic research
applied research
report
problem
problem statement
hypothesis
research methodology
internal sources
external sources
primary data
secondary data
survey method
personal interview
telephone survey

mail questionnaire
questionnaire design
questionnaire structure
structured questionnaire
unstructured questionnaire
probability sampling
nonprobability sampling
validity
reliability
observation method
experiment
simulation
direct plan
indirect plan
headings and subheadings

Chapter 11

- **Chapter Outline**

The Informal Short Report

- ***Learning Objectives***

After studying this chapter, you should be able to:
- Differentiate between a short and a long report.
- Describe the major focus of short reports.
- Select the appropriate short report form for a given situation.
- Identify and discuss the major guidelines for writing short reports.

Introduction

John Jackson, a recent graduate of State University, had just celebrated his first anniversary of working for a major manufacturing firm. Although John found his job challenging and satisfying, he was also experiencing mounting frustration. Shortly after beginning a temporary assignment in the plant's quality control department, John developed an idea for improving part of the quality control system on a production line. John's excitement and enthusiasm were soon dampened by lack of management action. Although he had discussed the idea on numerous occasions with his immediate supervisor, the idea appeared to get no further. After two frustrating months, John decided to take another approach. He began to assemble pertinent secondary data and to collect key primary data from quality control reports. When he was satisfied with his evidence, he prepared and submitted a written report to the supervisor. Shortly thereafter, the supervisor called John to his office and began with, "John, this is a brilliant idea. I have submitted it to our plant manager, and I'm positive that it will be implemented within the month."

A good report can help management solve problems.

Situations like this occur frequently in organizations. Despite the usefulness and importance of oral communications, written reports are sometimes more effective in encouraging or forcing action. Written reports are an important part of today's business world, especially regarding the reporting and interpreting of data. A well-researched and well-written report can greatly facilitate the problem-solving and decision-making process in organizations.

Reports fall into two general classifications—short or long. This chapter discusses and illustrates the major forms of short reports, examines how to determine which form of the short report to use, and presents general guidelines for preparing short reports.

SHORT REPORTS VERSUS LONG REPORTS

Before you begin writing a report, you should develop a feel for the length, format, and writing style that you will need to use. Although the distinction between the short and long report is some-

TABLE 11.1

General Guidelines for Short and Long Reports

	Short Reports	Long Reports
Format	Informal, with little (if any) preliminary and supplementary material. Supporting data included in body.	Formal, with much preliminary and supplementary material.
Nature	Less complex; some analytical, mostly informational.	Highly complex; very analytical, little informational.
Writing style	More personal: 1st person; colloquial expressions; abbreviations.	More impersonal: 3rd person; no contractions; no slang; no abbreviations; appears more objective.

what arbitrary, the basic characteristics of each are important and they are summarized in Table 11.1.

The Long Report

Long reports are formal and relatively complex.

A *long report* is any analysis or information presented in a complete formal structure that includes both preliminary and supplementary parts. The writing style is rather formal and impersonal. The nature of the research process leading to the long report is generally more complex and analytical. Busy executives normally prefer a direct organizational plan to help save time.

The Short Report

A *short report* is any analysis or information presented in a less formal arrangement. There is little preliminary or supplementary material, and any supporting data or information is kept brief and is included in the body of the report. The writing style is less formal and more personal. The nature of the problem necessitating the short report is generally less complex (perhaps one simple issue) and requires less analysis. In fact, many short reports are strictly informational in nature. An indirect organizational plan is normally used. However, more and more organizations are requiring a more direct approach even in short reports since executives want to know the recommendations up front.

The short report is more common than the long report in most organizations. The remainder of this chapter presents the major forms or types of short reports and discusses general guidelines for developing a short report.

MAJOR FORMS OF SHORT REPORTS

Although there are many forms or formats for short reports, the three major forms used in business are the memorandum report, the letter report, and the short manuscript report. Two other special short report forms that are quite common are the computer printout report and the standardized form report.

Memorandum Report

A *memorandum report* is an internal report that tends to be very informal. Since it is sent from one organization member to another, it is perhaps the most common report form used in business.

A memorandum report is usually prepared on standardized interoffice or letterhead stationery. The most common opening format is as follows:

TO:
FROM:
SUBJECT:
DATE:

Although a signature line is not normally included anywhere in the memo, the writer normally places his or her initials following their typed name at the top of the report.

Memorandum reports tend to be informal because they normally deal with routine, day-to-day issues. Consequently, introductory material is kept to a minimum. The main issues or facts are presented immediately following the subject line, as shown in Illustration 11.1.

ILLUSTRATION 11.1

A Memorandum Report

TO: Joe Curry, Principal
FROM: Mark White, Regional Maintenance Supervisor
DATE: May 1, 1986
SUBJECT: RECOMMENDATION FOR CAFETERIA LIGHT-
            ING AT HEBRON CHRISTIAN SCHOOL

THE PROBLEM

According to your instructions, I have analyzed the lighting needs for Hebron Christian School's cafeteria. The major objective was to recommend the lighting system that gave the best mix of economy and color rendition.

DESIGN CRITERIA

The priority of design criteria for the cafeteria lighting is:
1. Maintenance of 60 footcandles in the kitchen and at least 25 footcandles on the seating area.
2. Minimum life-cycle cost, assuming a 20-year life.
3. Color rendition suitable for plays and other performances.

The first of the criteria is the illumination design which cannot be changed. I was told that the second (life-cycle cost) should be weighted twice as heavily as the third (color).

CALCULATION RESULTS

The following table shows the results of my calculations for six different light sources. First cost is a function of the number of lamps and luminaires required to achieve the specified light levels. Energy cost is derived from the efficiency of the light source, and the color rendering index is taken from the IES standards. Maintenance cost is related to the number of lamps, rated lamp life, and cost per lamp replacement (including labor). Life-cycle cost assumes a 12 percent energy inflation rate, a 10 percent capital inflation rate, and 0 percent discount rate.

ILLUSTRATION 11.1 (continued)

TABLE 1
Calculation Results

Source	First Cost	Annual Energy Cost	Annual Maintenance	Life-Cycle Cost	CRI*
Incandescent	$5,000	$9,800	$1,200	$780,000	100
Fluorescent	3,500	1,800	85	140,000	70
Mercury vapor	6,000	2,500	180	195,000	65
Metal halide	5,400	1,400	180	115,000	75
High pressure sodium	4,550	1,100	130	90,000	40
Low pressure sodium	6,600	800	250	78,000	12

* Color Rendering Index

DECISION

For each light source, I have assigned points for cost and color. Cost points are proportional to the life-cycle cost as shown in Table 1, with the lowest receiving 10 points and the highest receiving 1 point. Color points are assigned according to the color rendering index, with the highest receiving five points and the lowest receiving one half point. The source with the highest resulting point total is the one which most closely complies with the design criteria and the client weighting, and should be selected. Table 2 displays these point assignments and totals.

TABLE 2
Point Assignment

Source	Cost Points	Color Points	Total
Incandescent	1.0	5.0	6.0
Fluorescent	9.0	2.9	11.9
Mercury vapor	8.3	2.7	11.0
Metal halide	9.4	3.2	12.6
High pressure sodium	9.8	1.4	11.2
Low pressure sodium	10.0	0.5	10.5

ILLUSTRATION 11.1 (concluded)

Based on this table, I suggest illuminating the cafeteria with metal halide lamps and luminaires, as they received the highest point total.

RECOMMENDATION

The cafeteria should be illuminated with metal halide lamps and luminaires. As my calculations show, these will best fit the design. Metal halide lighting will give the best mix of economy and color rendition when compared with the incandescent, fluorescent, mercury vapor, high pressure sodium, and low pressure sodium. If you approve of these results, please notify me so that I can begin work on the necessary drawings and specifications.

Letter Report

A *letter report* is simply a short report written in the style and format of a letter. The major function of a letter report is to disseminate information to someone outside the organization.

Although not common in normal letters, some (but not all) letter reports contain subject lines and subheadings. The first paragraph of a letter report normally contains the following items:

1. Authorization for the report.
2. Purpose (always include).
3. Statement of problem (if relevant).
4. Organization of report (if long enough).
5. Recommendations (if direct organizational plan).

The next paragraph or section typically describes the methodology and the facts that led to the recommendations. The final section contains the conclusions or recommendations. An example of a letter report is shown in Illustration 11.2.

Short Manuscript Report

A *short manuscript report* is less formal than the long reports, which will be discussed in the next chapter, but more formal than

ILLUSTRATION 11.2

A Letter Report

Dear Mr. Ray:

As a follow-up to our discussion of the need for training in the area of oral and interpersonal communication for your supervisory and middle-management personnel, I am pleased to present the following proposal.

THE PROBLEM

Management has perceived a need for improved communication performance on the part of supervisory and middle-management personnel to strengthen relationships between them and their subordinates.

A PROPOSED COURSE OF INSTRUCTION

Based on our experience, the following broad concept should be effective in producing better understanding and improved performance:

Teaching-Learning Method. The acquisition of interpersonal skills results from an activity-oriented training program in which students have an opportunity to apply theory through role playing, case discussion, and critical feedback. In this approach, the instructor is a learning facilitator rather than a lecturer. Frequent use of our video playback accompanied by instructor and group feedback reinforces learning.

Content. The following topics constitute the content core of the program:

1. Perception and self-concept.
2. A positive communication climate.
3. Sending skills.
4. Receiving skills.
5. Nonverbal skills.
6. Reducing communication barriers.
7. Resolving conflict.
8. Interviewing.
9. Small-group communication.
10. Power and persuasion.

Learning Materials. Because students seem to feel more comfortable when they have a textbook to guide them, we use the Verderber book, Interact. Additionally, case-problem handouts are provided for role playing and discussion.

ILLUSTRATION 11.2 (concluded)

Length of Course. The course consists of 12 two-hour sessions over a six-week period.

Number of Participants. Because of the activity orientation of the program, a maximum of 12 student participants is desirable.

COST

All teaching-learning materials will be provided by us and will include textbooks, handouts, video camera, and playback equipment. Based on a 12-session, 12-participant program, the total cost is $1,800. When two courses are offered on the same days, the total cost is $3,300.

Should you like to discuss implementation of the program, I will be pleased to meet with you at your convenience.

Sincerely,

R. M. McNitt

Enclosures: Biographical sketches of instructional staff.

the other short reports. The key element lending a more formal appearance to the short manuscript report is the title page, which the memorandum and letter reports do not have.

Since short manuscript reports frequently use the direct organizational plan, the first item is normally a brief summary or abstract, followed by a short introduction. The introduction generally includes statements of the purpose, problem, and organization of the report. Subsequent sections present the methodology, the findings, and the recommendations. A short manuscript report is shown in Illustration 11.3 (note that much of the descriptive material has been left out of this abbreviated version).

Special Reports

Although you yourself are likely to have to prepare reports using each of the three forms discussed earlier, you may also have to design formats for someone else to use in preparing two additional special types of reports.

ILLUSTRATION 11.3

A Short Manuscript Report

TITLE PAGE

AN ANALYSIS OF THE OPPORTUNITY FOR OFFERING
STRATEGIC MANAGEMENT SEMINARS
FOR MISSISSIPPI BANKERS

Submitted
to

Joe Carlisle
Senior Consultant

Prepared by

Ralph Rowel
Vice President for Research

and

Fred Rush
Vice President of Consulting Activities

August 25, 1986

1

ILLUSTRATION 11.3 (concluded)

A Short Manuscript Report

2

Summary
The results of this research project indicate that there is both a substantial need and a demand for a strategic management seminar by Mississippi bankers. Further, they feel that our organization can supply the needed expertise.

Introduction
This project, entitled "The Feasibility of Offering Strategic Management Seminars for Mississippi Bankers" began on May 5, 1986, and was completed on August 12, 1986. The objectives of this project, as stated in the original proposal were:

1. To study the demographic characteristics of banking presidents in Mississippi.
2. To study the corporate strategic planning process for banks in Mississippi.
3. To examine the relationship between organizational performance and both objective 1 and objective 2 above.
4. To assess the need for a strategic management seminar to be offered for presidents of Mississippi banks.

Methodology
The primary data needed for this project was gathered by using a mail survey. The questionnaire shown in Exhibit 1 was developed for this survey.

*   *   *   *   *

Findings
The bank presidents' responses are summarized in Table 2. Items 1 through 10 reveal that the sampled bank presidents perform strategic planning primarily alone. The data indicates that 63 percent of the respondents are the sole participants in the strategic decision-making process, 43 percent involve nonmanagers "very little," and 34 percent involve outsiders such as consultants, family, professors, or other businessmen "very little."

*   *   *   *   *

Recommendations
A seminar on strategic management for banks should be developed and offered through our College of Business. The seminar should be focused specifically on bank presidents and offered in the state capitol.

*   *   *   *   *

The *computer printout report* has become very common as the use of computers has become more widespread in business. Computer reports are particularly useful for routine, periodic reports. Since computers are used to gather, store, and analyze information, the information must be presented in a usable form. Even though you may not be involved with computer programming, you may have to design formats for presenting data. A computer printout report is shown in Illustration 11.4.

ILLUSTRATION 11.4

Computer Printout Report Example

```
              MISSISSIPPI STATE UNIVERSITY      SCHOOL OF ACCOUNTANCY      ENROLLMENT INFORMATION
Tue Dec 18  1984


SORTED BY    RECORD NO.   SEM/YEAR   COURSE   SECTION   PRE   REG   OFFIC   END   INSTRUCTOR   DOC/CPA   DOC/O   MBA/CPA
COURSES
             00350        F84        1413     01        42    50    34      26    THOMAS                          34
             00351        F84        1413     02        42    76    77      67    CAUSEY       77
             00352        F84        1413     03        42    50    57      50    THOMAS                          57
             00353        F84        1413     04        42    51    48      47    DAUGHTREY    48
             00354        F84        1413     05        42    48    42      38    KNIGHT, L.   42
             00355        F84        1413     06        16    48    45      32    ROBERTS
             00356        F84        1413     07        12    29    23      19    ROBERTS
             00357        F84        1413     08        42    52    45      37    DAUGHTREY    45
             00358        F84        1413     09        42    53    51      53    OWEN                            51
             00359        F84        1413     10        09    49    49      37    SEAY                            49
             00360        F84        1413     11        42    51    53      50    GREEN        53
             00361        F84        1413     12        42    49    45      39    DAUGHTREY    45
             00362        F84        1413     13        42    48    52      44    FESLER                          52
             00363        F84        1413     14        42    50    46      37    FESLER                          46
             00364        F84        1413     15        42    49    39      27    SEAY                            39
             00365        F84        1413     16        42    38    42      37    CHEATHAM     42

                                                        583   791   748     640                351   328

RECORDS SELECTED 00016
```

The **standardized form report** is often used for routine, periodic reports, especially by line or field personnel, such as production foremen or salespeople. The report is arranged for quick entry, formatted for checking or circling the current information or completing fill-in blanks. You may eventually have to prepare the specific format for a standardized form report. Your major objectives should be to make data entry and interpretation easy. An example of a standardized form report is shown in Illustration 11.5.

SELECTING A SHORT REPORT FORM

You must know your audience and . . .

Selecting the appropriate form for your short report requires that you ask and answer two basic questions. First, who is your audience? If, for example, your audience is someone inside your organization, the memorandum format would be best. Any of the other forms could be appropriate for someone outside your organization.

. . . your purpose.

Second, what is the purpose of your report? Although information can be transmitted via any of the report forms, routine data transmission for monthly production or sales figures is often done via the computer printout or standardized form. A report providing a detailed explanation of a complex situation or proposition (e.g., a sales proposition) might better use the letter report form. An analytical report presenting the results and recommendations of a research investigation might better use the short manuscript form.

GUIDELINES FOR WRITING SHORT REPORTS

A great deal of care should be exercised in planning and organizing a short report. The abbreviated length of the short report puts a premium on clearness, conciseness, and completeness. Since short reports are generally less than 10 pages long, there is little room for error. The following guidelines are offered.

1. *The short report should follow the principles of effective writing* discussed in Chapter 5 regarding completeness, conciseness, clarity, you attitude, tone, grammar and mechanics, and attractiveness.
2. *The purpose of the report should be clearly stated at the beginning of the report.*
3. *Making generalizations that cannot be supported by the data presented in the report should be avoided.*

ILLUSTRATION 11.5

Standardized Form Report Example

Monthly Sales Report

———— ————
Month   Year

Complete all blank spaces.

To:
From:
Date:

Sales volume

	Month	Previous Month	Month
	Year		Previous Year

Software
 Line PC
 PC 100
 PC 200
 PC 300
 PC 400

Hardware
 Line XT
 XT 100
 XT 200
 XT 300

Miscellaneous items

———— ———— ————
Month   Previous   Month
         Month

———— ————
Year   Previous
         Year

ILLUSTRATION 11.5 (concluded)

Sales volume (in dollars)
 Line PC
 Line XT $____ $____ $____
 Miscellaneous Sales

Inventory (in dozens)
 PC 100
 PC 200
 PC 300
 PC 400
 XT 100
 XT 200
 XT 300

Miscellaneous items

Comments and recommendations _____

_____

_____
        Signature

Have you completed all blank spaces?

4. The conclusions and/or recommendations of the report must be supported by the information.
5. The report should be written in a style that fits the relationship between the writer and the reader.
6. The indirect organizational plan is traditionally the preferred approach for the short report, but more and more executives are demanding the direct approach.
7. Information and analysis sufficient to enable the reader to respond in the desired manner should be included. In other

TABLE 11.2

Format Checklist for Short Reports

1. *Subject line.* State the subject of the report on the subject line in memorandum reports and letter reports (if needed).
2. *Introduction.* Clearly state the purpose of the report and the problem (if needed). If a problem statement is included, it should also be explained clearly.
3. *Body.*
   a. All facts should be presented accurately and impartially.
   b. Highlight key ideas by capitalizing, underlining, or indenting.
   c. Guide the reader through the report with headings and subheadings.
   d. Use topical or introductory paragraphs to begin each section.
   e. Use topical sentences in each paragraph.
4. *Ending section.*
   a. Select the appropriate ending format based on: a *summary* condensing the text material, *conclusions* evaluating the text material, and *recommendations* offering specific courses of action.
   b. The order of points in a summary should parallel the order of the text.
   c. Do not include new material.
   d. List and number multiple conclusions and recommendations.
5. *Appendix.* Appendixes should contain material that, while relevant to the report, is not crucial to the report's development and would therefore clutter the text.

words, make sure the reader can make the appropriate decision based on the information included.

Other suggestions are found in the checklist shown in Table 11.2.

You must pay special attention to your organization's practices and requirements regarding the formatting and structuring of short reports. For example, if your boss wants you to use a direct approach in a short report by putting the recommendations first, do it! These practices obviously differ from organization to organization.

You should follow your organization's guidelines when available.

Application Exercises

1. The following topics can be developed into reports of varying length and rigor. Specific details can be created by your instructor or you. Use your library to find additional relevant information.

a. Justify the implementation of a management by objectives (MBO) system for a firm.

b. Advise a country club on whether it should build an additional nine holes of golf or build new tennis courts.

c. Advise a church on whether it should renovate or destroy its old (unused) sanctuary.

d. Advise a rising executive on whether to buy his own condominium or part of a time-sharing agreement.

e. Advise a rising executive on whether to buy a new boat or install a swimming pool.

f. Advise a sales manager on whether to buy or rent a fleet of cars for the salespeople.

g. Justify your proposal to initiate an exercise program for executives of your company.

h. Justify the need for additional supervisory training in your firm.

i. Justify the need for additional communications training in your firm.

j. Justify the need for additional sales training in your firm.

k. Advise your company president on whether or not to initiate a flextime program for employees.

l. Advise a large department store on how to reduce shoplifting.

m. Advise a small specialty retail store on how to reduce shoplifting.

n. Recommend whether or not your company should use stress management training for its executives.

o. Advise a sales manager on whether or not to abandon the present straight salary compensation system in favor of a salary plus commission or straight commission.

p. Advise an office manager on whether or not to purchase word processing equipment.

q. Advise a professional typist on whether to purchase a dedicated word processor or a personal computer and word processing software.

r. Determine whether or not a new school building should have individual thermostat controls in each office and room.

   s. Advise the potential buyer of a small retail establishment on whether or not the store is priced appropriately.

   t. Advise a sales manager on which type of incentive gift should be offered customers.

   u. Advise a firm on whether or not it should use lie-detector tests in screening prospective employees.

   v. Advise your firm's president on whether or not your firm should establish its own in-house advertising department.

   w. Advise a firm on whether or not it should begin a program for hiring handicapped workers.

   x. Design a plan for employee grievances for your firm.

   y. Design a recruiting program focusing on college graduates for your firm.

   z. Present a report on the future of the electric automobile.

  2. Research a Fortune 500 corporation and write a report on the feasibility of investing in it. Use information from the firm's annual reports and 10-K reports.

Review Questions

1. Distinguish between a long report and a short report.
2. List and briefly describe the three major forms of short reports.
3. Discuss the memorandum report, including the major components.
4. Discuss the letter report, including the major components.
5. Discuss the short manuscript report, including the major components.
6. List and briefly describe the two major forms of special reports.
7. Name and defend the two basic questions that must be answered in selecting the appropriate form for your short report.

Key Terms

long report
short report
memorandum report
letter report
short manuscript report
computer printout report
standardized form report

Chapter 12

- *Chapter Outline*

The Formal Long Report

- ***Learning Objectives***

After studying this chapter, you should be able to:
- Discuss four major categories of long reports.
- Identify and discuss the major components of long reports.
- Understand the purpose of each long report component.

Introduction

Long reports are generally more complex than short reports.

Major research projects normally culminate in a formal ***long report***. An organization may have such a report written by an outside consulting firm or an internal research staff. Long formal reports are also written in university environments. Doctoral dissertations, master's theses, and many undergraduate term papers, for example, can be categorized as long formal reports. If you have not already had to write a long formal report, you probably will before you leave the university. When you move into the business world, you may on occasion be involved with a major research project that will require you to write a long formal report.

The long formal report is essentially an expansion of the short manuscript report, but normally it involves a more complex issue and is more analytical in nature. As a report grows in length, amount of analysis, and degree of complexity, you must increase your emphasis on helping the reader understand the report. To accomplish this, you must develop more extensive preliminary and supplementary components for the report. This chapter describes common types of formal reports, examines the major components of a long formal report, and illustrates a typical example of such a report.

COMMON TYPES OF LONG FORMAL REPORTS

Long formal reports can be grouped into four general categories: proposals, after-action reports, annual reports, and staff reports.

Long Proposals

A ***long proposal*** is most frequently used to make a sales proposition to an individual, a group, or another organization. It generally identifies the offering, its major strengths and benefits, and perhaps the contract terms.

Although sales proposals are often transmitted via a short letter or manuscript report, some situations require the inclusion of a great deal of preliminary and supplementary information. The short report can therefore quickly become a long report. Organizations dealing with complex, high dollar-value offerings must often use the long report form. It is not unusual, for example, for consulting and research firms to submit proposals ranging between 25 and 50 pages for projects such as feasibility studies or other investigations. Often, many people are involved in writing such a report, and in some cases, length is as important as content because it symbolizes a lot of work and information. These reports frequently include a great deal of general information, such as company background, major projects, sales, and other information that the researchers can obtain from available computer storage.

Long After-Action Reports

A *long after-action report* summarizes and highlights a specific event, activity, or project after its occurrence or completion. Although many after-action reports are short, the longer version is sometimes more appropriate for complex or sophisticated issues.

Consider the type of report you would write if your firm's president made the following comment: "While you are at the convention, keep your eyes and ears open for useful information." You would probably prepare and send a short report to the president. Compare that situation with your likely response to the following instructions:

> While you are at the convention, it is imperative that you find out several things. First, get a handle on the new pollution legislation. Can we fight it? Who will back us? If it is stacked against us, how will it impact us?
>
> Second, find out more about the new federal grant program. What is its major focus? Can we apply? How?
>
> Third, check out our new competition. Who are they? How strong are they? Who is backing them? What can we expect from them in the future?

Depending on the inclinations of your firm's president, your response to these instructions might entail a long formal report.

Long Annual Reports

The *long annual report* is perhaps the most familiar example of a long report. Corporations must generally publish a long, formal annual report at least once a year.

Perhaps the key component of a long annual report is financial data that summarizes the firm's activities during the previous year.

Annual reports can also contain a variety of other useful information, including a written overview of the previous year and descriptions of the firm's products, organizational structure, operating divisions, marketing activities, and future plans.

Note that the annual report does not focus on a single individual or group. Rather, it contains information that must be communicated to a broad audience, including stockholders, potential investors, the general financial community, employees, regulatory agencies, and university students and faculty. This broad audience makes writing the annual report relatively challenging.

Long Staff Studies

A *long staff study* involves a major problem that management has asked an individual or group to investigate. Such a study can be performed by internal or external individuals or groups.

Staff studies can sometimes involve a great deal of research over an extended period of time. Examples of staff studies include the feasibility of establishing a new plant in another part of the country, the financial impact of new government regulations, or an investigation of problems with employee turnover.

COMPONENTS OF THE LONG FORMAL REPORT

The following major components are normally found in long formal reports:

Preliminary parts
    Title fly
    Title page
    Letter of transmittal
    Table of contents
    List of tables and figures
    Abstract, summary, or synopsis
    Others
Body of report
    Introduction
    Discussion of findings
    Conclusions or recommendations
Supplementary parts
    Bibliography
    Appendix

Each of the components outlined above is discussed separately. Keep in mind, however, that not all situations or reports call for all of the components mentioned in this section.

Preliminary Parts

Preliminary material helps readers understand the report.

The preliminary parts discussed in this section are arranged in the order they would normally occur in a long report. Different situations and organization requirements, however, may require a different order.

Although it is a very important part of a report, the external cover is not included as part of the preliminary material. It should generally be designed to attract attention and physically hold the report together, and the binding should facilitate the turning of individual pages.

Title Fly.
The *title fly* simply contains the title of the report. The title must be stated in a complete and concise manner. The "five W" and the "how" guidelines can be quite helpful in designing a complete title. You should therefore consider the who, what, where, when, why, and how guidelines when designing your report title. An example of a title fly is shown at the end of the chapter.

Title Page.
Normally the *title page* immediately follows the title fly. It usually contains the following items:

- Title.
- The individual(s) who authorized the report, including their position or title and the name of the organization if appropriate.
- The author's name, position or title, and organization.
- The date the report is being submitted.

A well-designed title page is shown in the long report illustration at the end of this chapter.

Letter of Transmittal.
A *letter of transmittal* is often included when the author will not personally hand the report to the receiver. Since it is a substitute for interpersonal contact, the letter is generally written in a personal style and usually contains the following items:

- A statement referring to the authority that initiated the report (and research, if appropriate).
- A statement indicating the purpose of the report or project.

- A statement indicating any limitations regarding the project (e.g., limited funds or time).
- A brief statement indicating the major methods of collecting the information or conducting the project.
- A statement briefly summarizing the major findings and/or recommendations of the project may be omitted if a summary, a synopsis, or an abstract is included.

An example of a letter of transmittal is included in the illustration at the end of the chapter.

Table of Contents. The *table of contents* guides the reader through the organization of the specific sections of the report (an example is shown at the end of the chapter). The items listed in the table of contents are the headings and subheadings of the report. It should therefore be an extension of the writer's outline.

The length of a long report makes the table of contents important to the reader's understanding. It provides the reader with an overview of the report's contents, gives the order of presentation, and serves as a guide for finding specific information.

The table of contents provides an overview and helps locate information.

Busy executives often do not have time to read all of the long reports that cross their desks. They often seek an overview from the table of contents and synopsis, and they may use the table of contents to find those specific parts that they are particularly interested in.

The major components of a table of contents include:

- A listing of the preliminary parts that follow the table of contents.
- Outline captions which are the subheadings in the report with a page number for each caption or subheading (normally a dotted line extends from the subheading to the page number).
- All of the supplementary items or parts of the report.

An example of a table of contents is included in the illustration at the end of the chapter.

List of Tables and Figures. If a long report contains several tables and/or figures, a *list of tables and figures* should be positioned immediately following the table of contents. The list of tables and figures should include the title of each illustration and its page number in the report. An example of a list of tables and figures is included in the illustration at the end of this chapter.

Abstract.   Long reports often include some type of short summary before the body of the report, normally referred to as an *abstract*. (Other common names include synopsis, summary, executive summary, digest, or epitome.) As mentioned earlier, one of the primary purposes of the abstract is to summarize the major points for the busy executive who might not have the time to read the entire report.

The abstract is a short
summary of the report.

To write an effective abstract, you should review each major section of the report and include all major points of the report. The abstract essentially becomes a miniature report. The writing style must be concise and objective.

The organizational plan for the abstract can be either direct or indirect. With the indirect organizational plan, you would summarize major points included in each section of the report beginning with the introduction. With the direct organizational plan, you would begin by summarizing the conclusions and recommendations. Then, you would summarize the major points of the introduction and the remainder of the report.

Other Preliminary Parts.   Two other preliminary parts are sometimes included in a long report. First, a *letter of authorization* is the communication that formally approved the initiation of the project. This letter is not written by the author of the report. Rather, it is a copy of a letter received by the author from the person or organization requesting the report.

Second, a *preface* or *foreword* is included in some long reports. Although a distinction between a preface and a foreword is sometimes made, they are essentially the same. Their primary purpose is to transmit a report to an extremely broad audience.

A preface is usually written in a very personal manner and includes items such as expressions of indebtedness to those who helped in the project, different uses of the report, and perhaps how it might best be interpreted.

The Body of the Long Report

The body of a long report has a structure similar to the body of a short manuscript except it is more developed. As with the short report, the body of the long report can be broken up into major components.

Introduction.   The *introduction* should provide the reader with a background sufficient to understand the report. Before beginning to write the introduction, you should review the information included

The introduction should "read the reader into the situation."

in the preliminary parts of the report. The purpose of this review is to help determine the information that should be included in the introduction and how much it should be emphasized. If the preliminary parts of the report are extensive and well-written, the introduction can be less extensive.

The major components normally included in an introduction are described below. The list can serve as a checklist when writing a long report. The components are listed in a logical order, but the order can be modified to fit your specific situation.

1. Attention getter. Gaining your reader's attention early is important even in a long formal report. The first sentence and paragraph are especially critical for gaining attention. The best way to get a reader's attention is usually to show him or her the importance of the report.

2. Purpose. The purpose of the report should clearly state the reason the report was written and its major focus. The purpose is also sometimes referred to as the objective, goal, or problem statement. You can state the purpose directly, such as, "The purpose of this report is to. . . ." In other situations, you might state the purpose in the form of questions, such as, "The purpose of this report is to answer the following questions." Specific research objectives and hypotheses could then be specified later in the methodology section.

Your introduction must contain a clear statement of your purpose.

3. Scope. The scope of the report defines the boundaries or parameters of the project generating the report. If, for example, your report involved an investigation of employee absenteeism, your scope might include the entire organization, one plant only, the night shift only, or a specific category of workers. A well-written scope section helps the reader understand the remainder of the report and interpret the findings and recommendations.

4. Limitations. Practically all research projects and reports have certain limitations. Your discussion of limitations should be placed early in the report and should relate to the accuracy and validity of your findings. Limitations often arise due to factors such as small sample sizes, non-representative samples, poor response rates, respondent and interviewer bias, and statistical analysis procedures. Interpretation of the report's findings is severely compromised without a thorough discussion of the report's limitations.

5. Definitions. All terms that might be unfamiliar to the reader must be defined. If the terms are used throughout the report and are necessary for the reader to understand the general nature of the project, you should include a definitions subsection in the introduction. If the terms relate more closely to specific parts of the report, you can define them as they occur, perhaps with an explanatory footnote.

6. Background. Most long reports include a subsection that discusses the historical background of the report. Specifically, the situation leading up to the problem, the research, and the report are discussed. This section can include a review of similar problems, internal or external to the organization. Secondary research is often used to help develop this subsection.

In some reports, this subsection is of sufficient importance to be included as a separate major section (rather than as part of the introduction) commonly referred to as "Review of Literature." A good literature review can help the reader better understand how the problem evolved and can serve as the foundation for understanding the research methodology.

7. Research Methodology. This subsection describes the approach and procedures used to collect and analyze the data. The key issues normally include sample selection, questionnaire design, interviewing procedures, and statistical analysis tools. Similar to the background of the report, the research methodology subsection is sometimes so involved that it must be included as a separate major section.

8. Organization. The final subsection or component of the introduction involves a brief overview of the organization of the report. This subsection is particularly critical in a long report because it tells the reader what to expect.

Discussion of Findings. The *discussion of findings* is generally the longest section of a long report. Its purpose is to present and analyze the results of the research. The sheer mass of data gathered in most research projects makes the use of tables, figures, and other graphical aids critically important (graphical aids are discussed in Chapter 13). The effective use of headings and subheadings is also quite important in helping your reader follow the material.

Headings and subheadings are important in long reports.

You must make your writing easy for your audience to read and understand because the length and potential dryness of this section makes it quite easy for the reader to lose his or her concentration and attention.

Summary, Conclusions, and Recommendations

A long report can end in a variety of ways. It can have a summary, conclusions, recommendations, or a combination of these three components.

A *summary* briefly reviews and highlights each major point of the report. *Conclusions* essentially provide the answer(s) to the specific problem investigated. Conclusions are generally included in any type of analytical report. *Recommendations* suggest a course of action or follow-up to the report. For example, a specific solution to the research problem or suggestions for additional research might be presented.

When designing the end of your report, you should bear several key points in mind. First, your choice of writing a summary, conclusions, or recommendations section should be based on your overall purpose for the project. You might be charged, for example, with investigating a situation involving decreasing sales. The sales manager might want the situation analyzed and summarized, which implies that you would end your report with a summary. He might want the situation analyzed to determine the answer to a problem, implying that you should end with a conclusions section. Or, he might want you to analyze the situation and develop recommendations for action, implying that you should end with a recommendations section.

Second, all information included in any of the three ending sections must be substantiated by the report findings. If the reader cannot find this substantiation by relating the ending to the body of your report, he or she might wonder whether your report is biased or erroneous.

Third, your ending should flow logically from the purpose or objectives stated in the introduction. If you make this connection, you show that your objectives have been accomplished.

Supplementary Components

The final section of a long report is referred to as the supplementary or addenda portion of the report. The two primary supplementary components are the bibliography and the appendixes.

Bibliography.   The *bibliography* (or reference) section consists of a complete listing of all secondary research sources used to write the report. Appendix C at the end of this text includes a section on documentation that discusses the different forms for bibliographical entries and for footnotes.

Appendix.   Many long reports also include an *appendix* section. Any information that relates to or supports the report *indirectly* can be put in an appendix. Information that has a *direct* bearing on the report should naturally be included in the body of the report. Items commonly found in appendixes include questionnaires, interviewing guides, maps of sampled area, statistical tables, and computer printouts.

AN ILLUSTRATION OF THE COMPONENTS OF A LONG REPORT

Illustration 12.1 shows a staff feasibility study to highlight the major components of a long report discussed in this chapter. Note that only selected portions of the original report are included in the illustration. Also, remember that all possible components are not included in every long report.

ILLUSTRATION 12.1

A Long Report: Staff Feasibility Study
Title Fly

AN ANALYSIS OF THE TEXAS MARKET FOR METAL BUILDING
CONSTRUCTION AND THE FEASIBILITY OF LOCATING
A KELLY CORPORATION PLANT IN TEXAS

ILLUSTRATION 12.1 (continued)

Title Page

AN ANALYSIS OF THE TEXAS MARKET FOR METAL BUILDING
CONSTRUCTION AND THE FEASIBILITY OF LOCATING
A KELLY CORPORATION PLANT IN TEXAS

Authorized
by

Charles Q. Johnson, President
Kelly Corporation

Prepared
by

James Wingfield
Marketing Manager
Kelly Corporation

and

Sheila Gaston
Research Director
Kelly Corporation

July 15, 1986

ILLUSTRATION 12.1 (continued)

Letter of Transmittal

July 15, 1986

Charles Q. Johnson, President
Kelly Corporation
111 Main
Mayberry, Missouri 22222

Dear President Johnson:

As instructed by you on January 17, 1986, we have investigated the metal building market in Texas. The purpose of our investigation was to determine if it is presently feasible to locate a Kelly plant somewhere in Texas. Our field work was conducted in a manner intended to avoid alerting competitors of Kelly's possible intentions.

The major portion of our field work involved: (1) securing secondary data from the state capital to construct a profile of Texas, (2) examining additional trade data to analyze the building construction situation in Texas, (3) visiting with contractors and examining trade data to prepare a competitive analysis, and (4) discussions with Kelly personnel.

Due to a variety of factors influencing the potential profitability, we recommend that Kelly enter the Texas market on a limited basis. Specifically, Kelly should be able to establish a "beach head" with a limited capacity plant that would manufacture only primary structural components. Other components could be shipped from existing plants.

Respectfully,

James Wingfield
Marketing Manager

Sheila Gaston
Research Director

iii

ILLUSTRATION 12.1 (continued)

Table of Contents

TABLE OF CONTENTS

ILLUSTRATION 12.1 (continued)

Table of Contents

ILLUSTRATION 12.1 (continued)

Lists of Tables and Figures

LIST OF TABLES

ILLUSTRATION 12.1 (continued)

Lists of Tables and Figures

LIST OF FIGURES

ILLUSTRATION 12.1 (continued)

Summary, Abstract, or Synopsis

EXECUTIVE SUMMARY

The state of Texas has evolved into a major market for numerous consumer and industrial goods and services. Research has indicated that positive growth trends will continue for at least the next decade. Included in this growth is the increase in metal buildings sales, which has more than tripled in the past five years. Forecasts are for metal building demand to nearly double within the next five years. This market opportunity is too significant to be ignored in Kelly's future marketing plans.

Kelly's performance in the Texas market has been less than satisfactory as indicated by a continuously declining market share. Rather than attributing Kelly's negative performance to strong competition, it would be more appropriate to attribute it to lack of marketing efforts on Kelly's part.

Several strategic alternatives are available to Kelly:

1. Present marketing efforts can be continued. This alternative would do little to change the existing situation.
2. More aggressive marketing efforts with an emphasis on expanding the Kelly builder distribution network is a viable option. While this alternative would be beneficial, it would not achieve the 14 percent share objective.
3. Build a plant in Texas. This choice would provide Kelly with a strong presence in Texas and establish a base for increasing long-term market share in the state.

A complete manufacturing plant could not be supported by the Texas market demand. However, the market will support a miniplant. Building a miniplant in Texas is therefore the recommended solution. This miniplant would be a structural only type of plant. The decision to locate a plant in Texas must be made immediately.

viii

ILLUSTRATION 12.1 (continued)

Letter of Authorization

January 17, 1986

Dear Mr. Wingfield:

I am becoming increasingly concerned with our status in the Texas market. It appears that our present market share cannot be improved without locating a plant in the state. However, I cannot make such a decision without knowing more about its feasibility. Consequently, I want you and Miss Sheila Gaston to investigate this problem. Specifically, I want you to determine if it is presently feasible to locate a Kelly plant somewhere in Texas. Also, be sure to avoid alerting our competitors of Kelly's possible intentions. Your budget for this project is $5,000.

Sincerely,

Charles Q. Johnson, President
Kelly Corporation

ILLUSTRATION 12.1 (continued)

Introduction

SECTION I

INTRODUCTION

Purpose and Scope

This investigation was conducted to analyze the opportunities within the Texas metal building market. Kelly's market share of 7.3 percent is approximately one half of the stated strategic objective of 13 to 15 percent by 1989 as proposed in the 1986–1989 Strategic Planning Summary.

Specific recommendations for marketing strategies will be made to achieve the SBU strategic objectives.

Description of the Problem

A market share gap of 6 to 7 percent exists. Kelly must therefore double present market share within three years to reach the desired level.

History

Texas has increased in MBMA rankings of the 50 states from a position of 15th in 1977 to 2d in 1986. Shipments in 1986 of $61.4 million were exceeded only by California with a volume of $175.8 million.

1

ILLUSTRATION 12.1 (continued)

Body of Report (selected pages)

SECTION II

TEXAS PROFILE

The state of Texas grew at an exceptional economic pace during the 1970s. As the statistics and comments from various sources demonstrate, Texas has materialized as one of the most potent markets in the United States.

A report prepared by the Division of Economic Development for the state of Texas points to several economic aspects of the state's extraordinary growth.

1. Texas's population growth of 43.6 percent during the 1970s was 3.8 times the national population growth rate of 11.5 percent. Only four western states had larger population percentage increases.
2. In 1980, 87.9 percent of Texas residents resided in 18 Standard Metropolitan Statistical Areas (SMSA), a proportion much larger than the national SMSA rate of 74.8 percent.
3. Mining and manufacturing play smaller roles in the industrial structure of Texas employment and income than they do nationally. However, construction, trade, and services are larger sources of employment and income compared to the other 49 states.

3

ILLUSTRATION 12.1 (continued)

Body of Report (selected pages)

SECTION III

CONSTRUCTION MARKET IN TEXAS

Some analysts have identified the construction industry as a driving force in the Texas economy. As of 1980, the industry employed 263,900 and generated earned income of $4.6 billion. While Texas held a 4.0 percent share of national nonfarm employment generally, 6.l percent of the nation's construction industry jobs were in the state. The previous year, 7.3 percent of the value of construction contracts in the nation were for Texas construction—9.7 percent of the nation's residential construction contracts.

From 1970 to 1980 the rate of job growth for the Texas construction industry (52.0 percent) far exceeded those of the southeast (37.9 percent) and the national (21.1 percent). The construction needs of 43.4 percent more residents, 54.7 percent more tourists, and 61.5 percent more business establishments fueled this impressive growth.

Nevertheless, employment growth in the state's construction industry did not match that recorded by other divisions during the period. In fact, its employment growth rate ranked it behind services; finance, insurance, and real estate; government; and manufacturing. Its nonfarm employment role fell from 8.2 percent in 1970 to 7.4 percent in 1980; its earned income role during the same period fell from 9.3 percent to 7.8 percent.

25

ILLUSTRATION 12.1 *(continued)*

Body of Report (selected pages)

SECTION IV

METAL BUILDING MARKET IN TEXAS

In 1981 the state of Texas ranked second in the United States in metal building sales with $61,350,000. Over the past five years Texas has ascended from a ninth-place ranking in national sales to second place nationally. The share of the United States metal building market in Texas has grown from 2.9 percent (1976) to 5.3 percent (1981). As a share of the Columbus (Kelly) region, Texas's share of metal building demand has risen from 9.1 percent to 14.8 percent. Metal building sales in Texas have increased from $20,131,000 (1976) to $61,350,000 (1981), a 205 percent increase. Texas nonresidential construction during the same five-year period grew at a more rapid rate of 287 percent.

Industry forecasts for the metal building industry (based on F. W. Dodge's forecast) indicate an expected growth of 131 percent through 1987. Table IV–1 shows the F. W. Dodge nonresidential forecast, the national metal building forecast, and Texas's metal building forecast through 1987. Assuming Texas continues to account for approximately 5 percent of all metal building sales nationally and the ratio of metal building sales to total nonresidential construction in Texas remains at approximately .015, metal building sales should increase 131

ILLUSTRATION 12.1 (continued)

Body of Report (selected pages)

SECTION V

COMPETITIVE ANALYSIS

All major metal building manufacturers are represented in Texas, but the level of competition does not appear to be quite as intense as in other markets. Although the explanation for this lack of competitive intensity is not absolutely clear, a partial explanation involves metal building manufacturers focusing their attention on markets that are easier to penetrate because of location or a more attractive industrial base.

There are two regional metal building manufacturers within Texas. However, the dominant influence in Texas is from manufacturers with plants in Georgia and Alabama. See Figure V–1 for relative proximity of these plant locations. Selected data for the metal building manufacturers having significant influence is shown in Table V–1.

Highlights of Key Competitive Factors

Price. Price does not seem to be as strong a factor in Texas as in other parts of the country. Because of the location of Texas, relative to freight cost, small buildings are very price sensitive. Most manufacturers use a special factor for South Texas pricing in lieu of a specific pricing system.

Products. The present product offering of both Kelly and the industry seems to be quite adequate for the Texas market. The coastal climate does not place special demands on color.

47

ILLUSTRATION 12.1 (continued)

Body of Report (selected pages)

SECTION VI

PRESENT KELLY MARKETING STRATEGY

Kelly's present marketing strategy in Texas is essentially the same as in other states. The purpose of this section is to highlight specific details relative to the Texas market.

Products

Present product line is adequate for the Texas market; however, present builders are not taking optimum advantage of the new Korad Double-lam and Mecolok standing seam roof as these systems are being promoted strongly in south Texas. Special small buildings including ministorage and "T" hangars are not readily available within Kelly's product offering.

Pricing

No special discounting is being offered for Texas. The requirement for special estimates is frequent since the present price book does not offer specific price support for coastal markets requiring Standard Building Code (SBC) with 120 mph wind loading as South Texas Code requiring 30 psf live load and 120 mph wind load. Also, central inland Texas is not served by price book support requiring SBC with 100 mph wind loading. Small buildings (less than 6,000 ft.) are not competitively priced.

ILLUSTRATION 12.1 (continued)

Recommendations

SECTION VII

STRATEGY RECOMMENDATIONS FOR TEXAS MARKET

It has been shown that the potential market for metal buildings in Texas is quite good. The information available at this time indicates favorable growth trends for all nonresidential construction, including metal buildings.

Information regarding specific barriers to metal building construction was sought, such as building code restrictions, resistance by architects, resistance by customers, and lack of specialized products. None of these factors were found to represent a significant barrier to metal building construction.

Strategic Alternatives

Based on the notion that Texas represents an attractive market for Kelly, three basic strategic alternatives were evaluated: (1) maintain present efforts, (2) initiate an extensive builder acquisition program, and (3) locate a plant in Texas.

1. Maintain Present Efforts. Maintaining present efforts in terms of direction and character is an obvious alternative. The benefit of this alternative is that it involves minimum financial outlay. There appear to be two major problems

65

ILLUSTRATION 12.1 (continued)

Appendixes

APPENDIX 1

PROJECTIONS OF TEXAS POPULATION BY AGE AND SEX, 1980–2020

87

ILLUSTRATION 12.1 (concluded)

Bibliography

BIBLIOGRAPHY

U.S. Department of Commerce. Bureau of the Census. Current Population Reports. Series p-25, No. 796. Prepared by Executive Office of the Governor, Office of Planning and Budgeting, Revenue and Economic Analysis Section, Washington, D.C., 1983.

U.S. Department of Commerce. Bureau of the Census. Statistical Abstract of the United States, 1985. ES-292 report. Prepared by Texas Department of Labor and Employment Security, Division of Employment Security.

U.S. Department of Commerce. Bureau of Economic Analysis. County Business Patterns. Texas, 1986.

99

Application Exercises

1. You have just completed a long report that focuses on whether a local dress shop should add a line of high quality women's shoes. Prepare three different title pages for the report.

2. Your consulting group has just completed a long report for a client regarding the feasibility of opening a new pizza outlet in your city. Write a letter of transmittal. You will want to recognize the contributions of the group members, the director of the chamber of commerce (Lila Flowers), and a local SCORE representative (Sam Lucas).

3. For the situation in exercise 2, explain some possible additional subsections and material that could be added to your long report.

4. As the mayor of a large seaside city, you want the city's director of economic development to investigate the feasibility of establishing a business incubator. A *business incubator* is a low-cost facility for new businesses that also offers low-cost services (e.g., word processing, temporary office help). Its purpose is to help small new businesses survive their first year or two, when most failures occur. Write a letter of authorization to the director, John Haynes.

5. Select a real firm and assume that you are responsible for making recommendations to the president on what should be included in its annual report and on how the information should be presented. Prepare a memo in which you make your recommendations.

6. The president of a large regional retailer has approached you about conducting a research project. She doesn't feel that retailing firms are attracting their share of the top business students. She therefore wants to find out what business majors at your school think about retailers and a career in retailing. Prepare a questionnaire to submit for her approval.

7. Assume that you have just taken a job as a junior purchasing agent. Your first assignment involves investigating word processing equipment. Due to the nature of your firm, everyone seems to want a system built with personal computers, rather than dedicated word processors. Although very few executives and other potential users have had actual experience with word processing, everyone has an opinion. Your boss has directed you to find out which brand should be purchased—Apple, IBM, or Radio Shack.

Conduct this investigation and prepare the formal long report. Remember that few of the potential users have any experience and that your firm wants to get the most for its money.

Review Questions

1. Discuss the nature and characteristics of a long proposal.
2. Discuss the nature and characteristics of a long after-action report.
3. Briefly describe the major components of a long formal report.
4. Briefly describe the major preliminary parts of a long formal report.
5. Briefly describe the major components in the body of a long formal report.
6. Briefly describe the major supplementary parts of a long formal report.
7. Describe the items normally appearing on a title page.
8. Describe the items normally appearing in a letter of transmittal.
9. Discuss the rationale and character of an abstract.
10. Discuss the general nature of an introduction to a formal long report.
11. Briefly describe the components of an introduction.
12. Distinguish between a summary, conclusions, and recommendations.

Key Terms

long report
long proposal
long after-action report
long annual report
long staff study
title fly
title page
letter of transmittal
table of contents
list of tables and figures
abstract

letter of authorization
preface
foreword
introduction
discussion of findings
summary
conclusions
recommendations
bibliography
appendix

Chapter 13

■ *Chapter Outline*

Communicating With Graphics

- ***Learning Objectives***

After studying this chapter, you should be able to:
- Understand the meaning and significance of graphic communications.
- Describe the major considerations when planning for graphics in reports.
- Identify and discuss the major types of graphic aids.

Introduction

Graphic communications in reports involve any form of nontextual presentation, such as tables, figures, drawings, photographs, diagrams, graphs, models, and charts. The primary purpose of graphic communications is to help ensure clarity, thereby enhancing understanding. The importance of graphic communications is increasing because the volume of data available for most reports is also increasing.

The use of graphic communications can increase the overall effectiveness of your communication. Data presented in sentence form only can often be quite difficult to understand, and an overview may be practically impossible to grasp. Essentially, the old adage "a picture is worth a thousand words" is still appropriate.

A word of warning is needed at this point. Graphic communications should not be introduced in a report *unless* they are needed to clarify textual information. Inserting a table just because the data is available will only detract from understanding. This is becoming a more acute problem with the increasingly widespread usage of computers. Computer-generated graphics thrown indiscriminately into a report can easily overwhelm a reader and impair understanding.

This chapter focuses on ways to use graphic communications most effectively. The specific purpose is to show how graphic communications can be used effectively in written communication, particularly reports.

Graphic aids should be used when they can help clarify your message.

PLANNING FOR GRAPHICS

You should begin planning how to use graphic aids as early in the research and writing stages as possible. For example, you might need to consider the types of graphic aids that would best enhance understanding while you are planning your statistical analysis procedures. This consideration could influence the choice of specific procedures.

You must always keep in mind that the purpose of graphics is to aid the communication process. Graphic aids should therefore supplement the narrative material, not replace it.

Plan ahead for graphics.

You must also perform a cost/benefit analysis to determine whether the cost, time, and effort of preparing graphic aids is worth the benefit of having them in the report. For example, you may have to decide whether to spend several thousand dollars to include a color photograph in a report. If the color photograph does not improve communication significantly, it should not be used. A few simple tables or drawings would cost less and might actually communicate better.

There are several major graphic considerations on which you must make a decision. Each of these is discussed below.

Presenting Statistical Data Honestly

Perhaps you have heard the old adage "statistics don't lie." Hopefully, you understand by now that this is not completely true. In fact, a popular book entitled *How to Lie with Statistics* has addressed this issue. Statistics or numerical data can, in fact, be used to misrepresent a specific situation. Statistical misrepresentation can occur in three ways.

1. *Statistics can misrepresent through selective omission.* For example, specific data or information can be intentionally or unintentionally be left out of a graphic aid.
2. *Statistics can misrepresent through visual distortion.* Graphs, for example, can easily be constructed to mislead the reader.
3. *Statistics can misrepresent when meaningless descriptions are used.* Consider the meaning of "on the average." It could actually refer to the mode (the item occurring the most times), the median (the midpoint), or the mean (the arithmetical average).

It is critically important that data not be misrepresented. As you design a graphic aid, analyze it to determine whether it can be interpreted in more than one way. If it can, perhaps you should consider another way of presenting the data.

Choosing a Type of Graphic Aid

Remember your reader's frame of reference.

After you have decided to use graphic aids, you must then decide which types to use. The major consideration in this decision is your audience or the reader of the report. For example, if the reader's frame of reference is highly technical, a more complex graphic aid can be used. Conversely, if the reader is less educated, has a less sophisticated technical background, or demands simplicity, a simpler graphic aid should be designed. In general, the best graphic aid is the simplest and easiest one that your audience can understand—when in doubt, *keep it simple*!

Placement and Introduction of Graphic Aids

The specific placement of a graphic aid has a major impact on the effectiveness of the aid. If a graphic aid has a direct influence on the narrative, it should be placed close to where it is first mentioned in the narrative. More specifically, it should be placed either immediately following the paragraph in which it is first mentioned or at the top of the next page. If the graphic aid is relevant, but is of indirect benefit to the narrative, it should be placed in an appendix. Regardless of where it is placed, the narrative should specify exactly where the aid can be found.

Graphic aids should always be introduced or mentioned in the narrative or body of a report. Examples of acceptable methods for your reference to a graphic aid include:

- . . . (see Table 2).
- (See Table 2.)
- As shown in Table 2. . . .
- Table 2 presents. . . .

In addition to referring to the aid, you should provide some explanation or description of the aid or parts of it.

Size

A graphic aid should be large enough to be easily seen and interpreted. Conversely, it should not be so large as to take up space unnecessarily. Although most graphic aids take up one page or less, the sheer volume of data requires that some tables carry over to additional pages. Sometimes other items such as detailed flowcharts or schematics cannot fit on one page. These items are often prepared in such a way that the reader can unfold them to examine the entire graphic aid.

Color

Although color can add to the expense of a graphic aid, it can sometimes add significantly to the attention-getting qualities and understanding of a report. Like other graphic aids, however, it can be overdone. Too much color or too many colors can detract from understanding.

Use a graphic aid in the body of your report only if it has a direct benefit.

Always mention graphic aids in text.

Numbering

When numerous graphic aids are used in a report, a logical numbering system must be used. If a report has only three tables, they might be numbered: Table 1, Table 2, and Table 3. If the report is long enough to have multiple chapters with several tables in each chapter, your numbering sequence might include the chapter number along with sequential table numbers within each chapter. For example, tables in Chapters 2 and 3 of a long report might be numbered as follow:

Table 2.1
Table 2.2
Table 2.3
Table 3.1
Table 3.2
Table 3.3

Remember that a list of tables and figures is included in the preliminary components of your long report. The graphic aids will be shown in the order in which they are positioned in the report.

In addition to numbering, you must also decide what to call your graphic aids. For example, you can call all of the aids by one name, such as *Illustration* or *Figure*. You can also refer to each as accurately as possible, thereby numbering each type of aid sequentially. However, do not go overboard with this accuracy. Consider a report that has figures, tables, graphs, models, charts, and examples. If you labeled each type accurately, you would have six separate, sequential numbering schemes—Figure 1.1, Table 1.1, Graph 1.1, and so forth. This pattern is rather cumbersome and seldom facilitates understanding.

Title Captions

Each graphic aid should also have a complete and concise title. Title captions (and numbers) for tables are normally positioned at the top of the table. For other graphic aids the title captions are placed at the bottom.

Documentation

All graphic aids have a source. If the aid was drawn from a secondary source, the complete reference should be included at the bottom of the aid. The reference format used should be consistent

Always mention the source of a graphic aid.

with the footnote and bibliographic format being used for the report (see Appendix C). If the aid was constructed from primary research data generated for the report, you have the option of not including a source reference. We advocate, however, always including a source reference such as *Source: Research data*.

USING TABLES

A *table* is a presentation of data in column form. There are two major benefits of using tables. Data can be assimilated much more easily if it is presented in table form rather than in narrative form. Also, comparisons between data can be made more easily when data is presented in column form.

Tables help you compare specific data.

Table Construction

Constructing a table involves more than just throwing numbers together. The overall arrangement of a table has a large impact on its ability to communicate. A well-arranged table is shown in Table 13.1. The following guidelines should make the task easier for you.

1. Each table should include a table number and a clear, concise title positioned above the table.
2. Each vertical column should be identified clearly and concisely.
3. Any data included in any graphic aid for the purposes of comparison should be placed on a horizontal plane reading from left to right.
4. Fractions should be noted in decimal form.
5. A dash or abbreviated N/A (never a 0) should be used to indicate that the data is not available.
6. Sufficient white space should be included between columns to facilitate the reader's understanding of the table.
7. Totals and subtotals should appear wherever they facilitate the purpose and communication flow of the table. Totals can be computed for each column as well as each row. Normally, a ruled double line is used to highlight totals.
8. Footnote references to data in the table should be keyed with asterisks, daggers, and so forth.

Types of Tables

There are two basic types of tables, the dependent table and the independent table. The *dependent table* is actually considered part of

TABLE 13.1

Example of a Well-Arranged Table

Table Number
Table Title

Item Name	Column Name	Major Umbrella Heading		
		Column Name	Column Name	Column Name
Item 1	XXX	XXX	XXX	XXX
Item 2	XXX	XXX	XXX	XXX
Item 2	XXX	XXX	XXX	XXX
.	.	.	.	.
.	.	.	.	.
.	.	.	.	.
Total	XXX	XXX	XXX	XXX

Footnotes:

Source:

the text and is positioned as such. It follows its first mention immediately and does not have to have a number and title caption.

Most tables are independent tables. An ***independent table*** is one that stands by itself. When an independent table is needed to fully understand the narrative, it should be positioned as close to its first reference as possible, and no further away than the next page. If it is important in understanding the overall research process but is not directly helpful for understanding the narrative, the independent table can be located in the appendix. Independent tables should be numbered and titled and should follow the guidelines mentioned above. Table 13.1 is an example of an independent table.

USING CHARTS

In contrast to tables, ***charts*** do not normally present detailed, specific information. Whereas the purpose of a table is to present specific data, the purpose of a chart is to indicate major *trends* or situations at a glance. For example, depending on the nature of the

Charts give quick, visual indications of trends.

chart, the reader should be able to quickly determine whether the sales level is constant, increasing, or decreasing and at what rate. Also note in the subsequent examples that the title of a chart is normally placed at the bottom of the chart.

The three major types of charts are bar charts, pie charts, and line charts.

Bar Charts

You need to use a *bar chart* when you want to show the relative size or level of variables with different types of bars (see Illustration 13.1). The length of each bar normally indicates quantity. Varying both the length and width of the bars should be avoided to reduce confusion. The bars can be positioned either vertically or horizontally.

Although bar charts can be quite effective in providing the reader with quick, general indications, remember that they do not reflect quantities with the precision and accuracy of tables. A quick glance

ILLUSTRATION 13.1

Example of a Bar Chart

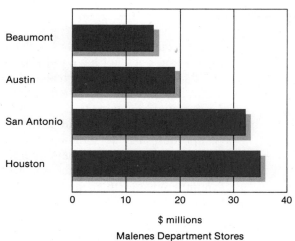

$ millions

Malenes Department Stores

Comparison of sales

Source: Primary Data.

ILLUSTRATION 13.2

Example of a Multiple Bar Chart

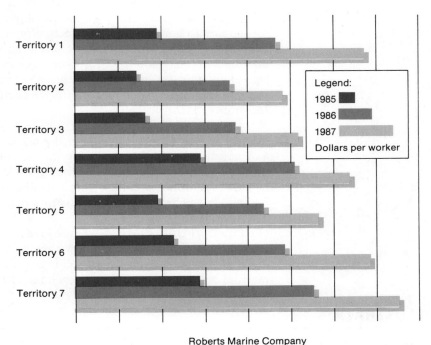

Roberts Marine Company
Average annual earnings, 1985-1987

Source: Primary Data.

Bar charts are good for showing comparisons of relative level or size.

at Illustration 13.2, for example, should show you that sales in Houston are approximately twice as great as sales in Beaumont. You can, however, increase the precision of bar charts by placing the actual sales figures inside the bars themselves.

There are four basic variations of the bar chart: (1) simple bar chart, (2) multiple bar chart, (3) bilateral bar chart, and (4) subdivided bar chart.

Simple Bar Chart.   A *simple bar chart* is used when you want to show a comparison of the differences in quantity or level of a single variable by varying the length of the appropriate bars. A simple bar chart was shown in Illustration 13.1.

Multiple Bar Chart. A ***multiple bar chart*** is used when you want to show a comparison of the differences in quantity or level of multiple variables by varying the length of the appropriate bars. This type of chart is obviously more sophisticated than the simple bar chart and is more difficult to construct. You should try to minimize the number of variables shown on a multiple bar chart.

The key to constructing an effective multiple bar chart involves helping the reader differentiate between the various types of information presented. Multiple bar charts are often multicolor, with a legend defining the color of each variable. Other multiple bar charts use different cross-hatching patterns for each variable, as shown in Illustration 13.2.

Bilateral Bar Chart. A ***bilateral bar chart*** shows both positive and negative quantities, normally for one or a few variables. All positive quantities are shown on the same side of a zero-line and all negative quantities are shown on the other side. An example of a bilateral bar chart is shown in Illustration 13.3.

Subdivided Bar Chart. A ***subdivided bar chart*** divides each bar into various components as shown in Illustration 13.4. Note that distinguishing colors or cross-hatchings are needed to clearly separate the components and that a legend is also needed. This type of

ILLUSTRATION 13.3

Example of a Bilateral Bar Chart

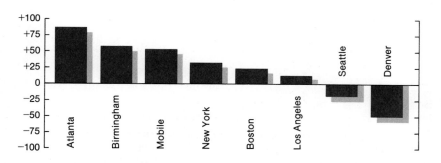

Huddleston & Sons
Percentage change in net income, 1985–1987

Source: Primary Data.

ILLUSTRATION 13.4

Example of a Subdivided Bar Chart

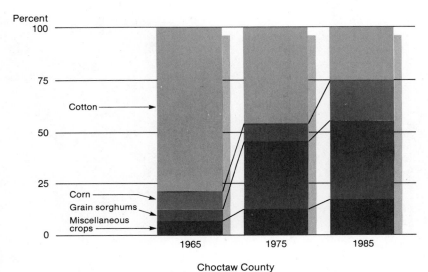

Choctaw County

Percentage breakdown of crop cash income

chart is sometimes referred to as a ''component'' or ''segmented'' bar chart.

Pie Charts

Use a *pie chart* when you want to show various components' relative share of a whole variable. The whole pie or circle is 100 percent, with each component having a lesser percentage of the 100 percent total. Each component is normally identified with a distinct color or cross-hatching pattern. To help further reduce potential confusion, each component's share or percentage should be noted, as shown in Illustration 13.5.

Pie charts are good for showing percentages or relative share.

Line Charts

Use a *line chart* (sometimes referred to as a curved chart) when you want to show a comparison of the level of a series of variables

ILLUSTRATION 13.5

Example of a Pie Chart

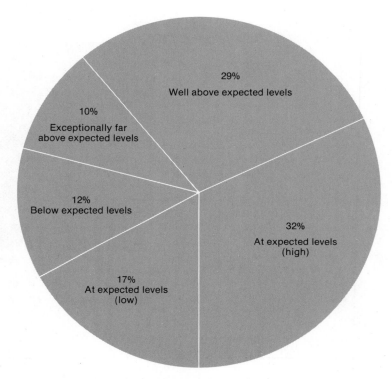

29%
Well above expected levels

10%
Exceptionally far
above expected levels

12%
Below expected levels

32%
At expected levels
(high)

17%
At expected levels
(low)

Percentage of people whose overall averaged rating was:
below, at, above or far above expected levels

by representing each variable with a line. One of the primary uses of line charts is to show changes over time. A line chart is shown in Illustration 13.6. A matrix or grid is normally used to plot the level of each variable.

The key advantages of a line chart include the ability to present a large quantity of information on one chart, use multiple lines or curves to compare related variables, and construct them easily.

Although line charts are easy to construct, it is also easy to make them confusing. Always begin charts at the zero point. Remember

ILLUSTRATION 13.6

Example of a Line Chart Comparing More than One Series

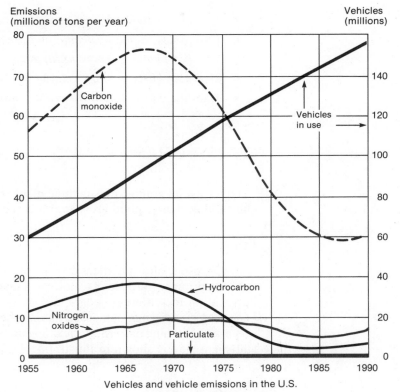

Emissions
(millions of tons per year)

Vehicles
(millions)

Vehicles and vehicle emissions in the U.S.

Actual and projected, 1955-1990

Source: National Petroleum Council.

that charts are supposed to show relative quantities or levels. If a line chart starts at any point other than zero, it cannot show relative quantity. When the variable quantities are such that it is impractical to put them on the same scale, you might still begin at zero and break the scale immediately.

Keep the scales uniform. For example, if the vertical axis begins with one eighth of an inch representing $1,000, then one eighth of an inch should represent $1,000 the entire length of the axis. In other words, do not change the vertical axis so that half of it has one sixteenth of an inch representing $1,000.

The following list shows when you might want to use each type of graphic aid:

- Use *charts* to show *trends*.
- Use *tables* to show *specific and precise data*.
- Use *bar charts* to show *relative trends* with the size of bars.
- Use *pie charts* to show *relative shares of the whole*.
- Use *line charts* to show *relative changes over time*.

OTHER GRAPHIC AIDS

Other useful graphic aids include maps, pictograms, organization charts, flowcharts, photographs, and cutaways.

Maps

Maps, especially statistical maps, are a common form of graphic aid. The primary purpose of a statistical map is to show quantitative information for different geographic areas. The quantitative differences can be shown in numerous ways, such as with colors, shading, or a cross-hatching pattern. A clear legend is obviously important. A statistical map is shown in Illustration 13.7.

Pictograms

A *pictogram* is simply a bar chart made with pictures, as shown in Illustration 13.8. The picture chosen to represent units should be relevant to the topic area. The coins shown in Illustration 13.8, for example, are obviously relevant to profits. Similarly, a picture of an orange would be appropriate for a pictogram showing the leading orange producing states. Obviously, the pictures should be of equal size.

Organization Charts

Organization charts show the authority relationships or the chain of command from the top executive all the way down to the first-line supervisors, as shown in Illustration 13.9. This is a very common graphic aid that can be found in most organizational policy or procedural manuals. The primary justification of an organization chart is

ILLUSTRATION 13.7

Example of a Statistical Map

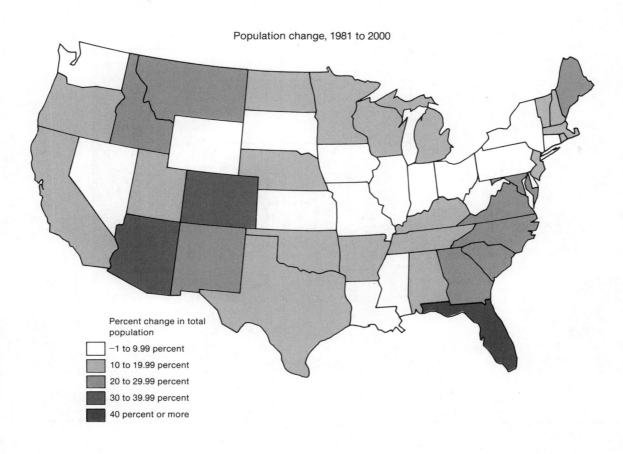

Population change, 1981 to 2000

Percent change in total
population

☐ −1 to 9.99 percent
▢ 10 to 19.99 percent
▢ 20 to 29.99 percent
▢ 30 to 39.99 percent
▢ 40 percent or more

that it can show an organization's structure and the interrelation-
ships between components much more easily than words can.

Flowcharts

A *flowchart* is generally a diagram showing the key steps and
activities of a process. You could, for example, make a flowchart
depicting the steps and activities involved in registering for classes
each semester. Illustration 13.10 shows a hypothetical decision tree
in a flowchart format.

ILLUSTRATION 13.8

Example of a Pictogram

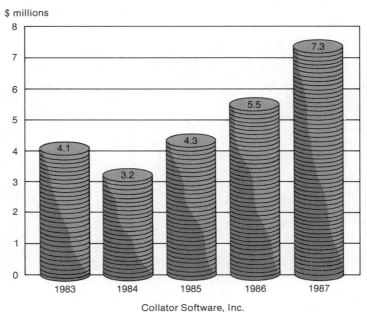

Collator Software, Inc.

Annual net profits after taxes

Source: Primary data.

Photographs

Photographs can sometimes show the details or tone of a situation better than any other graphic aid. Rapid advances in photographic equipment and procedures in recent years has led to the increased use of photographs as graphic aids. Note, however, that it can be quite expensive to include photographs in reports that have to be reproduced in printed form.

Cutaways

A *cutaway* can be of a drawing or a photograph. It is often used to show or compare components of machinery and other equipment as shown in Illustration 13.11. This type of graphic aid is frequently

ILLUSTRATION 13.9

Example of an Organization Chart

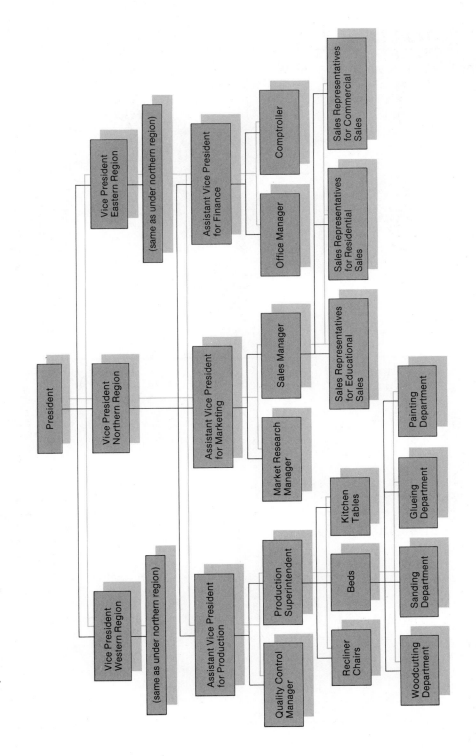

ILLUSTRATION 13.10

Example of a Flowchart

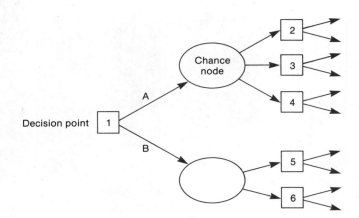

ILLUSTRATION 13.11

Example of a Cutaway

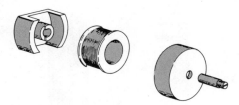

ILLUSTRATION 13.12

Examples of Computer Graphics

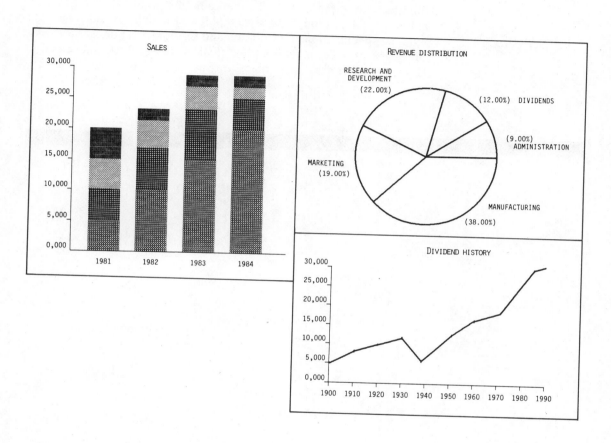

used in technical manuals. An ***exploded cutaway*** can be used to show individual components.

COMPUTER GRAPHICS

Perhaps the major current and future trend in communication graphics involves ***computer graphics***. With improvements in computer graphic technology coming almost daily, integrating sophisticated graphic aids into reports becomes increasingly possible.

Graphic aids such as tables, bar charts, pie charts, line charts, and others can be computer designed and constructed. Once you have the computer graphics software package, you provide raw data (numbers) as input and "tell" the computer what type of graphics aid you need. Although overly simplified, the point is that you provide the specifications for your aid and the computer does the work. This type of aid can save a great deal of time, effort, and money. Examples of computer graphics are shown in Illustration 13.12.

Application Exercises

1. The following tabular data represents an individual's expenditures for food for each week of the year:

January	$25	$28	$35	$22	$27
February	23	30	24	22	
March	24	32	32	19	
April	26	22	34	21	
May	24	23	35	22	30
June	54	18	10	19	
July	57	21	14	29	
August	27	20	20	20	
September	49	25	25	21	
October	23	24	25	45	24
November	22	23	60	22	
December	10	20	75	5	22

    a.   Write a sentence introducing this table.
    b.   Prepare a title.
    c.   Provide a source note.
    d.   Rearrange or add to the table to facilitate interpretation (e.g., compute averages).

2. Use the data in exercise 1 as the basis for preparing a pie chart. Is this a good use of a pie chart? Why or why not?

3. Use the data in exercise 1 as the basis for preparing a simple bar chart. Is this a good use of simple bar chart? Why or why not?

4. Use the data in exercise 1 as the basis for preparing a multiple bar chart. Is this a good use of multiple bar chart? Why or why not?

5. Use the data in exercise 1 as the basis for preparing a bilateral bar chart. Is this a good use of bilateral bar chart? Why or why not?

6. Use the data in exercise 1 as the basis for preparing a subdivided bar chart. Is this a good use of subdivided bar chart? Why or why not?

7. Use the data in exercise 1 as the basis for preparing a line chart. Is this a good use of the line chart? Why or why not?

8. Use the data in exercise 1 as the basis for preparing a pictogram. Is this a good use of the pictogram? Why or why not?

9. Which of the above graphic aids (1–8) is best for presenting the information in exercise 1? Defend your answer.

10. Assume that the pictogram in exercise 8 is part of a larger report. Write the section in which the pictogram might appear. Remember that the section should explain the pictogram.

11. Obtain a copy of a corporate annual report that contains graphic aids. Prepare a one-page memo explaining how the graphic aids agree or disagree with the principles in this chapter and pointing out additional opportunities for graphic aids.

Review Questions

1. Discuss the purpose and importance of graphic communications.
2. When should graphic communication be used?
3. Where should a graphic aid be placed?
4. Discuss the appropriate size for a graphic aid.
5. How should graphic aids be numbered?
6. Discuss the documentation of graphic aids.
7. Discuss the three major problems associated with misrepresentation by statistics.
8. Justify the use of tables in a report.
9. Discuss the proper arrangement of a table.
10. Distinguish between dependent and independent tables.
11. Distinguish between a table and a chart.
12. List and describe the three basic types of charts.
13. Describe and illustrate the four basic types of bar charts.
14. What are the key advantages of a line chart?

Key Terms

graphic communications
table
dependent table
independent table
chart
bar chart
simple bar chart
multiple bar chart
bilateral bar chart
subdivided bar chart

pie chart
line chart
map
pictogram
organization chart
flowchart
photograph
cutaway
exploded cutaway
computer graphics

Part V

Improving Oral Communication Skills

Oral and written communication skills are equally important in organizational settings. Remember that most managers spend more time communicating orally than they do in written form. Consequently, efforts to improve communications must also focus on oral communication.

This section focuses on three key situations that require oral communication skills. Chapter 14 deals with conducting effective interviews. Chapter 15 covers conducting effective group meetings. Chapter 16 discusses delivering effective oral presentations. Dictating skills are discussed in Appendix E.

Chapter 14

- ## *Chapter Outline*

Conducting Effective Interviews

- ***Learning Objectives***

After studying this chapter, you should be able to:
- Understand the common types of interviews conducted in organizations.
- Discuss the major strategies for effective interviewing.
- Identify and discuss the key steps in the interviewing process.
- Practice the major communication skills needed for effective interviewing.

Introduction

As mentioned previously, most individuals (including managers) devote more time to oral communications than to written communications. Furthermore, a great deal of time devoted to oral communications involves interviewing or conducting interviews. An *interview* is:

> a face-to-face exchange of information that has a predetermined purpose and a clear structure.

An interview is, therefore, much more than a casual conversation such as one you might have with a classmate or friend. It includes, in addition to job interviews, such exchanges as salesman-to-prospect, superior-to-subordinate, and accountant-to-client. The key distinguishing characteristic is that interviews possess a predetermined purpose and a clear structure.[1]

Although interviewing occurs frequently in organizations, consider the following observation.

> If you . . . tend to believe that interviewing comes naturally—like swimming to a dog—think of your recent experiences: the inept company recruiter who kept answering his own questions, the car sales representative who was determined to sell you a large sedan when you wanted a small economy car, the counselor who told you all of his problems instead of listening to your problems, the public opinion interviewer who asked biased questions, the encyclopedia salesperson with the canned pitch.

To most people, interviewing does not necessarily come naturally. However, it can be improved with study and practice.

Your initial participation in an interview will probably be as the interviewee when you enter the job market. Later, you will become involved more as an interviewer in the role of a recruiter, salesperson, or accountant. To help you better understand the interview process we will begin the discussion in this chapter from the interviewer's perspective. Chapter 18 discusses interviewing from the interviewee's perspective. Specifically, this chapter examines five major areas: common types of interviews, the importance of conducting an effective interview, interviewing strategy, the interviewing process, and interviewing skills.

Interviews are more than casual conversations.

COMMON TYPES OF INTERVIEWS

Although there are many specific types of interviews, most can be grouped into one of five basic categories: employment interviews, exit interviews, performance appraisal interviews, disciplinary interviews, and persuasive interviews.

Employment Interviews

An *employment interview* is one of the most important aspects of the hiring process. It is designed to obtain information about how well the applicant will do on a specific job. As an interviewer, you must attempt to determine whether there is a match between the abilities and skills of the applicant (or interviewee) and the job requirements.

There are two basic types of employment interviews. The purpose of the first, a *screening employment interview,* is to obtain specific answers to specific questions, primarily regarding whether applicants have the minimum desired qualifications. The purpose of the second, the *follow-up employment interview,* is to get a more in-depth interview that will answer the why questions.

A successful employment interview helps ensure that the right individual is hired for the right job. Conversely, a poorly conducted employment interview can result in a variety of negative situations. A promising employee prospect might discover that the job is not what he wanted or had understood it to be, and he might seek employment elsewhere. Or, an applicant might be hired for the wrong job because of a poor match between the individual's qualifications and the job requirements. Or, an unqualified or undesirable individual might be hired. It is the role of the interviewer to avoid these situations by conducting an effective interview in which the right person is selected for a job.

> The objective of employment interviews is to match people and jobs.

Exit Interviews

An *exit interview* is an important means of obtaining feedback to assist the organization in developing an improved environment for its employees. A successful exit interview can help management discover why individuals are leaving the organization. An effective interviewer will listen for verbal cues and observe nonverbal cues to determine reasons the person is leaving. These reasons might be a sign of trouble in the organization.

> Exit interviews help determine why people leave your organization.

A poorly conducted exit interview will yield no useful information and can actually be damaging. It can make a bad situation worse by causing the dissatisfied former employee to spread rumors that harm the organization's reputation.

Performance Appraisal Interviews

A *performance appraisal interview* is a regularly scheduled (normally annual) discussion between a superior and a subordinate. The subordinate's performance for the previous period is discussed and, sometimes, objectives for the forthcoming period are selected. This interview can have a large impact on an individual's professional growth if his or her strengths and weaknesses are discussed accurately, rationally, and constructively. It is also important because it often influences the subordinate's raises and promotions.

A poor performance appraisal interview can result in rewarding undeserving individuals or not rewarding deserving individuals. Either of these situations could lead to decreased morale, decreased productivity, increased employee turnover, and perhaps even legal action.

Information and motivation can be provided in performance appraisal interviews.

Disciplinary Interviews

A *disciplinary interview* is also a discussion between a superior and a subordinate, but it is not regularly scheduled and usually involves unacceptable subordinate performance or behavior. It is frequently a high-stress interview for both parties.

An effective disciplinary interview should pinpoint and correct the employee's undesirable actions. It should also result in improved relations between the boss and the subordinate. Ineffective disciplinary interviews, however, can increase employee antagonism and frustration, which can lead to low morale and performance, high employee turnover, and perhaps even legal action.

Disciplinary interviews should correct rather than punish.

Persuasive Interviews

A *persuasive interview* is designed to convince someone to accept an idea or take a specific action. Perhaps the most obvious example of a persuasive interview is the salesperson attempting to sell a product. In some situations, the interviewer must consider the employment interview as a persuasive interview. Other examples of persuasive interview situations include convincing your boss to buy a new piece of equipment, convincing employees to work overtime or contribute to a "flower fund," or convincing management that your annual budget should be increased.

Remember to present your listener's benefits.

An ineffective persuasive interview obviously results in the interviewer not accomplishing his or her immediate objectives. Further, if the interview is very badly done, antagonism can develop. This is often referred to as "burning your bridges" and reduces the probability of future success.

STRATEGIES FOR EFFECTIVE INTERVIEWING

To conduct an effective interview, you must choose the right interviewing strategy. Two major interviewing strategies are (1) the directive interview strategy and (2) the nondirective interview strategy.

Directive Interview Strategy

A *directive interview strategy* uses a structured approach for the interview. Closed-end questions are the major tool, and emphasis is on yes-no answers and other brief responses. A directive interview is characterized by questions such as:

- Have you been involved in extracurricular activities during your college career?
- Is your grade average above 3.0?
- Are you willing to relocate?
- Are you willing to travel?
- Did you work part-time while going to school?

Use the directive interview strategy if you need to maintain control of the interview.

The directive interview strategy has two major advantages. First, the interviewer can easily maintain control of the interview. Second, the structured nature of the interview typically generates more valid (comparable) data.

The major weakness of this strategy is that it rarely allows room for probing. Specifically, the interviewer generally finds it more difficult to determine the reasons or reasoning behind the various responses.

Nondirective Interview Strategy

A *nondirective interview strategy* is an unstructured approach in which open-end questions are much more important than closed-end questions. Probing and paraphrasing skills are, therefore, important. Nondirective interviews are characterized by questions such as:

- What kind of extracurricular activities have you pursued during your college career?
- How well have you done in school?
- How do you feel about relocating?
- How do you feel about travel?
- What kind of work experience do you have?

The nondirective strategy allows the interviewee much more control of the interview than he or she has in an interview using a directive strategy. The role of the interviewer is often one of an empathetic, nonjudgmental listener.

Use the nondirective strategy when you need in-depth information on selected topics.

The primary advantage of the nondirective interview is that it allows the interviewer to explore selected topics in great depth. The primary disadvantages are that it is more time-consuming, is more costly, and requires more skillful interviewers. In addition, the data may lack validity or comparability (i.e., with other interviews).

Which Strategy Is Best?

The best strategy is the one that best fits the interviewer's needs. For example, assume that you are a personnel director for a company and that you must interview a large number of people for an entry-level training program. On the first interview, your objective is to determine whether each applicant has the basic qualifications for your program. For this interview, you would probably want to use a directive interview strategy. On subsequent interviews, you would want to find out more about the applicants' attitudes and abilities. Since you would want the applicants to talk more, you would probably use a nondirective interview strategy.

THE INTERVIEWING PROCESS

Although there are many different types of interviews, the basic interviewing process remains the same. Five key steps can be identified:

1. Planning the interview.
2. Establishing favorable relationships.
3. Communicating the purpose.
4. Soliciting feedback.
5. Closing the interview.

Planning the Interview

Planning the interview ahead of time is obviously a critical part of the interviewing process. Effective planning involves answering the following key questions.

What is the purpose of the interview? You must define your objective or desired results for the interview. This definition forms the basis for choosing an appropriate strategy.

What is the best interview strategy? You must select the interview strategy that has the best chance of accomplishing your stated purpose or objective. For example, if your purpose involves obtaining specific information about a prospective employee (a screening employment interview), you would probably need to select the directive interview strategy.

What is the interviewee's frame of reference? Although the time devoted to anticipating the interviewee's frame of reference will vary considerably, it is sometimes critically important. For example, if you are planning a disciplining interview, you would probably spend a great deal of time trying to understand the events and issues leading up to the present situation.

Where should the interview be conducted? The environment in which the interview is conducted can influence the overall tone of the interview. Consider the differences in conducting a disciplinary interview in the boss's office, the employee's office, or a neutral location. The possibility of interruptions should be minimized. This requirement can influence not only the location but also the timing of the interview.

As mentioned above, the amount of planning needed will vary from interview to interview. You must ensure that sufficient time is available to think through the upcoming interview and to answer detailed questions.

Plan interviews carefully to achieve your objectives.

Establishing Favorable Relationships

One of the most important aspects of opening an interview is establishing a favorable relationship with the interviewee. Without a favorable relationship, the probability of conducting an effective interview is hindered tremendously.

Perhaps the key benefit of establishing a favorable relationship is that it reduces stress. Many interviewing situations have a great deal of stress or tension for one or both parties of the interview. The reduction of stress is particularly important because an interview involves the exchange of information. High levels of stress can greatly reduce the two-way flow of information. (An exception would be a "stress interview" for applicants for jobs that involve high stress, such as labor negotiators. In that case, a stressful climate is intentionally maintained to see how an individual copes with stress.)

Building a trusting relationship early in the interview helps reduce stress. Two points discussed earlier in this text can be quite helpful in establishing a trusting relationship. First, follow the indirect approach used for the no letter in Chapter 8. Specifically, begin the interview with a pleasant topic.

Second, remember the six communication behaviors leading to a supportive climate that were discussed in Chapter 2.[3]

Put the interviewee at ease.

---

1. **Nonevaluative:** nonjudgmental; based on descriptions of facts rather than on personalities.
2. **Problem oriented:** emphasis on solving problems and preventing their reoccurrence.
3. **Nonmanipulative:** oriented toward sincerity and freedom from deception.
4. **Empathetic:** attempting to understand others' frames of reference.
5. **Equitable:** participants have mutual trust and respect.
6. **Open-minded:** individuals are open to views that differ from their own.

Communicating the Purpose

Although the need for communicating the purpose of the interview may appear obvious, many interviewers fail to do so. Employees, for example, are often called into the boss's office without being told the purpose beforehand. In addition to creating stress, the employee tends to spend the initial moments of the interview trying to figure out the purpose of the interview. Unless the superior comes directly to the point, much valuable time can be lost and miscommunication can occur. Even when an indirect interview is planned, the purpose of the interview should be stated early.

Early communication of the purpose removes a potential communication barrier.

Soliciting Feedback

At the heart of most interviews is the need to solicit feedback. The questions asked during the interview should be designed to provide you with the information you need. This is the phase in which you implement the interviewing strategy chosen during the planning step and apply the interviewing skills that will be discussed in the next section.

In addition to listening to the answers to your questions, you should also attempt to gather nonverbal feedback (discussed in

Notice both verbal and nonverbal feedback cues.

Chapter 3). A good candidate, for example, normally maintains steady eye contact; uses appropriate voice modulation and inflection; demonstrates a high energy level through hand gestures, smiles, and general body movement; and responds to questions easily.[4]

Closing the Interview

Bringing the interview to an effective close is important. It is frequently a difficult task, however, primarily because of the different frames of reference brought to the interview by each party. For example, the interviewer and the interviewee may perceive completely different points as being the most important. To avoid this problem, either person can use a feedback mechanism such as, "Richard, to make sure that we are 'reading from the same sheet of music,' tell me what you think our major objective is."

This is the time for the interviewer to review any follow-up actions agreed on during the interview. After the interview, it is often desirable to follow up with a letter, particularly regarding major points and actions.

SKILLS FOR EFFECTIVE INTERVIEWING

Now let's examine the major skills you need to conduct effective interviews. These skills allow the interviewer to obtain more information from the interviewee. The three basic skills are listening, accepting, and reflecting. Accepting and reflecting skills depend on good listening skills and are particularly important for nondirective interviews. However, all three skills should be used throughout each step of the interviewing process.

Listening Skills

Good listening skills allow you to obtain information. They also allow you to apply your accepting and reflecting skills (discussed in the next two sections).

Being a good listener requires more than just remaining silent and forcing your mind not to wander (as discussed in Chapter 3). You must be an active listener, maintaining interest and quiet enthusiasm. However, you should not show active support (which elicits dependency) or judgment (which generates defensiveness). You should adopt a body position and facial expression indicative of attention. You should also accept pauses and help keep the conversation going with statements (in a nondirective interview) such as

Listening is an active rather than a passive activity.

"Uh-huh . . . ," "I see . . . ," "I don't understand," and "Tell me more about that." Most important, you must make sure you understand what it is that the interviewee is trying to get across, and this often involves both verbal and nonverbal skills.

Accepting Skills

Accepting feelings implies that you assume a nonevaluative or nonjudgmental posture during the interview. Acceptance helps build a trusting relationship that encourages the interviewee to talk further. If the interviewer is evaluating or judging the interviewee's feelings and attitudes as irrelevant or unimportant, the interviewee may sense this nonacceptance and limit further communication or respond antagonistically.

If acceptance isn't communicated, a communication barrier is created.

You should strive to neither agree nor disagree with the interviewee. The interviewee's feelings about the relevant issues may be the most important facts gleaned from the interview. At most, you might seek to clarify your perceptions of the interviewee's feelings with statements such as, "I gather that you really miss the people you used to work with," or "You really felt bad about that, didn't you?"

Reflecting Skills

Reflecting feelings is sometimes referred to as the *mirror technique*. This technique essentially involves restating the interviewee's ideas in a declarative form and in the interviewer's own words, such as, "You often feel that your boss doesn't listen to you." This is accomplished best by avoiding yes-no questions, questions that probe for facts (e.g., "How did you get the impression that your boss ignored you?"), and those that question the interviewee's judgment or competence (e.g., "Why would you feel that the boss didn't listen to you?").

Reflecting skills help encourage the interviewee to open up.

When reflecting feelings, you should reflect only thoughts that have been expressed. If more than one is expressed, reflect only the last one mentioned.

In reflecting back the interviewee's thoughts, you (as an interviewer) contribute three important elements to the interview. First, you become a more active listener. Second, the interviewee is encouraged to remain in charge of the interview process. Third, the interviewee is stimulated to explore his or her feelings in more depth.

Application Exercises

1. Organize into groups of three students. Conduct three 5-minute interviews. Each student will alternate roles: interviewer, interviewee, observer. The objective is to find out as much as possible about the interviewee's background. At least one of the three interviews should be directive and one should be nondirective. Write a one-page report on the interviews, concentrating on the effect of each type of strategy.

2. Interview a local retailer about his or her advertising practices. Prepare a one-page report on the interview.

3. Select a topic of general interest. Prepare two lists of 10 questions each. Make all questions in one of the lists leading questions and make all questions in the other list neutral questions. Have five people respond to each of the lists of questions. Write a one-page report analyzing the responses to these two types of questions.

4. Select a well-known personality and prepare a list of 20 questions you would like the person to answer. Have another student play the role of the well-known personality. Ask each of your 20 questions and follow up each question with two probing questions.

5. Interview someone who conducts employment interviews. Find out what kind of interviewing strategy and techniques the person uses. Compare the responses to what has been presented in this chapter. Write a one-page report on your interview.

6. Interview someone who conducts exit interviews. Find out what kind of interviewing strategy and techniques the person uses. Compare the responses to what has been presented in this chapter. Write a one-page report on your interview.

7. Interview someone who conducts performance appraisal interviews. Find out what kind of interviewing strategy and techniques the person uses. Compare the responses to what has been presented in this chapter. Write a one-page report on your interview.

8. Interview someone who conducts performance appraisal interviews. Find out what kind of interviewing strategy and techniques the person uses. Compare the responses to what has been presented in this chapter. Write a one-page report on your interview.

9. Interview someone who is involved in the occupation you wish to pursue. Prepare a list of questions to use during the interview. Find out as much about the job as possible (educational requirements, job description, working conditions, and so forth). Write a report (five-page maximum) on your interview, including the results of the interview and your perceptions of the interviewing process.

Review Questions

1. Discuss the concept of interviewing, being sure to distinguish between an interview and a conversation.
2. List and briefly describe each of the five basic types of interviews.
3. Discuss the purpose and need for each of the basic types of employment interviews.
4. Discuss the rationale for conducting exit interviews.
5. Discuss the rationale for conducting performance appraisal interviews.
6. Discuss the potential impact of an ineffective disciplinary interview.
7. Discuss the potential impact of an ineffective persuasive interview.
8. Distinguish between a directive and a nondirective interview strategy.
9. Discuss the advantages and disadvantages of a directive interview strategy.
10. Discuss the advantages and disadvantages of a nondirective interview strategy.
11. List and briefly describe the five key steps of the interviewing process.
12. Discuss the key questions that must be addressed when planning an interview.
13. Discuss the rationale for establishing favorable relationships in an interview.
14. Discuss the rationale for communicating the purpose of the interview.
15. Discuss how good listening skills facilitate an interview.
16. Discuss why accepting feelings is an important aspect of interviewing.
17. Discuss the concept of reflecting feelings.

Key Terms

interview
employment interview
screening employment interview
follow-up employment interview
exit interview
performance appraisal interview

disciplinary interview
persuasive interview
directive interview strategy
nondirective interview strategy
accepting feelings
reflecting feelings

Notes

1. Patricia Bradley and John E. Baird, *Communication for Business and Professions,* 2d ed. (Dubuque, Iowa: Wm. C. Brown, 1983), pp. 129–30.

2. Ibid., p. 135.

3. Jack R. Gibb, "Defensive Communications," *The Journal of Communications,* 2, no. 3, September 1961, pp. 141–48.

4. Helen Carl, "Nonverbal Communication during the Employment Interview," *The ABCA Bulletin,* 43, December 1980, p. 14.

Chapter 15

■ *Chapter Outline*

Conducting Effective Small Group Meetings

- ***Learning Objectives***

After studying this chapter, you should be able to:
- Explain the advantages and disadvantages of using small group meetings in organizations.
- List and discuss the major skills needed to plan group meetings.
- List and discuss the major skills needed to conduct an effective small group meeting.
- List and discuss the major skills needed to effectively follow-up a small group meeting.

Introduction

You have probably already spent many hours in various types of small group meetings. If your experience has been typical, you have also discovered that small group meetings are not always successful or pleasant. Do not expect the business world to be any different. The following are typical of comments repeated daily in offices across the country:

> "Oh no, not another committee meeting!"
>
> "George, I have spent six hours today involved in committee meetings and to be frank with you, I'm not sure that we have accomplished anything worthwhile."

Meetings, however, do not have to be a waste of time. They are, after all, an important part of conducting business. This chapter focuses on the primary skills needed to conduct effective small group meetings.

To conduct a meeting effectively, a group rather than a *collection of individuals* is needed. A **group** has the following characteristics:

1. The number of participants must be small enough so that each is aware of and can react to the other participants.
2. An overall group purpose exists.
3. Each participant has a sense of belonging or membership and identifies with other group members.
4. Oral interaction exists.
5. Individual behavior is based on norms, values, and procedures accepted by all members.[1]

There are three main reasons for conducting small group meetings: (1) to deliver information, (2) to receive information, and/or (3) to analyze a problem. The essence of a group meeting, therefore, involves an exchange of information, generally to help identify or solve a particular problem.

Information exchange is critical.

The success of a small group meeting depends largely on appropriate information exchange. The quality of the meeting, therefore, relates directly to the quality of communication during the meeting.

Before addressing the skills needed to conduct effective group meetings, it is necessary to look at the advantages and disadvantages of small group meetings. This will help you understand why it is important to know how to conduct *effective* small group meetings.

ADVANTAGES AND DISADVANTAGES OF SMALL GROUP MEETINGS

Managers spend a lot of their time planning, conducting, and participating in small group meetings, specifically committee meetings. These meetings are too often considered by the participants as a waste of time and, sometimes, as unnecessarily stressful. However, do not expect committee meetings to disappear—as organizations have become more concerned with participative organizational climates, input from internal groups has become an increasingly important part of management's decision-making process. Small group meetings are a needed and integral part of our business system.

Committee meetings are here to stay.

Advantages

Organizations benefit from committee meetings in three general ways. First, the quality of decisions made by committee can be better than the quality of individual decisions. You have probably heard the old saying, "Two heads are better than one." This is usually true—especially when the decisions affect a business and its employees. A group setting can also bring together input from a variety of sources. The functional areas of marketing, production, finance, and personnel, for example, might meet to discuss new product ideas. Each would discuss the effect on his or her department, thus making for a more informed decision than if only one department's opinions were considered. This process eliminates a great deal of individual bias.

Committee meetings allow joint decision making, . . .

Second, a problem that is analyzed and/or resolved by a committee can have a positive impact on the organization's climate. One reason is that when members of an organization are asked to participate in a group, the participants may feel more important. Essentially, it can be a positive stroke because the organization has asked the participants for their opinions. For example, if representatives of all functional areas were invited to a meeting to discuss new products, a more trusting and supportive organizational climate would result. However, if new product decisions were made without consulting with one or more of the functional areas, a climate of distrust could develop.

. . . can improve organizational climate, and . . .

Committee membership can, therefore, improve the morale of individuals, which then enhances the climate of the entire organization.

Third, potential resistance to decisions is often reduced. Employees are more likely to accept a committee decision when they were on the committee or were represented by one of their fellow workers or colleagues. Also, they will often be more heavily committed to implementing the group's decision. For example, if every functional area contributed input to launching a new product, all would be more committed to making that product a success.

. . . create greater commitment.

Disadvantages

There are two major disadvantages of group meetings over other means of communication, and these disadvantages help explain why there is so much frustration associated with committee meetings. Committee meetings are costly. This expense is inherent in the small group process because of the time needed to prepare, announce, and conduct the meeting. Obviously, an individual can often make a decision quicker and with much less expense than can a group.

Committee meetings can be costly and . . .

Committee meetings can also generate or contribute to an unfavorable organizational climate. This is largely caused by high levels of stress, frustration, and antagonism created by the meeting. People leave meetings feeling frustrated for a variety of reasons:

. . . damage the organizational climate if not conducted properly.

- They may feel that nothing has been accomplished and, therefore, that their time has been wasted.

- They may be frustrated with the difficulties associated with coming to closure. Effective closure implies that an agreement has been reached. Without effective closure, much infighting can occur, resulting in bitterness and frustration.

- Unequal participation may cause frustration among the participants. If not given an equal chance to participate, group members may feel that they have been railroaded or forced into conclusions or decisions they do not agree with. When this occurs, group decision making is damaged and is usually replaced by individual decisions.

The rest of this chapter focuses on ways to ensure that your small group or committee meetings work to everyone's advantage and not to their disadvantage. Your chances of conducting an effective group meeting will be enhanced if you carefully work through three distinct phases: the planning phase, the meeting phase, and the follow-up phase. Each of these phases is discussed next with emphasis on the skills needed to successfully perform each step.

THE PLANNING PHASE

Good meetings do not just happen. They are the result of much thought and planning.

Determine Whether a Meeting Is Necessary

You must first determine whether a meeting is necessary. For example, could the overall objectives be accomplished with telephone conversations, written correspondence, or face-to-face oral conversations? Remember that meetings are time-consuming and can be expensive. They should be avoided when other less expensive and time-consuming means can accomplish the same objectives.

Don't have a meeting unless it is necessary.

Define the Meeting's Purpose(s)

Once you have determined that a meeting is necessary, you must define the purpose or purposes of the meeting. The purpose should be as specific as possible to show those attending what kind of results are expected from the meeting. To avoid confusion and promote efficiency, a meeting should generally have only one major purpose. For example, production supervisors might meet to discuss possible improvements in quality control procedures—additional purposes might reduce the quality of discussion. A well-defined purpose helps maintain focus and promotes shorter, more efficient meetings.

Develop a well-defined purpose.

Choose a Meeting Strategy

Once you have defined your meeting's purpose, you must select the strategy or technique that can best accomplish your objectives. You can choose from two extreme techniques: the interacting group strategy or the nominal group strategy.

In *interacting group strategy,* the meeting's leader presents the problems or issues to the group and then leads the group in discussion. This is a traditional approach to group meetings, and you probably have participated in meetings of this kind. An interacting group can be extremely unstructured or somewhat structured depending on the issues, the group members, and the leader. For example, a club president might introduce the possibility of a fund drive to help a disadvantaged family. He may then either withdraw from the discussion or dominate it.

The success of this strategy depends on the leader's skills and the individual group members. Unless the leader has good group leadership skills, this type of meeting can be dominated by one or a few individuals, and closure (a final decision) is difficult to achieve.

In the *nominal group strategy* the group leader uses a highly structured approach, which facilitates rather than controls the group process.

The nominal group strategy overcomes a number of the critical problems associated with the typical interacting group strategy. The nominal group strategy forces equal participation and makes closure (or arriving at a final consensus) much easier to accomplish. This strategy typically involves the following steps:

1. *Present the problem.* The group leader presents the problem to the group in writing and orally to ensure that everyone understands the problem.
2. *Generate ideas silently.* Time is allowed for each group member to write down as many ideas as he or she can generate.
3. *Record ideas.* The leader follows a round-robin approach by taking one idea at a time from each group member. This circular approach continues until all ideas are recorded (perhaps on a chalkboard or flip chart).
4. *Discuss ideas.* The group is now ready to discuss the ideas. The leader reads each idea to the group in order to clarify it. There is no discussion at this time as to whether it is either a good or bad idea.
5. *Vote.* A vote is taken to identify those ideas the group thinks are most important. For example, the leader might ask each group member to write down the five ideas he or she thinks are most important.[2]

Whether the interacting group strategy or the nominal group strategy would be most effective depends primarily on the specific purpose of the group meeting. A nominal group strategy tends to be better when you want to ensure equal participation from members or if idea generation is critical. Pretend, for example, that you are the chairperson of a committee responsible for recommending areas for severe budget cutting to the president of your company. You must conduct the first committee meeting, and you are apprehensive because of the dominating personalities of two committee members. The nominal group strategy would probably be a better choice in this

Equal participation is enhanced with nominal groups.

Nominal groups are good for idea generation.

case because it enhances idea generation while reducing the probability of one or two members dominating the discussion.

Determine Group Composition and Size

Your group should be composed only of individuals who can make a positive contribution to accomplishing the purpose of the meeting. If you have the authority to select each group member, you should select individuals who are capable of experiencing and promoting beneficial face-to-face interactions, psychological relationships, and common interests (such as in a goal). Note, however, that you may have to consider inviting certain individuals to avoid potential negative factors. For example, political and protocol issues can necessitate inviting certain individuals who will not or cannot make a positive contribution to the group. When this occurs, you may have to revise your group strategy. For example, if you expect an individual to try to dominate the group discussion, you probably should choose a nominal group strategy.

Large group meetings are naturally more difficult to conduct. Generally, larger groups have more complex patterns of interaction and require more formalized procedures to manage efficiently.

Optimum small group size has been a subject of controversy. Usually the lower limit is set at 3 (2 is a dyad), with some authorities setting the upper limit at 20. The most *common* sizes are five, seven, and nine. The key to effectiveness, however, is that the group size in a particular situation encourage face-to-face interaction, psychological relationships, and some degree of common interest (often involving a shared goal).[3]

Select the Group Leader

Now that the group is chosen, you must select the leader or facilitator. Successful group leaders tend to have strong interpersonal skills, those relating to listening and using feedback mechanisms (discussed in Chapter 3). The successful group leader/facilitator also tends to be patient, tactful, and unbiased. Essentially, this individual must be a good communicator to enable him or her to stimulate and motivate idea generation.

Group leaders need strong interpersonal communication skills.

The actual selection of the group leader is normally made by the person who put the group together—the boss. In fact, the boss will often assume the leadership role. Although this usually ensures that the group will address the key issues, it can also create problems. For example, group members are aware of the superior's authority and dominance and are often less likely to participate openly. When this lack of participation is expected to be a problem, the leadership role should be delegated to someone else.

Choose a Notification Method

Next you must determine the best way to let the participants know that a group meeting has been called. It is critically important that the individuals receive this notification far enough in advance to prepare for the meeting, including arranging their calendar of activities. Two or three days is generally considered the minimum time to allow participants to plan to attend a meeting.

The notification or announcement of a meeting should contain an agenda and should include:

1. Date, time, and place of the meeting.
2. Purpose or objective of the meeting.
3. List of specific items to be discussed at the meeting.
4. List of individuals who will attend the meeting.

Illustration 15.1 presents a typical memo announcing a committee meeting.

Multiple channels of communication are usually used to announce meetings. A telephone call the day of or the day before the meeting can often greatly enhance attendance.

Use multiple channels.

Ensure Physical Arrangements

Finally you must make sure that the physical arrangements for the meeting are optimal. Consider the following scenario:

> Group participants begin to arrive at the meeting room five minutes before the appointed time, only to find the door locked. The group leader arrives one minute late to find everyone else standing around waiting. Finally 10 minutes later, the group leader has found a key and unlocked the door, and the participants file into the room. They find that the air conditioner has not been turned on, coffee cups and ashtrays remain from a previous meeting, chairs are scattered in a grid pattern rather than around the conference table, the chalkboard has not been erased, the slide projector is missing, and the expected coffee urn is missing.

How would you like to be the leader of this meeting? The variety of irritants here are all factors that could contribute to an unfavorable climate, which in turn could reduce the flow of communication between participants and thereby damage group performance.

The key point is that you must plan ahead and make specific arrangements to ensure that the physical environment is desirable. Your considerations should include: room reservation, room size, seating capacity, seating arrangements, availability of audiovisual equipment (e.g., projectors, microphones, easels, chalkboards, po-

ILLUSTRATION 15.1

A Memo Announcing a Committee Meeting

DATE: December 5, 1987

TO: Management Development Committee

FROM: Mrs. Dora Herring

SUBJ: Conference, December 20, 1987
        2:00 P.M., Conference Room Number 3

Topic for Discussion:

    Shall the Acme Company establish a Management Development and Training department (MD&T)?

Specific Items for Discussion:

1. Advantages of a MD&T unit for salaried and hourly personnel.
2. Disadvantages of a MD&T unit for salaried and hourly personnel.
3. Staff required.
4. Cost (first two years).
5. Other business.

Distribution:

S. A. Jowes	R. T. Blue
W. H. Morris	H. L. Thomas
J. J. Jones	D. R. Arnold
D. S. Cochran	W. E. Mondy

diums), and refreshments. Although these items may appear to be elementary, they are important. Efficient arrangements can greatly enhance group performance. Similarly, shortcomings create a barrier to group effectiveness.

Seating arrangements are particularly important. The basic alternatives for arranging a group meeting are shown in Illustration 15.2. Each alternative is discussed below.

1. *Circle arrangement:* Allows for maximum interaction among all group members.
2. *Lecture arrangement:* Minimizes interaction and participation by group members; normally used for lectures.
3. *Rectangle arrangement:* Allows for moderate participation and interaction; interaction is easier to control and direct than in circle arrangement; used for a seminar or with conference tables.
4. *U-shape arrangement:* Allows for moderate participation and interaction; interaction is easier to control and direct than in circle arrangement; similar to rectangle arrangement.

You should choose the arrangement that is most compatible with your objectives for the meeting. For example, if the purchasing manager simply wants to give information to her 12 buyers on a new purchasing procedure, the lecture arrangement would probably be most appropriate. However, if the purchasing manager desired input from the buyers on the design of a new purchasing procedure, the circle arrangement would probably be more appropriate.

THE MEETING PHASE

The major factors that you should consider in conducting a group meeting are discussed next.

Develop a Favorable Climate

You should strive to develop a favorable climate early in the meeting. This is much easier to establish if you have conducted the planning phase properly and have provided for an adequate seating arrangement and a comfortable room temperature. These additional considerations will help you get your meeting off to a good start:

- Begin the meeting on time. (You should also strive to end the meeting as close to the published time as possible.)
- Open the meeting with a pleasant attention getter. It should make the members feel that their participation is important

Arrange room to promote desired interaction pattern.

ILLUSTRATION 15.2

Group Meeting Arrangements

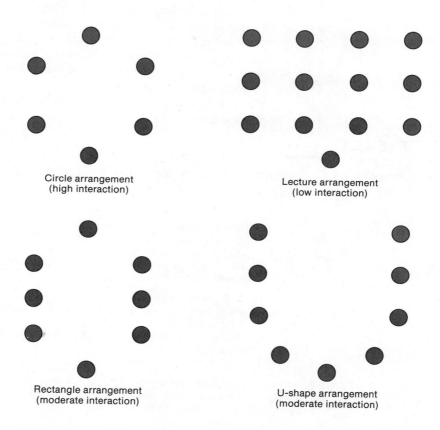

Circle arrangement
(high interaction)

Lecture arrangement
(low interaction)

Rectangle arrangement
(moderate interaction)

U-shape arrangement
(moderate interaction)

and appreciated. Try such words as, "Thank you for attending—with your collective experience and expertise, we should be able to solve this crucial problem quickly and efficiently."

- Go over the details of the agenda, even though the agenda is written out for the participants.

- Mention the purpose or objectives of the meeting, specific items to be discussed, and the anticipated time frame.

Encourage Participation

Remember that one of the primary purposes of having a group meeting is to obtain input from a variety of individuals.

Watch out for members who tend to dominate the discussion. There are two basic strategies for dealing with this problem. First, if you have anticipated this problem, you can select and implement a nominal group approach. As discussed earlier, this approach is very structured and forces equal participation.

Second, you can prompt more reticent group members to contribute by asking appropriate questions. Table 15.1 provides examples of good questions.

TABLE 15.1

Examples of Questions that Can Aid Group Discussion

To Define Problems:
1. As I understand it, the problem is . . . . Does anyone have additional information on this issue?
2. Would anyone care to suggest facts we need to better understand the issues involved?

To Broaden Participation:
1. We've heard from some of you. Would others who have not spoken like to add their ideas?
2. How do ideas presented so far sound to those of you who have been thinking about them?
3. What other issues related to this problem should we discuss?

To Limit Participation (directed to a dominating participant):
1. We appreciate your ideas, but perhaps we should now hear from others. Would some of you who have not spoken care to add your ideas to those already expressed?
2. You have made several good comments and I wonder if someone else might like to ask a question or make a statement?
3. Since all of the group has not yet had an opportunity to speak, I wonder if you would hold your comments until a little later?

To Focus Discussion:
1. Where are we in relation to the decision we need to make?
2. Would you like to have me review my understanding of what's been said and where we are?
3. That's an interesting comment. However, I wonder if it relates exactly to the problem that's before us?
4. As I understand it, this is the problem. . . . Are there additional comments before we come to a decision?

ILLUSTRATION 15.3

Example of Typical Minutes of a Meeting

Minutes of Meeting

TO: Mr. David Ware, Production Supervisor

FROM: Mr. Charles Z. Hill, Vice President

DATE: August 25, 1986

SUBJ: Minutes of meeting
August 24, 1986, 2:00 P.M.,
Brazilian Conference Room

Present: J. Barker, D. Williams, D. Jones, C. Edwards, G. Bell,
F. Wynn, G. McMinn, L. Thompson

Summary of Discussion:

1. Early retirement alternatives
2. Flextime alternatives
3. Additional employee lounge in Sector G

Decisions Reached:

1. Early retirement not approved
2. Flextime not approved
3. Additional employee lounge continued to September
   meeting

Action Items:

Description	Responsibility	Date
Investigate possible locations	G. McMinn	9–15
Budget analysis	D. Williams	9–10
Obtain employee ideas	C. Edwards	9–15

Closing the Meeting

A good closing to a meeting is just as important as a good opening. You want people to leave the meeting feeling that something was accomplished that they can support, even though they might not agree with all the specific issues.

It generally helps if you will summarize the key issues, review any conclusions or decisions, delineate any follow-up activities or tasks that should be accomplished prior to the next meeting, and mention the date and time of the next activity.

Close on a positive note.

THE FOLLOW-UP PHASE

Although the face-to-face aspects of your group meeting are now over, two key post-meeting activities are necessary. First, you should prepare and distribute the *minutes* of the meeting to all participants and to other concerned or interested parties.

Minutes are generally prepared in the form of a memo. You should include the participants' names, date of the meeting, subject, time, major items discussed, and decisions reached. An example of typical minutes is shown in Illustration 15.3.

Second, you should perform an assessment of the meeting. This simply involves an analysis (perhaps with other meeting organizers) of whether the meeting accomplished its purpose and whether anything was learned that might help in conducting future meetings.

Application Exercises

1. Organize into groups of four students. Select a common problem or issue for discussion without appointing a group leader. Examples of common problems are: (*a*) What are the characteristics of a good teacher? (*b*) Should college athletes be paid as professionals? (*c*) What is the value of a college degree? After discussing the problem, write a one page report on the development of communication in your group. Pay particular attention to the various roles assumed by individuals.

2. Repeat exercise 1, but assign and rotate the leader's role.

3. Repeat exercise 1, but use groups of eight students. Evaluate the effect the group size had on the meeting.

4. Attend a meeting of your local city council and observe the interaction of council members. Write a one-page report.

5. Attend a group meeting on campus and critique the meeting. Pay particular attention to times when the leader could have done something different to enhance the quality of the meeting. Write a one-page report.

6. Pick a topic that is familiar to a small group of five to six individuals and practice using the nominal group technique.

7. Pick another topic and use a typical interacting group format. Compare the differences between your process in this group with the nominal group technique.

Review Questions

1. Discuss the basic purposes for conducting small group meetings.
2. Discuss the major advantages of small group meetings.
3. Discuss the major disadvantages of small group meetings.
4. List and briefly describe the three major phases of a small group meeting.
5. List and briefly describe the six major aspects of good prior planning for a small group meeting.
6. Compare and contrast the interacting group strategy and the nominal group strategy.

7. Discuss the basic procedure for using a nominal group strategy.
8. Distinguish between a group and a collection of individuals.
9. Discuss the major factors that can help create a favorable climate for a group meeting.
10. Discuss the key issues regarding the encouragement of participation.
11. Discuss the importance of a good follow-up phase.

Key Terms

group
interacting group strategy
nominal group strategy
circle arrangement
lecture arrangement

rectangle arrangement
u-shape arrangement
minutes

Notes

1. Andre Delbecq, Andrew Van de Ven, and David Gustafson, *Group Techniques for Program Planning* (Glenview, Ill.: Scott, Foresman, 1975), pp. 67–69.

2. John K. Brilhart, *Effective Group Discussion* (Dubuque, Iowa: Wm. C. Brown, 1978), pp. 20–21.

3. Patricia Hayes Bradley and John E. Baird, Jr., *Communication for Business and the Professions* (Dubuque, Iowa: Wm. C. Brown, 1983), p. 200.

Chapter 16

Effective Oral Presentations

■ *Learning Objectives*

After studying this chapter, you should be able to:
■ Explain the major benefits of learning how to deliver a good oral presentation.
■ Discuss the major skills needed for an effective oral presentation.
■ Describe the key components of an effective oral presentation.
■ Practice the major skills involved in conducting an effective oral presentation.

Introduction

Oral presentations by college graduates are common today. Professionals generally have expertise in some subject and therefore may receive invitations to speak to a wide range of groups. As one speech writer noted:

> On an average day in Los Angeles there are 25,000 audiences meeting. In New York, it's 40,000 a day, ranging all the way from PTAs and high school assemblies to conventions, garden clubs, and service clubs. And they all want a speaker.[1]

Your ability to develop and deliver an effective oral presentation can have a dramatic effect on your future success because speech making plays a vital role in businesses. More and more oral presentations are made to groups within an organization. Specific proposals regarding such matters as budgets, sales campaigns, product improvements, and innovative ideas can be presented orally to decision-making groups. More firms are also finding out that speeches to outside groups can often be more effective than using the mass media because there is time to say more and an opportunity for face-to-face questions and answers. These situations include public forums, congressional hearings, conventions, and industry conferences.[2]

Despite the fact that oral presentations are made frequently, far too many presentations are done very poorly.[3] Just because a person is well versed on a subject does not guarantee a good presentation. Inadequate planning and delivery can turn good material into a confusing and boring monologue.

In addition, many individuals experience a great deal of stress when faced with the prospect of delivering an oral presentation. Uncontrolled stress can destroy even the most well-planned presentation.

You can improve the quality of oral presentations and reduce the stress involved in giving a presentation by improving your skills. This chapter focuses on helping you develop those basic skills needed to deliver an effective oral presentation.

Good oral presentation skills are important for business people.

Good skills can help reduce stress by building confidence.

BENEFITS OF GOOD
ORAL PRESENTATIONS

An oral presentation generally has one or a combination of the following purposes: to deliver information, to persuade, or to entertain. You may already have delivered an oral presentation in one of your classes for one (or more) of these purposes. You are quite likely to encounter additional opportunities in the future. Good oral presentations generate a variety of potential benefits, including stress reduction, enhanced self-esteem, job acquisition, professional success, and improved organizational image.

Stress Reduction

As mentioned earlier, the prospect of delivering an oral presentation to a group creates a great deal of stress for many individuals. In fact, a survey of 3,000 Americans found that most feared making an oral presentation. While only 19 percent admitted to fearing death, 41 percent feared giving presentations.[4] To help illustrate this issue, consider the following story:

Many people fear oral presentations.

You are a young executive and have just agreed to give a noon luncheon presentation to the local Kiwanis Club. You notice that every time you begin thinking about the presentation, you start to feel rather anxious. The frequency and intensity of the anxiety or stress increases as you get closer to the time of the presentation. On the day of the presentation, your stress level is so high that you are actually considering backing out of the speech.

When you arrive, they ask you to sit in front of the audience at the head table, and then they shove a dinner in front of you. After picking over your food for interminable minutes, you are finally introduced as the guest speaker.

You stand up (knees feeling rather weak), step up to the podium, and look out at the audience. To help hide your visible stress symptoms, including pounding heart, rivers of perspiration, and trembling hands, you grab the podium in a death grip. Your voice squeaks and cracks as you determinedly begin the presentation; this further increases your stress level. Soon, however, your trembling hands begin to affect the stability of the podium. You hold on even tighter and haltingly read through the entire speech in 15 minutes, then gratefully stumble back to your seat.

You experience tremendous relief that you made it through the speech, but you find that you do not feel particularly good about it. You know that you did a dreadful job and that you embarrassed yourself and your organization. Your self-esteem and confidence are low, and you are fearful that word of your fiasco will get back to your boss. You vow that you will never again deliver an oral presentation to a group.

Experiencing stress before and during an oral presentation is perfectly natural! Your burden is to reduce and control stress, rather than attempt to eliminate it. In fact, many excellent speakers feel that stress—as long as it is under control—contributes positively to an oral presentation.

Reducing and controlling stress is predicated on two basic factors. First, you must have developed the skills necessary to deliver an effective oral presentation. Second, you must have the confidence that you can deliver an effective oral presentation. This confidence comes largely from good preparation and experience. Essentially, one good presentation leads to another.

Enhanced Self-Esteem

Most people find that delivering oral presentations has a strong impact on their psychological state. Delivering a good oral presentation tends to enhance self-esteem. Similarly, giving a poor oral presentation (assuming the presenter recognizes it as poor) lowers self-esteem and undermines self-confidence.

Job Acquisition

The ability to give a good oral presentation can sometimes help you in your job acquisition efforts. Although most of your oral communications with prospective employers will involve one-on-one communication, opportunities for formal or informal presentations sometimes arise. Consider the following true story:

> Jay had recently obtained his bachelor's degree and had arranged an interview with a major U.S. corporation for an entry-level sales job. He was met at the airport late one afternoon by a company representative. After dinner, he was taken to his hotel and given a loose-leaf sales guide and flip chart. Jay's host told him to look it over because he would be asked to talk about it the next day. Taking the comment seriously, Jay spent several hours studying the guide and practicing with the flip chart.
>
> Jay's interview began with several short sessions with individual managers. After about an hour, he was ushered into a small conference room and asked to deliver the sales presentation from the sales guide to six people. Less than 10 minutes into the presentation, he was asked to stop and step outside. Jay was crestfallen.
>
> About five minutes later, however, Jay was invited back into the room and offered the job. Unknown to Jay, he had been competing

with five other prospective employees, four of whom were receiving their MBA degree. All six prospects had been given identical sales material and the same vague instructions. Jay was told that obviously he was the only one who was both prepared and skilled enough at oral presentations to handle the job.

Professional Success

As you pursue your profession, you are quite likely to be called on to deliver presentations in a variety of situations. You may have to make committee reports to management councils, clubs, and associations; present proposals to management councils, clients, and government agencies; or give overviews of reports that you have prepared.

The quality of your oral presentations will have a strong influence on the impressions that you make and on your ability to succeed.[5] Good oral presentation skills can separate a good employee from an average employee.

Improved Organizational Image

Your organization's image depends strongly on its representatives. When you give a presentation to a group outside your organization, *you* are the representative of your organization. Your actions therefore directly influence the organization's image. If you deliver an effective and interesting presentation, both your image and your organization's image are enhanced.

THE FOUNDATION OF AN EFFECTIVE PRESENTATION

An effective presentation is based on two key building blocks. First, you must have *adequate knowledge* of the subject matter. Not only does knowledge provide the ammunition for the presentation, it also builds confidence and reduces stress.

Second, you must have the necessary *oral communication skills*. Superb technical knowledge without the required delivery skills leads to a boring and sometimes confusing presentation. Knowledge is of little value unless it is communicated effectively to the audience. To communicate clearly you need to fully develop each component of an oral presentation.

THE KEY COMPONENTS OF AN EFFECTIVE PRESENTATION

An effective oral presentation is composed of three basic components—introduction, body, and close.

Introduction

Your *introduction* sets the stage for the remainder of your presentation. If it is done properly, you will have your audience's attention. The audience will know the purpose of your speech and generally what to expect. Thus, your introduction should consist of three key parts: the attention getter, the purpose, and the overview of the organizational plan.

Your *attention getter* might involve an issue or situation with which the audience can identify, perhaps a rhetorical question, or a humorous story. Your attention getter should relate to your overall topic. For example, one well-known speaker often opens his seminar on communication skills by simply bellowing "Woo-Pig—Soooiiii!" After getting everyone's attention, he then goes on to discuss the implied communication value of this one drawn-out word. Many in the audience recognize his bellow as the Arkansas Razorback "hog call," and they can discuss a variety of implied meanings.

Never use excuses or disclaimers to introduce your presentation. Avoid openings such as:

> "I don't know much about this subject, but we will muddle through the best we can."
>
> "I have very little to add to what has already been said, but. . . ."
>
> "I'm not sure why I was asked to talk on this topic, but. . . ."

Be positive.

Such openings set a negative tone for your presentation.

Once you have your audience's attention, you should relate the *purpose* of your presentation. If you do not, your listeners will spend time trying to figure out just what you are trying to tell them instead of concentrating on what you are saying. While they are trying to grasp your purpose, they may be missing an otherwise good presentation.

Stating the purpose is the first step of an old speakers' cliché, "Tell them what you are going to tell them, then tell them, and then tell them what you have told them."

Next, you should provide your listeners with an ***organizational overview***. Your basic approach or framework should be outlined for your audience. This is especially critical if several key topics must be developed during the presentation and then brought together and integrated at the end. You might structure your overview statement as follows: "I'm going to talk to you about inflation, interest rates, and unemployment. Then, I will show you how they interact to influence our economy."

Body

The ***body*** of your presentation normally accounts for about 75 percent of your presentation time. In planning the content, you should first transform your general topic and purpose into a ***central theme***. For example, assume that you are to talk to a group of employees. Your planning might involve the following sequence:

1. General topic: Customer relations.
2. Purpose: Improve employees' customer relations skills.
3. Central theme: The key to improving customer relations involves improving skills that "stroke the customer's feelings."

The central theme is stated in one sentence, which can be quite helpful. Further, the full central theme can sometimes be recalled via the use of one key word. In this case it might be the word *feelings*.

As you develop the body of your presentation you will incorporate both main ideas and supporting ideas. ***Main ideas*** are those key topics that are used to buttress the central theme. A common rule of thumb is that most individuals cannot retain more than four or five main ideas. The customer relations central theme, for example, might be developed with the following main ideas:

Limit your presentation to a few main ideas.

1. Customers patronize a given organization because they *feel* like it.
2. Positive and negative strokes have an impact on customers' feelings.
3. Verbal and nonverbal skills are needed for positive stroking.

Supporting ideas are used to explain, substantiate, prove, and reinforce the main ideas. Your support can assume the form of statistics, examples, analogies, and quotations. In choosing the various forms of support, you should consider questions such as the following:

For Statistics:
Will the audience understand the statistics?
Will the audience believe the statistics?

For Examples:
Will the audience understand the example?
Is the example clearly related to the central theme and main ideas?

For Analogies:
Is the analogy appropriate?
Will the audience be able to relate the analogy to the main idea?

For Quotations:
Will the audience recognize the individual being quoted?
Will the audience recognize the individual being quoted as an authority on the subject?

The body of your presentation must follow a logical sequence. Alternative logical sequences may be chronological, cause-and-effect, deductive, inductive, or problem-and-solution developments.

Close

Your *close* can take the form of a summary, conclusions, and/or recommendations. If a summary is appropriate, your major objective should be to fix the central theme in the minds of the audience. If your presentation has been an examination and interpretation of a body of evidence, a summary of the evidence *and* your conclusion would be appropriate. In other situations, you might need to state recommendations, such as suggesting a specific course of action, proposing a solution, or requesting approval.

THE ORAL PRESENTATION SKILLS

A variety of oral presentation skills are discussed in this section. The framework for our discussion involves three basic phases: (1) planning and preparation, (2) delivery, and (3) follow-up.

Planning and Preparation

Planning and preparing for an oral presentation require a myriad of specific tasks. These tasks focus on planning the content and on planning the actual delivery.

Planning Your Content.   There are four key steps in planning your content. First, *define your topic*. Sometimes you might be asked to give a presentation on a specific topic or central theme, while other times you may be free to choose your own topic and central theme. In either situation, you must carefully define the boundaries of the topic and the central theme. For example, assume that you are a personnel director and have been asked to speak to a collegiate organization on jobs. What will you talk about? You could interpret the topic as any of the following:

1. How to find a job.
2. Job alternatives in business.
3. Job alternatives in personnel management.
4. A forecast of job availability.
5. Job possibilities at ABC Corporation.

When receiving a general or vague request, you must ask enough questions to get a clear understanding of what the request actually means.

Second, *research your topic*. You have perhaps one or two topics for which you could plan an effective presentation without gathering additional information. Unfortunately, most of your oral presentations will probably be on topics for which you do not have all of the information you need. Refer to Chapter 10 for specific research steps.

Third, *anticipate your listeners' frames of reference*. The objective of your research is to provide you with knowledge. It is a comforting feeling when you step up to a podium and know that you know more about your specific topic than your audience does. The key to this feeling lies in anticipating the audience's frame of reference. You should also try to anticipate exactly what the audience wants or needs to know about your topic. For example, undergraduate students, doctoral students, and professors have different frames of reference—you would therefore need to deliver a different presentation to each group on the topic, "The Job Market."

Fourth, *organize your presentation*. The information you have assembled must be presented in a logical order or sequence. If your listeners cannot easily follow your presentation, you will probably lose their attention. A good outline can help you develop a logical organizational plan.

Planning Your Delivery.   Unfortunately, this aspect of planning a presentation is usually the most neglected one. A poor delivery can destroy a presentation, even if you are knowledgeable and the content is superb.

Seek a common frame of reference with your audience.

One of the primary factors influencing the type of delivery you should use is the facility in which you will be making your presentation. You need to know the following:

1. How large is the room?
2. How large is the room relative to the audience size?
3. Will the room be arranged in lecture style? Conference style? Circular?
4. Is there a podium?
5. Is there an electronic speaker system?
6. What kind of lighting is available?
7. Will ashtrays and water be made available?
8. Are there adequate electrical outlets for audiovisual equipment?

Although you, as a speaker, may not have much influence or control over the answers to the above questions, you need to know the answers so that you can tailor your presentation to the conditions.

Second, you should analyze the need for incorporating visual aids into your delivery. Visual aids help you appeal to more senses. You must determine which types would help improve your presentation and whether or not they are available.

Visual aids can help clarify your major points.

In choosing visual aids, remember that your objective is to use those that improve your presentation. Visual aids can add vitality and polish your presentation.

There are, however, certain problems inherent in using visual aids. They can be overused. Too many or too many different types can create confusion. Audiovisual equipment can create immense stress for a speaker. You may have to bring your own equipment, which might involve logistical problems. And you must have contingency plans for emergencies such as the slide projector bulb blowing out during your presentation.

Be in control of your visual aids—plan for contingencies to help reduce stress.

If you provide handouts for the audience, you must allow time for the audience to read the material. They are going to read it anyway, so you must plan for this in order to maintain control of your presentation.

Actual Delivery

If you plan well and prepare well, your presentation should be relatively easy to deliver. To make it even easier, follow these five tips:

1. Project enthusiasm.
2. Use eye contact effectively.

3. Use visual aids effectively.
4. Handle questions effectively.
5. Obtain feedback.

Project Enthusiasm.   Enthusiasm is internal energy that is manifested primarily through nonverbal communication. Projecting enthusiasm is important for several reasons. It is contagious. If you project enthusiasm, your audience is likely to reflect your attitude by also showing enthusiasm.

Your enthusiasm helps you obtain and maintain audience attention. And enthusiasm serves as a positive outlet for stress. Essentially, stress is energy. An unenthusiastic speaker with a high level of stress might experience trembling hands and a wavering voice. Enthusiasm, however, can help rechannel this energy to achieve a positive effect. The enthusiastic speaker can redirect stress-generated energy by moving around the podium or stage, using more emphatic gestures, and varying voice inflection.

Use Eye Contact Effectively.   Eye contact is critical in all forms of oral communication. An audience may feel that a speaker who does not maintain eye contact is shy, devious, or simply does not know what he or she is talking about. The effect is quite negative. Conversely, the effective use of eye contact has a positive influence because it makes people feel good, important, and involved.

Effective use of eye contact during an oral presentation helps make individual members of the audience feel that you are communicating to them one-on-one. It also helps maintain audience attention and interest.

Three techniques will help you maintain good eye contact. First, do not overuse your notes. If you have prepared properly, your notes should consist of no more than a brief outline. The more details you integrate into your notes, the more likely it is that you will keep your head buried in them.

Second, do not look at one spot in the back of the room, on the ceiling, or out the window. This practice will make you appear mechanical and uninterested.

Third, try to look directly at each individual in the audience in a random pattern. Your objective should be to try to achieve frequent eye contact with every individual in the audience, not just the three or four right in front of you.

Use Visual Aids Effectively.   Blending visual aids into your talk must be done smoothly. The following is a list of do's and don'ts for the use of visual aids:

Audiences like to listen to enthusiastic speakers.

Good eye contact can help you hold the audience's attention.

1. Make sure that everyone can see the visual aid. Avoid small visual aids (in relation to room size) or lines and words that are too small or light to be seen at a distance.
2. Present a minimum number of ideas on each visual aid. A visual aid is supposed to clarify, not confuse.
3. Organize the visual aids to fit your presentation. For example, don't put yourself in a situation where you have to shuffle through a stack of transparencies to find the right one during your presentation.
4. Allow sufficient time for each visual aid to be seen without destroying your allotted time table.
5. Explain each visual aid, including how it relates to or supports your main ideas.
6. Talk to the audience, not the visual aid. Remember that the audience will look at the visual aid when you look at it.
7. Emphasize the visual aid by pointing to it with words and actions.
8. Do not block anyone's line of vision with a projector or easel.

Handle Questions Effectively. Questions from the audience can be one of the major sources of speaker stress. However, effective handling of questions can sometimes be the highlight of an oral presentation. There are a variety of ways to handle questions effectively.

1. Recognize that questions will arise.
2. Anticipate and prepare for as many specific questions as possible. To do this, you must have accurately anticipated the audience's frame of reference.
3. If you do not know the answer to a question, say so.
4. Allow ample time for answering questions both during and after your presentation.
5. Make sure that you understand the question. It is good practice to repeat and perhaps rephrase the question. Thus, you ensure that both you and the entire audience has heard the question accurately.

Feedback can help you adjust your presentation to the audience's interest.

Obtaining Feedback. You must be alert to the feedback provided by the audience during your presentation. Obtaining feedback requires that you *be sensitive to audience-generated nonverbal cues.* The primary benefit of obtaining feedback is that it allows you to vary your presentation to match audience interest. Factors such as content, depth of analysis, organization, and use of humor can be varied. For example, if you detect that your audience is not particularly interested in the point you are presently covering, move on to something else. Conversely, if you sense that you have hit upon a hot topic, you might consider further elaboration or additional examples.

Follow-up

The last major phase of the oral presentation involves the *follow-up*. Your follow-up should focus on evaluating your presentation. Determine the answers to these three key questions. First, did you accomplish the purpose of your presentation? You might determine this from introspection, evaluating the audience's questions, or simply asking selected audience members after the meeting.

Second, in what areas was your presentation lacking? The checklist shown in Illustration 16.1 can help you evaluate your presentation.

ILLUSTRATION 16.1

Checklist for Evaluating Your Presentation

1. Did you use an effective attention getter?
2. Did your order of presentation lead logically to the close?
3. Did you use language specifically adapted to the audience?
4. Did you articulate clearly, pleasantly, and with proper emphasis?
5. Did you use proper grammar and pronunciation?
6. Were you enthusiastic and confident?
7. Did you use nonverbal language effectively?
8. Did you use eye contact effectively?
9. Did you effectively control your stress level?
10. Did you use enough examples, analogies, and stories to make the presentation interesting?
11. Did you incorporate visual aids effectively?
12. Did you handle questions, including hostile ones, effectively?
13. Did you state conclusions and recommendations quickly and clearly?

Third, you should seek ways and means for improving your presentation skills. You should formulate a specific strategy for improvement. Your strategy might simply be to do more extensive preparation for the next presentation. Greater strides, however, can normally be made through *practice*. For example, you might join an organization devoted primarily to enhancing its members' public speaking abilities, such as Toastmasters. Other alternatives include taking a speech class and practicing on your own or with a sympathetic friend.

Application Exercises

1. Assume that you are planning to deliver an oral presentation to a group of incoming freshmen. Your topic is "The Benefits of Majoring in Business" or "How to Survive in Business School." Develop a detailed outline of your presentation.

2. Assume that you are planning to deliver an oral presentation to a group of supervisors in your firm. Your topic is "The Importance of Effective Communication." Develop a detailed outline of your presentation.

3. Select someone you consider to be experienced and adept at delivering oral presentations. Interview this individual to find out what kind of techniques he or she uses to help reduce the stress of delivering an oral presentation.

4. Attend a meeting in which one or more oral presentations are delivered. Critique the presentations, discussing areas that could be improved.

5. Assume that you are to deliver a presentation to a group of businesspeople on the topic, "Personal Selling Skills." Develop five different attention getters for your introduction.

6. Develop a purpose and central theme for the following general topics:

- **a.** Reducing employee turnover.
- **b.** Reducing shoplifting.
- **c.** Improving employee morale.
- **d.** Improving profitability.
- **e.** Management by objectives.
- **f.** Increasing customer traffic.
- **g.** Reducing job stress.

7. Develop three main ideas for each of the general topics listed in exercise 6.

8. You are to develop a five-minute presentation on the topic, "Reducing the Dropout Rate in Universities." Develop five different outlines for this presentation, following each of these sequences:

- **a.** Chronological.
- **b.** Cause-and-effect.
- **c.** Deductive.
- **d.** Inductive.
- **e.** Problem-and-solution.

9. Outline a presentation to a group of travel agents on the topic, "Why You Should Vacation in My State." Describe the types of visual aids you would use.

10. Select a recognized television personality and list the gestures he or she uses to command attention. Identify and discuss those that are distracting.

11. Choose one of the outlines developed in exercise 8 and demonstrate how and where you would encourage participation during your presentation.

12. Select a speaker (e.g., politician, teacher, preacher) who you feel is very effective. Make a list of reasons that you feel make that person so effective.

Review Questions

1. Discuss the two major problems with oral presentations.
2. Discuss the major purpose(s) of an oral presentation.
3. List and briefly describe the potential benefits of an oral presentation.
4. How can stress be reduced and controlled?
5. How do oral presentations relate to job acquisition?
6. How do oral presentations relate to potential professional success?
7. How do oral presentations relate to an organization's image?
8. Discuss the two key ingredients of an effective presentation.
9. What is the basic purpose of an introduction in an oral presentation?
10. List and describe the three key parts of an introduction.
11. Discuss the need for and relationship between main ideas and supporting ideas.
12. What is the purpose of a close and why is it important?
13. List and discuss the four key steps involved in planning your content.
14. Discuss the major aspects of planning your delivery.
15. List and discuss the five basic skills that can aid you in the actual delivery of an oral presentation.
16. Discuss the importance of projecting enthusiasm.
17. Describe three skills for improving your eye contact during an oral presentation.
18. Discuss the concept of follow-up as it relates to oral presentation.

Key Terms

introduction
attention getter
purpose
organizational overview
body

central theme
main ideas
supporting ideas
close
follow-up

Notes

1. C. A. Boyle, "A Few Words About Speeches," *Vital Speeches of the Day,* September 1, 1975, p. 687.

2. Randall Capps, Carley H. Dodd, and Larry James Winn, *Communication for the Business and Professional Speaker* (New York: Macmillan, 1981), p. 172.

3. G. Busse, "Ghostwriters in the Executive Suite," *TWA Ambassador,* June 1978, pp. 42–45.

4. Richard Huseman, James Lahiff, and John D. Hatfield, *Business Communication: Strategies and Skills* (Hinsdale, Ill.: Dryden Press, 1981), p. 273.

5. Phillip V. Lewis, *Organizational Communication: The Essense of Effective Management* (Columbus, Ohio: Grid, 1980), p. 217.

Part VI

Improving Career Communication Skills

Part VI is designed to help you assimilate the knowledge and skills discussed in Parts I through V and apply them specifically to job search and career situations. Chapter 17 focuses on the research aspects of the overall career process. Chapter 18 focuses on both the oral and written communication skills needed in the job search process.

Chapter 17

- ## *Chapter Outline*

INTRODUCTION
CONDUCT A SELF–ANALYSIS
  Testing
  Personal Inventory
SELECT A JOB TARGET
ANALYZE THE JOB MARKET

Careers and Research

- **Learning Objectives**

After studying this chapter, you should be able to:
- Explain the steps involved in the career process.
- Conduct a self-analysis.
- Select a job target.
- Analyze the job market.

Introduction

Your communication skills can help you select the right job target.

Before studying specific career communication skills, you must have a thorough understanding of the overall career process. This brief, but important, chapter presents an overview of the career process. Your career process involves combining research skills and communication skills to analyze career alternatives, to determine career objectives, and to begin searching for a job.

You will find that both research and communication skills will be important in your career process. For example, you will need to gather and analyze information about your talents and interests and relate that information to potential employers and careers. Only when your research is complete will you be ready to focus your communication skills directly on potential employers.

Illustration 17.1 presents the career process model used to structure and integrate this chapter and Chapter 18. Note that the first three steps of the model focus on career planning and the related research skills. The last three steps (covered in Chapter 18) then focus on the job search and its related communication skills.

ILLUSTRATION 17.1

Career Process Model

I.	Conduct a self-analysis	
II.	Select a job target	Research Skills
III.	Analyze the job market	
IV.	Prepare a resume	
V.	Prepare an application letter	Communication Skills
VI.	Prepare for job interview	

CONDUCT A SELF-ANALYSIS

Identifying an appropriate career and the appropriate entry-level job involves matching *you* with desirable opportunities. Therefore, you must first conduct a *self-analysis* to identify your individual skills, interests, and abilities. One leading career consultant refers to this as the *career discovery process.*

Study your strengths and weaknesses to help find the career path that is right for you.

Most people begin their career planning facing a major barrier. How many times have you heard or made a statement such as this: "I just don't know what I want to do." Actually, this is not an unusual condition for young people. One of the major purposes of a self-analysis is to help you solve this dilemma. Essentially, it can help you choose one or more career objectives. A *career objective* simply states the overall results you expect from a career and sets the general direction for the remainder of your planning.

Consider the following quote:

> The problem with most resumes is not so much the form of them, although that is bad enough, it is deeper than that. It's that the people who write them aren't really in touch with who they are—what they have to offer—their magnificence, if you will, and it shows. Tell them not to rush into the resume right away—to sit back and take inventory first.[1]

This quote, provided by an employment manager for one of the nation's largest corporations, emphasizes the significance of conducting a thorough self-analysis. It focuses on the need for introspection and taking a personal inventory.

You must look at what you are, what you have done, what you have done well, and what you like to do. Essentially, you need a list of your major interests and skills. There are two major approaches for conducting a self-analysis: (1) testing and (2) personal inventory.

Testing

A wide variety of tests are available to help in your career discovery. Most of these tests focus on identifying your interests, your personal attributes or personality characteristics, or your specific skills. You may have taken one, for example, in high school to help you choose a major in college.

The Strong Vocational Interest Blank is an example of an *interest test.* It compares your interests with the interests of people in a variety of careers. You might find from taking this test, for example, that your interests are similar to people who are successful in the fields of real estate sales, insurance sales, and computer sales. You might also find that your interests are not like those people who have been successful in fields such as chemistry, engineering, and architecture.

The Minnesota Multi-Faceted Personality Inventory and the Wonderlich Personality Inventory are examples of *personality tests.* Tests such as these can help you identify your major personality attributes or characteristics. For example, you can find out whether you are primarily an introvert or an extrovert. This bit of information might help you focus on jobs and careers that are more compatible with your preferred mode of behavior.

There are a plethora of *skills tests.* These tests are typically designed to determine your strengths in such areas as typing, reading, listening, and many others.

Tests such as these can normally be administered by career counselors and clinical psychologists, or they may be available from university placement and career counseling centers.

It should be pointed out that there is some question about the validity of some of these tests. Essentially, you should view the tests as *indicators* rather than as the unquestioned truth.

Personal Inventory

The second major approach involves your own *personal inventory.* Your objective in making a personal inventory is to determine your interests and skills based on your past experiences. For exam-

---

ILLUSTRATION 17.2

Personal Inventory Work Sheet

1. What are the things you do best? Are they related to people, data, things?

   _____ related to _____
   _____ related to _____
   _____ related to _____

2. Do you express yourself well and easily?
   Orally: Yes _____ No _____
   In writing: Yes _____ No _____

3. Do you see yourself as a leader of a group or team?
   Yes _____ No _____
   Do you see yourself as an active participant of a group or team?
   Yes _____ No _____

ILLUSTRATION 17.2 (concluded)

Do you prefer to work on your own?
Yes _____ No _____

Do you like supervision?   Yes _____ No _____

4. Do you work well under pressure?   Yes _____ No _____
   Does pressure cause you anxiety; in fact, is it difficult for you to work well under pressure?   Yes _____ No _____

5. Do you seek responsibility?   Yes _____ No _____
   Do you prefer to follow directions?   Yes _____ No _____

6. Do you enjoy new ideas and situations?
   Yes _____ No _____
   Are you more comfortable with known routines?
   Yes _____ No _____

7. In your future, which of the following things are most important to you:
   _____ a. Working for a regular salary.
   _____ b. Working for a commission.
   _____ c. Working for a combination of both.

8. Do you want to work a regular schedule (e.g., 9 A.M. to 5 P.M.)?   Yes _____ No _____

9. Are you willing to travel more than 50 percent of your working time?   Yes _____ No _____

10. What kind of environment is important to you?
    a. Do you prefer to work indoors?   Yes _____ No _____
    b. Do you prefer to work outdoors?   Yes _____ No _____
    c. Do you prefer an urban environment (population over a million)?   Yes _____ No _____
       Population between 100,000 and 900,000?
       Yes _____ No _____
    d. Do you prefer a rural setting?   Yes _____ No _____

11. Do you prefer to work for a large organization?
    Yes _____ No _____

12. Are you free to move?   Yes _____ No _____
    Are there important "others" to be considered?
    Yes _____ No _____

Source: Adapted from Joan M. Bowser, ed., *The CPC Annual,* Career Planning and Placement Guide for College Graduates (Bethlehem, Pa.: The College Placement Council, 1984), p. 8.

ple, you might use reflective thinking or introspection to generate a list of the things you like to do and the things that you have done well. A personal inventory worksheet such as that shown in Illustration 17.2 can help.

The following books provide a variety of specific, effective approaches to help you make your personal inventory:

1. *The Perfect Resume* by Tom Jackson.
2. *Guerrilla Tactics in the Job Market* by Tom Jackson.
3. *What Color is Your Parachute?* by Richard Bolles.
4. *The Professional Job Changing System* by Robert Jameson.
5. *The CPC Annual* (Career Planning and Placement Guide for College Graduates) by The College Placement Council, Inc.

SELECT A JOB TARGET

Once you have completed your self-analysis, you are ready to begin matching your interests and skills with an appropriate job target. A ***job target*** is a particular work description or title in a given field or discipline. It is not a specific job position or opening; it is a job title for which there could be many potential employers.

Match your interests and skills to help find the right job.

The following approach uses personal inventory procedures (steps 1 and 2) as the beginning point for helping you select a job target:[2]

1. Make a list of 25 things you like to do. This list can involve either work or leisure activities. Label it Interest Areas.
2. Make a second list of 25 problems that you can solve in your everyday life. This is essentially a list of results that you can produce or things that you can do. Label it Skill Areas.
3. Rank each list according to each item's importance to you. Select the top five items from each list.
4. List the top five skills and interests on the grid shown in Illustration 17.3.
5. Select 10 intersections of skills and interests that could be translated into jobs.

The result of this process will be a list of major job targets. For example, a skill in writing and an interest in broadcast media might imply careers in areas such as advertising or public relations. Additional examples are shown in Illustration 17.4.

ILLUSTRATION 17.3

Example of a Job Skills and Interests Grid

Top 5 interests	Top 5 skills	1.	2.	3.	4.	5.
1.						
2.						
3.						
4.						
5.						

Source: "Job Grid," from *The Perfect Resume* by Tom Jackson. Copyright © 1981 by Tom Jackson. Reprinted by permission of Doubleday & Company, Inc.

ANALYZE THE JOB MARKET

Once you have selected a job target, you should begin gathering and analyzing information about specific types of positions and opportunities. Finding desirable job openings is extremely important, but it is not easy. Consider the following quote:

> One key to your success will be your ability to find the openings. If you rely solely on the published job market—the locally advertised jobs—you may be looking for a long time. Less than 10 percent of all professional managerial and executive jobs are advertised in local media.[3]

Another career consultant reports that 85 percent of the available jobs are not advertised.[4]

The job market research process involves discovering the names of employers who, in their normal course of business, generally hire

ILLUSTRATION 17.4

Examples of Matching Skills and Interests to Job Targets

The skill of *negotiating*
and
The interest in *working with people*

could combine in the following job possibilities:
1. *Labor negotiator*
2. *Arbitrator*
3. *Marriage counselor*

The skill of *purchasing/buying*
and
The interest in *business systems*

could combine in the following job possibilities:
1. *Office manager*
2. *Purchasing agent*
3. *Systems planner*

The skill of *communication*
and
The interest in *travel*

could combine in the following job possibilities:
1. *Travel agent*
2. *Tour guide*
3. *Convention planner*

The skill of *typing and shorthand*
and
The interest in *dancing*

could combine in the following job possibilities:
1. *Secretary to theatre manager*
2. *Assistant to dance instructor*
3. *Assistant editor-dance magazine*

Source: "Resume Writing Rules," from *The Perfect Resume* by Tom Jackson. Copyright © 1981 by Tom Jackson. Reprinted by permission of Doubleday & Company, Inc.

---

people for positions that fit your stated job target. Sources of information are many:

Your research skills are important.

1. Present and back issues of the *College Placement Annual*.
2. Present and past listings in your university placement office.
3. Classified telephone directories.
4. Business and professional directories.
5. Trade journals.
6. Professional associations.
7. Experts in the field, such as alumni, professors, or authors.
8. Leads provided by placement directors.
9. Classified sections of newspapers.
10. Advertisements in business newspapers, such as *The Wall Street Journal* and *Barron's*.

You should use sources such as those listed above to compile a list of potential employers for each of your job targets.

Once you have done the above, you are ready to use your communication skills to help you find a satisfying career. The following list contains some techniques for organizing information about possible employers for each job target:

- You should use a quick reference system for listing each company, such as with 8 by 10 index cards.
- Write the complete name and address of each company, including the names of people to contact. This may be someone other than the personnel director (such as the sales manager or production manager).
- If you have multiple job targets, code each card to a job target category and develop a file of cards for each category.
- Put such general information about the firm on the back of each card as primary industry and financial condition.
- Include specific information about each company, such as types of job openings.

You can now take this job target and company needs file and begin the process of contacting firms and selling yourself.

Application Exercises

1. Investigate the availability and variety of self-analysis tests on your campus. Have at least one test administered in each of the following categories: interest inventories, personality tests, and skills tests. Write a one-page report summarizing the results and comparing the results with your prior conceptions.

2. Prepare a report organized around the five steps associated with Illustration 17.3.

3. Prepare a one page explanation of how your present major is preparing you to pursue the job target(s) identified in exercise 2.

4. Choose a particular job market and conduct your own research. Consult at least 1 each of the 10 sources listed in this chapter. Prepare a one-page report on your research, with particular emphasis on the expected availability of jobs in the future.

Review Questions

1. List the six steps of the career process model. Briefly discuss the first three steps.
2. Discuss the purpose of a self-analysis.
3. Discuss the testing approach to self-analysis.
4. Discuss the self-evaluation approach to self-analysis.
5. Discuss the concept of a job target.
6. How can a job target be developed?
7. Discuss the job market research process.

Key Terms

self-analysis
career objective
interest test
personality test

skills test
personal inventory
job target

Notes

1. Tom Jackson, *The Perfect Resume* (Garden City, N.Y.: Anchor Books, 1981), p. 19.

2. Tom Jackson, *Guerilla Tactics In The Job Market* (Garden City, N.Y.: Anchor Books, 1981).

3. Robert J. Jameson, *The Professional Job Changing System* (Parsippany, N.J.: Performance Dynamics, 1978), p. 7.

4. Jackson, *Guerilla Tactics In The Job Market.*

Chapter 18

- ***Chapter Outline***

Examining Career Communication Skills

- **Learning Objectives**

After studying this chapter, you should be able to:
- Identify the major errors made in resume writing.
- Recognize the major elements of a good resume.
- Explain when to use the major types of resume formats.
- Write an effective cover letter.
- Understand when and how to use an alternative to the resume—the application letter.
- Use the major skills involved in participating in an effective job interview.

Introduction

Show employers their benefits from hiring you.

By now, you should know what you are selling and to whom you intend to sell it. This chapter discusses the communication skills involved in the following career-search activities: (1) resume writing, (2) application letters, and (3) interviewing.

Before beginning your communication efforts, you should consider Tom Jackson's universal hiring rule: *Any employer will hire any individual as long as the employer is convinced that the hiring will bring more value than it costs.*[1] Consequently, your overall purpose in communicating with potential employers is to show them that you can make a positive contribution to their firm. The best way to accomplish this is to target all of your communications toward satisfying a specific employer's needs. The importance of good targeting is highlighted in the following brief story:

> An east coast executive had done a mailing of 1,500 resumes and did not receive a single interview. He retained a consultant to rewrite the materials and 90 days later another 300-piece mailing was launched. The result was 22 interviews which culminated in four job offers. Needless to say, the importance of superior, creative work, combined with proper target selection was critical.[2]

RESUME WRITING SKILLS

A good *resume* is an integral part of an effective job search. You will need a resume regardless of the nature of your original contact with a potential employer.

A resume (also sometimes called a data sheet or a vita) is simply a written summary of facts about you. The relevant facts include your skills, interests, and experience. These facts should be presented in a way that shows the prospective employer that you are *results-oriented* and can be of value to the firm.

Common Errors

First, let's examine some of the most common errors found on resumes. According to a survey of employers, career counselors, and employment agencies, the 10 most common errors on resumes are:

1. *Too long:* the preferred length is one page.
2. *Disorganized:* information is scattered and hard to follow.
3. *Poorly typed and printed:* unprofessional and hard to read.
4. *Overwritten:* paragraphs and sentences are too long.
5. *Too sparse:* gives only dates and job titles with no additional information.
6. *Not oriented for results:* does not show what was accomplished on the job.
7. *Too many irrelevancies:* height, weight, sex, health, and marital status are not needed on today's resumes.
8. *Misspellings, typographical errors, poor grammar:* proofread with extreme care.
9. *Tries too hard:* fancy typesetting and binders, photographs, and exotic paper stocks distract from the clarity of the presentation.
10. *Misdirected:* too many resumes arrive on employer's desks unrequested and with little or no apparent connections to the organization—cover letters help avoid this.[3]

Avoid these common mistakes.

Most of these errors can be avoided by adhering to the characteristics of effective writing discussed in Chapter 5. Some specific resume writing rules are shown in Table 18.1.

Consider the poorly written resume in Illustration 18.1. It violates many of the characteristics of good writing. Now, consider the resume shown in Illustration 18.2. This is a much better presentation of the candidate's background. Although the facts are basically the same, the two resumes differ significantly in quality.

Elements of the Resume

The specific elements included in a resume vary from individual to individual and from job target to job target. The elements depend on the amount of an individual's experience and other important factors. The basic elements include:

- Resume heading
- Career or job objective
- Education
- Work experience
- Career-related experience

- Military experience
- Extracurricular activities
- Personal items
- Other information
- Date available

Resume Heading.   The heading of your resume should begin with the word *Resume*. It should also include your name, campus address, permanent address (if different), and complete telephone numbers.

Career or Job Objective.   This section is optional and should not be included if you have *not* concisely defined your career goals or job target. If your objectives are very specific, you should make a brief statement describing exactly what you are looking for—possibly a specific job title or titles. If your goals are very broad, you may want to state your career objective in the cover letter or wait to discuss it during your interview.

TABLE 18.1

Resume Writing Rules

1. Keep sentences and paragraphs short (no paragraphs should exceed 10 lines).
2. Use indented and bulleted statements (i.e., with * or < before each) where appropriate, rather than complete sentences.
3. Use simple terms rather than complex expressions that say the same thing.
4. Use quantities, amounts, dollar values where they enhance the description of what you did (e.g., increased sales by $50,000 per year).
5. Put strongest statements at the top, working down from that.
6. Have someone with good English skills check for spelling, punctuation, and grammatical errors.
7. Avoid excessive use of *I*.
8. Do not include hobbies or avocational or social interests unless they clearly contribute to your work abilities.
9. Avoid purely personal evaluations; be objective and results oriented. For example, say, "I have finished three major research projects," rather than, "I am an intelligent and diligent researcher."

Source: Tom Jackson, *The Perfect Resume* (Garden City, N.J.: Anchor Books, 1981), p. 77.

ILLUSTRATION 18.1

A Poor Resume

Poor appearance.

Doesn't emphasize
what the applicant has
done.

CONFIDENTIAL

RESUME

Name: Ben Wilder   Age: 45
Address: 1111 Rockhill Avenue   Height: 5′ 8″
              Provo, Utah   Weight: 165
Phone: (222) 333-4444   Marital Status: Married,
                                                                          3 sons
                                                     Health: Good

JOB OBJECTIVE: Position as a Manufacturing Supervisor

EMPLOYMENT:
1985 to Present   Present position is Machine Operator
1973 to 1985   Packaging Equipment where I worked in a
United Pkg.   small shop overhauling equipment.
Co.
1965 to 1973   Production Department, United Pkg. Co.

EDUCATION:
Woodrow High School, 1959
Interplant Courses—1966 to 1970
Itawamba County Community College—Industrial Management

Education.   List the schools you have attended beginning with
the most recent, because it is the most important. Include the name
of the school, location, dates of attendance, degree(s) earned, and
your major/minor(s). You may also briefly describe your curricu-
lum, abilities, skills, and accomplishments as they relate to the type
of employment you are seeking. Unless there is enough information
to add a separate section, you might also want to include information about your grades and whether you financed all or a portion of
your college expenses.

Work Experience.   List your present and previous employers,
beginning with the present or most recent employer. Include the

ILLUSTRATION 18.2

A Good Resume

Emphasizes specific responsibilities and skills.

Ben Wilder
1111 Rockhill Avenue
Provo, Utah 56788
(222) 333-4444

WORK EXPERIENCE
United Packaging Company, 1965 to Present
Machine Operator: Operate a wide variety of manufacturing and packaging equipment. Manage records of all related activity—hours, material, and total costs. Handle inventory control of machine parts and equipment.

Mechanic: Worked in a small shop overhauling packaging and other equipment. Scheduled planned maintenance for all equipment and maintained associated records.

Stock Clerk: Handled complete inventory of various raw materials, primarily boxes and cartons. Responsible for ordering, maintaining, and issuing material and all related records.

EDUCATION
Itawamba County Community College—Industrial Management Interplant Courses—Electrical, heat seal, tool and die, and pulp and paper equipment maintenance

name, the location (city and state are enough), your job title, and your major responsibilities. Briefly summarize the skills you acquired from each job and any significant accomplishments or results (e.g., employee of the month). If you have held many different jobs, you may want to be selective as to which to include on the basis of relative importance to your current goals and the recentness of the jobs. This section can also be entitled Experience or Employment.

Career-Related Experience. Many new college graduates do not have sufficient work experience to include on a resume. However, special class projects, internships, volunteer jobs, and extracurricular activities may have provided valuable and marketable skills. Follow the instructions discussed for Work Experience for this section. If the section would not be too large, you might consider a combined section for Career-Related and Work Experience.

Military Experience.   This experience can be listed separately or included under work experience. Include the branch, years in service, rank, special assignments, awards, distinctions, pertinent skills, and knowledge acquired.

Extracurricular Activities.   This is usually presented in list form and is sometimes called Awards and Interests, Professional Affiliations, Community Activities, or Hobbies and Interests. Include offices held or any additional responsibilities relative to your field of interest. Do not abbreviate names of clubs and/or Greek organizations.

Personal Items.   This section is optional because laws prohibit employers from obtaining this type of information unless it is job related.

Other Information.   This can be a vital section that tells the employer how to learn more about you. If you have (or will have) a credential file, a simple statement such as References Available upon Request will suffice. Or, you might want to list your references with addresses and phone numbers. (Your references should be job related.)

Date Available.   This is a short, but important, section. It helps the firm understand how to project you into their schedule of human resource needs.

Resume Format

The overall format of your resume also has a strong influence on its effectiveness. The key issues to consider are length, arrangement, and paper and duplication.

Length.   Limit your resume to one or two pages; many employers prefer one-page resumes. Exceptions are made for those with graduate degrees and/or extensive and important experience. A crisp style allows for inclusion of much information within the length limitations.

Arrangement.   Select the type of outline and form that is most appropriate for the amount of information you must include. The best resumes are simple, consistent, and uncluttered. The use of underlining and capitals to accent headings adds to the distinctiveness of your resume. Several revisions will probably be necessary to arrive at a form (and length) you find both attractive and easy to read.

Paper and Duplication. A standard size sheet (8 ½ by 11) of high quality white paper is easy to handle and is usually a good choice. You have several choices for printing or duplicating your resume. Each resume can be typed individually, but this can be time-consuming and expensive. If you have access to a word processor, many copies can be made relatively quickly. Offset type printing is inexpensive, attractive, and frequently used when many copies are needed. Copier copies are usually more expensive but are appropriate and frequently used. When choosing a printing option, remember that you do not want to give the impression that a copy you send is one of hundreds mailed.

Language and Your Resume

You should try to avoid using full sentences in your resume, with the exception of your career objectives. Rather, you should use brief, descriptive phrases. Also avoid using first person singular (I, me, my, mine). Be matter of fact without praising yourself. For example, "Awarded Outstanding Student-Teacher Honor" is much better than, "I received the Outstanding Student-Teacher Award."

Resume Types

Resumes come in three basic types: chronological, functional, or targeted. You should use the one that best describes you to a prospective employer. The three basic resume types are discussed below.

Use a chronological resume if the job is a logical next step in your career path.

Chronological Resume. In a *chronological resume,* all major sections and the items within the sections are presented in reverse chronological order. It is best to use this approach when your career direction is clear and the job target is directly in line with your work history. It emphasizes continuity and career growth. It is also easy to follow.

Note in Illustration 18.3 that the job history is spelled out beginning with the most recent job. Note also that the most recent job receives the most space. Titles and organizations are emphasized, and the duties and accomplishments within those titles are described.

***ILLUSTRATION* 18.3**

A Chronological Resume

Jack Raber
415 Spring Road
Bellweather, Alabama 94226
(333) 888-8888

WORK EXPERIENCE:

1980 to Present   White's Department Stores, Inc.
                                Birmingham, Alabama

Divisional Controller: Reported directly to the Chief Financial Officer. Managed cash funds, prepared consolidated corporate tax returns for seven companies and financial review of major subsidiaries. Designed and prepared a monthly sales comparison report for corporate executives. Cosupervisor of a 12 member staff that handled all facets of accounting for a $25 million company.

Chronological format highlights a good work history.

1979 to 1980   Anderson, Clayton, Inc.
                              Houston, Texas

Corporate Auditor: Reported directly to the Assistant Corporate Controller. Conducted operational and financial audits within the Treasurer's Office and five operating divisions. Developed a report with findings and recommendations for the CEO of each division and numerous management personnel.

1972 to 1979   Stephens, Wade & Company
                              Certified Public Accountants
                              Dallas, Texas

Supervising Senior: Joined the professional staff as an assistant accountant. Reported directly to partners and managers. Planned, supervised, and completed numerous audit assignments.

AWARDS, ACCREDITATIONS, MEMBERSHIPS:

1976   Certified Public Accountant, Alabama
1972   William Simmons Award in Taxation
            American Institute of Certified Public Accountants
            Alabama State Society of Certified Public Accountants

EDUCATION:
1972, B.S. in Accounting, Auburn University

Use a functional resume to orient major aspects of your background toward your job target.

Functional Resume.   The *functional resume* highlights major areas of accomplishment and strength. You can organize it in an order that best supports your work objectives and job targets. As you can see in Illustration 18.4, actual titles and work history are in subordinate positions (and can even be left off entirely).

The functional resume is best used in cases of career change, career redirection, first job search, or reentry into the job market. It is also effective when you wish to play up a particularly strong area of ability.

Use a targeted resume to focus your specific abilities and achievements on your job target.

Targeted Resume.   The *targeted resume* focuses on a specific job target, such as accountant for a transportation firm or salesperson for a major computer firm. If you have multiple job targets, you should prepare multiple targeted resumes. As shown in Illustration 18.5, a targeted resume lists only capabilities and supporting accomplishments that relate to the job target listed at the top.

You should use a target resume only when you are clear about your job targets and are willing to go for them. This approach makes a very impressive case for the one selected job target, but remember that it is at the expense of other possibilities. It also helps you demonstrate a thorough understanding and ability of the targeted area.

Review Your Resume

Once your resume is prepared, you must review and scrutinize it carefully, asking yourself three general questions:

1. *Are there gaps?* For example, if your four-year degree program took six years to complete, are those two extra years accounted for elsewhere in your resume, such as in Experience or in Military Experience? If not, a brief explanation in the Education section is appropriate.
2. *Is the slant (or emphasis) appropriate?* For example, a candidate for a management position should elaborate on previous activities relating to managerial skills as opposed to a long explanation of a waiter/waitress position.
3. *Are your descriptions adequate?* Curriculums vary from university to university, and summer jobs are not always clearly defined by their titles. Make sure your experiences are easily understood by employers by using brief yet descriptive phrasing.

A slightly longer resume critique form is shown in Table 18.2.

ILLUSTRATION 18.4

A Functional Resume

Susan Herndon
888 Carpet Street
Dallas, Texas 23456
(222) 333-0000

CORPORATE LAW
Extensive study of corporation structure, including legal rights, obligations, and privileges. Acted as agent for several corporations in various transactions. Studied decisions, statutes, and ordinances of quasi-judicial bodies.

REAL ESTATE LAW
Handled sale and transfer of real property. Instituted title searches to establish ownership. Drew up deeds, mortgages, and leases. Acted as trustee of property and held funds for investment.

This functional resume emphasizes ability and potential rather than work history.

INSURANCE LAW
Advised management of insurance company on legality of insurance transactions. Studied court decisions and recommended changes in wording of insurance policies to conform with law and/or to protect company from unwarranted claims. Advised claims department personnel of legality of claims filed on company to insure against undue payments. Advised personnel engaged in drawing up of legal documents, such as insurance contracts and release papers.

WORK EXPERIENCE
1981 to Present   National Underwriter's Company, Inc.—Insurance Services Office Supervisor

EDUCATION
1979   LLB, Tulane University Law School—Insurance Law, Corporate Law, Estate Planning, Income Taxation
1976   B.A., Louisiana State University

ILLUSTRATION 18.5

Example of Targeted Resume

Daryl R. Hollis
5555 Lucky Street
Jonesville, Illinois 44829
(555) 888-6787

Job Target: Elevator Engineer for Private Firm

ABILITIES:
- Providing professional services in research, development, and designing of elevators for large, complex buildings.
- Providing design for alterations and renovations of many styles of elevators.
- Full designing from start to finish of freight elevators, adaptable to many situations.
- Designing high-rise hotel elevators with special consideration to sound and lighting design.
- Designing complete elevation systems for shopping centers, including escalators.
- Designing elevation systems for hospital and rest home facilities conforming to full health and safety standards.

This targeted resume stresses what you can do or your capabilities for a specific job target.

ACHIEVEMENTS:
- Created designs for all county buildings and alterations thereto.
- Planned, organized, directed, and reviewed all engineering functions of my department's jurisdiction.
- Designed elevators for office buildings, data processing facilities, police stations, power plants, and other facilities.
- Produced schematics, feasibility studies, reports, and cost estimates.

WORK HISTORY:
- 1979 to Present—Richardson County Department of Buildings and Grounds, County Engineer
- 1972 to 1979—Bill Rials & Associates, Associate Engineer

PROFESSIONAL AFFILIATIONS:
- Corporate member—A.S.E.
- Member—Illinois State Association of Engineers

EDUCATION:
- 1970—Illinois College
- 1971—License, State of Illinois

TABLE 18.2

Resume Critique Form

Overall Appearance. Do you want to read it?

Layout. Does the resume look professional, well typed and printed, good margins, and so forth? Do key points stand out?

Length. Could the resume tell the same story if it were shortened?

Relevance. Has extraneous material been eliminated?

Writing Style. Is it easy to get a picture of your qualifications?

Accomplishments. Are your accomplishments and problem-solving skills emphasized?

Completeness. Is all important information covered?

Bottom line. How well does the resume accomplish its ultimate purpose of getting the employer to invite you for an interview?

Source: Gloria Reeves, ed., *Mississippi State University Placement Manual* (Rahway, N.J.: University Communications), p. 8.

Cover Letters

A *cover letter* is normally included when you mail a resume to a prospective employer. The basic purpose of the cover letter is to communicate a specific, personalized message about your potential value to the organization. In effect, the cover letter (1) introduces you and your resume to the prospective employer, (2) serves as an attention getter, and (3) encourages the employer to read your resume. A poorly written cover letter can completely negate all the time and effort you have expended on developing a resume. Several key techniques can help you write effective cover letters.

A good cover improves the chances of your resume being read.

Address It to a Specific Individual.
Write and mail your cover letter to a specific name. The most appropriate person to send your cover letter and resume to is the person who will be making the hiring decision. Addressing your cover letter to Personnel Director should never be done. Appropriate names can often be found in company literature and trade association publications. For example, the American Society of Personnel Administrators publishes a list of personnel directors. If you have trouble finding the appropriate name, a simple telephone call to the firm will often be successful.

Use a Personal Tone.
You should strive to use a personal tone in your cover letter. The opening line is particularly critical. It must

not give the impression that it is a standardized form letter mailed to hundreds of employers. Try to make your opening unique in that it specifically relates to the organization to which you are writing. Study the following good opening lines: "One of my management professors, Dr. Kinson, mentioned to me that your firm is experiencing tremendous growth." Or, "I see that you are planning to open a new manufacturing facility in the Stockton area." Also, avoid self-aggrandizement. You want to sound like a professional, not a huckster or a peddler.

Communicate Your Value.   Your cover letter should use the you attitude as you communicate your potential value or benefit to the organization. You should, for example, mention specific key skills that relate to the organization's needs. This also shows the employer that you are really interested in his or her firm and that you have done your homework. Such a statement might read, "My two years of experience in recruiting and selecting personnel could help you as you begin staffing for your new plant in the Stockton area."

Ask for the Sale.   Remember that your job search is a selling situation and that you are selling yourself and your skills, knowledge, and interests. Further, the purpose of your cover letter and resume is to help you obtain a job interview. In closing a sales presentation for a tangible product, you would naturally ask for the sale. In closing your cover letter, you should also ask for the job interview. The following closing illustrates this point: "I am going to be in the Stockton area the second week in May and would like to meet with you at your convenience during that week. I will call you around the first of April to set up a convenient date and time." Illustration 18.6 shows a results-oriented cover letter written by a young college graduate seeking his first job.

AN ALTERNATIVE TO THE RESUME—THE APPLICATION LETTER

Use a letter of application when your resume does not present a clear picture of your potential value.

A *letter of application* can be sent in lieu of a resume and cover letter. An application letter is a detailed letter to a particular employer that focuses on areas where you can be of value to that employer. It can be especially valuable when your resume (which is primarily a historical summary) does not present a clear picture of your potential value. It tends to be more forward looking, which is especially valuable when you have been out of the job market for a time or are trying to change careers.

The primary rationale for using an application letter is that the

ILLUSTRATION 18.6

A Cover Letter

Dear Mr. Kraft:

Software International's plans for expansion have been widely publicized, and it's clear that it is progressing rapidly. Your firm is very attractive to me and I believe that I can make a solid contribution . . . immediately . . . as part of your junior marketing management team. Without intending to appear overly confident, here is why:

A recent cum laude graduate, I have worked for the last three years on a part-time basis as Assistant to the Marketing Director at Hayden and Company. My earnings there have allowed me to finance my education.

In this capacity, I was exposed to a variety of marketing and promotion problems and learned how to deal creatively with them. In the absence of a senior executive, I was given complete responsibility for marketing to commercial users.

I am 22 years old, single, and interested in working with the kinds of challenges faced in the software industry. I have a BA in Business Administration from the University of Georgia (3.1 out of a possible 4.0 grade average).

Enclosed is a copy of my resume. If you can use someone with my talents, enthusiasm, and experience, I would appreciate the opportunity to speak with you personally.

Sincerely yours,

letter is sometimes better able to capture attention and create employer interest, as highlighted in the following quote:

> The combination of a cover letter and a standard resume will rarely produce as many interviews as a well-written letter. In a letter you can tailor your presentation to each target. You can discuss what you can do or arouse curiosity. Besides, resumes make it easier for readers to discover a reason for disqualifying you.[4]

A good application letter addresses specific employer needs that you have discovered through your research. It provides enough factual information to avoid the need for a resume, and it demon-

ILLUSTRATION 18.7

A Good Letter of Application

This application letter is results oriented and . . .

Dear Mrs. Kane-Smith:

I believe my extensive experiences with all-terrain vehicles and equipment would help your growing firm. Some of my recent accomplishments are:

- Managed an Arctic re-engineering and test program involving a wide variety of equipment. Performed duress tests and developed and prepared new profiles and reports to satisfy government contract requirements. Contract was completed within budget requirements and maintainability and reliability was improved 15 percent.
- Managed the experimental group and supervised three design engineers' efforts to construct a new prototype for a non-wheeled, remote-controlled system. The system is performing satisfactorily and will be upgraded in the near future.
- Supervised all aspects of several field tests including acceptance tests of new terrestrial and extraterrestrial motorized systems. Systems were completed within cost allocations and have operated satisfactorily.

My education includes a degree from Ouachita Institute of Technology and additional engineering and computer-assisted design courses on company and manufacturers' premises.

. . . reader oriented.

I would like to meet with you and see how I might make a contribution to your organization. I will call you in a week or so.

Very truly yours,

strates your abilities as much as it describes them. It is best used by those who have little or no work experience and who are willing to do the required research. Illustration 18.7 shows an example of a good letter of application.

INTERVIEWING SKILLS

Your interviewing skills are obviously important, as illustrated by the following quote:

Never beg for a job, you won't get it. Also, once you have got the interview and first impressions in, personality will be far more critical than your actual credentials. The first five minutes of any interview are usually as important as all other minutes combined.[5]

Jameson goes on to say that:

A winning formula for most interviews? Here it is. Handsome clothes, a hearty handshake, a quick smile, sincerity, genuineness, and an alive interest and enthusiastic personality. These things ideally combined with a talent for providing smooth articulate answers to the interview questions. . . .[6]

You need to develop your interviewing skills in three basic areas: preparation, the interview itself, and follow-up.

Preparation

Preparation should begin with the realization and admission that *you cannot go into an interview and try to "wing it."* Interviewers simply ask too many questions that require forethought and planning.

Find out as much as possible about the employer. Even though you should already have a sizable amount of information from your job search activities, you may need to seek additional facts, such as finding out more about their products and/or services, where they are located, and how stable they are.

Another key aspect of preparation involves following the proper procedures for arranging an interview. You must exercise care to avoid irritating the recruiter, by being overbearing or late, or by failing to provide complete or accurate information. If your interview is in your school's placement center, arrive early to be sure that you understand its procedures and that all paperwork has been completed. If your interview is in the employer's office, make proper arrangements by phone or letter. If an application blank is required, complete it. Be sure that you are on time, in the correct office, and able to remember the interviewer's name.

Finally, you should have the necessary paperwork ready. Take several extra copies of your resume. Since most questions are usually drawn from your resume, you should carefully review the resume. Try to anticipate as many questions as possible. Fifty questions recruiters frequently ask are shown in Table 18.3. You could also try to rehearse your interview with friends.

The Interview Itself

Interviews vary considerably. Most hiring procedures for entry-level positions, for example, include not one but two interviews.

Review your self-evaluation and the information you have collected about the firm.

TABLE 18.3

Fifty Questions Recruiters Frequently Ask

1. What are your long-range and short-range goals and objectives? When and why did you establish these goals. How are you preparing yourself to achieve them?
2. What specific goals, other than those related to your occupation, have you established for yourself for the next 10 years?
3. What do you see yourself doing five years from now?
4. What do you *really* want to do in life?
5. What are your long-range career objectives?
6. How do you plan to achieve your career goals?
7. What are the most important rewards you expect in your business career?
8. What do you expect to be earning in five years?
9. Why did you choose the career for which you are preparing?
10. Which is more important to you, the money or the type of job?
11. What do you consider to be your greatest strengths and weaknesses?
12. How would you describe yourself?
13. How do you think a friend or professor who knows you well would describe you?
14. What motivates you to put forth your greatest effort?
15. How has your college experience prepared you for a business career?
16. Why should I hire you?
17. What qualifications do you have that make you think that you will be successful in business?
18. How do you determine or evaluate success?
19. What do you think it takes to be successful in a company like ours?
20. In what ways do you think you can make a contribution to our company?
21. What qualities should a successful manager possess?
22. Describe the relationship that should exist between a supervisor and subordinates.
23. What two or three accomplishments have given you the most satisfaction? Why?
24. Describe your most rewarding college experience.
25. If you were hiring a graduate for this position, what qualities would you look for?
26. Why did you select your college or university?
27. What led you to choose your field of major study?
28. What college subjects did you like best? Why?
29. What college subjects did you like least? Why?
30. If you could do so, how would you plan your academic study differently? Why?
31. What changes would you make in your college or university?
32. Do you have plans for continued study? An advanced degree?
33. Do you think that your grades are a good indication of your academic achievement?
34. What have you learned from participation in extracurricular activities?
35. In what kind of a work environment are you most comfortable?
36. How do you work under pressure?
37. In what part-time or summer jobs have you been most interested? Why?

TABLE 18.3 (concluded)

38. How would you describe the ideal job for you following graduation?
39. Why did you decide to seek a position with this company?
40. What do you know about our company?
41. What two or three things are most important to you in your job?
42. Are you seeking employment in a company of a certain size? Why?
43. What criteria are you using to evaluate the company for which you hope to work?
44. Do you have a geographical preference? Why?
45. Will you relocate? Does relocation bother you?
46. Are you willing to travel?
47. Are you willing to spend at least six months as a trainee?
48. Why do you think you might like to live in the community in which our company is located?
49. What major problem have you encountered and how did you deal with it?
50. What have you learned from your mistakes?

Source: Developed by Dr. Frank Endicott. Reprinted in Gloria Reeves, ed., *Mississippi State University Placement Manual* (Rahway, N.J.: University Communications), p. 562.

The First Interview.   The *first interview* is the screening or introductory interview. It is usually relatively formal, lasts around 30 minutes, and is conducted by a personnel specialist (especially for a large firm). The interviewer usually tells a little about the organization and allows a few minutes for answering questions and inviting the applicant to add information.

Styles vary considerably from the very formal to the informal. In a *formal interview (directive),* the interviewer has a set list of questions and asks every applicant the same questions. In an *informal interview (nondirective),* the recruiter asks broad, general questions to elicit open-ended answers. The goal of most recruiters is to get the interviewee to do most of the talking, but some recruiters simply cannot be quiet (your listening skills are obviously critical when facing these recruiters).

Not only are listening skills important, but speaking skills are also critically important. You simply must plan to talk during your interview. A reserved personality does not help at this point. Nonverbal communication is also important. Look the person in the eye, dress appropriately (but do not go overboard), develop a good, firm handshake, and learn to read the recruiter (e.g., if the recruiter tells jokes, laugh—if the recruiter is a lecturer type, pay attention). Table

Be prepared for any type of interview.

TABLE 18.4

Advice for Interviewees

1. *Be enthusiastic.* Being cool gives an appearance of being uninterested. Many employers think that enthusiasm is the most important quality for entry-level job candidates.
2. *Use good nonverbal cues.* Avoid weak handshakes, poor eye contact, slouching, smoking, and poor grooming—each can give an interviewer a negative impression.
3. *Be positive.* Avoid being negative and critical.
4. *Do not give excuses for weak areas in your record.* Work on developing acceptable reasons.
5. *Do not ask about salary in the initial interview.*
6. *Be clear as to what the next step will be after the interview.*
7. *Be ready to start an interview since studies have shown that first impressions are lasting impressions.*
8. *Be sure to get names and addresses so following up is easy.*

18.4 provides additional advice on how to conduct yourself during the interview.

The Second Interview. Success in the first interview usually leads to a *second interview.* The key factor in obtaining a second interview is whether the interviewer can match you with a specific job. If what you want and the training you have is precisely what the employer needs, the major element is in place.

The second interview is usually at the employer's location and is most often with the department in which you would work. This interview is often longer than the first interview, perhaps a half to a whole day. It usually involves a tour; meeting many people; and discussion of housing, community and recreational facilities, and salary and benefits. Private firms usually pay expenses for this trip, but public agencies usually require that the individual pay. Since the second interview is longer, a nondirective strategy is often used, and both parties get to know each other better.

Before leaving for the second interview, several potential trouble spots need your consideration. There are many arrangements to be made—travel, motel, meals, clothes, money, classes missed, and so forth. Get all the details straight when the company's invitation is issued. Some firms make most of the arrangements, while others expect the candidate to handle them and present the bill. Be sure to get it clear because this involves your money. Keep up with three categories of expenses: travel, food, and lodging. For travel, get receipts or keep track of mileage. For lodging, get receipts. For food, keep good figures.

Finally, try to avoid last-minute cancellations. Organizations usually go through considerable time and expense to arrange these visits.

Follow-Up

Follow-up is also an important part of your overall interviewing process. Effective follow-up involves both oral and written communication skills. You might want to call your prospective employer to thank him or her for the interview or for the opportunity to talk to them about a job. Or you might want to send a follow-up letter. There are four basic types of follow-up letters:

1. Thank you letter.
2. Inquiry letter.
3. Acceptance letter.
4. Refusal letter.

Employers like applicants who show interest in the job *and* in the firm.

Follow-Up Thank You Letter.   *Follow-up thank you letters* are generally short and focus on generating goodwill. This type of letter shows the employer that you are interested in his or her company. You should express your appreciation for the interview, indicate your interest in the firm, and perhaps mention something special regarding your personal interaction with the individual. Your close should focus on generating goodwill and on asking for the sale. An example of a good thank you letter is shown in Illustration 18.8.

Follow-Up Inquiry Letters.   A *follow-up inquiry letter* asks about the status of your application. It is generally used when there has been an unexpectedly long time lapse since you have heard from the firm. This type of letter should follow the basic format of the letter of inquiry discussed in Chapter 6.

Essentially, you should read the interviewer back into the situation by referring to the interview. You might also mention that you want to make a job decision fairly soon and need to get a response from them. Again, your close should focus on generating goodwill and show your continued interest in the organization.

Follow-Up Acceptance Letter.   A *follow-up acceptance letter* is written to tell the firm that you are accepting their job offer. It

ILLUSTRATION 18.8

Example of a Good Thank You Letter

Note the personal tone and strong expression of interest in the company.

Dear Mr. Clark:

I appreciated the opportunity to talk with you on March 15. The candid information you shared with me about Ellis Consumer Products, Inc. was excellent, and I am excited about the possibility of applying my education and experience to the position we discussed.

If I can provide you with any additional information, please let me know. I look forward to visiting with you at your home office.

Sincerely,

ILLUSTRATION 18.9

A Good Follow-Up Acceptance Letter

Dear Miss Milletelo:

I am very pleased to accept your offer to enter McRae's Junior Executive Program as outlined in your letter of April 3. I understand that the starting salary is $23,000 and that I am to report to your headquarters in Jackson on June 1.

As you requested, I am enclosing your packet of employee forms.

I look forward to meeting the challenges of the job and I shall make every attempt to fulfill your expectations.

Sincerely,

ILLUSTRATION 18.10

A Good Letter of Rejection

Dear Mrs. Collins:

After considerable thought, I have finally reached a decision about your offer of employment as outlined in your April 16 letter. Although this has been a very difficult decision for me, I feel that I have made the correct one for this point in my career. My present position appears to offer the most long-run promotion opportunities. I have therefore decided not to accept your offer.

Thank you for your time, effort, and consideration. Your confidence in me is sincerely appreciated.

Sincerely,

---

should follow the format of the favorable response letter discussed in Chapter 7. Essentially, put the yes at the beginning of the letter, and keep the message short and to the point. A good example of a follow-up acceptance letter is shown in Illustration 18.9.

Follow-Up Refusal Letter.   A *follow-up refusal letter* is more difficult to write than a letter of acceptance. It should follow the format of the unfavorable response letter discussed in Chapter 8. Essentially, give the explanation before the refusal. Use the indirect approach and end the letter with a goodwill statement thanking them for the time they devoted to you. An example of a good letter of rejection is shown in Illustration 18.10.

Application Exercises

1. College graduates can usually go to work for more than one type of firm. An accountant, for example, might work for a public accounting firm or for an industrial firm such as Exxon Corporation. Prepare chronological resumes for two different types of firms. Use realistic data about yourself and your major.

2. Prepare functional resumes for two different types of firms. Use realistic data about yourself and your major.

3. Prepare targeted resumes for two different types of firms. Use realistic data about yourself and your major.

4. Prepare cover letters for three different types of firms that you could go to work for.

5. Prepare a letter of application for two different types of firms that you could go to work for.

6. Choose a firm for which you could eventually interview. Use any sources you can to gather data on the firm that you could use in an interview. Write a report with this information (five-page maximum).

7. Find out from your placement office what kinds of paperwork you need to bring to a job interview. Prepare this paperwork.

8. Organize into teams of three students. Have one student play the role of an interviewer using the questions in Table 18.3. The second student should be the interviewee. The third student simply observes and critiques afterward. Alternate roles. This exercise can be especially beneficial if the interviewees can later view their performance on videotape.

9. Assume that you have just returned from an interview with Mr. James Goodman of the ABC Corporation. Write him a follow-up thank you letter.

10. Assume that you have been waiting for the XYZ Corporation to contact you regarding a second interview you had four weeks ago. Write a follow-up inquiry letter.

11. Assume that you have been offered a job with the JKL Corporation. Write a follow-up letter of acceptance.

12. Assume that you have been offered a job with the RST Corporation. Write a follow-up letter of refusal.

Review Questions

1. Should a career or job objective be included on a resume? Discuss your answer.
2. What should be included in the Education section of your resume?
3. What should be included in the Work Experience section of your resume?
4. List and briefly describe the key issues relative to resume format.
5. List and briefly describe the three basic resume types.
6. When should the chronological resume be used?
7. When is the functional resume best used?
8. When is the targeted resume best used?
9. Discuss the three basic questions you should address when reviewing your resume.
10. What is the purpose of a cover letter?
11. Provide detailed advice for writing a cover letter.
12. What is a letter of application? Justify its use.
13. Discuss the preparation phase of interviewing for a job.
14. Discuss a first interview.
15. Distinguish between formal and informal interviews.
16. Discuss a second interview.
17. List and discuss four types of follow-up letters.

Key Terms

resume
chronological resume
functional resume
targeted resume
cover letter
letter of application
first interview
formal interview

informal interview
second interview
follow-up
follow-up thank you letter
follow-up inquiry letter
follow-up acceptance letter
follow-up refusal letter

Notes

1. Tom Jackson, *The Perfect Resume* (Garden City, N.Y.: Anchor Books, 1981), p. 51.

2. Robert J. Jameson, *The Professional Job Changing System* (Parsippany, N.J.: Performance Dynamics, 1978).

3. Jackson, *The Perfect Resume,* p. 51.

4. Jameson, *The Professional Job Changing System,* p. 8.

5. Ibid.

6. Ibid.

Appendix A
Basic English Grammar for Business Writers

This appendix was coauthored by Janet Dolan. Dr. Dolan has a Ph.D. in English, an M.B.A., and two years of postdoctoral study in business. She is presently a professor of business and communication at Pfeiffer College, North Carolina.

DIAGNOSTIC TEST*

Directions: Correct any of the following sentences that you feel are incorrect. Place a C in front of those sentences that you feel are correct.

1. Employees are usually given a set amount of time for lunch, however, many of them take longer than the allotted time.
2. Along a lonely stretch of the sea coast, where the solitary sea gulls wheel and swoop.
3. Before the hen could sit, the farmer gathered the eggs.
4. In the first act she lies the pillow on the floor and raises to her feet.
5. After the raft had sank, the men continued on foot.
6. Hundreds of dusty text books were lying on the floor of his office.
7. The bugs were eaten by the birds.
8. Business ethics are the study of standards of conduct in business dealings.
9. The teacher let each student pick their term paper topic.
10. Did the car dealer hand the warranty to yourself or to your wife?
11. The neighbor which saved the children from the fire was badly burned.
12. Come have lunch with Joan and I.
13. Its true that Duke University took it's name from a wealthy benefactor.
14. I was real angry at her last week.
15. It sure cannot be denied that this year's team is one of the baddest we've ever had.

* Solutions to this diagnostic test are contained in the Instructors Manual.

INTRODUCTION

One word in the English language almost always makes students groan and make faces—**GRAMMAR.** Yet, a working knowledge of the rules of English grammar makes what you write and say much more understandable.

Most disciplines have rules and conventions that govern the way subject matter is used. Thumb through any mathematics textbook and notice the numerous rules that apply to the use of numbers. Browse through a chemistry text and note the laws and axioms that appear in each chapter. Grammar is the term used to refer to the rules that define how words fit together to form correct clauses, phrases, and sentences.

There is nothing awesome about grammar. As with any discipline, you need to learn the basic rules and key terms so that you can communicate effectively. Bear in mind that grammar and its rules are arbitrary in nature; rather than worry about *why* a rule exists, accept it as the way words are handled. Adopting this attitude toward the rules of grammar should remove most of the negative or indifferent feelings you may have regarding the subject.

This appendix discusses the parts of speech, parts of a sentence, types of sentences, and common grammatical errors.

THE PARTS OF SPEECH

The English language has eight parts of speech:

- Nouns
- Pronouns
- Verbs
- Adverbs
- Adjectives
- Prepositions
- Interjections
- Conjunctions

Nouns

Nouns name things, persons, places, or ideas. They can appear in sentences as subjects, objects, direct objects, appositions, subject complements, or objects of prepositions. There are five basic types of nouns.

Proper nouns name a particular person, place, thing, or idea. For example,

> *Dr. Carpenter* teaches *management*.

Common nouns name one or more members of a class or group. For example,

> The *teachers* met in the *cafeteria*.

Collective nouns, which are by nature singular, name whole groups. For example,

> The student *senate* was convened at 10 o'clock.

Abstract nouns designate qualities, concepts, or beliefs. For example,

> *Humor* is lacking in most textbooks.

Concrete nouns name things that are experienced through one or more of the human senses. For example,

> The *odor* of the lilacs hung heavy in the air.

Pronouns

Usually, **pronouns** are used in place of nouns. However, indefinite pronouns do not refer to specific nouns. There are four basic types of pronouns.

Personal pronouns are either singular or plural and refer to a person, a group of people, or an object. They are:

	Singular	Plural
First Person	I, me, mine	we, us, ours
Second Person	you, yours	you, yours
Third Person	he, she, it, him, her, his, hers, its	they, them theirs

For example,

> *I* want to register for class.
> Did *you* take statistics?
> *She* gave *him* the brush-off.
> *It* doesn't matter now.

Demonstrative pronouns (this, these, that, those) are used to designate particular persons or objects. *This* and *these* refer to objects that are near, while *that* and *those* are used to refer to distant objects. For example,

> *This* calculus book is mine.
> *That* book is Sam's.
> *These* books are damaged.
> *Those* are in good shape.

Indefinite pronouns are usually singular in nature and do not refer to particular persons or things. For example,

> *Anyone* may take Accounting I.
> *Nobody* cheated on the test.
> *One* should always work the assigned algebra problems.

Interrogative pronouns are used in questions. The interrogative pronouns include which, what, who, whom, whoever, whomever, and whose. For example,

> *Which* calculator is Bob's?
> *What* are you doing this weekend?

Verbs

Verbs are words that express action, describe a state of being, or designate a condition. There are four basic types of verbs.

Action verbs portray action. For example,

> The car *zoomed* down the hill.
> I *ran* to my economics class.

Linking verbs show condition. For example,

> The entire class *was* sleepy.

State of being verbs naturally describe a state of being. For example,

> The Business Department *is* in this building.

Helper verbs are used in conjunction with main verbs. For example,

> The school choir *has gone* on tour.
> The classroom *is located* in the basement.

Verbs have three principle parts: the **infinitive,** the **past tense,** and the **past participle.** Each of these three principle parts are listed in dictionary entries. **Regular verbs** form the past tense and past participle by adding *d*, *ed*, or *t*. **Irregular verbs** change form in the past tense and past participle. Familiarity with these verbs comes through usage, and sometimes through memorization. Consider the following examples:

	Regular	Irregular
Infinitive	help	ring
Past tense	helped	rang
Past participle	helped	rung

Transitive verbs take an object, whereas **intransitive verbs** do not. For example,

> **Transitive:** The student wrote the term paper.
> **Intransitive:** The rain fell on the plain.

Some verbs are particularly bothersome, such as lie and lay, sit and set, and rise and raise. *Lay, set,* and *raise* take objects, whereas *lie, sit,* and *rise* do not. *Lie* means to recline or to be situated, while *lay* means to place. *Sit* means to be seated while *set* means to place or to arrange. *Rise* means to get up, while *raise* means to lift or to elevate. For example,

> *Lie* back in bed.
> *Lay* the paper on my desk.
> *Sit* in my chair.
> *Set* the table for dinner.
> I like to *rise* early.
> The ROTC Cadet *raised* the flag.

Adverbs

Some **adverbs** express place or time, while others limit, qualify, or describe verbs, adjectives, and other adverbs. Quite a few adverbs are formed by adding *ly* to adjectives. For example,

> She answered *hesitantly.*
> Let the cat *out.*

Adjectives

Words that are descriptive in nature and that modify nouns or pronouns are called **adjectives.** *The, a,* and *an* are also classified as adjectives. For example,

> *The red* notebook contains my business law notes.
> *A beautiful* Irish Setter ran across the field.

There are four basic types of adjectives.

Predicative adjectives follow linking verbs and are used to modify the sentence subject. For example,

> The professor looked *tired.*
> The desks in this room are *old.*

Possessive adjectives are similar to the pronouns *my, your, our, his, its,* and *their.* These adjectives refer to specific nouns. For example,

> *Your* exam was well written.

Demonstrative adjectives have the same form as demonstrative pronouns but modify nouns. For example,

> *That* student procrastinates.

Indefinite adjectives are similar to indefinite pronouns. For example,

> *Every* student received an F.

Prepositions

Prepositions join nouns or pronouns to other words in a sentence to form prepositional phrases. Prepositional phrases most often function as adjectives or adverbs. For example,

> The student ran *through the hallway.*
> *Before class,* the teacher made an assignment.

Interjections

Interjections are words that express strong emotion or surprise, such as *Bam! Biff! Pow!* in the old Batman comic books. Here is another example,

> *Well,* if that doesn't beat all!

Conjunctions

Conjunctions are used to connect words, clauses, and phrases. There are two basic types of conjunctions.

Coordinating conjunctions connect parts of a sentence that have equal rank. For example,

> Frank *and* Bill play lacrosse. (Joins two nouns.)

We waited for you, *but* you didn't come home. (Joins two independent clauses.)

Subordinating conjunctions are used to add a dependent element—one that cannot stand alone as a sentence—to a sentence. For example,

When he finished his homework, he went to the movies.

THE PARTS OF A SENTENCE

To qualify as a complete **sentence,** a group of words must have a subject and a verb, have a complete meaning, and be able to stand by itself. Additions to the subject and verb of a sentence are **direct objects** (words that receive the action of the verb), **indirect objects** (*to* or *for* understood), adjectives, adverbs, and the other parts of speech.

A complete sentence is also an **independent clause.** Clauses are groups of words that have subjects and verbs. Some of them cannot function as sentences and are called **dependent clauses.**   Two independent clauses can be joined by a conjunction, such as:

The class was over *and* the students left.

The following sentence illustrates a dependent adverbial clause and an independent clause:

When the class was over, the students left.

Phrases are groups of words that do not have both a subject and a verb. The various types of phrases include:

Noun phrase: *The new Marketing professor* started this term.

Appositive phrase: The Golden Gate bridge, *a magnificent structure,* is in San Francisco.

Verb phrase: The gym floor *is being varnished.*

Prepositional phrase serving as an **adjectival phrase:** The door *to the building* is locked.

Prepositional phrase serving as an **adverbial phrase:** The snow fell *on the campus.*

Gerund phrase: *Flying in a storm* is scary.

Participial phrase: *Troubled by her low grades,* she decided to study more.

Infinitive phrase: Formula notes *to be used when taking the test* must be on 3 by 5 cards.

THE TYPES OF SENTENCES

Sentences fall into four categories. **Simple sentences** have one independent clause. For example,

> The professor gave a boring lecture.

Compound sentences have two or more independent clauses joined by conjunctions or semicolons. For example,

> The business policy course is required and it is always full.
> The organizational behavior class is popular; students clamor to be admitted.

Complex sentences have an independent clause and one or more dependent clauses. For example,

> When the new recreational complex opened, most students took advantage of the facilities.

Compound-complex sentences have a compound sentence and one or more dependent clauses. For example,

> When he finished his speech, the guest speaker stayed and the students asked him questions.

COMMON ERRORS STUDENTS LOVE TO MAKE

Sentence Fragments

Many students are prone to using dependent clauses, which do not have a subject and a verb, as sentences. One way to avoid this error is to deliberately check your sentences for both a subject and a verb and the absence of any other word that creates subordination. For example,

> When the *speech* (subject) *was* (verb) over.

When is a subordination conjunction and its use creates a dependent clause. The following sentence is an independent clause:

> The *speech was* over.

Comma Splices

When two independent clauses are joined by a comma instead of a conjunction or a semicolon, the error is called a **comma splice.** A comma splice is shown in the following example,

Two independent clauses should not be joined with a comma, the error is called a comma splice.

Run-On Sentences

A **run-on sentence** occurs when at least two complete sentences are combined. For example,

I saw her downtown she was buying a necklace and she said she would be here tonight.

Subject-Verb Agreement

A hard and fast rule of grammar is that *singular* subjects take *singular* verbs and *plural* subjects take *plural* verbs. Be careful when using collective nouns because they take singular verbs when the group is referred to *as a unit,* such as, The *class was* restless today. Also, remember that titles of books and films are regarded as singular and take singular verbs, such as:

Principles of Management is an excellent text.
The Maltese Falcon was filmed in black and white.

When a sentence begins with *there* or *here,* the verb agrees with the subject of the sentence.
For example,

There *are magazines* which are particularly useful to business students.
Here *is* a new *issue* of *Business Week.*

Cases of Pronouns

There are four cases of pronouns: nominative, objective, reflexive, and possessive. The role a pronoun plays in a clause determines the case to be used.

Nominative case is used when the pronoun is acting as the subject of the verb. For example,

Jane and *I* prepared the report.

Objective case is used when the pronoun is acting as the object of a preposition or takes the action of a verb. For example,

Give a copy of the term paper to *her.*

Reflexive case is used when the pronoun refers to a noun used earlier in the sentence. For example,

Bob prefers to do the work *himself*.

Possessive case is used to signify ownership. For example,

This briefcase is *mine*.

The cases of pronouns are as follows:

	Singular	Plural
Nominative	I, you, he, she, it	we, you, they
Objective	me, you, him, her, it	us, you, them
Reflexive	myself, yourself, himself, herself, itself	ourselves, yourselves, themselves
Possessive	mine, yours, his, hers, its	our, yours, theirs

Remember that *its* without an apostrophe (') is the possessive pronoun; *it's* with an apostrophe is the contraction of the verb form *it is*. The two words are not interchangeable.

Punctuation

Many students have trouble using correct punctuation. We often suspect that they operate on the premise that commas are inserted at places where one would take a breath if reading the sentence out loud! The following rules can be quite helpful:

- Use commas between two independent clauses joined by a conjunction (and, but, or, nor, for, so, yet). For example: She ran all the way, but she was still late.
- Use commas between words, phrases, and clauses in a series. For example: They chose blue, pink, and gold for the color scheme of the prom.
- Use commas after long introductory clauses or phrases. For example: At the end of the three-hour class, I was ready for a nap.
- Use commas to set off nonrestrictive appositives. For example: Dr. Franks, the economics professor, is the head of the department.
- Use commas with parenthetical elements. For example: They finished the test, they believed, in record time.
- Use commas with unusual word order. For example: The man, tall and lithe, swung out of the saddle.
- Use commas with degrees, titles, dates, places, and addresses. For example: (1) John Smith, Ph.D., joined the faculty in September; (2) On Friday, October 12, fall break be-

gins; and (3) Tucson, Arizona, is the location of the University of Arizona.

- Use commas for contrast or emphasis. For example: I want the third edition, not the second.

Do not use commas:

- Between subjects and verbs.
- Between compound elements.
- Between dependent clauses.
- In comparisons.
- Before the first parenthesis.
- After coordinating conjunctions.
- To set off restrictive clauses, appositives, or phrases.

The Semicolon

Use **semicolons** between two independent clauses and between items in a series. For example,

> Manhattan, Kansas, is near Ft. Riley; it is also the home of Kansas State University.
>
> In her desk Sally found a ballpoint pen, which was dry; several 13 cent stamps, which were stuck together; and an old driver's license, which had expired.

The Colon

Use **colons** to introduce formal series, before quotations, and before statements. For example,

> Prepare the following items: a resume, a biographical sketch, and a brief summary of your career objectives.
>
> John Kennedy said: "Ask not what your country can do for you; ask what you can do for your country."

The Dash

Practice using the **dash.** It can add spice to your writing style. It functions to designate interruptions, parenthetical comments, or special emphasis. For example,

> The movie is excellent—really excellent—you should see it!
>
> The blame can be placed on only one person's shoulders—yours.

Brackets

Square **brackets,** not parentheses, are used to enclose interpolations within a quotation. For example,

Slowly but surely [italics mine] we are polluting our environment.

Word Usage

Students apparently get conflicting advice regarding the use of big words. Big words are sometimes appropriate—when they are accurate, when you are comfortable using them, and, most of all, when your receiver will easily understand them. When in doubt, use the smaller word in your business communications.

The following rules of thumb can also help:

- Avoid the use of highly technical words.
- Do not use trade jargon or shoptalk that has meaning only to those in the same profession or discipline.
- Avoid split infinitives, such as "to quickly go."
- Balance sentences by matching phrases, clauses, verbs, and other parts of speech.
- Aim for a variety of sentences in what you write.
- Avoid dangling modifiers, such as: After he blew up the chemistry lab, the Dean suspended the student. (Who blew up the lab?)

Do not make shifts in tense, person, number, or voice. Use present tense with present tense, singular person with singular person, singular number with singular number, and active voice with active voice. For example,

Tense shift: The teacher *was* energetic, but his students *are* lazy.

Person shift: When *we* left class, *you* could feel the tension.

Number shift: *One* may cheat on a test and then *they* deny doing so.

Voice shift: A chapter *is read* by the girl and then *she outlines* it.

We advocate the consistent use of the active voice. One way to remember the distinction between active and passive voice is the following sentence:

The active wife is actively pushing her passive husband into the shoe store.

Commonly Misspelled Words

absence	criticize	incidentally	preparation
accidentally	deferred	incredible	prevalent
accommodate	definite	independence	privilege
accumulate	description	inevitable	probably
acquaintance	desperate	intellectual	professor
acquitted	dictionary	intelligence	pronunciation
advice	dining	interesting	prophecy
advise	disappearance	irresistible	prophesy
all right	disappoint	knowledge	quantity
altar	disastrous	laboratory	quiet
amateur	discipline	laid	quite
among	dissatisfied	led	quizzes
analysis	dormitory	lightning	recede
analyze	eighth	loneliness	receive
annual	eligible	maintenance	recognize
apartment	eliminate	maneuver	recommend
apparatus	embarrass	manufacture	reference
apparent	eminent	marriage	referred
appearance	encouraging	mathematics	repetition
arctic	environment	may	restaurant
argument	equipped	maybe	rhythm
arithmetic	especially	miniature	ridiculous
ascend	exaggerate	mischievous	sacrifice
athletic	excellence	mysterious	salary
attendance	exhilarate	necessary	schedule
balance	existence	ninety	secretary
beginning	experience	noticeable	seize
believe	explanation	occasionally	separate
benefited	familiar	occurred	sergeant
boundaries	fascinate	omitted	severely
Britain	February	opportunity	shining
business	fiery	optimistic	siege
calendar	foreign	parallel	similar
candidate	formerly	paralyze	sophomore
category	forty	pastime	specifically
cemetery	fourth	performance	specimen
changeable	frantically	permissible	stationary
changing	fulfill or fulfil	perseverance	stationery
choose	generally	personnel	statue
chose	government	perspiration	studying
coming	grammar	physical	subtly
commission	grandeur	picnicking	succeed
committee	grevious	playwright	successful
comparative	height	possibility	supersede
compelled	heroes	practically	surprise
conceivable	hindrance	precede	temperamental
conferred	hoping	precedence	tendency
conscience	humorous	preference	their
conscientious	hypocrisy	preferred	thorough
control	immediately	prejudice	

Source: Watkins/Dillingham: *Practical English Handbook*, Sixth Edition. Copyright © 1982 Houghton Mifflin Company. Used with permission.

ILLUSTRATION A.2

Principal Parts of Some Troublesome Verbs

Infinitive	Past Tense	Past Participle
arise	arose	arisen
awake	awoke, awaked	awoke, awaked
be	was	been
bear (to carry)	bore	borne
bear (to give birth)	bore	born, borne
begin	began	begun
bid (offer)	bid	bid
bid (order or say)	bade	bidden
bite	bit	bitten, bit
blow	blew	blown
break	broke	broken
bring	brought	brought
burst	burst	burst
catch	caught	caught
choose	chose	chosen
come	came	come
deal	dealt	dealt
dig	dug	dug
dive	dived, dove	dived
do	did	done
drag	dragged	dragged
draw	drew	drawn
dream	dreamed, dreamt	dreamed, dreamt
drink	drank	drunk
drive	drove	driven
drown	drowned	drowned
eat	ate	eaten
fall	fell	fallen
find	found	found
flee	fled	fled
fly	flew	flown
forget	forgot	forgotten, forgot
freeze	froze	frozen
get	got	got, gotten
give	gave	given
go	went	gone
grow	grew	grown
hang (to execute)	hanged	hanged
hang (to suspend)	hung	hung
have	had	had
hear	heard	heard
know	knew	known

ILLUSTRATION A.2 *(concluded)*

Infinitive	Past Tense	Past Participle
lay	laid	laid
lead	led	led
lend	lent	lent
let	let	let
lie	lay	lain
light	lighted, lit	lighted, lit
lose	lost	lost
pay	paid	paid
pay (ropes)	payed	payed
plead	pleaded, pled	pleaded, pled
prove	proved	proven, proved
raise	raised	raised
ride	rode	ridden
ring	rang, rung	rung
rise	rose	risen
run	ran	run
say	said	said
see	saw	seen
shine (to give light)	shone	shone
shine (to polish)	shined	shined
show	showed	shown, showed
shrink	shrank, shrunk	shrunk
sing	sang, sung	sung
sink	sank, sunk	sunk
sit	sat	sat
slide	slid	slid
sow	sowed	sown, sowed
speak	spoke	spoken
spit	spat, spit	spit, spat
spring	sprang, sprung	sprung
stand	stood	stood
steal	stole	stolen
stink	stank, stunk	stunk
swim	swam, swum	swum
swing	swung	swung
take	took	taken
tear	tore	torn

Spelling

There is really only one way to learn to spell correctly—*practice*. In addition, you must remember *i* before *e* except after *c* and buy and use a recent, hardcover edition of a good dictionary. Illustration A.1 presents a list of the most commonly misspelled words in the English language.

Difficult Verbs

Irregular verbs can be somewhat unusual in their conjugations. Illustration A.2 contains a list of irregular and difficult verbs. Often the best thing to do is to memorize these verbs. Remember—the dictionary gives the principal parts of verbs.

CONCLUSION

This appendix is admittedly a capsulized discussion of basic English. We heartily recommend that you purchase a good English grammar workbook and then work the exercises.

One final word—there is only one way to learn to write well—WRITE AND EDIT, WRITE AND EDIT, and then WRITE AND EDIT some more.

Appendix B
Business Letters and Memos: Form and Style

This appendix was coauthored by Janet Dolan. Dr. Dolan has a Ph.D. in English, an M.B.A., and two years of postdoctoral study in business. She is presently a professor of business and communication at Pfeiffer College, North Carolina.

BUSINESS LETTERS

Business letters are written messages that are sent to individuals or groups outside the organization. The appearance or format of a letter has become standardized by convention in that certain forms have become generally acceptable.

No matter which of the acceptable forms you choose for a letter, the appearance of a particular letter is of primary importance. When you send a letter, that letter represents both you and your organization. A neat, well-organized letter helps create a positive impression on the receiver.

To ensure that your letters create a favorable impression, you should pay careful attention the following points: stationery, layout, different parts, punctuation styles, and format.

Stationery

The most generally accepted color for business stationery is white, but more companies are beginning to use various pastels. Regardless of the color used, the paper should be of good quality, preferably 25 percent rag content and from 16 to 20 pounds in weight.

Many organizations purchase stationery that has the organization's logo or emblem impressed on the paper as a watermark. The standard letterhead size is 8½ by 11 inches. Envelopes should match the stationery in quality and type of printing.

Layout

A business letter should be visually well balanced on the paper. Think of your margins as a *frame* that sets off your printed message, much like a picture frame sets off a work of art. Side margins are generally 1 ½ inches, and top and bottom margins are approximately 2 inches.

Different Parts

Most people expect a business letter to have certain parts. The traditional parts include:

- Letterhead
- Date
- Inside address
- Attention line
- Salutation
- Subject line
- Body
- Complimentary close
- Signature
- Reference line
- Enclosure line
- Copy line

Illustration B.1 shows these traditional parts of a common business letter.

Letterhead.   Many firms hire professional artists to create an original and distinctive **letterhead.** Regardless of who designs the letterhead, it should tell *who* the firm is, *where* the firm is, *how* to contact the firm by telephone or telex, and it may possible include a line devoted to *what* the firm does. In large firms different officers, departments, or divisions place an appropriate name on the letterhead, such as "Office of the President" or "Personnel Office."

Date.   Every business letter *must* have a **date line.** It should be typed two or more lines below the letterhead. Depending on the style of letter used, it can begin on the left margin, end on the right margin, or be centered. Illustrations B.1, B.2, and B.3 show different date line positions.

Dates may be expressed in one of two ways: "January 4, 1986" or "4 January 1986." Do not use all figures, such as "1/4/86." The first figure can be interpreted as either the month or the day of the month.

ILLUSTRATION B.1

Parts of the Business Letter (Full Block Style)

Heading	who what where
Date	_____ (4 line spaces)
Inside address	_____ _____ (double space)
Salutation	_____ (double space)
Body	(single space body) (double space between paragraphs) (double space)
Complimentary close	_____ (4 line spaces)
Signature **Typed name** **Title**	_____ (double space)
Identifying initials	_____ (double space) (double space)
Enc. or cc.	_____

ILLUSTRATION B.2

Modified Block Style

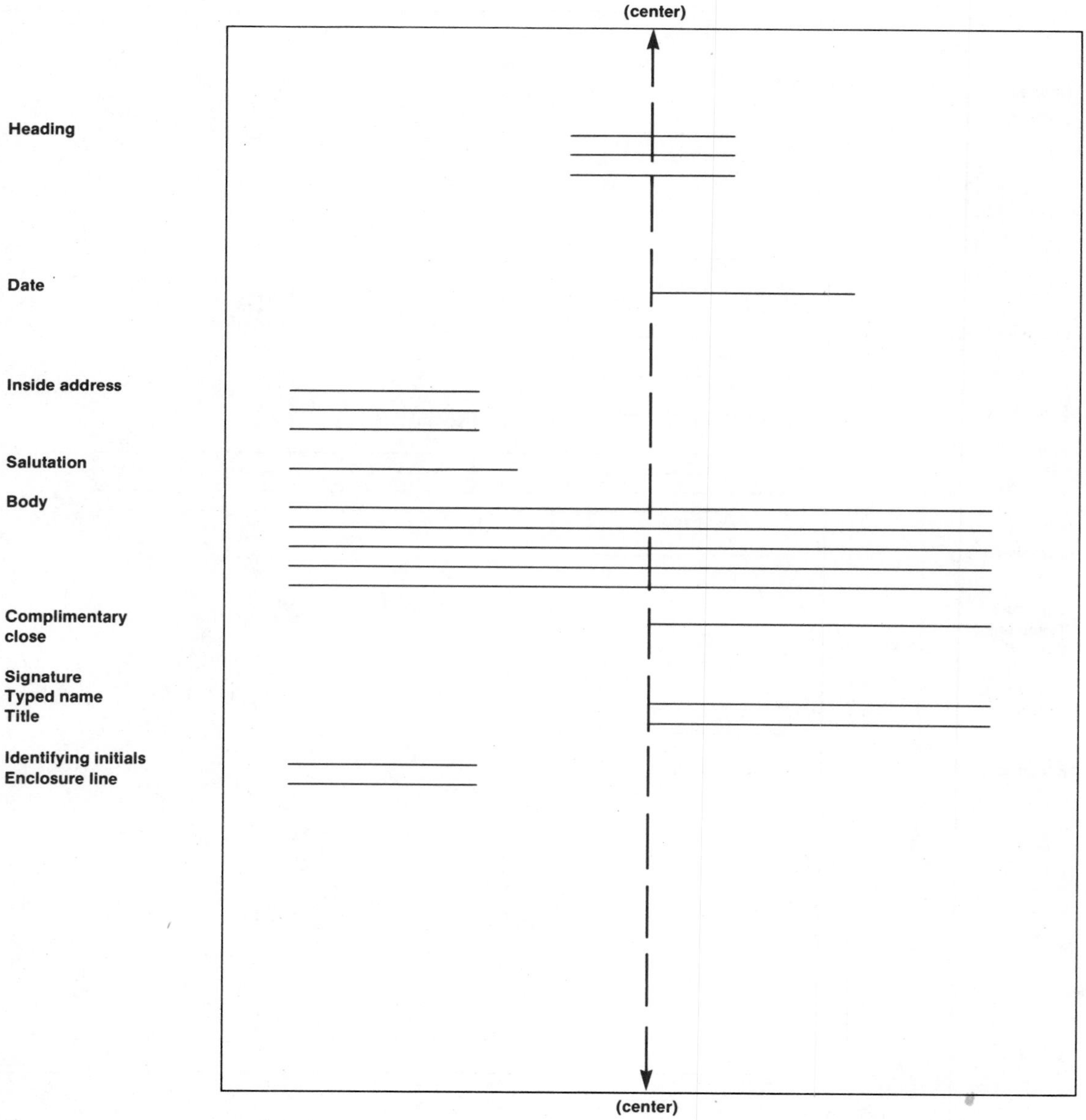

ILLUSTRATION B.3

Modified Block Style with Indented Paragraphs

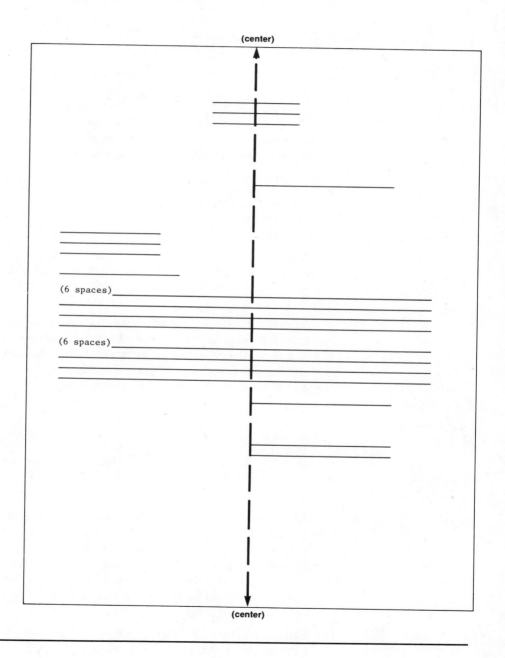

Inside Address. The **inside address** should include several parts:

- The addressee's title (such as Mr., Mrs., Miss, Dr., Professor, Sgt., Gen.) and full name.
- The addressee's professional title (such as President, Director, Comptroller).
- The organization's name.
- The street address or mailing address.
- The city, state, and zip code.

If you get confused with certain complicated addresses, a good rule of thumb is to proceed from the specific to the general. The following illustrates an acceptable inside address:

Dr. David Avery
President
Avery Medical Supplies
1234 McCain Avenue
Grayson, MI 56789

It is acceptable to abbreviate state names; standard abbreviations can be obtained from your post office. You should also include one or two spaces between the state abbreviation and the zip code.

Attention Line. An **attention line** has traditionally often been included immediately following the inside address to direct the letter to a particular person or department. More and more, however, this information is included in the inside address. Both a traditional style and a more modern usage are shown below:

Traditional	Modern
Murray College	Director of Admissions
1400 School House Lane	Murray College
Concord, NC 28025	1400 School House Lane
Attention: Director of Admissions	Concord, NC 28025

Salutation. The degree of formality for your **salutation** depends on your personal relationship with the recipient. It is acceptable to use the recipient's first name if you know him well. Otherwise, you should maintain formality by using the recipient's title and last name, such as "Dear Mr. Smith:" or "Dear Mrs. Feltz:." The salutation should be typed two lines below the inside address.

Subject Line. A **subject line** should tell the recipient what the letter is about. Although it can often be omitted, it can be helpful in such instances as in reference to an insurance policy number or to a previous letter. A subject line should be short and positive. The potential danger of using a subject line is that it can sometimes add an air of excessive formality.

The subject line should appear two lines below the salutation. The use of terms such as *re, in re,* and *reference* is becoming obsolete. The use of "Subject:" is now preferred.

Body.   The **body** of your letter contains the information you intend to convey. Each paragraph should be typed single-spaced within and double-spaced between paragraphs. Varying the length of paragraphs helps give your letter a more pleasing appearance.

Complimentary Close.   Standard **complimentary closes** have evolved over the years. In the 1800s, for example, the following close was common: "With all best wishes, I remain yours truly, . . ." This type of close is now considered archaic. Simplicity is now the rule. Commonly used closes include: Sincerely, Sincerely yours, Cordially, and Cordially yours. Your close should reflect the degree of formality expressed throughout your letter.

Signature.   It is customary to leave four lines below the complimentary close for your written **signature.** Your typewritten signature appears on the fourth line, with your title on the fifth line.

Your organization's name can be included in the complimentary close. When included, it should be positioned two lines below the complimentary close and typed in capital letters as follows:

Sincerely yours,

ACME PRODUCTION COMPANY

Leonard Flynn
President

Reference Line.   When someone other than the sender types a letter, the typist's initials are generally placed on the **reference line.** Normally, the typist's initials are placed after the sender's initials and are separated by a slash (/) or colon (:). The following forms are generally acceptable:

- DOR:jks
- DOR/jks
- dor:jks

- dor/jks
- jks (sender's initials omitted)
- s (first initial of typist's last name)

Enclosure Line. An **enclosure line** is needed when your letter includes additional material. The number of pieces of additional material is noted one or two lines below the reference line. Acceptable enclosure line forms include:

- Enclosure
- Picture enclosed
- Two enclosures
- enc
- Enc.
- enc:2
- enc: 1. Map
       2. Check

Copy Line. When you send a copy of a letter to additional people, you should note the fact on the original letter. The **copy line** is typed one or two lines below the preceding line (the enclosure line, reference line, or signature). While the traditional notation is "cc" (referring to carbon copies), it is more common today to use a single "c" (referring to copies). Acceptable copy line forms include:

- cc: Personnel Department
- c Jane Smith
- C Accounting Department
- Copies to: Joe Brown
           Jane Smith
           Mack White

Punctuation Styles

The two most common styles of punctuation are *open* and *closed*. These two styles are shown in Illustration B.4.

Format

Business letters generally use one of three basic formats: *full block, modified block,* or *modified block with indented paragraphs.* These formats are shown in Illustrations B.1, B.2, and B.3.

ILLUSTRATION B.4

Styles of Punctuation

Open punctuation

Inside address

Salutation

Body

Complimentary close

Closed punctuation

Inside address

Salutation, followed by
a colon

Body

Complimentary close

Other Considerations

You will sometimes need to prepare a letter on blank stationery (does not have a letterhead). When doing so, you should type in a complete return address. Illustration B.5 shows the use of modified block style and full block style on blank paper.

ILLUSTRATION B.5

Heading on Blank Stationery

Modified block style

Return address

Street address
City and State
Date

Inside address

Full block style

Return address

Street address
City and State
Date

Inside address

ILLUSTRATION B.6

Envelope Format Showing Mailing Notations

The Common mailing notations are:
- **Certified mail**
- **Registered mail**
- **Special delivery**
- **Personal**
- **Confidential**

```
Return Address
_____
_____

NOTATION IN CAPS                          NOTATION IN CAPS

                        Stamp


              Recipient's Name
              and Address
              _____
              _____
```

Notations are placed <u>above</u> the recipient's name and address to allow the Post Office's optical scanners to "read" the address.

```
Return Address
_____
_____

NOTATION IN CAPS                          NOTATION IN CAPS

                        Stamp


              Recipient's Name
              and Address
              _____
              _____
```

ILLUSTRATION B.7

Folding the Letter

**Folding to fit
a large envelope**

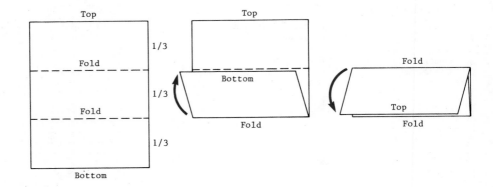

**Folding to fit
a small envelope**

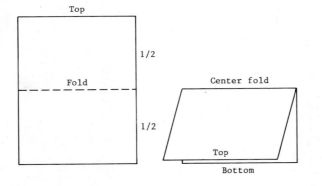

ILLUSTRATION B.8

Memo Formats

Horizontal heading

```
To:                    Date:

From:                  Subject:
```

Vertical heading

```
To:
From:
Date:
Subject:
```

You might also have occasion to include special mailing notations on envelopes, such as: Certified Mail, Registered Mail, Special Delivery, Personal, or Confidential. Illustration B.6 shows the proper placement of mailing notations. Notice that the notations are typed in capital letters.

You must also consider the proper way to fold a letter, depending on the size of the envelope. Effective folding procedures are shown in Illustration B.7.

MEMOS

Memos are written communications that are sent to someone *inside* your organization. Since memos are not intended for public viewing, they generally (1) have a more informal tone, (2) are initialed rather than signed, and (3) are written on less expensive paper than that used for letters.

Many organizations use colored paper for memos to distinguish them from letters. Most organizations use preprinted memo forms. Some of these forms have two parts, including a space for a reply.

All memos follow a basic format. The heading normally includes four points:

- To:
- From:
- Date:
- Subject:

Illustration B.8 shows two common memo formats.

The key points to remember when writing memos include:

- Memos should be short, usually only one page in length.
- The subject line should state what the memo is about.
- One memo should cover only one subject.
- If the recipient is called upon to do something as a result of the memo, the action should be stated clearly, and any time constraints should be noted.
- Important parts of the memo should be emphasized by underlining, using all capital letters, enclosing in boxes, or using different colors of ink.
- Memos are not substitutes for handwritten notes or telephone calls. The first question to ask before writing a memo is: Is this memo *really* necessary? Don't bury your organization in an avalanche of paper.

Appendix C
Footnote and Bibliography Format

INTRODUCTION

When you use secondary information (from another published or unpublished source) in a report, you should clearly specify the original source. This documentation is done with footnote and bibliography entries. This appendix discusses the major aspects of footnotes and bibliography references.

Before studying the proper form and format, you should understand four key points. First, since published written material is considered real property, using the material without giving due credit to the author and publisher amounts to stealing. Use without proper documentation is called *plagiarism*.

Second, there are a variety of acceptable footnote and bibliography forms used in report writing. No particular variation or form is considered to be the correct form.

Third, select a form that is complete enough to allow your reader to locate the source.

Fourth, use the form you select consistently throughout your report.

Now, let's look at footnote and bibliography forms, beginning with the footnotes.

FOOTNOTES

Footnotes are generally used in four situations.[1] In two situations, a **reference footnote** is used: (1) to cite the authority for statements (both facts and opinions) in text, and (2) to make cross-references. In two other situations, a **content footnote** is used: (1) to make incidental comments, such as to amplify or qualify textual discussion with material you feel is worthwhile but that would interrupt the flow of the text; and (2) to give acknowledgments.

One of your most challenging tasks involves determining what information needs to be footnoted. The following guidelines can help:

- Information and opinions that are solely your own do not have to be footnoted.

- Information quoted verbatim from another source must be enclosed in quotation marks ('') and footnoted, for example: According to Petersen, ''Time is an asset that must be managed.''[33] Also note that if a direct quote consumes three or more lines in your report, it should be single-spaced and indented five spaces from each margin.

- Information taken from another source that you paraphrase should be footnoted, but it does not have to be enclosed in quotes. However, information that is considered to be common knowledge in the field does not have to be footnoted. For example, if you wanted to state that the balance sheet normally contains data on assets, liabilities, and owners equity, a footnote would not be necessary.

Reference Footnotes

There are two major forms for reference footnotes, the traditional method and the modern journal method. Let's first look at the traditional method of footnoting.

Traditional Method of Footnoting.   The traditional method of footnoting involves placing each footnote at the bottom of the page on which the cited information appears. A raised footnote number, called a **superscript**, is placed at the end of the relevant passage. The superscript number tells the reader that the preceding material came from a secondary source that is shown at the bottom of the page.

The most commonly used variations of the traditional method of footnoting follow.

For a book reference:

> John Ivancevich and William Glueck, *Foundations of Personnel/Human Resources Management,* rev. ed. (Plano, Texas: Business Publications, Inc., l983), p. 163.

For a journal or periodical article:

> Larry Smeltzer and Steven Golen, ''Transmission and Retrieval of Information: Statements and Hypotheses for Research,'' *Journal of Business Communication,* Vol. 21, No. 1 (Winter l984), pp. 81–92.

For unpublished papers:

> Henry Spence, ''Behavior Patterns in Rigid Organizations'' (unpublished doctoral dissertation, Louisiana Tech University [Ruston], June l985), p. 144.

For a governmental publication:

> United States Department of Agriculture, *Dry-Farming Possibilities for Guayule in California* (Washington, D. C.: United States Government Printing Office, 1986), p. 55.

For unpublished speeches and interviews:

> Jerry K. Smith, "Getting Your Money's Worth," speech presented at the meeting of the National Consumer Finance Association, Chicago, Ill., April 3, 1985.

> Avery Lewis, Vice-President, Arkansas Federal Savings and Loan Association, Fayetteville, Arkansas, Personal interview, April 7, 1985.

In addition to the above examples, the following Latin abbreviations are used in the traditional form of footnoting to keep you from having to repeat a footnote that has been used previously.

Ibid.   **Ibid.** is used when information is quoted from the same source two times in succession, such as:

> [18] Garry D. Smith, Danny R. Arnold, and Bobby Bizzell, *Strategic Management,* (Boston: Houghton Mifflin, 1985), p. 88.
> [19] Ibid., p. 90.

The second footnote pertains to page 90 of the *Strategic Management* textbook. If it had been on the same page, the p. XX is omitted.

Op. cit.   **Op. cit.** is also used when the information being cited is from a previously cited source, but when there is at least one intervening footnote from a different source. For example,

> [14] Walter Shell, "Improving Students' Proofreading Skills," *Journal of Business Education,* Vol. 57 (May 1982), p. 304.
> [15] William Davidson, "Structure and Performance in International Technology Transfer," *Journal of Management Studies,* Vol. 20 (October 1983), p. 453.
> [16] Shell, op. cit., p. 306.

Footnote 16 refers to page 306 of the source cited in footnote 14.

Loc. cit.   **Loc. cit.** is used when information is quoted from the same page of a source two or more times regardless of whether or not there are intervening footnotes. Page numbers therefore do not have to be used in a loc. cit. footnote. The following example illustrates the use of loc. cit., ibid., and op. cit.

[1] Joseph A. Stone, *Editing Your Newspaper* (New York: Alfred A. Knopf, 1967), p. 311.

[2] William D. Thomas, *Effective Radio Advertising* (New York: Macmillan, 1976), p. 171.

[3] Ibid.

[4] Ibid, p. 177.

[5] Stone, op. cit., p. 314.

[6] Thomas, op. cit., pp. 211–15.

[7] Stone, loc. cit.

Footnote 7 refers to page 314 of the Stone book cited in footnote 5.

Modern Journal Method of Footnoting

While the traditional method of footnoting is decreasing in popularity, the modern journal method of footnoting is gaining in popularity. It is simple, easy to understand, and easy to type.

This modern approach involves grouping the footnote entries at the back of each chapter or at the back of the report. Frequently used headings include Footnotes, References, and References Cited.

Numbers are used in the text to refer to a specific source, such as:

"Telecommunication is more media oriented while teleconferencing is more participant oriented."(3)

The number three in parentheses (3) following the sentence tells your reader that the corresponding source is entry three in the reference section. Note that the page number can also be included in the text along with the reference. For example, (3:94) would tell your reader that the material came from page 94 of reference number three.

In the references section, the number is used to refer to the source. For example,

3. John Penrose, "Telecommunications, Teleconferencing, and Business Communications," *Journal of Business Communications,* Vol. 21, No. 1 (Winter 1984), p. 94.

A popular variation of the above modern journal style involves listing the sources in alphabetical order in the references section. The reference in the text consists of (at least) the author's last name; the publication date and page number are sometimes included. For example,

"A facsimile machine transmits and receives images." (Penrose, 1984, p. 95)

Content Footnotes

Content footnotes are also referred to as discussion footnotes and explanatory footnotes. As mentioned earlier, these footnotes contain information that does not follow the textual flow. Content footnotes are often used to clarify how a term is being used. For example,

> * Note that the terms *merchandise, goods, offerings,* and *products* are used interchangeably.

As shown in the example, an asterisk (*) rather than a number is often used to identify a content footnote.

BIBLIOGRAPHY FORMATTING

A bibliography is a list of sources from which you obtained information for your report. All reference footnote sources are included in a bibliography or references section.

When many sources are included in a bibliography, it may be divided into categories for easier referencing. The categories can include books, periodicals, newspaper articles, unpublished materials, interviews, and miscellaneous.

Although footnote and bibliography entries are similar, there are some basic differences. The key difference is that the author's last name is put first in a bibliography entry. This and other differences are illustrated in the following example:

BIBLIOGRAPHY

Books
1. Aronson, Elliot. *The Social Animal.* San Francisco: W. H. Freeman, 1972.
2. Harris, Thomas A. *I'm OK — You're OK.* New York: Avon Books. Published by arrangement with Harper & Row Publishers, Incorporated, 1973.

Articles
1. Cater, Douglas. "The Communications Revolution—What Social-Political Consequences?" *Current,* Vol. 3, No. 15, October 1973, pp. 36–40.

CONCLUSION

Perhaps the most important point to retain from this appendix is to *include sufficient information in a consistent format*. To obtain additional, more detailed information, you should refer to a current edition of a generally accepted "form and style manual." Two popular manuals are:

1. Campbell, William Giles, and Stephen Ballou. *Form and Style: Theses, Reports, Term Papers*. Sixth ed. Boston: Houghton-Mifflin, 1979.
2. Turabian, Kate. *A Manual for Writers of Term Papers, Theses, and Dissertations*. Fourth ed. Chicago: University of Chicago Press, 1973.

Notes

1. Kate Turabian, *A Manual for Writers of Term Papers, Theses, and Dissertations,* Fourth ed. (Chicago: University of Chicago Press, 1973), p. 78.

Appendix D
Legal Considerations in Organization Communications

This appendix was coauthored by Dennis Eshee, J. D., professor of applied legal studies at Mississippi State University and city judge.

INTRODUCTION

Your organization will be concerned with what you write and say as part of your job for a variety of reasons. One of the major reasons involves the potential for communication-related litigation and the use of communication as evidence in other legal actions. Since ignorance of the law is not a defense, you must at least be familiar with the key legal concepts.

Although a comprehensive treatment is not possible, this appendix attempts to provide a general overview of key legal concepts that can influence your communications. If you find yourself in a delicate or complicated situation, you should consult an attorney to advise you on specific details. The concepts addressed in this appendix are:

- Defamation
- Fraud
- Contracts
- Warranties
- Invasion of privacy
- Copyrights
- Employment
- Credit and collections
- Use of the mail
- Packaging and labeling

Each discussion concludes with a section of implications for communicators.

DEFAMATION

Defamation arises from the publication of a false and malicious statement that tends to injure one's character, fame, or reputation. **Publication** is also a legal term and is a critical part of the definition; it involves transmitting a defamatory statement to a third party. Written defamation is referred to as **libel.** Oral defamation is referred to as **slander.**

Note that three key elements must be present for a statement to be a defamation. First, the statement must be untrue. Truth is usually an acceptable defense to a defamation suit.

Second, the statement must be communicated to a third party (publication). For example, assume that you tell Mr. Dull that you consider him to be an incompetent computer programmer. Since this is your opinion and a third party is not involved, a successful legal action would be unlikely. However, assume that you tell Mr. Sharp that Mr. Dull is an incompetent computer programmer. If Mr. Dull can prove injury, he has a much better chance for successful litigation.

Third, the statement must cause some injury. The injury can involve issues such as contempt, ridicule, or disrepute. Defamation relative to requested recommendations is discussed later in this appendix.

A variety of words have been judged as defamatory. The following is a sampling of those that you should avoid or use with caution:

bankrupt	inferior
blackmailer	insolvent
Communist	kickbacks
corrupt	liar
crook	misappropriation
deadbeat	misconduct
dishonest	misrepresentation
disreputable	profiteer
drug addict	quack
faker	queer
falsified	racketeer
forger	shyster
fraud (fraudulent)	swindler
gouged money	thief
grafter	unchaste
has a social disease	unworthy of credit
hypocrite	worthless
incompetent	

Implications for Communicators

Increasingly, the burden of proof relative to defamatory statements rests with the communicator. The major implications of this situation include the following:

- Avoid making statements that could be construed as defamatory.
- Make sure that all of your communications are accurate and truthful.
- Your statements, especially those that are responses to requests for information about people (such as letters of recommendation), must be made in good faith and without intentional deceit or malice.
- When providing unfavorable information, make it obvious that you are trying to protect the individual as much as possible, such as by indicating that the information was requested and that it should be kept confidential.

FRAUD

Stated simply, **fraud** results from misrepresentation or concealment. The following factors must be present.

First, a misstatement must be made with the intent to deceive. In other words, a critical fact must be deliberately concealed or falsely represented. For example, the statement "The Wunder Extruder costs less than any of its competitors" can be acceptable. However, if the cost of all necessary peripheral devices and the cost of installation is included in the list price of competing extruders and is not included in the list price of the Wunder Extruder, the statement may be fraudulent. Opinions, judgments, or predictions of the future normally do not constitute fraud. For example, saying "This is a real bargain" is generally acceptable.

Second, the misrepresentation must be of a material existing fact. The degree of importance is of little consequence. A fact is considered material if knowledge of the fact would have changed the defrauded party's actions, in entering into such actions as a contract or an agreement.

Third, the individual making the false representation must know it to be false or make it recklessly without regard to its truth. You must therefore avoid (a) deliberate false statements, (b) deliberate concealment of material facts, (c) deliberate acts to mislead another person, and (d) statements made without prior determination of truth or falsity.

Fourth, the misrepresentation must induce action and cause damage or injury. In other words, an agreement or contract must arise due to the misrepresentation. Further, the defrauded party must also be able to prove injury.

Implications for Communicators

The implications for communicators regarding fraud include these:

- You must be particularly careful to avoid false statements in advertising communications regarding prices, performance capability, quality, and character of goods and services.
- You must exercise care in using statements by people misrepresented as experts.
- You must avoid transmitting false information in credit letters.
- You should know that, in general, fraud can be avoided if you are to the point and honest.

CONTRACTS

Contract law deals with the creation, transfer, and disposition of rights through legally enforceable promises. A **contract** may be defined as a promise or set of promises. The law recognizes the performance of a contract as a duty and will furnish a remedy for the breach of a contract. A valid contract requires that four conditions be present.

First, there must be an **agreement** between the contracting parties. The agreement consists of an **offer** from one party and the **acceptance** of the offer by another party.

Second, **consideration** must be present. The consideration is that price (either tangible or intangible) bargained for by each party. Each party receives or gives up something of value according to the terms of the agreement.

Third, the contracting parties must be **competent.** Essentially, each party must have the capacity to contract by being of legal age and not insane. Otherwise, the contract may be avoided by the incompetent party.

Fourth, the contract must be formed for a **legal purpose.** The subject matter of the contract must comply with the law and public policy.

Implications for Communicators

In all communications, oral or written, care should be taken to avoid the appearance of entering into a contract when a contract is not desired. Key points include the following:

- Avoid language that could be interpreted as being an offer or acceptance.
- Avoid language that could be construed as inviting an offer or inviting acceptance when it is not desired.
- Determine the organization's objective before communicating. Be clear on whether your firm wants to enter a contract or to merely negotiate.
- Know the legal capacity of the individual you are dealing with. Find out if he or she is authorized to enter into contracts on behalf of his or her organization.
- Ascertain the legality of the proposal.
- Obtain the opinion of legal counsel when in doubt.

WARRANTIES

When an organization sells goods (or services), it assumes various obligations concerning the nature, title, and quality of the goods being sold. When such an obligation actually helps induce the sale, it is called a **warranty.**

The warranty obligation can be stated expressly or simply implied by the seller. An **express warranty** exists when the seller explicitly states an assurance of the quality or performance of the good. An **implied warranty** is not stated by the seller, but may consist of an obvious fact that the buyer relies on, such as the implication that the seller can convey clear title to the goods being sold. Express warranties are more obvious and easier to prove in litigation.

Note that simply exaggerating the merits of a product does not necessarily constitute an implied warranty. That tactic is referred to as *puffery*. Such statements are considered personal opinions or value judgments.

A **full warranty** guarantees that products will be repaired or replaced by the seller without charge within a reasonable time if there is a defect. A **limited warranty** places certain restrictions on the seller's obligations—it must be placed in a conspicuous position so that buyers are not misled.

Implications for Communicators

The major implications for communicators regarding warranties include these:

- Avoid any actions regarding express or implied warranties that you cannot substantiate, particularly in sales letters.
- Ensure that your warranties are in compliance with federal laws. For example, warranties on products costing $5 or more must disclose the warranty terms in simple and readily understood language. Warranties on products costing over $15 must be labeled "full" or "limited."
- Product presentations contained in brochures and pamphlets have been construed to be express warranties.

INVASION OF PRIVACY

Invasion of privacy involves the unconsented, unprivileged, and unreasonable intrusion into the private life of an individual. Note that invasion of privacy does not have to meet the same requirements as defamation—publication, falsehood, and injury. The invasion of privacy is somewhat analogous to trespass in that individuals have right to freedom from mental and physical anguish resulting from the invasion. Several key aspects should be noted:

- The use of a person's name, picture, or other identifying information without their permission is construed as invasion of privacy.
- The right of privacy may be violated if records, reports, and letters are read by persons not entitled to examine them.
- Citizens now have greater access to previously unavailable government files.

Implications for Communicators

The potential hazards regarding invasion of privacy have several implications for organizations.

- Make sure that all information you have about customers is accurate, especially if someone else may see it.

- If you want to use a picture or the identity of an individual in your promotional efforts, have the individual sign a properly prepared and notarized or witnessed release form.
- Since your competitors have the right to access certain information that you have to file with governmental agencies, you must attempt to meet the requisites of the filing regulations without revealing sensitive data.

COPYRIGHTS AND COPYING

The intent of a **copyright** is to protect published material (for a limited time) from unauthorized copying or publishing. The copying of copyrighted material without permission of the copyright owner is forbidden, except for certain limited "fair use" privileges and single copies made for noncommercial purposes.

A wide variety of documents and items cannot be copied in some circumstances. Some of these are:

Treasury notes.

Federal Reserve notes.

National Bank currency.

Certificates of indebtedness.

Silver and gold certificates.

Paper money.

U.S. savings bonds.

Internal Revenue stamps.

Postage stamps.

Postal money orders.

Bills, checks, or drafts for money drawn by or upon authorized officers of the U.S.

Certificates of citizenship or naturalization.

Passports.

Immigration papers.

Obligations or securities of any foreign government, bank, or corporation.

Draft registration cards.

Badges, identification cards, passes, or insignia carried by military or members of the various federal departments and bureaus (e.g., FBI).

Implications for Communicators

The implications for communicators regarding copyrights and copying include these guidelines: (1) Do not copy large segments of materials from another's work and use them commercially. (2) Avoid copying any government-related document without specific clearance.

EMPLOYMENT

This section focuses on potential communication hazards relative to employment; specifically, it addresses an organization's preemployment inquiries. The primary constraints are provided by Title VII of the *Civil Rights Act* (of 1964) and the related amendments of 1972 and 1978. These regulations prohibit discrimination in employment as to hiring, firing, compensation, termination, and conditions or privileges of employment on the basis of race, color, religion, sex, or national origin.

Implications for Communicators

Note that discrimination is forbidden, not the asking of certain questions. However, in many instances, asking the questions implies the intent to discriminate. In employment interviews and letters requesting information, you must be careful when asking questions about credit and employment. The list of general suggestions in Table D.1 for fair and unfair preemployment inquiries meets the federal Uniform Guidelines on Employee Selection Procedures.

TABLE D.1

Examples of Fair and Unfair Preemployment Inquiries

Subject	Fair Preemployment Inquiries	Unfair Preemployment Inquiries
Age	Birth date in some states; only whether applicant is of legal age in others.	Any inquiry that implies discrimination without job-related justification.
Arrests	None.	All inquiries relating to arrests.
Citizenship	Whether applicant is prevented from lawfully becoming employed in this country because of visa or immigration status. Whether applicant can	Requirement before hiring to present birth certificate, naturalization, or baptismal records. Any inquiry that would divulge lineage, ancestry,

TABLE D.1 *(continued)*

Subject	Fair Preemployment Inquiries	Unfair Preemployment Inquiries
	provide proof of citizenship, visa or alien registration number after being hired.	national origin, descent, or birthplace.
Convictions	Inquiries concerning specified convictions that relate reasonably to fitness to perform particular job being applied for, provided that such inquiries be limited to convictions for which date of conviction or of prison release is within seven years of job application date.	Inquiries that would divulge convictions that (*a*) do not relate reasonably to fitness to perform particular job or (*b*) do not relate solely to convictions for which date of conviction or of prison release is within seven years of job application date.
Family	Whether applicant can meet specified work schedules or has activities, commitments, or responsibilities that may prevent meeting work attendance requirements.	Specific inquiries concerning spouse, spouse's employment or salary, children, child care arrangements, or dependents.
Handicap	Whether applicant has certain specified sensory or physical handicaps that relate reasonably to fitness to perform particular job. Whether applicant has any handicaps or health problems that may affect work performance or that employer should take into account in determining job placement.	Any inquiry that is not based on actual job requirements.
Height and weight	Inquiries as to ability to perform actual job requirements. Being of a certain height or weight will not be considered to be a job requirement unless the employer can show that no employee with the ineligible height or weight could do the work.	Any inquiry that is not based on actual job requirements.
Marital status	None.	Whether applicant is married, single, divorced, separated, engaged, widowed, etc.; whether Mr., Mrs., Miss, Ms.
Military	Inquiries concerning education, training, or work experience in the armed forces of the United States.	Type or condition of military discharge. Experience in other than U.S. armed forces. Request for discharge papers.
Name	Whether applicant worked for this firm or a competi-	Inquiry into original name where it has been

TABLE D.1 (concluded)

Subject	Fair Preemployment Inquiries	Unfair Preemployment Inquiries
	tor under a different name; if so, what name. Name under which applicant is known to references if different from present name.	changed by court order or marriage. Inquiries about name that would divulge marital status, lineage, ancestry, national origin.
National origin	Inquiries into applicant's ability to read, write, and speak foreign languages, when such inquiries are based on job requirements.	Inquiries into applicant's lineage, ancestry, national origin, descent, birthplace, or mother tongue. National origin of parents or spouse.
Organizations	Inquiry into organization memberships, excluding any organization the name or character of which indicates race, color, creed, sex, marital status, religion, or national origin or ancestry.	Requirement that applicant list all organizations, clubs, societies, and lodges to which he or she belongs.
Photographs	May be requested after hiring for identification purposes.	Request that applicant submit photo, mandatorily or optionally, before hiring.
Pregnancy	Inquiries as to duration of stay on job or anticipated absences that are made to males and females alike.	All questions as to pregnancy, and medical history concerning pregnancy and related matters.
Race or color	None.	Any inquiry concerning race or color of skin, hair, eyes, etc.
Relatives	Names of relatives already employed by this company or by any competitor.	Names and addresses of any relative other than those listed as proper.
Religion or creed	None.	Inquiries about applicant's religious denomination or affiliations, church, pastor, parish, religious holidays.
Residence	Inquiries about address to the extent needed to facilitate contacting the applicant.	Names or relationship of persons with whom applicant resides. Whether applicant owns or rents home.
Sex	None.	Any inquiry.

Source: Excerpts from *Preemployment Inquiries and Screening,* Washington State Human Rights Commission, July 1977 and November 1982.

CREDIT AND COLLECTIONS

Credit and the subsequent billings and collections have become an integral part of our society. Consequently, many federal and state laws now focus on ensuring that consumers are treated fairly in credit transactions. Much of an organization's compliance with these regulations involves its communications with consumers. The major issues are discussed briefly.

Privacy

Individual privacy is protected by the *Fair Credit Reporting Act* (of 1970). Reporting agencies such as credit bureaus must tell the consumer the names and addresses of those to whom information is reported. Further, any organization that provides information about an individual to a third party or makes subjective statements about another individual's credit may be liable under the act.

False Information

The individual's right to have accurate credit information reported is also enforced by the *Fair Credit Reporting Act* (of 1970). A consumer can have false information stricken from the files of creditors and credit bureaus. Although consumers have the right to know what kinds of information are in their files, they do not have access to the files.

Full Disclosure

The consumers' right to receive full disclosure about the stipulations of their credit agreement is covered by the *Truth in Lending Act* (of 1969). Advertisers of credit must also specify the credit terms clearly and conspicuously.

Discrimination

Discrimination in the granting of credit is covered by the *Equal Credit Opportunity Act* (of 1974). Essentially, creditors are forbidden to discriminate in the granting of credit on the basis of a person's sex, marital status, color, race, national origin, age, or because the individual has taken action under the provisions of the act. This act also requires that refusals of credit must be in writing. Consequently, you must be extremely careful when writing letters refusing credit.

Complaints

Complaints about credit are addressed by the *Fair Credit Billing Act* (of l974). Consumers have the right to receive speedy attention on complaints about their bills. Creditors must send customers printed instructions twice a year explaining inquiry procedures; many therefore now include detailed descriptions on their bill statements about how to inquire about your bill.

Collecting Debts

Debt collection practices are addressed by the *Fair Debt Collection Practices Act* (of l978). Unreasonable means of collecting debts are prohibited and considered an invasion of privacy. For example, an organization cannot mail materials that falsely imply that a lawsuit has been filed.

Implications for the Communicator

The acts introduced above have many implications for communicators. Key implications include the following:

- Since state statutes vary, investigate those in your state.
- Make statements about consumers and their credit situation very cautiously, and ensure that any information transmitted is reliable and substantiated.
- Because of the regulations, do not try to make up your own credit forms—use readily available standard forms that have been checked by legal counsel.
- When refusing credit, write your refusal—include non-discriminatory reasons for the refusal.
- Be cautious about asking questions that could be construed as discriminatory.
- Make sure that no collection letter violates any state statutes.

USE OF THE MAIL

Organizations using the U.S. Mail must be aware of certain restrictions. These restrictions apply to five basic issues.

First, using the U.S. Mail to defraud is a crime. Essentially, any false statements sent through the mail to secure credit, sell stock, obtain funds from an insurance company, or broadcast a cure for an illness are illegal.

Second, the mail can unintentionally serve as the publication vehicle leading to defamation. If statements of an unfavorable nature are enclosed in a letter, and it is probable that the letter will be seen by others, this can lead to charges of defamation against the sender.

Third, the mailing of certain *unmailable materials* may violate the U.S. postal laws. Examples of unmailable materials include letters and printed matter concerning lotteries, obscene literature, extortion threats, and solicitation of illegal business.

Fourth, although sending unordered merchandise through the mail is not illegal unless it is sent COD, consumers are not obligated to pay for such unordered merchandise. The consumer who receives unordered merchandise can (1) return to sender, (2) destroy after a reasonable length of time, or (3) treat the unordered merchandise as an unconditional gift if living in a state where the law applies.

Fifth, the sending of unsolicited credit cards through the mail is illegal.

Implications for the Communicator

Organizations must obviously be careful in their use of the U.S. mail. The major implications are these:

- Make sure that all statements in mailed material are true and reliable.

- In sending any unfavorable, potentially damaging information such as past due notices, enclose them in envelopes that prohibit unauthorized viewing and label the envelope personal or confidential.

- If you are in doubt about the mailability of any particular material, you may submit a request to the Office of the General Counsel, Mailability Division, Post Office Department, Washington, D.C. 20260. Rulings are furnished as promptly as circumstances permit.

- Make sure that you have a valid request for any mailed merchandise and credit cards.

PACKAGING AND LABELING

Another communication task many organizations must address involves the labeling of products. The intent of the *Fair Packaging and Labeling Act* is to ensure that consumers receive accurate information and are safe from being misled about the product. Essentially, it gives the Federal Trade Commission (FTC) authority to regulate the nature of the language on labels.

Implications for the Communicator

The major implication is that organizations must strive to avoid language that can mislead consumers. Not only must the product be described accurately and clearly, words such as *large* and *family size* must be used carefully.

Appendix E
International Business Communications

This appendix was coauthored by C. Kendrick Gibson, Dean of the School of Business, Henderson State University, Arkadelphia, Arkansas.

INTRODUCTION

As recently as 20 years ago, international communications were of concern to only a few people, most of whom worked for our national government. Today, the business community has become more actively involved in communicating with foreign countries. Foreign trade, both exporting and importing, has become an increasingly significant part of our economy.[1]

U.S. firms are involved with governments and businesses in foreign countries in many different ways, including:

- Negotiating with potential sources of supply.
- Negotiating with potential distributors.
- Building a plant in a foreign country.
- Applying for licenses to distribute.
- Negotiating with potential buyers of your firm.

The key point is that opportunities for the college graduate to become more involved in international business are increasing. You might even obtain an overseas assignment some day. Along with your opportunities will come the problems of communicating (both verbally and nonverbally) with foreign business people.

Presently, international business communications are not being carried out particularly well. According to one congressman, the inability of U.S. business people to communicate effectively with business people overseas may explain a large part of our trade deficit.[2] Specifically, Japanese and American business negotiations have been cited as having major communication difficulties and breakdowns.[3]

The purpose of this appendix is to discuss the major barriers to effective international business communications as well as to suggest some key gateways to overcoming these barriers.

BARRIERS TO EFFECTIVE
INTERNATIONAL COMMUNICATIONS

International communications naturally involves different cultures. Culture is the accumulated experiences of a given society or nation that results in group-accepted behaviors or norms. When a business person from one culture or society communicates with an individual from another culture, international communication takes place. Since the accumulated experiences of individuals in one culture differ from the experiences of someone from a different culture, the major barrier to international communications involves *different frames of reference.*

Putting a message into a receiver's frame of reference is the major challenge for organizations operating in other countries. Unless this is accomplished, organizations face an almost insurmountable communication barrier.

The task of formulating messages appropriate for a specific individual's frame of reference is difficult enough in your own country. This difficulty is multiplied many times when your receiver has a different cultural background. Consider the following comparison of a typical person from a Western culture with one from a Third World culture.[4]

A member of a Western culture, principally the United States, is likely to equate time and money with success. Wealth and power are the tools used to solve most problems. In addition, this person:

- Thinks that democratic processes or majority rule is the best form of government.
- Reveres technology.
- Sees competition as good.
- Thinks winning is an important goal.
- Values material possessions, the scientific method, efficiency, organization, specialization, and separation of work activities from leisure.
- Is likely to be fairly aggressive, direct, impatient, and self-amused when communicating.
- Regards business topics as the principal topic of most opportunities to interact with others and tries to avoid discussion of family or personal matters.

In a contrast, imagine a Third World person with the following cultural norms communicating with the above person. The Third World person:

- Views speed and efficiency as irrelevant or negative.
- Views material possessions, competition, and winning as unimportant.
- Obtains power and status from extended family relationships.
- Views democracy, technology, progress, and development with suspicion and cynicism.
- Gives little thought to changing living conditions since these are the result of destiny.
- Is passive, indirect, patient in communications.
- Places a higher value on family and friends than upon business.
- Wants to be much closer to the other individual and uses more gestures in communicating.

Clearly, then, one's frame of reference is shaped by the culture surrounding the individual. No one can avoid the process of learning the symbols and signs that govern communication with others. It becomes painfully clear to the international traveler or business representative that the differences are almost beyond comprehension. Before we go on to discuss how to close this cultural gap, let's examine a few more cultural differences that create communication barriers.

Verbal Barriers

Channel Selection Barriers.   Cultures vary as to which communication channel (oral versus written) is most appropriate for a given situation. For example, where an American business person might not think twice about sending a written thank you note to a business customer, a Japanese business person would be more likely use a personal visit. If the Japanese business person did use a thank you note, he would be likely to include an apology such as: "Please excuse me for lack of formality in thanking you by this note instead of paying a personal call."[5]

Language Barriers.   Even though English is the predominate language used in international business transactions, language is a major barrier. Frequently, a common English word is used in international communications, yet the word can mean different things in different cultures. One recent study, for example, found that the word *profit* held different meanings for American and Japanese business people. Americans were more likely to associate personal gain with profit than were their Japanese counterparts.[6]

Nonverbal Barriers

Cultural norms dictate appropriate forms of nonverbal behavior. Differences in acceptable nonverbal behavior can also create communication barriers.

Body Language. Acceptable body language varies widely from culture to culture. Consider the following examples:[7]

- India: A wink is considered an insult.
- Certain countries in Far East: Eye contact is to be avoided, and the OK sign (using the thumb and forefinger to make a circle) is considered bad.
- Thailand: The feet are considered the lowest or most rejected part of the body—to allow the sole of the foot or toe of the shoe to point to another is a major error.

There are many other examples of body language that differs from what you are used to, including facial expressions, bowing, gestures, and the wearing of shoes in the home.

Personal Space and Touching. Americans tend to be very reserved relative to their personal space, generally preferring to avoid contact. As discussed in Chapter 3, our personal zone extends to about 4 feet and our preferred distance for transacting business is from 4 to 12 feet.

In some countries, however, being within the four-foot zone is important to the perceived quality of the discussion, such as in those cultures that begin and end business conversations with handshakes. Conversely, the norm in other countries is further and may be specified in different situations. For example, men in South America are morally bound to maintain a distance of at least five feet from the women they interact with.[8]

Many Middle Eastern cultures are very touching oriented. Frequent touching, holding hands, and hugging are normal in male/male and female/female interactions. In the Arabic culture, honesty and sincerity is communicated when the odor of each individual's breath is shared; refusal to breathe in another's face is suspicious.[9]

In Thailand, the head is considered the soul or life force of the individual. Consequently, patting someone's head or touching the head accidentally is a major violation of the individual's personality.[10]

Voice.   Tone of voice is also a way that respect may be shown in many countries. The use of regular voice levels to discuss personal or family matters may be considered indiscreet. In some countries, silence is viewed as a sign of respect. Personal matters are simply not discussed with strangers. It would be impolite to speak to elders unless addressed by them first. In addition, scolding or reprimanding an elderly employee in public embarrasses the employee and all other younger employees in the area.

Time.   Americans dislike to wait. We are a society geared to hurry, hurry, hurry. Good time management is considered an asset, and waiting is generally not considered part of good time management. However, in Latin American cultures, waiting does not have a negative connotation. You might wait in an outer office for a couple of hours in Mexico and still find the Mexican business person interested in your meeting and not apologetic at all.[11]

BRIDGING THE FRAME OF REFERENCE GAP

Many organizations attempt to teach their employees the basics of international business, economics, and language.[12] However, this knowledge does not seem to be enough. Today, reacting to different cultural communication behaviors is more important. Unfortunately, teaching acceptance of others and their customs and mores is quite difficult. Most training programs appear to do a poor job regarding the feelings and reactions that are necessary to bridge the communications gap.

One linguistics professor who spent 20 years principally in Japan observed that effective intercultural communicators:[13]

- See the person first; see him as a representative of the culture second.
- Know people are good.
- Know the values of other cultures, and his own.
- Can control his bodily reactions to different foods, odors, and so forth.
- Speaks with hopefulness and candor.
- Has inner security and can be different comfortably.

Other researchers have suggested that what is really desired in the international arena is an array of personal characteristics or behaviors, such as:[14]

- The ability to communicate respect.
- The ability to be nonjudgmental.
- The ability to show sympathy.
- The capacity to be flexible.
- The ability to practice taking turns.
- Tolerance for ambiguity.

SUMMARY

Doing business in other cultures offers great opportunities as well as great risk of failure. To enhance the possibilities for success, business people must recognize that the frames of reference resulting from cultural influences are so significantly different as to make it seem impossible to communicate. Managers would be wise to go slowly, avoid jumping to conclusions, and study some of these differences before attempting to close the deal.

These are some of the major skills you will need:

- Learn the language.
- Learn cultural differences and anticipate them in communication exchanges.
- Exercise 100 percent responsibility attitude toward communication.
- Exercise the interpersonal communication skills discussed in the text: active listening, feedback, seeking a common frame of reference, using multiple channels, and using nonverbal cues (see Chapter 3).

Most of these communication skills must be *practiced* rather than simply read about or studied. Training programs that use role-playing and video-feedback techniques tend to be more successful in preparing American business personnel to close the cultural gap.

Notes

1. Louis Kraar, "The Multinationals Get Smarter about Political Risk," *Fortune,* March 24, 1980, p. 100.

2. Henry H. Rodkin, "Ten Rules To Live (and Sell) by Overseas," *Sales and Marketing Management,* April 2, 1984, pp. 63–64.

3. R. B. Peterson and J. Y. Shimada, "Sources of Management Problems in Japanese–American Joint Ventures," *Academy of Management Review,* no. 3 (1978), pp. 796–804.

4. Brent D. Ruben, "Human Communication and Cross-Cultural Effectiveness," *International and Intercultural Communication Annual,* December 1977, pp. 95–103.

5. Saluro Haneda and H. Shima, "Japanese Communication Behavior as Reflected in Letter Writing," *Journal of Business Communication,* 19 (1982), p. 23.

6. Jeremiah J. Sullivan and N. Kameda, "The Concept of Profit and Japanese–American Business Communication Problems," *Journal of Business Communication,* 19 (1982), p. 38.

7. Robert Shuter, *Understanding Misunderstandings,* (New York: Harper & Row, 1979), pp. 60–80.

8. Ibid.

9. Ibid.

10. Suriya Smutkupt and La Ray M. Barna, "Impact of Nonverbal Communication in an Intercultural Setting: Thailand," *International and Intercultural Communications Annual,* Volume III (1976), pp. 131–38.

11. Edward T. Hall, "The Silent Language in Overseas Business," *Harvard Business Review,* May–June 1960.

12. Philip R. Harris and Dorothy L. Harris, "Intercultural Education for Multinational Managers," *International and Intercultural Communication Annual,* Volume III (1976), pp. 70–85.

13. William S. Howell, "Can Intercultural Communication Be Taught In a Classroom," in *Readings in Intercultural Communication,* Volume II, ed. David Hooper, (LaGrange, Ill.: Intercultural Network, 1977), pp. 3–14. Ruben, p. 98.

Appendix F
Effective Dictation Skills

INTRODUCTION

Written communications such as memos, letters, and reports have long been part of our business system. Executives can normally choose from three basic approaches to get their thoughts into written form—handwriting, typing, or dictating. Handwriting has traditionally been the most common method for preparing written communications. Typing (directly by the executive) has been used by some executives, but has been somewhat limited because many business people do not type efficiently or find that concentrating on typing detracts from their ability to compose the message. The third method, dictation, has become an increasingly popular approach. The purpose of this appendix is to present a variety of helpful dictating skills.

TYPES OF DICTATING

Dictating is oral composition in that it allows you to get your thoughts on paper by talking, rather than by typing or handwriting. **Dictation** can be defined as:

> the recording and storage of a message using either automatic equipment or the manual skills of shorthand so that it can be transcribed in written form to the receiver at a later date.

Face-to-Face Dictation

Dictation has historically occurred live in that you would dictate to your secretary or stenographer. The stenographer would use his or her shorthand skills to quickly write the message. Later, the shorthand would be transcribed into English by hand and typed or just typed directly.

Face-to-face dictation has four major advantages:

1. You do not have to rely on your handwriting or typing skills.
2. If your stenographer/secretary is sufficiently proficient, you

do not have to worry as much about spelling and grammar skills. Remember, however, the final results are still your responsibility, not your secretary's.

3. It allows immediate feedback from your secretary. This can be especially important—if your secretary cannot understand your meaning, then your reader may also encounter difficulties.

4. Secretaries often know enough about a firm's operations to supply additional ideas for content or format.

Face-to-face dictation, however, has two major drawbacks. First, face-to-face dictation can occur only when a person with the relevant stenography skills is available when and where you need to dictate. This issue is particularly limiting in certain situations, such as when you are traveling. Second, it can limit your creativity. If your normal rate of speech is faster than the stenographer's ability to take the dictation (which is the normal situation), your thought processes can also slow down. These two problems have led to decreased usage of face-to-face dictation in many organizations.

Machine Dictation

More and more organizations are turning from face-to-face dictation to **machine dictation.** As implied, machine dictation involves composing your message and speaking so that it is recorded by a tape recorder. The resulting cassette recording can then be transcribed (replayed and typed) by a secretary.

The two major advantages of machine dictation are: (1) Dictating to a machine is more convenient in many situations, particularly when traveling, driving to work, or waiting for a secretary who might be busy on another project. It can therefore make effective use of otherwise lost time and capture creative thoughts as they occur. (2) Creativity can be allowed to flow. Your flow of ideas is limited by your rate of speech rather than by a secretary's shorthand speed.

The major limitations of machine dictation include the facts that machine dictation does not provide instant feedback from your secretary, and the written message is not available until the cassette is transcribed by a secretary. Technological progress may soon alleviate the last limitation with commercially feasible talking word processors. When available, you will be able to dictate a message and have the word processor immediately transcribe your oral message into written form and display it on a CRT screen. You can then edit or print immediately.

THE DICTATING PROCESS

Your ability to dictate messages efficiently may have dramatic impact on your overall level of productivity. Your machine dictation skills will be particularly important. The major dictating skills are discussed below relative to the three major phases of dictating—preparation, actual dictation, and follow-up.

Preparing to Dictate

The first major phase of the dictating process involves preparation before you begin the actual dictation. Effective preparation is critical to successful dictation. Six steps in the preparation phase are discussed next.

Gather Information. After you have decided to write a letter, memo, or report, you should begin your activities by gathering all needed information. Your research process should be complete. Once the actual dictating begins, you will want your ideas to flow naturally and without interruption.

Organize Your Message. It is critical that you determine what you want to say and the order in which you want to say it. The outlining procedures discussed in Chapter 4 should be quite helpful. For more complex writing (such as a report), you might need an extensive and detailed outline. For a less complex message (such as a memo), your outline might consist merely of a few notes jotted on scratch paper. Your outline for responding to a letter might simply be notes jotted in the margins of the letter itself. The key point is to get your thoughts down in the right order so that you can dictate smoothly without unnecessary interruptions.

Provide Instructions. All preliminary instructions and information should be provided before you begin dictating your message. You should therefore determine needed directions and include them as part of your outline. These directions might include memo or letter format, addresses, subject lines, title page format, enclosures, or special mailing instructions.

Prepare Your Secretary. Preparing your secretary is extremely important for developing an effective working relationship. Remember that your secretary must interpret your instructions and your message. He or she may be able to provide valuable suggestions for saving time and trouble for both of you, particularly during the editing process.

Plan Your Time.   Plan your time to minimize interruptions. Interruptions can slow down your dictating, obstruct your flow of creativity, and create disjointed word flow. Many business people set aside a certain time each day for dictation; all visitors and calls are held during this period.

Become Familiar with Equipment.   It is also important to become familiar with your dictating equipment, including special features. For example, some recorders have a button or switch for recording either dictation or a conversation (i.e., a conference speaker). The conversation or conference mode will pick up voices over long distances, but it is very narrowly focused—dictation will not be picked up in this mode unless the microphone is pointing directly at you. You should also check equipment even if you are familiar with it. Many people who dictate have at one time dictated a letter (or chapter) only to find nothing recorded due to a machine malfunction.

Actual Dictation

Now you should be ready to begin your actual dictating. Recall that any special instructions for your secretary should already have been prepared. Some of the instructions might be dictated at the beginning, while others should be written to alert your secretary before he or she begins transcribing. For example, if you want a letter typed on special letterhead paper, your secretary should be forewarned. Six points need to be remembered as you begin dictating.

Do Not Nitpick.   When dictating, do not be overly concerned with achieving absolute preciseness in grammar, wording, punctuation, and sentence structure. The most important issue at this point is to get your ideas on paper; you can edit a rough draft later. Getting your ideas on paper is easier if you will force yourself to dictate your message all the way through, especially if you are dealing with a letter or memo. For longer reports, you should consider dictating an entire chapter or section without stopping.

Speak Clearly.   You must speak clearly into your microphone. Pronunciation and diction must also be understandable. A common error is to allow the voice to trail off at the end of words and sentences. Another common error involves turning the dictating machine off before completing a sentence.

Speak at Your Normal Rate.   You should speak at your normal or natural rate. Unfortunately, many people slow their rate of speech in an attempt to speak more clearly. This change of tempo can actually cause you to mispronounce more words.

Mention Major Punctuation.   Major punctuation should be included as part of your dictating. For example, you can indicate the position or location of periods, paragraph endings, semicolons, dashes, and others. Remember, however, to avoid getting so bogged down with punctuation that your creativity is hindered.

Avoid the Irrelevant.   You should refrain from inserting extraneous comments in your dictation. Comments such as the following should be avoided:

> "Well, wait a minute. . . .I'm not sure that I want to include that."
> "Wonder if he will get a laugh out of that comment?"
> "Mary, what do you think about that last comment? Should I include it or not?"

Comments such as these serve only to confuse your transcriber. If you have relevant side comments, however, make yourself some reminder notes while you are dictating. You can then refer to the reminder notes during the editing phase.

Include References.   References are generally needed in reports. You should include full references as you dictate, even though the reference is to be positioned at the end of the report. Moving the reference later is easy. Finding the needed source later in an office full of papers, notes, other reports, and books can be surprisingly difficult.

Follow-Up

Your dictating process does not end when you turn the machine off. In addition to ensuring that the message gets into the hands of a qualified transcriber, there are several other points to consider.

Giving Special Instructions.   You probably should remind the secretary of any special instructions mentioned earlier. Items such as special enclosures, mailing instructions, and expected completion time might be mentioned at the end of your cassette.

Editing.   All written material should be edited, particularly dictated material. Shorter documents such as letters and memos might only need proofreading and light editing. Longer and more complex documents such as reports generally need heavy editing and some rewriting. In either case, compare the final version with your initial outline to ensure that all necessary points are included.

Maintaining Good Relationships.   Your dictating process will be no more efficient than your secretary. It is therefore quite important that you maintain a good working relationship with your secretary. Take the time to tell him or her how much you appreciate their efforts. A simple personal touch such as, "Thank you very much, Valerie, for transcribing these letters" can help maintain a good working relationship.

DICTATION ILLUSTRATIONS

This section contains illustrations of both good and bad dictating practices. The first illustration demonstrates poor dictating (side comments are in italics):

> Dear Mr. McGlone: *Well, let's see. . . .How about this opening?* The enclosed check for $450.33 . . . *Is that right? . . .* is my way of showing you that you made the right decision in buying from us. *That should make the old buzzard happy.* Our satisfaction-guaranteed-or-money-back policy means much to us . . . *I wish we didn't have to do it.*

Imagine the secretary's difficulty in transcribing the above message. An illustration of good dictating is shown below:

> *Instructions: This letter will acknowledge Bell & Sons' last order. Get the address from the purchase order, number 17.* Dear Mr. Bell: One thousand 5 *hyphen* pound boxes of pre *hyphen* cracked Fancy Desirable pecans should be in your store sometime Friday morning *period*. They were shipped today via Smithe *that's s-m-i-t-h-e* Motor Freight *period*. As you requested in your October 5 order *comma*, the $3,000 *parenthesis* Invoice #5555 *parenthesis* was credited to your account *period, paragraph*. Your customers should really like these pecans *period*. They are the best we have shipped this year *period*. Thanks *comma*, Mr. Bell *comma*, for another opportunity to serve you *period*. Sincerely *type it for my signature*.

Many dictating machines have a special feature (button or switch) that can be activated while you are recording to alert the secretary that the next few words are instructions. The alerting signal is normally a buzz.

Dictation, like all communication skills, takes practice, practice, and more practice.

Index

This book has been set Linotron 202, in 10 and 9 point Times Roman, leaded 2 points. Part numbers and titles are 48 point and 24 point Helvetica. Chapter numbers and titles are 42 point and 20 point Helvetica. The size of the type page is 35 by 48 picas.